MW01379367

Hadoop Essentials:
A Quantitative Approach

Henry H. Liu

𝒫 **PerfMath**

ISBN-13: 978- 1480216372

ISBN-10: 1480216372

10 9 8 7 6 5 4 3 2 1
20130201

To My Family

Table of Contents

Preface

WHY THIS BOOK

Hadoop is a distributed computing platform for dealing with large datasets. It has not only demonstrated its practical values in real applications such as data mining, Web searching, online photo postings in the social media industry, and so on, but also stirred up wide interests in the academic circle. For example, many universities have started offering Hadoop classes to their CS students. However, it has been challenging for both developers and CS students to learn Hadoop. This challenge results from the fact that Hadoop seems to evolve at a faster pace than other software technologies and its inner workings are retrofitted more often than others. On the other hand, online Hadoop API documentations and tutorials do not seem to teach Hadoop from a systematical, consistent perspective. There are several Hadoop texts available, but they either provide outdated information, or lack consistency in presenting Hadoop.

Given the above observations, I strongly feel that there should be a more effective and efficient approach to learning Hadoop. The new approach should be as *quantitative* as possible. The inner workings should be explained mostly based on the readily reproducible logs and observable artifacts such as the logs and reports produced by Hadoop itself. Another quantitative measure is that Hadoop APIs, rather than verbose textual explanations, which could be subjective and unreliable, should be used to reveal what are working behind the scene. These are the motivations for the author to write this book in the hope that it would offer another perspective about how one can learn Hadoop more effectively and efficiently.

WHOM THIS BOOK IS FOR

Obviously, this book is for those who are interested in learning Hadoop. No matter what role you play on your team, a developer, or a manager, this text will help you gain truly applicable Hadoop skills in a most efficient and relevant manner, mostly because of its unique, *quantitative* approach.

The book is especially suitable to be used as a supplementary text for a Hadoop course offered in many colleges to upper-division undergraduate and graduate students who may even benefit more from the quantitative approach itself than the knowledge about Hadoop. This applies to software developers as well.

HOW THIS BOOK IS ORGANIZED

This book consists of the following two parts:

- **Part I Setting the Stage**. In chapter 1 of this part, a gentle introduction to the Hadoop MapReduce framework is given to help you get an idea on the overall Hadoop landscape. Then, a step-by-step procedure is given about how to set up a Hadoop development environment and run the sample SpendingPattern MapReduce program in local mode. Chapter 2 is dedicated to setting up Hadoop in a four-node Linux cluster to run the same SpendingPattern MapReduce program in fully distributed mode. This part serves as a springboard for us to jump into Hadoop in Part II as is described next.
- **Part II The Hadoop MapReduce Framework**. This is the major part of this book. Using the SpendingPattern sample application at each step, we explore how various Hadoop infrastructural elements and classes come into play to make a MapReduce program work. The subjects covered in this part include the HDFS, Hadoop job orchestration and workflows, basic MapReduce programming, and Advanced MapReduce programming. This part also covers Hadoop streaming, administration and performance tuning.

SOFTWARE AND HARDWARE

I am a firm believer that there is no better way to learn about a technical subject than actually experiment with it yourself and gain the first-hand experience. If you decide to take a hands-on approach, you need a Mac OS X machine or a Linux PC with all necessary software installed. Ideally, you should have four Linux machines for setting up a Linux cluster to run Hadoop in fully distributed mode. This actually is not too hard to achieve if you have a few outdated Windows PCs and you can easily convert them into Linux as I did. Chapters 1 and 2 provide details about how to set up and run Hadoop in local mode and in fully distributed mode.

HOW TO USE THIS BOOK

There are three ways to use this book:

1) Follow the steps laid out logically in the text and learn progressively from simple to complicated Hadoop concepts and MapReduce programming techniques. For a best possible learning experience, trying out the exercises at the end of each chapter is strongly recommended.
2) Use the sample application as your learning base for trying out more advanced Hadoop technologies to suit your specific needs.
3) Take a cursory look just for a general understanding about Hadoop.

TYPOGRAPHIC CONVENTIONS

Times New Roman indicates normal text blocks.

Italic indicates *emphasis*, *new terms*, *definitions*, *email addresses*, *file names*, *file extensions*, and *URLs* in general.

Calibri font indicates code listings, scripts, and all other types of programming segments.

```
Courier indicates programming elements outside a program or script as well as everything related to executing a program or script such as commands, entries on an HTML form, etc.
```

HOW TO REACH THE AUTHOR

All errors in the text are the author's responsibility. You are welcome to email your questions and comments to me at *henry_h_liu@perfmath.com.* Your valuable feedback will be greatly appreciated.

THE BOOK'S WEBSITE

This book has a companion website at http://www.perfmath.com for downloads and updates.

Henry H. Liu, PH. D.

California

Autumn, 2012

Acknowledgements

First, I would really like to thank the self-publishing vendors I have chosen for making this book available to my readers. This is the most cost-effective and efficient approach for both readers and author. Computer and software technologies evolve so fast that a faster publishing path is beneficial for all of us.

My gratitude extends to my wife Sarah and our son William, as I could have not been able to complete this book without their support and patience.

I would also like to thank my audience for valuable feedback and comments to help me make this book better and better over time.

Part I Setting the Stage

To help you get a smooth warm-up on learning Hadoop, this first part includes the following two chapters:

- Chapter 1: Introduction to Hadoop. This chapter has two objectives:

  o Helping you comprehend what Hadoop is for, the origin of Hadoop, Hadoop release history, and Hadoop infrastructural and ecosystem components;

  o Helping you get to know about Hadoop as quickly and as early as possible by walking you through a SpendingPattern Hadoop MapReduce program and running it in local and in pseudo-distributed mode so that you would get some first-hand experience in Hadoop. This is a better approach to learning Hadoop than just reading a verbose text about what Hadoop is.

- Chapter 2: Setting up a Linux Hadoop cluster. This second chapter details how to set up a Linux cluster to run Hadoop in fully distributed mode, which emulates a real Hadoop environment in production as can be found typically in many big companies. To some extent, Hadoop is all about performance and scalability when processing large datasets, so it's the preferred approach to developing and testing Hadoop in such a mini-cluster environment.

All in all, I always advocate learning by getting your hands dirty as early as possible. The book is written this way to help you learn Hadoop more effectively and efficiently than letting you spend most of your time *reading* a verbose text. Let's begin with an introduction to Hadoop next.

1 Introduction to Hadoop

Hadoop has quickly become one of the most interesting subjects in data mining, parallel computing and Java. It is interesting not only practically but also academically. Large companies like Google, Apple, Amazon, Microsoft, Yahoo, and Facebook, and so on, depend on Hadoop for their daily operations. Many universities around the world offer Hadoop class to their CS major students. Hadoop represents a new, paradigm shift in processing large volumes of data – from structured to unstructured. It provides us with various opportunities for pushing the limits of the state-of-the-art hardware and software technologies in solving real world computing challenges.

In this first chapter, we first explain what *Hadoop* is about. Then, we explore a few core concepts associated with Hadoop with an example. We wrap up this chapter by actually demonstrating how to set up an experimental Hadoop environment that runs in local mode. The next chapter demonstrates how to set up a Hadoop cluster with four Linux systems in a home office or classroom environment based on OpenSuse 12.1, which you can easily replicate for your own Hadoop learning and exploration. It is also the common base on which all Hadoop concepts and features are explored in this book.

Let us begin with a brief overview of Hadoop next.

1.1 OVERVIEW

This section provides a brief overview of Hadoop to help you understand what Hadoop is for, its name origin, its infrastructural elements and complementary components, and its release history. We will get deeper about Hadoop from a technical perspective in the second section of this chapter.

1.1.1 What is Hadoop for?

Hadoop (http://hadoop.apache.org/) is one of the software projects hosted at the Apache Software Foundation. Its major objective is to provide an open-source software platform for reliable, scalable, distributed computing in the area of data mining, which attempts to look for useful patterns in large datasets. One real world data mining scenario used throughout this text is to look for spending patterns based on the credit card transactions of customers. The better a credit card company knows about its customers' spending habits, the better it can target its customers with promotions and advertisements. A credit card company can also look for unusual transactions from large volumes of pre-authorization requests to identify fraudulence as early as possible. I once got a call from my credit card company inquiring if I made several transactions on a day in Spain, one of which was a purchase of gas worth $7000. Of course it was not from me, as I had never travelled there or even knew anybody there (I still wonder who did it and how he/she did it. That's partially the reason why I chose spending pattern as the use scenario for Hadoop in this book). This kind of unusual-event discovering is termed "*anomaly detection*" in data mining parlance.

In general, you would find Hadoop potentially useful if you have large volumes of data to process on a regular basis, although the patterns to look for may vary from context to context. A question is why traditional database techniques are not used for data mining applications when large datasets are involved. That is mainly because the datasets that Hadoop deals with are mostly unstructured. It's too cumbersome to shuffle large volumes of unstructured data measured in petabytes in and out of a traditional database system, although traditional database vendors would be happy to do so for their business purposes if you ask for (in fact, databases like Oracle do support storing large text or binary files with proper column types). The nature and scale of unstructured datasets to be processed call for more appropriate solutions like Hadoop that offers reliable, scalable performance that cannot be matched by traditional database technologies.

1.1.2 The Origin of Hadoop

Hadoop is a by-product of the Apache Lucene project, which, in addition to text indexing and searching APIs, includes an open source web search engine named Nutch. In order to make Nutch more scalable, Doug Cutting and his team at Yahoo! implemented the concepts of MapReduce and a distributed file system for Nutch, based on papers published by Google (see the *Recommended Reading* section at the end of this chapter about those two Google papers). It is said that the implementation was named *Hadoop* after a stuffed yellow elephant toy of Cutting's kid.

Hadoop started at Yahoo! in 2004. Initially, it ran on a 20-node small cluster. By May 2009, it reached a milestone of sorting a terabyte dataset in 62 seconds with 1406 nodes, 8000 maps, 2600 reduces, and 1 replication. It also sorted a petabyte dataset in 16.25 hours with 3658 nodes, 80,000 maps, 20,000 reduces, and 2 replications (http://developer.yahoo.com/blogs/hadoop/posts/2009/05/hadoop_sorts_a_petabyte_in_162/). We discuss more about the concepts of Hadoop's maps, reduces and replications in the next section.

1.1.3 Hadoop Release History

To learn about Hadoop release history, a good start point is to visit the Hadoop download page at http://hadoop.apache.org/common/releases.html#Download. Figure 1.1 shows what's available there as of this writing. As you see, there are basically two *stable* releases:

- 0.20.203.X – legacy stable version
- 1.0.X – current stable version, 1.X release.

This book uses the 1.0.3 release, which can be obtained by clicking on the "Download a release now!" link in Figure 1.1. Clicking on the suggested mirror location of http://apache.mirrors.tds.net/hadoop/common/ would bring up a page similar to Figure 1.2. Clicking on the directory of *hadoop-1.0.3/* would eventually lead to all available options as shown in Figure 1.3.

As you can see from Figure 1.3, Hadoop releases are mostly for Linux and Mac OS X (another flavor of UNIX in case you are less familiar with Mac OS X). Production Hadoop runs on Linux, but development can be either on Linux or Mac OS X. One can also develop Hadoop on Windows, but it requires installing Cygwin for SSH, which makes it less desirable. For this book, I did sample development on a Mac OS X machine, but actually ran Hadoop on a Linux cluster consisting of four Linux machines, all of which run on OpenSuse 12.1 (three 32-bit and one 64-bit dual boot with Windows 7). More information on my Mac OS X and Linux cluster is provided later.

After you decide whether you would develop Hadoop on Mac OS X or Linux, you can download the proper Hadoop release based on the proper extension shown in Figure 1.3. For my Mac OS X, I downloaded *hadoop-1.0.3.bin.tar.gz* as shown in Figure 1.3 and untarred it with a sequence of clicks to a directory in *~henry/dev*. More detailed instructions on how to get Hadoop up and running will be presented later. For now, let's see what had been installed with this version of Hadoop 1.0.3 and what complementary components can be installed in the next section.

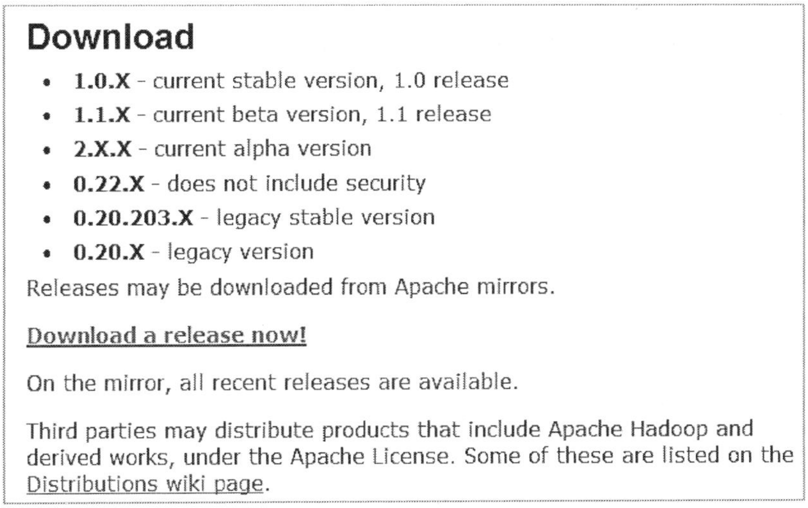

Download

- **1.0.X** - current stable version, 1.0 release
- **1.1.X** - current beta version, 1.1 release
- **2.X.X** - current alpha version
- **0.22.X** - does not include security
- **0.20.203.X** - legacy stable version
- **0.20.X** - legacy version

Releases may be downloaded from Apache mirrors.

Download a release now!

On the mirror, all recent releases are available.

Third parties may distribute products that include Apache Hadoop and derived works, under the Apache License. Some of these are listed on the Distributions wiki page.

Figure 1.1 Latest Hadoop download

Hadoop Releases

Please make sure you're downloading from a nearby mirror site, not from www.apache.org.

We suggest downloading the current stable release.

Older releases are available from the archives.

Name	Last modified	Size	Description
Parent Directory		–	
alpha/	18-Jul-2012 17:19	–	
hadoop-0.20.2/	01-Mar-2010 13:01	–	
hadoop-0.20.203.0/	04-May-2011 12:30	–	
hadoop-0.20.204.0/	02-Sep-2011 19:13	–	
hadoop-0.20.205.0/	07-Oct-2011 19:01	–	
hadoop-0.21.0/	23-Aug-2010 11:56	–	
hadoop-0.22.0/	03-Dec-2011 19:45	–	
hadoop-0.23.0/	03-Nov-2011 04:34	–	
hadoop-0.23.1/	18-Feb-2012 01:22	–	
hadoop-1.0.1/	14-Feb-2012 16:11	–	
hadoop-1.0.2/	27-Mar-2012 13:46	–	
hadoop-1.0.3/	08-May-2012 19:48	–	
hadoop-2.0.0-alpha/	15-May-2012 21:17	–	
hadoop-2.0.1-alpha/	18-Jul-2012 17:19	–	
stable/	08-May-2012 19:48	–	
KEYS	05-Jul-2012 17:34	126K	
readme.txt	05-Jul-2012 17:34	95	

Figure 1.2 Hadoop releases

Index of /hadoop/common/hadoop-1.0.3

Name	Last modified	Size	Description
Parent Directory		-	
hadoop-1.0.3-1.i386.rpm	08-May-2012 15:19	36M	
hadoop-1.0.3-1.i386.rpm.asc	08-May-2012 18:49	827	
hadoop-1.0.3-1.i386.rpm.mds	08-May-2012 18:49	1.1K	
hadoop-1.0.3-1.x86_64.rpm	08-May-2012 15:37	32M	
hadoop-1.0.3-1.x86_64.rpm.asc	08-May-2012 18:49	827	
hadoop-1.0.3-1.x86_64.rpm.mds	08-May-2012 18:49	1.1K	
hadoop-1.0.3-bin.tar.qz	08-May-2012 15:35	33M	
hadoop-1.0.3-bin.tar.qz.asc	08-May-2012 18:49	827	
hadoop-1.0.3-bin.tar.qz.mds	08-May-2012 18:49	1.1K	
hadoop-1.0.3.tar.qz	08-May-2012 15:35	60M	
hadoop-1.0.3.tar.qz.asc	08-May-2012 18:49	827	
hadoop-1.0.3.tar.qz.mds	08-May-2012 18:49	958	
hadoop_1.0.3-1_i386.deb	08-May-2012 15:20	36M	
hadoop_1.0.3-1_i386.deb.asc	08-May-2012 18:49	827	
hadoop_1.0.3-1_i386.deb.mds	08-May-2012 18:49	1.1K	
hadoop_1.0.3-1_x86_64.deb	08-May-2012 15:39	32M	
hadoop_1.0.3-1_x86_64.deb.asc	08-May-2012 18:49	827	
hadoop_1.0.3-1_x86_64.deb.mds	08-May-2012 18:49	1.1K	
releasenotes.html	08-May-2012 20:17	282K	Hadoop 1.0.3 Release Notes

Figure 1.3 Hadoop release 1.0.3

1.1.4 Hadoop Essential Elements and Components

Figure 1.4 shows a typical Hadoop 1.0.3 install, taken from my Mac OS X machine. You may recognize immediately what got installed, with some of the notable directories such as *bin, libexec, sbin, conf, contrib, lib,* and *webapps*, and so on. Note the directories under the *contrib* directory. These are additional features such as *streaming* that work with the Hadoop MapReduce framework.

Figure 1.5 shows the contents of the directories of *bin, sbin, conf,* and *webapps*. Note further the files in the *bin* and *conf* directories. We will refer back to some of the directories and files displayed here later when we discuss how to configure and start up/shut down Hadoop in local mode or in cluster mode.

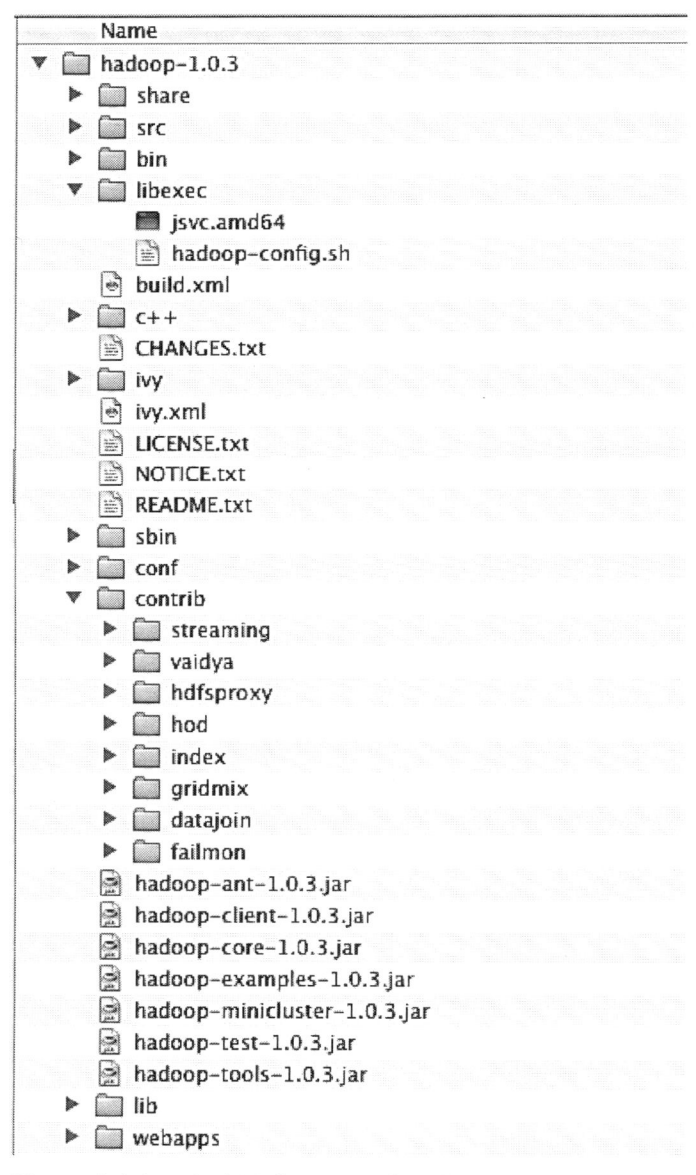

Figure 1.4 A typical Hadoop 1.0.3 install

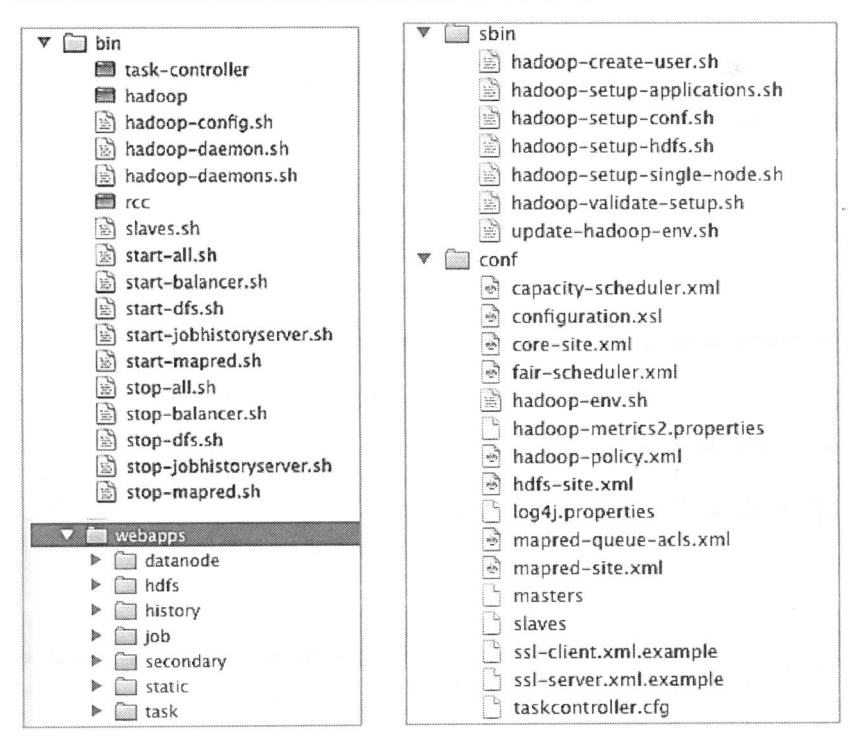

Figure 1.5 Hadoop scripts and configuration files

As a generic data mining platform for large datasets, in addition to its essential elements that come from a single download, Hadoop takes an army of complementary components to help facilitate MapReduce programming and extend its functionality. Although these complementary components are not needed if you just want to put up a simple sample to see how Hadoop's core function of MapReduce works, they are mostly necessary in production environment in order to achieve the highest possible efficiency with Hadoop. Table 1.1 shows a brief summary of the essential elements and the complementary components that work with Hadoop in general.

Table 1.1 Hadoop Essential Elements and Complementary Components

Essential/Component	Function
Essential:Core	A common set of utilities including FileSystem, RPC, and serialization libraries.
Essential:MapReduce	A programming model and software framework for developing highly reliable, parallel, scalable data mining applications that work on large datasets.

Essential:HDFS	Hadoop Distributed File System (HDFS) is the Hadoop storage file system for creating multiple replicas of data blocks and distributing them on compute nodes of a cluster of any size.
Component:Avro	A data serialization system.
Component:Cassandra	A database choice for supporting linear scalability and high availability without compromising performance. According to Apache, many large companies have been using it.
Component:Chukwa	A data collecting and monitoring toolkit for monitoring and analyzing the health of large distributed Hadoop systems.
Component:HBase	The Hadoop database as a distributed, scalable, big data store that supports structured data storage for large tables.
Component:Hive	A Hadoop data warehouse system for data summarization and ad-hoc queries.
Component:Mahout	A machine learning library consisting of a core set of algorithms for clustering, classification and batch based collaborative filtering.
Component:Pig	A compiler for producing sequences of map-reduce programs with its own high-level language.
Component:Zookeeper	A coordinator for maintaining configuration information, naming, providing distributed synchronization, and providing grouping services.

1.2 HADOOP ILLUSTRATED

In this section, we cover the following subjects:

- Setting up a local Hadoop environment
- MapReduce sample context: credit card spending pattern
- A simple MapReduce program
- Running the spending pattern MapReduce program

After finishing this section, you would have a better first-hand experience with Hadoop than just reading a verbose text about what Hadoop *is about*. I have tried to make the procedures as precise as possible so that you can easily replicate this environment for developing and running MapReduce programs. Note that this book was originally written based on a Mac OS X development environment and now updated with instructions on how to develop Hadoop MapReduce programs on Linux as an alternative to Mac OS X. If you prefer Linux to Mac OS X, refer to Appendix A and skip Sections 1.2.1.

1.2.1 Setting up a Local Hadoop Environment

First off, for your reference, my Mac OS X system for my Hadoop development was a Mac Mini with the specs as shown in Figure 1.6. All samples presented throughout this book were developed and verified in local mode on this Mac before deployed on a 4-node Linux cluster, which will be presented in the next chapter.

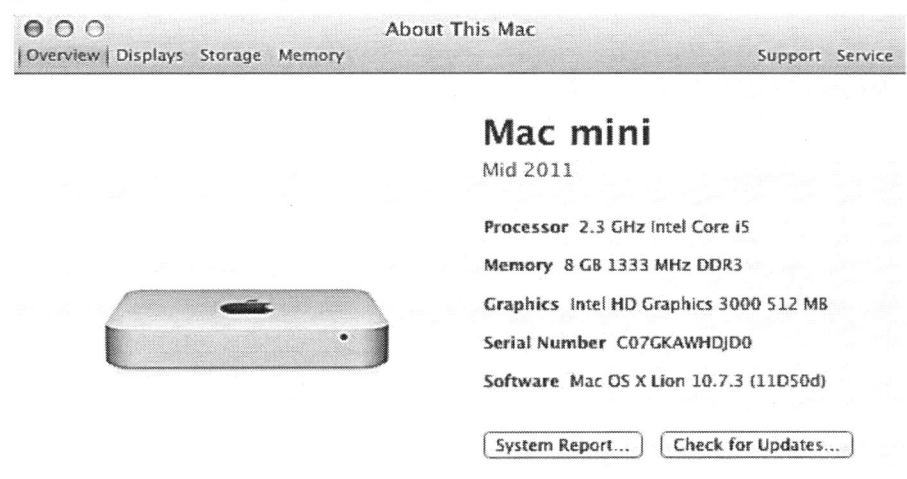

Figure 1.6 My Mac Mini for running Hadoop 1.0.3 in local mode

Setting up a local Hadoop environment on Mac OS X is easy. First, verify that a JDK is installed properly by running the command of *java –version* at a command prompt. On my Mac, it returned java version "1.6.0_29" which is quite up-to-date, so I just left it alone. However, this is a JDK installed by Apple by default out of the box at the location */System/Library/Java/JavaVirtualMachines/1.6.0.jdk/Contents/Home*, and you need to create a soft link by executing the following command and verify it with the second command as shown below:

```
$ ln –s /System/Library/Java/JavaVirtualMachines/1.6.0.jdk/Contents/Home
/Library/Java/Home
$ ls –l /Library/Java/Home
```

Next, download a proper Hadoop release of your choice (throughout this book, we use the Hadoop release hadoop-1.0.3.bin.tar.gz as illustrated in Figure 1.3). In my case, I moved the entire unpackaged hadoop-1.0.3 directory to the directory of $HOME/dev/.

Now set the following environment variables:

■   In your ~/.bash_profile file, add the following lines (Remember to replace my user name with your username in setting HADOOP_INSTALL. You may also notice that some other texts suggest setting the Hadoop environment variable as HADOOP_HOME instead of HADOOP_INSTALL. HADOOP_HOME is deprecated and use HADOOP_INSTALL instead.):

```
JAVA_HOME=/System/Library/Java/JavaVirtualMachines/1.6.0.jdk/Contents/Home
HADOOP_INSTALL=/Users/henry/dev/hadoop-1.0.3
PATH=$PATH:$HADOOP_INSTALL/bin:$HADOOP_INSTALL/sbin
export JAVA_HOME
export PATH
```

■   In your hadoop-env.sh in the conf folder as shown in Figure 1.5, add the following line:

```
export JAVA_HOME=/Library/Java/Home
```

This is because somehow Hadoop 1.0.3 looks for a JDK at the above location by default. Next, run a hadoop version test at a command prompt, and you should get an output similar to the following, which means that your Hadoop is ready to run in local mode (note that mc81511 is the hostname of my Mac).

mc815ll:hadoop-1.0.3 henry$ **hadoop version**
Hadoop 1.0.3
Subversion https://svn.apache.org/repos/asf/hadoop/common/branches/branch-1.0
-r 1335192
Compiled by hortonfo on Tue May 8 20:31:25 UTC 2012
From source with checksum e6b0c1e23dcf76907c5fecb4b832f3be
mc815ll:hadoop-1.0.3 henry$

The next step is to create a Maven/Eclipse project for the MapReduce programs presented throughout this book.

1.2.2 Setting up a Maven/Eclipse Hadoop Development Environment

This section describes how to set up a Maven/Eclipse project for our Hadoop samples. Depending on whether you are familiar with Maven and Eclipse, two options are available:

1)   Importing the MyHadoop-1.0.3 project as an existing Maven project downloadable from this book's website at http://www.perfmath.com/download.htm and skipping the rest of this section.

2)   Creating an initial, bare-minimum Hadoop project structure with Maven and Eclipse. With this option, I'll explain why we choose certain options and why we need to modify some of the default settings. Note that if you are not interested in going through this

exercise, feel free to skip it and move to the next section after you import my MyHadoop-1.0.3 project into your Maven-enabled Eclipse IDE.

No matter which option you take, it's necessary to verify/install Maven and enable it on the Eclipse IDE on your Mac, as described next.

Verifying or Installing Maven on your Mac OS X

Throughout the book, we use Maven 3 for all our MapReduce program development. It's very likely that you already have Maven installed on your Mac out-of-the-box. You can check it out by executing the "*mvn --version*" command at your bash shell prompt. For your reference, here is what I got on my Mac with the above command:

```
mc815ll:MyHadoop-1.0.3 henry$ mvn --version
Apache Maven 3.0.4 (r1232337; 2012-01-17 00:44:56-0800)
Maven home: /Users/henry/dev/apache-maven-3.0.4
Java version: 1.6.0_37, vendor: Apple Inc.
Java home: /System/Library/Java/JavaVirtualMachines/1.6.0.jdk/Contents/Home
Default locale: en_US, platform encoding: MacRoman
OS name: "mac os x", version: "10.7.5", arch: "x86_64", family: "mac"
```

However, if your Maven version is too old or you do not have Maven installed on your Mac, you can install it on your Mac as follows:

1. Download the latest version of Maven 3, which was 3.0.4 at the time of this writing, from http://maven.apache.org/download.html (I picked the file *apache-maven-3.0.4-bin.tar.gz* for my Mac).

2. Untar the file, for example, to a directory like *$HOME/dev/apache-maven-3.0.4*, in my case.

3. Set Maven environment variables. For example, in my case, I added the following lines at the end of my *.bash_profile* file and executed the command of "*source $HOME/.bash_profile*":

```
export M2_HOME=$HOME /dev/apache-maven-3.0.4
export M2=$M2_HOME/bin
export PATH=$M2:$PATH
```

4. To verify your Maven install, execute the command of "*maven --version*" at a bash prompt.

The next step is to enable Maven on Eclipse, as is discussed next.

Enabling Maven on Eclipse

The Maven plug-in for Eclipse is named *m2eclipse or m2e*. It is now bundled with the latest Indigo version (2011 release) and Juno version (2012 release) of *Eclipse Java EE IDE for Web Developers*. Next, I assume that you already installed Indigo or Juno on your Mac, or download and install it if not.

To enable Maven plug-in on your Eclipse IDE, complete the following steps:

- Open up your Eclipse IDE. Click *Help → Install New Software…* In the dialog box of *Available Software*, enter http://download.eclipse.org/releases/juno and click *Add*, as shown in Figure 1.7. Under the *Collaboration* category, make sure you select the two m2e entries as well as all the check boxes in the *Details* pane underneath. Click *Next* and finish the install.
- After Eclipse is restarted, open up the *Available Software* dialog box again. Click the link `already installed`. Verify your m2e install as shown in Figures 1.8 (*Features* tab) and 1.9 (*Plugin Details*).

You are ready to use Maven 3 with Eclipse now.

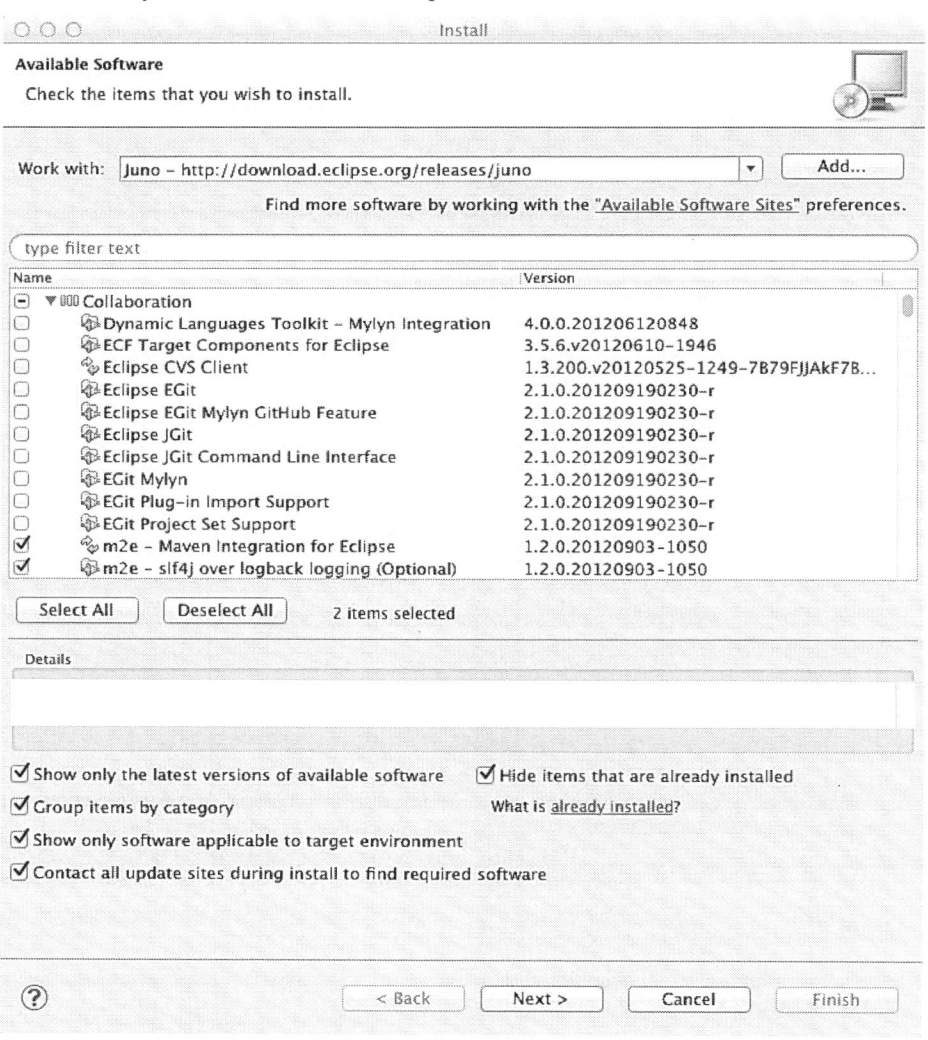

Figure 1.7 Maven plug-in m2e bundled with Eclipse Juno

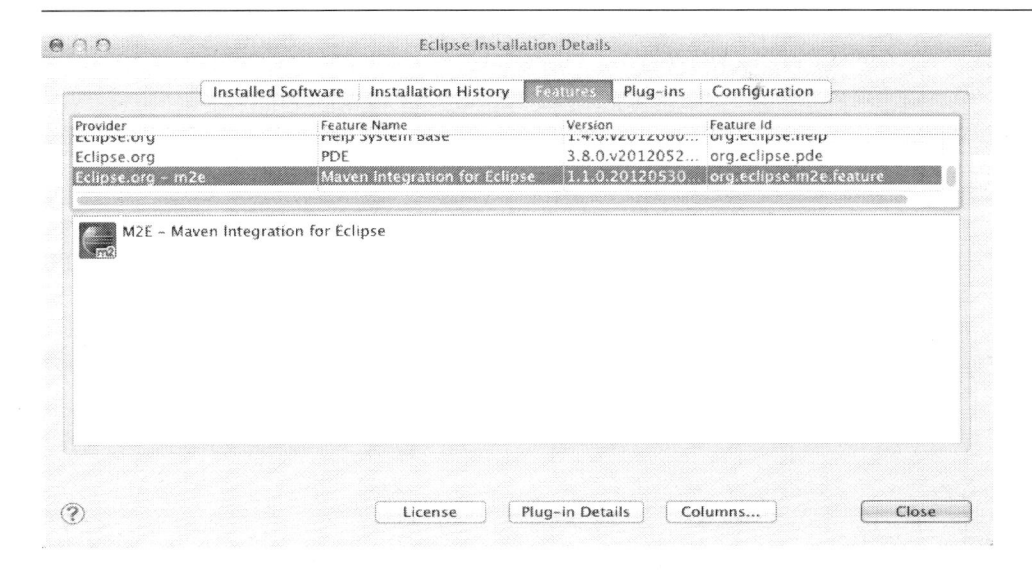

Figure 1.8 Maven plug-in m2e under the Eclipse Juno *Features* tab

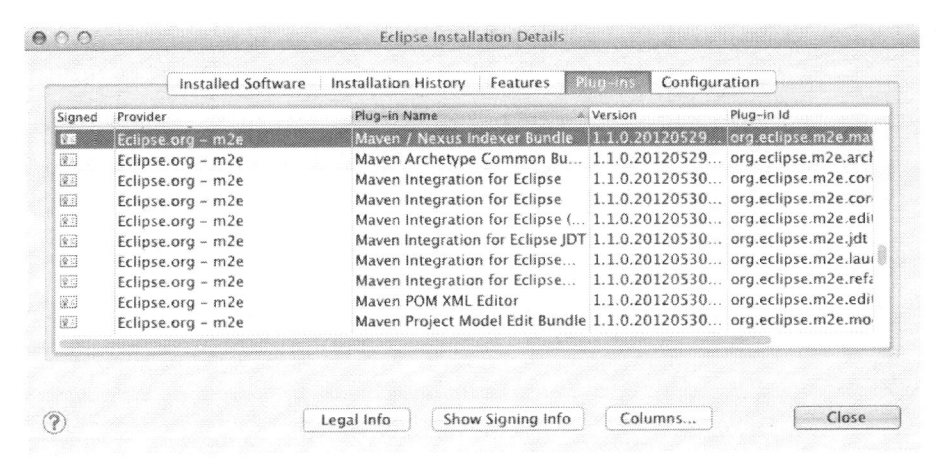

Figure 1.9 Maven m2e plug-in details under the Eclipse Juno Plug-ins tab

Next, either import my MyHadoop-1.0.3 project into your Maven-enabled Eclipse IDE and jump to Section 1.2.3 afterwards if you are not interested in learning how to create an initial, bare-minimum Hadoop project, or skip importing MyHadoop-1.0.3 project into your Eclipse IDE and create MyHadoop-1.0.3 project on your Eclipse by executing a series of Maven commands.

Importing MyHadoop-1.0.3 Project into your Eclipse IDE

To import MyHadoop-1.0.3 Project into your Eclipse IDE, follow the below procedure:

- Download and unzip my MyHadoop-1.0.3 project from this book's website available at http://www.perfmath.com/download.htm and unzip it to the workspace of your Eclipse IDE with "MyHadoop-1.0.3" as the top project directory.
- Open your Eclipse IDE. Click File → Import... → Maven → Existing Maven Projects as shown in Figure 1.10. Click Next.
- Select the root directory as shown in Figure 1.11. Make sure only the top pom.xml file is selected; otherwise, all four modules will be imported at the same level as the MyHaoop-1.0.3 project and you will have to manually delete them. Click Finish.
- Change to the MyHadoop-1.0.3 directory and execute the following command and verify that your build process is successful with similar output as shown in Figure 1.12:

$mvn clean package −DskipTests −Dhadoop.version=1.0.3

You can jump to Section 1.2.3 now.

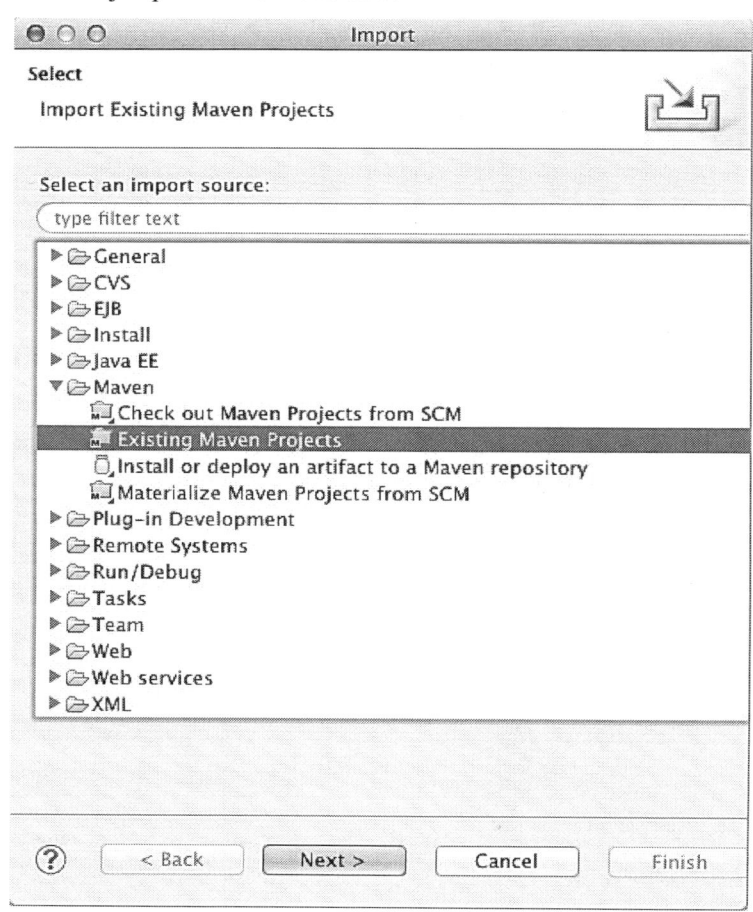

Figure 1.10 Importing MyHadoop-1.0.3 project as an existing Maven project

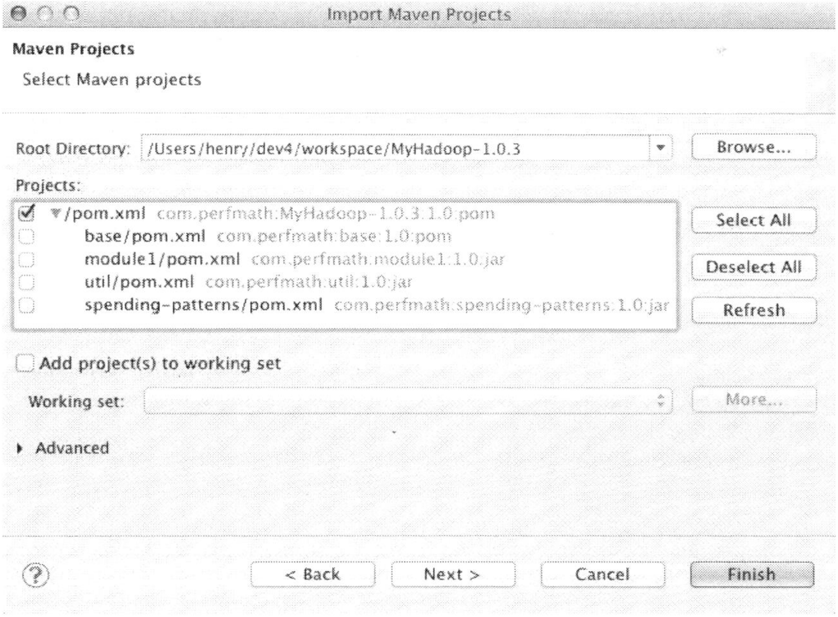

Figure 1.11 Select the downloaded MyHadoop-1.0.3 project

```
[INFO]
[INFO] ------------------------------------------------------------------------
[INFO] Building Root 1.0
[INFO] ------------------------------------------------------------------------
[INFO]
[INFO] --- maven-clean-plugin:2.4.1:clean (default-clean) @ MyHadoop-1.0.3 ---
[INFO] ------------------------------------------------------------------------
[INFO] Reactor Summary:
[INFO]
[INFO] Base ............................................... SUCCESS [2.827s]
[INFO] Module1 ............................................ SUCCESS [7.005s]
[INFO] Util ............................................... SUCCESS [0.444s]
[INFO] Spending Patterns .................................. SUCCESS [2.746s]
[INFO] Root ............................................... SUCCESS [0.003s]
[INFO] ------------------------------------------------------------------------
[INFO] BUILD SUCCESS
[INFO] ------------------------------------------------------------------------
[INFO] Total time: 13.267s
[INFO] Finished at: Sat Dec 29 19:48:01 PST 2012
[INFO] Final Memory: 15M/81M
[INFO] ------------------------------------------------------------------------
mc815ll:MyHadoop-1.0.3 henry$ ▊
```

Figure 1.12 Verifying building MyHadoop-1.0.3 is successful

Creating the Initial Hadoop Project Structure Using Maven/Eclipse on Mac OS X

This section describes how to create an initial Hadoop project structure using Maven/Eclipse on OS X. Note that this project was created based on my username of *henry* and workspace location at *~henry/dev2/workspace*. You should make proper changes to suit your environment accordingly in step 1 shown below.

1) Change to your workspace directory (e.g., ~henry/dev2/workspace in my case) at a bash command prompt.

2) Execute the following Maven command:

   $mvn archetype:generate -DgroupId=com.perfmath -DartifactId=MyHadoop-1.0.3

3) For the prompt '*Choose a number or apply filter (format: [groupId:]artifactId, case sensitive contains): 239:*', accept the default number, which corresponds to '*remote -> org.apache.maven.archetypes:maven-archetype-quickstart (An archetype which contains a sample Maven project.)*' Note that this is a generic archetype and the number (239 in this case) might differ from environment to environment. Select 5 and 1.0 for the next two prompts to be consistent with the MyHadoop-1.0.3 project I created initially when writing this book or choose 6 and 1.1 as the latest default settings, respectively. This really doesn't matter much because the pom.xml files will have to be overwritten later with the downloaded MyHadoop-1.0.3. project. The contents provided in this section are for demo purposes only so that you would understand better later about the structure of the MyHadoop-1.0.3 project you download from this book's website. Use the default settings for all remaining prompts until done.

4) Create a new Eclipse project with the name "MyHadoop-1.0.3" by following the steps of *File → New → Project → General → Faceted Project* (Select Facet Java as shown in Figure 1.13, which enables Java Content Assist. Also make sure you select Java JDK 1.6).

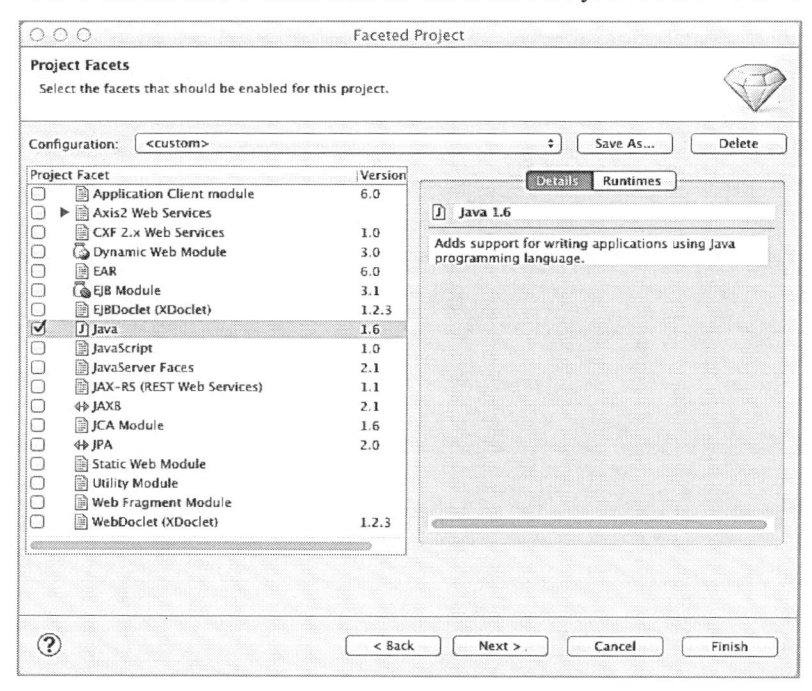

Figure 1.13 Creating a Java faceted project on Eclipse (2012 release named Juno in my case)

5) Delete the `src` and `build` folders.

6) Open the `pom.xml` file to change the packaging of your parent project from `jar` to `pom` to make it look like the following (this is because this is a top project directory without having its own java files directly underneath it):

<packaging>pom</packaging>

7) From the command line, change to the `MyHadoop-1.0.3` project directory and create the following modules by following the same procedure for creating the parent project of `MyHadoop-1.0.3` as shown in steps 2 and 3 above:

$mvn archetype:generate -DgroupId=com.perfmath -DartifactId=base
$mvn archetype:generate -DgroupId= com.perfmath -DartifactId=profiles
$mvn archetype:generate -DgroupId= com.perfmath -DartifactId=module1
$mvn archetype:generate -DgroupId= com.perfmath -DartifactId=util
$mvn archetype:generate -DgroupId= com.perfmath -DartifactId=spending-patterns

8) Verify that the newly created modules have been added automatically to your parent `pom` as follows (select the *pom.xml* tab rather than the *Overview* tab to view the `pom.xml` file):

<modules>
  <module>base</module>
  <module>profiles</module>
  <module>util</module>
  <module>module1</module>
  <module>spending-patterns</module>
</modules>

9) Refresh your `MyHadoop-1.0.3` project by hitting the F5 key and you should see all the above five modules created underneath it.

10) Install the project in your local repository and generate the eclipse files (note that if you want to delete a Maven project, delete it on Eclipse instead of manually on the local filesystem to prevent corrupting your Maven repository):

$mvn install
$mvn eclipse:eclipse

The second command of "`mvn eclipse:eclipse`" as shown above would generate eclipse configuration files such as `.project` and `.classpath` files, etc. In general, we do not need to manually edit these files, so we would not detail them further here.

At this point, you should see an output similar to Figure 1.14. You might wonder what a *reactor* is there on the second line of Reactor Summary. According to http://maven.apache.org/guides/mini/guide-multiple-modules.html, a Maven reactor is a mechanism that handles multi-module projects, which does the following:

■ Collecting all the available modules to build
■ Sorting the modules into the proper build order
■ Building the modules in order

This probably is sufficient for us to know all about a reactor at this point.

```
[INFO] ------------------------------------------------------------------------
[INFO] Reactor Summary:
[INFO]
[INFO] MyHadoop-1.0.3 .................................. SUCCESS [1.021s]
[INFO] base ........................................... SUCCESS [0.131s]
[INFO] profiles ....................................... SUCCESS [0.027s]
[INFO] module1 ........................................ SUCCESS [0.033s]
[INFO] util ........................................... SUCCESS [0.046s]
[INFO] spending-patterns .............................. SUCCESS [0.059s]
[INFO] ------------------------------------------------------------------------
[INFO] BUILD SUCCESS
[INFO] ------------------------------------------------------------------------
[INFO] Total time: 2.032s
[INFO] Finished at: Wed Aug 22 18:17:15 PDT 2012
[INFO] Final Memory: 6M/81M
[INFO] ------------------------------------------------------------------------
```

Figure 1.14 Creating a multi-module Maven/Eclipse project on Mac OS X

Note that if you get the following WARNING from the above command:

Workspace defines a VM that does not contain a valid jre/lib/rt.jar: /System/Library/Java/JavaVirtualMachines/1.6.0.jdk/Contents/Home,

apply the workaround as posted at http://doc.nuxeo.com/display/CORG/Maven+usage as follows and then re-run the mvn eclipse:eclipse command:

```
$ cd /System/Library/Java/JavaVirtualMachines/1.6.0.jdk/Contents/Home
$ sudo mkdir -p jre/lib
$ sudo ln -
↪/System/Library/Java/JavaVirtualMachines/1.6.0.jdk/Contents/Classes/classes.jar
↪jre/lib/rt.jar
```

Note that the last command was broken into three lines because of the line width limitation with the book, and you should type it as one line and execute it at a command prompt. If you encounter any issues, double-check your *Eclipse Java Build Path Classpath Variables* (accessible by clicking Eclipse / Preferences) against my setup as shown in Figure 1.15.

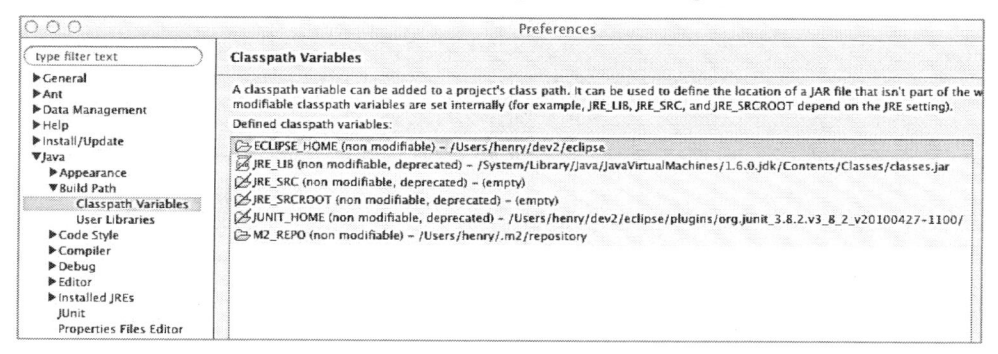

Figure 1.15 Eclipse *Preferences*: Java Build Path Classpath Variables on a Mac OS X machine

Verify that Eclipse Java Content Assist works. You can check it out by opening up one of those automatically created App.java Java source file, typing in, for example, "System." somewhere in a block as shown in Figure 1.16, to see if a Template Proposals dialog box shows up. If it shows up, it means that Eclipse Java Content Assist is working. Otherwise, you may see a pop-up as shown in Figure 1.17, indicating that Java Content Assist is not working.

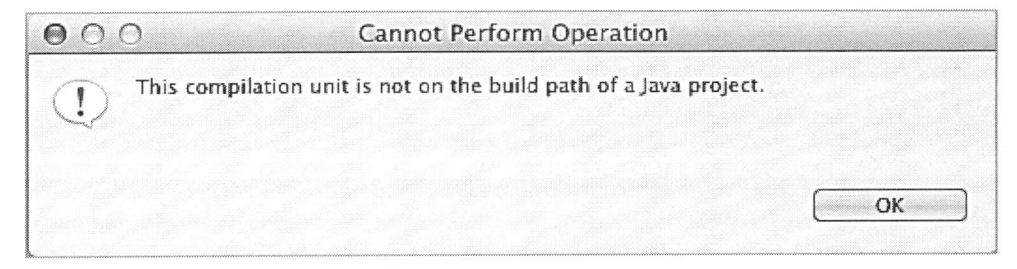

```
*App.java ⊠

    package com.perfmath;

  /**
    * Hello world!
    *
    */
    public class App
    {
        public static void main( String[] args )
        {
            System.out.println( "Hello World!" );
            System.|
        }
    }
```

o class : Class<java.lang.System>
ℱ err : PrintStream – System
ℱ in : InputStream – System
ℱ out : PrintStream – System
o arraycopy(Object arg0, int arg1, Object arg2
o clearProperty(String arg0) : String – System
o console() : Console – System
o currentTimeMillis() : long – System
o exit(int arg0) : void – System
o ac() : void – System

Press '^Space' to show Template Proposals

Figure 1.16 Eclipse Java Content Assist feature

⊖ ◯ ◯   Cannot Perform Operation

(!)   This compilation unit is not on the build path of a Java project.

                                                    OK

Figure 1.17 An indicator that Eclipse Java Content Assist is not working

Since Eclipse Java Content Assist is an indispensable feature for developing Java programs on the Eclipse IDE, you need to get it fixed if it is not enabled. One workaround is to start with the project's Properties dialog, and then enable *Project Facets/Java* as shown in Figure 1.18.

Now, delete the App.java file in each module. Your MyHadoop-1.0.3 project should look similar to Figure 1.19.

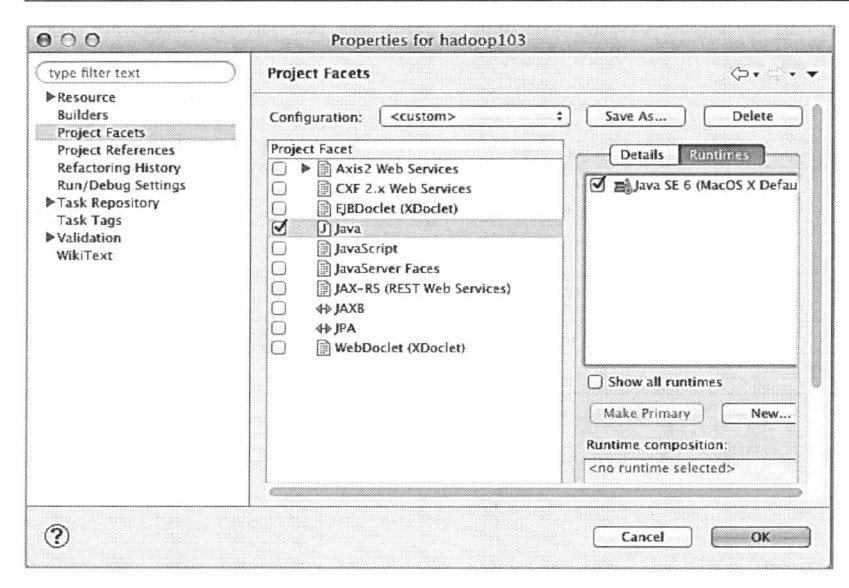

Figure 1.18 Enabling Java Content Assist by enabling Java facet for the project

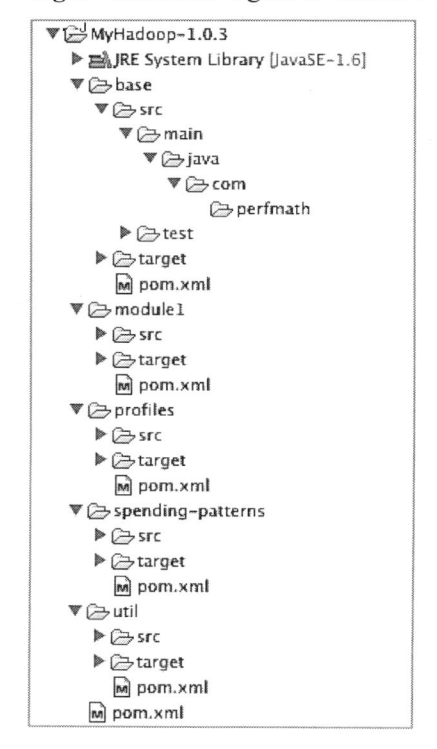

Figure 1.19 MyHadoop-1.0.3 project structure

At this point, download my MyHadoop-1.0.3 project from my website at http://www.perfmath.com/download.htm and overwrite your MyHadoop-1.0.3 project with my MyHadoop-1.0.3 project (or you can delete your MyHadoop-1.0.3 project and go back to the "*Importing MyHadoop-1.0.3 Project into your Eclipse IDE*" option to import my Hadoop-1.0.3 project into your Eclipse IDE).

The MyHadoop-1.0.3 project created above sets the stage for developing Hadoop programs. If you are new to Maven and Hadoop, it's beneficial to get familiar with the logistics of setting up various pom.xml files so that you can compile and package your Hadoop programs trouble-free. Otherwise, feel free to skip the next section and jump to the section about how to create the first Hadoop sample.

1.2.3 Maven pom.xml Files for the Hadoop Project

In the previous section, we created five modules, each of which has a special purpose as described below:

- **base**: This module defines all Maven plug-ins and all non-Hadoop dependencies, shared among all other modules. Listing 1.1 shows the pom.xml file for this module. Out of those Maven plug-ins, the compiler plug-in is for compiling Java sources, the failsafe and surefire are related to running JUnit tests, while the enforcer plug-in is for environmental constraint checking such as Maven and JDK versions. The dependencies include logging and apache commons.
- **profiles**: This module defines all Hadoop dependencies required by all Hadoop programs. These dependencies are specified in terms of *profiles*. A profile defines a group of dependencies that can be activated at build time through an element of <activation> inside the pom.xml file. For example, in the pom.xml file shown in Listing 1.2, two profiles are specified: hadoop-1.0.3 and hadoop-1.0.2. By passing in the profile in the form of –Dhadoop.version=<version-number> at build time when an mvn command is issued, for example, mvn package –Dhadoop.version=1.0.3, the designated profile will be used. This is convenient when you want to build a package using different versions of the same framework.
- **util**: This module centralizes all utility programs for all Hadoop programs. As is shown in Listing 1.3, its parent is specified with a <relativePath> tag pointing to the profiles' pom.xml file, which is because the profiles module is at the same directory as the util module level rather than one level higher. Also note that util's packaging is specified as jar since it contains Java sources.
- **module1**: We use this module to demonstrate how to develop our first Hadoop MapReduce program, which processes customer credit card spending activities. As is shown in Listing 1.4, its parent is also specified with a <relativePath> tag pointing to the profiles' pom.xml file. The packaging format for this module is specified as jar as well since it contains Java sources.
- **spending-patterns**: This module aggregates and packages all Hadoop modules into one jar file to be executed in a Hadoop environment. As is shown in Listing 1.5, its pom.xml file contains a Maven assembly plug-in, which packages all Hadoop programs in a jar file with the help of an assembly descriptor as shown in Listing 1.6. This jar file will include all

modules with the groupId of *com.perfmath* as specified in Listing 1.6. The jar name will *be spending-patterns.jar* as specified in Listing 1.5. We will see later how a Hadoop MapReduce program is run using this jar file throughout all samples contained in this book.

Listing 1.7 shows the parent pom.xml file, which specifies all modules included for this project. Figure 1.20 shows the relationships among these modules based on how their pom.xml files are set.

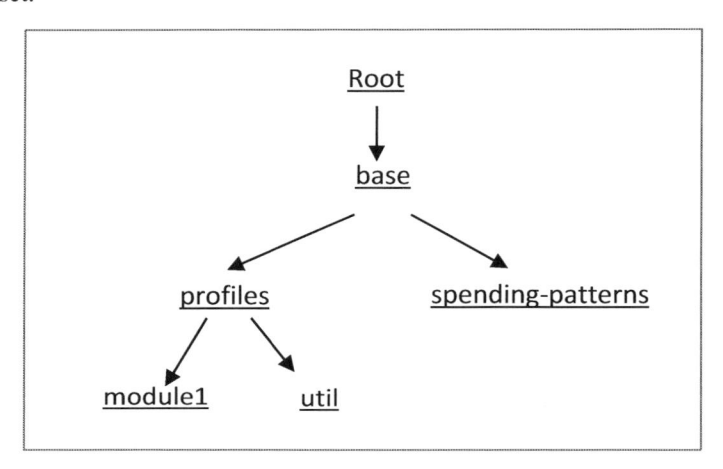

Figure 1.20 Relationships among the modules of the MyHadoop-1.0.3 project

Having explained how these pom.xml files work, we are ready to develop our first Hadoop MapReduce program next.

Listing 1.1 Base pom.xml

```
<?xml version="1.0"?>
<project xsi:schemaLocation="http://maven.apache.org/POM/4.0.0
http://maven.apache.org/xsd/maven-4.0.0.xsd"
xmlns="http://maven.apache.org/POM/4.0.0"
  xmlns:xsi="http://www.w3.org/2001/XMLSchema-instance">
 <modelVersion>4.0.0</modelVersion>
 <modelVersion>4.0.0</modelVersion>
 <groupId>com.perfmath</groupId>
 <artifactId>base</artifactId>
 <packaging>pom</packaging>
 <version>1.0</version>
 <name>Base</name>
 <url>http://maven.apache.org</url>

 <properties>
  <project.build.sourceEncoding>UTF-8</project.build.sourceEncoding>
```

```xml
    <project.reporting.outputEncoding>UTF-8</project.reporting.outputEncoding>
</properties>

<dependencyManagement>
   <groupId>log4j</groupId>
   <artifactId>log4j</artifactId>
   <version>1.2.15</version>
   <exclusions>
    <exclusion>
     <groupId>javax.mail</groupId>
     <artifactId>mail</artifactId>
    </exclusion>
    <exclusion>
     <groupId>javax.jms</groupId>
     <artifactId>jms</artifactId>
    </exclusion>
    <exclusion>
     <groupId>com.sun.jdmk</groupId>
     <artifactId>jmxtools</artifactId>
    </exclusion>
    <exclusion>
     <groupId>com.sun.jmx</groupId>
     <artifactId>jmxri</artifactId>
    </exclusion>
   </exclusions>
   </dependency>
   <dependency>
    <groupId>org.slf4j</groupId>
    <artifactId>slf4j-api</artifactId>
    <version>1.5.11</version>
   </dependency>
   <dependency>
    <groupId>org.slf4j</groupId>
    <artifactId>slf4j-log4j12</artifactId>
    <version>1.5.11</version>
   </dependency>
   <dependency>
    <groupId>junit</groupId>
    <artifactId>junit</artifactId>
    <version>4.10</version>
    <scope>test</scope>
   </dependency>
   <dependency>
    <groupId>org.apache.commons</groupId>
    <artifactId>commons-exec</artifactId>
    <version>1.1</version>
   </dependency>
   <dependency>
    <groupId>commons-io</groupId>
```

```
      <artifactId>commons-io</artifactId>
      <version>2.0.1</version>
    </dependency>
  </dependencies>
</dependencyManagement>

<build>
 <plugins>
  <plugin>
   <groupId>org.apache.maven.plugins</groupId>
   <artifactId>maven-compiler-plugin</artifactId>
   <version>2.3.2</version>
   <configuration>
    <source>1.6</source>
    <target>1.6</target>
   </configuration>
  </plugin>
  <plugin>
   <groupId>org.apache.maven.plugins</groupId>
   <artifactId>maven-enforcer-plugin</artifactId>
   <version>1.0.1</version>
   <executions>
    <execution>
     <id>enforce-versions</id>
     <goals>
      <goal>enforce</goal>
     </goals>
     <configuration>
      <rules>
       <requireMavenVersion>
        <version>[3.0.0,)</version>
       </requireMavenVersion>
       <requireJavaVersion>
        <version>1.6</version>
       </requireJavaVersion>
      </rules>
     </configuration>
    </execution>
   </executions>
  </plugin>
  <plugin>
   <groupId>org.apache.maven.plugins</groupId>
   <artifactId>maven-failsafe-plugin</artifactId>
   <version>2.9</version>
   <executions>
    <execution>
     <id>integration-test</id>
     <goals>
```

```
          <goal>integration-test</goal>
         </goals>
       </execution>
       <execution>
        <id>verify</id>
        <goals>
         <goal>verify</goal>
        </goals>
       </execution>
      </executions>
     </plugin>
     <plugin>
       <groupId>org.apache.maven.plugins</groupId>
       <artifactId>maven-surefire-plugin</artifactId>
       <version>2.5</version>
       <configuration>
        <argLine>-Xmx1024m</argLine>
       </configuration>
     </plugin>
    </plugins>
   </build>
  </project>
```

Listing 1.2 Profiles pom.xml

```
<?xml version="1.0"?>
<project xsi:schemaLocation="http://maven.apache.org/POM/4.0.0
http://maven.apache.org/xsd/maven-4.0.0.xsd"
xmlns="http://maven.apache.org/POM/4.0.0"
  xmlns:xsi="http://www.w3.org/2001/XMLSchema-instance">
  <modelVersion>4.0.0</modelVersion>
 <parent>
   <artifactId>base</artifactId>
   <groupId>com.perfmath</groupId>
   <version>1.0</version>
   <relativePath>../base/pom.xml</relativePath>
 </parent>
 <groupId>com.perfmath</groupId>
 <artifactId>profiles</artifactId>
 <packaging>pom</packaging>
 <version>1.0</version>
 <name>Profiles</name>
 <url>http://maven.apache.org</url>
 <profiles>
  <profile>
    <id>hadoop-1.0.3</id>
    <activation>
     <property>
      <name>hadoop.version</name>
```

```xml
    <value>1.0.3</value>
  </property>
</activation>
<properties>
  <hadoop.version>1.0.3</hadoop.version>
</properties>
<dependencies>
  <dependency>
    <groupId>org.apache.hadoop</groupId>
    <artifactId>hadoop-core</artifactId>
    <version>${hadoop.version}</version>
  </dependency>
  <dependency>
    <groupId>org.apache.hadoop</groupId>
    <artifactId>hadoop-test</artifactId>
    <version>${hadoop.version}</version>
  </dependency>
  <!-- Required to run -->
  <dependency>
    <groupId>log4j</groupId>
    <artifactId>log4j</artifactId>
  </dependency>
  <dependency>
    <groupId>com.sun.jersey</groupId>
    <artifactId>jersey-core</artifactId>
    <version>1.8</version>
  </dependency>
  <dependency>
    <groupId>org.codehaus.jackson</groupId>
    <artifactId>jackson-mapper-asl</artifactId>
    <version>1.5.2</version>
  </dependency>
  <dependency>
    <groupId>org.apache.mrunit</groupId>
    <artifactId>mrunit</artifactId>
    <version>0.8.1-incubating</version>
    <classifier>hadoop100</classifier>
    <scope>test</scope>
  </dependency>
</dependencies>
<build>
  <plugins>
    <plugin>
      <groupId>org.apache.maven.plugins</groupId>
      <artifactId>maven-compiler-plugin</artifactId>
    </plugin>
  </plugins>
</build>
```

```xml
    </profile>

    <profile>
     <id>hadoop-1.0.2</id>
     <activation>
      <property>
       <name>hadoop.version</name>
       <value>1.0.2</value>
      </property>
     </activation>
     <properties>
      <hadoop.version>1.0.2</hadoop.version>
     </properties>
     <dependencies>
      <dependency>
       <groupId>org.apache.hadoop</groupId>
       <artifactId>hadoop-core</artifactId>
       <version>${hadoop.version}</version>
      </dependency>
      <dependency>
       <groupId>org.apache.hadoop</groupId>
       <artifactId>hadoop-test</artifactId>
       <version>${hadoop.version}</version>
      </dependency>
      <!-- Required to run -->
      <dependency>
       <groupId>log4j</groupId>
       <artifactId>log4j</artifactId>
      </dependency>
      <dependency>
       <groupId>com.sun.jersey</groupId>
       <artifactId>jersey-core</artifactId>
       <version>1.8</version>
      </dependency>
      <dependency>
       <groupId>org.codehaus.jackson</groupId>
       <artifactId>jackson-mapper-asl</artifactId>
       <version>1.5.2</version>
      </dependency>
      <dependency>
       <groupId>org.apache.mrunit</groupId>
       <artifactId>mrunit</artifactId>
       <version>0.8.1-incubating</version>
       <classifier>hadoop100</classifier>
       <scope>test</scope>
      </dependency>
     </dependencies>
    </profile>
```

```
</profiles>
</project>
```

Listing 1.3 util pom.xml

```xml
<?xml version="1.0"?>
<project xsi:schemaLocation="http://maven.apache.org/POM/4.0.0
http://maven.apache.org/xsd/maven-4.0.0.xsd"
xmlns="http://maven.apache.org/POM/4.0.0"
  xmlns:xsi="http://www.w3.org/2001/XMLSchema-instance">
 <modelVersion>4.0.0</modelVersion>
 <parent>
  <groupId>com.perfmath</groupId>
  <artifactId>profiles</artifactId>
  <version>1.0</version>
  <relativePath>../profiles/pom.xml</relativePath>
 </parent>
 <groupId>com.perfmath</groupId>
 <artifactId>util</artifactId>
 <packaging>jar</packaging>
 <version>1.0</version>
 <name>Util</name>
 <url>http://maven.apache.org</url>
</project>
```

Listing 1.4 module1 pom.xml

```xml
<?xml version="1.0"?>
<project xsi:schemaLocation="http://maven.apache.org/POM/4.0.0
http://maven.apache.org/xsd/maven-4.0.0.xsd"
xmlns="http://maven.apache.org/POM/4.0.0"
  xmlns:xsi="http://www.w3.org/2001/XMLSchema-instance">
 <modelVersion>4.0.0</modelVersion>
 <parent>
  <artifactId>profiles</artifactId>
  <groupId>com.perfmath</groupId>
  <version>1.0</version>
  <relativePath>../profiles/pom.xml</relativePath>
 </parent>
 <groupId>com.perfmath</groupId>
 <artifactId>module1</artifactId>
 <packaging>jar</packaging>
 <version>1.0</version>
 <name>Module1</name>
 <url>http://maven.apache.org</url>
 <dependencies>
  <dependency>
   <groupId>junit</groupId>
```

```
    <artifactId>junit</artifactId>
    <version>3.8.1</version>
    <scope>test</scope>
  </dependency>
 </dependencies>
</project>
```

Listing 1.5 spending-patterns pom.xml

```xml
<?xml version="1.0"?>
<project xsi:schemaLocation="http://maven.apache.org/POM/4.0.0
http://maven.apache.org/xsd/maven-4.0.0.xsd"
xmlns="http://maven.apache.org/POM/4.0.0"
  xmlns:xsi="http://www.w3.org/2001/XMLSchema-instance">
 <modelVersion>4.0.0</modelVersion>
 <parent>
  <artifactId>base</artifactId>
  <groupId>com.perfmath</groupId>
  <version>1.0</version>
  <relativePath>../base/pom.xml</relativePath>
 </parent>
 <groupId>com.perfmath</groupId>
 <artifactId>spending-patterns</artifactId>
 <version>1.0</version>
 <name>Spending Patterns</name>
 <url>http://maven.apache.org</url>
  <dependencies>
  <dependency>
   <groupId>com.perfmath</groupId>
   <artifactId>util</artifactId>
   <version>1.0</version>
  </dependency>
  <dependency>
   <groupId>com.perfmath</groupId>
   <artifactId>module1</artifactId>
   <version>1.0</version>
  </dependency>
 </dependencies>
 <build>
  <plugins>
   <plugin>
    <artifactId>maven-assembly-plugin</artifactId>
    <version>2.2.1</version>
    <executions>
     <execution>
      <id>make-assembly</id>
      <phase>package</phase>
      <goals>
       <goal>single</goal>
```

```
        </goals>
        <configuration>
         <descriptors>
          <descriptor>src/main/assembly/jar.xml</descriptor>
         </descriptors>
         <finalName>spending-patterns</finalName>
         <outputDirectory>${project.build.directory}/../..</outputDirectory>
         <appendAssemblyId>false</appendAssemblyId>
        </configuration>
      </execution>

    </executions>
   </plugin>
  </plugins>
 </build>
</project>
```

Listing 1.6 assembly descriptor jar.xml

```
<assembly xmlns="http://maven.apache.org/plugins/maven-assembly-
plugin/assembly/1.1.2"
  xmlns:xsi="http://www.w3.org/2001/XMLSchema-instance"
  xsi:schemaLocation="http://maven.apache.org/plugins/maven-assembly-
plugin/assembly/1.1.2 http://maven.apache.org/xsd/assembly-1.1.2.xsd">
 <id>jar</id>
 <formats>
  <format>jar</format>
 </formats>
 <includeBaseDirectory>false</includeBaseDirectory>
 <dependencySets>
  <dependencySet>
   <outputDirectory>/</outputDirectory>
   <useProjectArtifact>true</useProjectArtifact>
   <unpack>true</unpack>
   <scope>runtime</scope>
   <useTransitiveDependencies>false</useTransitiveDependencies>
   <includes>
    <include>com.perfmath:*</include>
   </includes>
  </dependencySet>
 </dependencySets>
 <fileSets>
  <fileSet>
   <directory>target/classes</directory>
   <outputDirectory>/</outputDirectory>
  </fileSet>
 </fileSets>
</assembly>
```

Listing 1.7 parent pom.xml

```xml
<?xml version="1.0" encoding="UTF-8"?>
<project xmlns="http://maven.apache.org/POM/4.0.0"
xmlns:xsi="http://www.w3.org/2001/XMLSchema-instance"
xsi:schemaLocation="http://maven.apache.org/POM/4.0.0
http://maven.apache.org/maven-v4_0_0.xsd">
 <modelVersion>4.0.0</modelVersion>
 <groupId>com.perfmath</groupId>
 <artifactId>MyHadoop-1.0.3</artifactId>
 <packaging>pom</packaging>
 <version>1.0</version>
 <name>Root</name>
 <url>http://maven.apache.org</url>
 <dependencies>
  <dependency>
   <groupId>junit</groupId>
   <artifactId>junit</artifactId>
   <version>3.8.1</version>
   <scope>test</scope>
  </dependency>
 </dependencies>
 <modules>
  <module>base</module>
  <module>module1</module>
  <module>util</module>
  <module>spending-patterns</module>
 </modules>
</project>
```

1.2.4 Developing Our First Hadoop MapReduce Sample Program

Every Hadoop MapReduce program has two questions to answer:

- **Dataset**: What dataset does it work on?
- **Pattern**: What pattern does it attempt to discover?

Although the size of a dataset that a Hadoop MapReduce program processes could be huge in a real use scenario, the data format typically is simple. For example, in our use scenario for developing our first Hadoop MapReduce sample program, most records of credit card transactions follow the format of *Transaction Date | Description | Amount | Comments*, as is shown in Figure 1.21. Whether there are hundreds of records or hundreds of millions of records, the format remains the same. This peculiarity characterizes the datasets that most Hadoop applications operate on.

Although each transaction record is simple, it contains very interesting information such as when the transaction occurred, at which store and which city the transaction occurred, and how much was spent with that transaction. Although one isolated transaction may not mean much, the transactions over a period of one or two months might be sufficient to form a spending pattern or patterns. However, we are not concerned with the number of patterns too much yet – we are concerned with one thing only at this point: How do we write a Hadoop MapReduce program to find the maximum amount spent at each store given a credit card transaction data file?

```
Name of Report: 0812

Transaction Date        Description      Amount   Comments
08/02/2012       MEMBERSHIP FEE AUG 12-JUL 13     $0.00
07/21/2012       TARGET        00010983 SUNNYVALE         CA      -$5.11
07/20/2012       PAYMENT -$1330.33
07/20/2012       TRU HOLIDAY EXPRESSQPS SUNNYVALE          CA      -$10.74
07/13/2012       TARGET        00010983 SUNNYVALE         CA      -$6.27
07/10/2012       TARGET        00010983 SUNNYVALE         CA      -$36.04

Card ending in  8742
Transaction Date        Description      Amount   Comments
08/01/2012       MEG*LEGOLANDCALIFORNIA 760-918-5346  CA $220.00
08/01/2012       PRETZEL TIME SUNRISE    CUPERTINO CA    $5.69
08/01/2012       TOYS R US #5808     QPS CUPERTINO CA    $9.67
07/31/2012       WAL-MART #1760          SUNNYVALE       CA      $28.13
07/31/2012       MCDONALD'S F20253       SUNNYVALE       CA      $4.08
07/31/2012       SAFEWAY STORE 00017947 SUNNYVALE        CA      $10.39
07/30/2012       IDEAL CUTS              SUNNYVALE       CA      $12.00
07/29/2012       CENTURY THEATRES 41QPS SUNNYVALE        CA      $17.00
07/29/2012       SAFEWAY STORE 00017947 SUNNYVALE        CA      $3.37
07/29/2012       SAFEWAY STORE 00017947 SUNNYVALE        CA      $5.78
```

Figure 1.21 Credit card transaction data sample

Our first task is to replicate an arbitrary number of credit card transactions based on a limited number of real transactions over a period of several months. For this purpose, I developed a simple MapIncrease.java program, which is shown in Listing 1.8. The MapIncrease.java file is in the module1 module at src/main/java/com/perfmath, and the credit_card_tx_0.txt file can be found in the in0 directory from the downloaded MyHadoop-1.0.3 project. Copy these two files to a separate directory, compile and run as described next.

The MapIncrease program is run with two command line arguments: the initial, seed transaction data file and the number of transactions to make up. The logic of this program is simple: first, it extracts the descriptions of all transaction records to form keys in a *while-loop*; and then, it creates the specified number of transaction records in a *for-loop*. On an Intel core i5 Windows 7 PC, I created 2M transaction records within 40 seconds with the following command:

```
cmd> java MapIncrease credit_card_tx_0.txt 2000000
```

At the end of the run, a data file named *credit_card_tx_0_out.txt* of 114 MB was created at a throughput of 2.85 MB/second. This data file will be used for our first Hadoop MapReduce program to be discussed next (note that this program is available in the download for this book).

Listing 1.8 MapIncrease.java

```java
import java.io.BufferedReader;
import java.io.FileReader;
import java.io.FileWriter;
import java.io.IOException;
import java.io.PrintWriter;
import java.text.DateFormat;
import java.text.DecimalFormat;
```

```java
import java.text.SimpleDateFormat;
import java.util.ArrayList;
import java.util.Date;
import java.util.StringTokenizer;

public class MapIncrease {
    public static PrintWriter writer = null;
    public static BufferedReader reader = null;
    public static String dataFileIn = "credit_card_tx_0.txt";
    public static String dataFileOut;
    public static ArrayList<String> keys = new ArrayList<String>();
    public static int numOfKeys = 0;

    public static void main(String[] args) throws InterruptedException {
        String line = "";
        dataFileIn = args[0];
        dataFileOut = dataFileIn.substring(0, dataFileIn.lastIndexOf("."))
                + "_out.txt";
        long numOfTxs = Long.parseLong(args[1]);
        writer = createWriter(dataFileOut);
        long startTime = System.currentTimeMillis();

        try {
            reader = new BufferedReader(new FileReader(dataFileIn));
            while ((line = reader.readLine()) != null) {
                if (line.trim().contains("/") && !line.trim().isEmpty()
                        && !line.trim().startsWith("//")) {
                    addKeys(line);
                }
            }

        } catch (IOException ioe) {
            System.out.println(dataFileIn + " not found");
        }
        numOfKeys = keys.size();
        System.out.println("number of keys: " + numOfKeys);

        for (long i = 0; i < numOfTxs; i++) {
            String key = getKey();
            writeTx(key);
            if (i % 100000 == 0) {
                System.out.println ("number of Txs written: " + i);
            }
        }
```

```java
        writer.close ();
        long totalTimeInSec = (System.currentTimeMillis() - startTime) / 1000;
        System.out.println ("Total time in seconds: " +  totalTimeInSec);
        if ( totalTimeInSec > 60) {
            long totalTimeInMin = totalTimeInSec / 60;
            System.out.println ("Total time in minutes: " +  totalTimeInMin);
        }
        System.out.println ("Tx writing rate = " + (numOfTxs
                / totalTimeInSec) +"/sec");
    }

    public static PrintWriter createWriter(String fileName) {
        PrintWriter writer = null;
        try {
            writer = new PrintWriter(new FileWriter(fileName), true);
        } catch (IOException ioe) {

        }
        return writer;
    }

    public static String getKey() {
        int index = (int) (Math.random() * numOfKeys);
        return keys.get(index);
    }

    public static void writeTx(String key) {
        DateFormat df = new SimpleDateFormat("MM/dd/yyyy");
        DecimalFormat myFormatter = new DecimalFormat("###.##");

        long offset = (long) (1000 * 3600 * Math.random()) * 24 * 365 * 5;
        long currTime = System.currentTimeMillis();
        String txDate = df.format(new Date(currTime - offset));
        float amount = (float) (99.99 * Math.random());
        if (key.contains("PAYMENT")) amount = - amount;
        writer.println(txDate + "\t" + key + "\t" + myFormatter.format(amount));
    }

    public static void addKeys(String line) {
        StringTokenizer st = new StringTokenizer(line, "\t");
        String txDate = st.nextToken();
        String description = st.nextToken();
```

```
        String amount = st.nextToken();
        if (!keys.contains(description)) {
            System.out.println("added key: " + description);
            keys.add(description);
        }
    }
}
```

At this point, I am more anxious to help you get this first Hadoop MapReduce program up and running in a standalone Hadoop environment. Remember that a Hadoop MapReduce programs typically consists of three classes: a mapper class, a reducer class, and a driver class. Next, let us briefly review what we have with this simple Mapper program, the goal of which is to find the maximum amount spent at a store.

The Hadoop framework elements used in this simple Mapper program as shown in Listing 1.9 are as follows:

- It extends the Hadoop `Mapper` class with four typed parameters of `LongWritable`, `Text`, `Text`, and `FloatWritable` types, which are Hadoop data types. The first `LongWritable` is a key identifying every transaction record, while the next Text takes reach record as the *value*. The last two types of `Text` and `FloatWritable` are for out-going keys and values from the mapper for the *description* and *amount* fields, respectively.
- Each transaction record is parsed and then written out with the `context.write` statement as is highlighted at the end of the `if-block`. This step forms *n* <key, value> pairs to be processed by the Reducer program as is discussed next, where *n* is the total number of transaction records. Therefore, we can say that the function of the Mapper is to transform the original data into key-value pairs that Hadoop understands and processes in the subsequent *reduce* stage of MapReduce.

Listing 1.9 The first MapReduce example: the Mapper

```
import java.io.IOException;
import java.util.StringTokenizer;
import org.apache.hadoop.io.FloatWritable;
import org.apache.hadoop.io.LongWritable;
import org.apache.hadoop.io.Text;
import org.apache.hadoop.mapreduce.Mapper;

public class SpendingPatternMapper
  extends Mapper<LongWritable, Text, Text, FloatWritable> {

  @Override
  public void map(LongWritable key, Text value, Context context)
    throws IOException, InterruptedException {

  String line = value.toString();
```

```
  if (!line.contains ("PAYMENT")) { // filter PAYMENT line
  StringTokenizer st = new StringTokenizer (line, "\t");
  String tranxDate = st.nextToken();
  String description = st.nextToken();
  float amount = Float.parseFloat(st.nextToken());
  context.write(new Text(description), new FloatWritable(amount));
  }
 }
}
```

The Hadoop Reducer program shown in Listing 1.10 is as simple as the Mapper program as discussed above:

■ It extends the Hadoop Reducer class with four typed parameters of Text, FloatWritable, Text, and FloatWritable types. Note that the first pair of *Text-FloatWritable* is set up for the input *key-value* pairs from the Mapper class, while the second *Text-FloatWritable* pair is set up for the output *key-value* pairs from the Reducer program.

■ Each input key-values pair is processed and then is written out with the context.write statement as is highlighted at the end of the reduce method. For this program, the processing logic is to find the maximum amount spent at a store based on all transactions occurred at that store, passed in as key-values (one *key* with a series of *amount* values) from the mapper class discussed previously.

Listing 1.10 The first MapReduce example: the Reducer

```
import java.io.IOException;

import org.apache.hadoop.io.IntWritable;
import org.apache.hadoop.io.FloatWritable;
import org.apache.hadoop.io.Text;
import org.apache.hadoop.mapreduce.Reducer;

public class SpendingPatternReducer
  extends Reducer<Text, FloatWritable, Text, FloatWritable> {

 @Override
 public void reduce(Text key, Iterable<FloatWritable> values,
   Context context)
   throws IOException, InterruptedException {

 float maxValue = Float.MIN_VALUE;
 for (FloatWritable value : values) {
  maxValue = Math.max(maxValue, value.get());
 }
```

```
    context.write(key, new FloatWritable(maxValue));
  }
}
```

The last piece is the Hadoop driver program, which is shown in Listing 1.11. Its execution logic is as follows:

- First, it creates a Hadoop Job with the setJarByClass and setJobName methods.
- Then, it sets the input path and output path through Hadoop's InputFormat and OutputFormat classes, respectively.
- The next a few lines set the mapper class, reducer class, output key class, and output value class.
- At last, it waits until the job is complete.

If you are new to programming, you might wonder how come it is so simple to write a Hadoop MapReduce program. That's what it means by a *framework* – the Hadoop framework does all behind the scene. Let's see what Hadoop does behind the scene by running this simple Hadoop MapReduce program next.

Listing 1.11 The first MapReduce example: the driver

```
import org.apache.hadoop.fs.Path;
import org.apache.hadoop.io.FloatWritable;
import org.apache.hadoop.io.Text;
import org.apache.hadoop.mapreduce.Job;
import org.apache.hadoop.mapreduce.lib.input.FileInputFormat;
import org.apache.hadoop.mapreduce.lib.output.FileOutputFormat;

public class SpendingPattern {

  public static void main(String[] args) throws Exception {
    if (args.length != 2) {
      System.err.println("Usage: SpendingPattern <input path> <output path>");
      System.exit(-1);
    }

    Job job = new Job();
    job.setJarByClass(SpendingPattern.class);
    job.setJobName("Spending Pattern");

    FileInputFormat.addInputPath(job, new Path(args[0]));
    FileOutputFormat.setOutputPath(job, new Path(args[1]));

    job.setMapperClass(SpendingPatternMapper.class);
    job.setReducerClass(SpendingPatternReducer.class);
```

```
    job.setOutputKeyClass(Text.class);
    job.setOutputValueClass(FloatWritable.class);

    System.exit(job.waitForCompletion(true) ? 0 : 1);
  }
}
```

At this point, if you have not done so, you might want to download the source code of this book at http://www.perfmath.com and manually drop these Java source files located in the module1 directory into the same directory in the Hadoop project you created.

1.2.5 Running Hadoop in Local or Standalone Mode

For development and debug purposes, you can run Hadoop in local or standalone mode. In this case, there is no need to configure Hadoop and no daemons need to run in the background. The three configuration files in Hadoop's conf directory, core-site.xml, hdfs-site.xml, and mapred-site.xml, do not contain any parameter settings. This will become clear after we describe how to set up Hadoop to run in pseudo-distributed mode in the next section.

To run this MapReduce program on Hadoop, we need to package it into a jar file. This is accomplished with the following command executed at a bash shell prompt in the MyHadoop-1.0.3 project directory:

```
$mvn clean package –DskipTests –Dhadoop.version=1.0.3
```

After the above step, you should see a spending-patterns.jar file. You can copy this jar file to your $HADOOP_INSTALL directory and run it by executing the following command (you may also need to make sure or copy the credit_card_tx_0_out.txt file to the in0 directory of your $HADOOP_INSTALL directory):

```
$hadoop jar spending-patterns.jar SpendingPattern in0/credit_card_tx_0_out.txt out0
```

With the above command, *SpendingPattern* is the Hadoop driver program (Listing 1.11), *in0* is the *input* directory that contains the input data file of *credit_card_tx_0_out.txt* with 200k credit card transaction records produced with the *MapIncrease* program (Listing 1.8) discussed previously, and *out0* is the directory for final reduce output. Keep in mind that the output directory for each run must not exist before the run is launched.

Listing 1.12 shows the complete Hadoop MapReduce output from the job submitted as described above. It is contained in a file named part-r-00000 located in the *out0* directory as specified when the job was submitted. This file contains the maximum amount spent at each store based on the 200k transactions contained in the input file. Note the maximum amount is $99.99 for most of the stores, which is because it is the maximum amount hard-coded in the MapIncrease program. This artificial effect is less important here.

Listing 1.12 The Reducer output for the first MapReduce example (44 items)

```
mc815ll:MyHadoop-1.0.3 henry$ cat out0/part-r-00000
76 10115095          SUNNYVALE    CA    99.92
76CR5754SUNNYVALE10080067 SUNNYVALE    CA   99.97
99 RANCH #1776       SAN FRANCISCO CA    99.99
BABIES R US #6447 QPS SUNNYVALE     CA   99.98
BR/TOGO'S #332475 Q35 SUNNYVALE     CA 99.94
CENTURY THEATRES 41QPS SUNNYVALE    CA    99.98
CUTEGIRL.COM         CUPERTINO CA  99.95
CVS PHARMACY #9923    SUNNYVALE     CA 99.99
Chinese Gourmet Expres CUPERTINO CA   99.98
DISH NETWORK-ONE TIME  800-894-9131 CO 99.99
DISNEY RESORT-WDTC    ANAHEIM      CA 99.99
DOLRTREE 1228 00012286 SUNNYVALE     CA    99.98
GROCERY OUTLET OF FO   SUNNYVALE     CA 99.93
GYMBOREE  504850050483 SUNNYVALE    CA    99.98
IDEAL CUTS           SUNNYVALE     CA 99.93
KOHLS #0663          SUNNYVALE     CA    99.99
KP INTERNATIONAL MARKE MILPITAS CA  99.97
LORI'S GIFTS STORE#233 SAN FRANCISCO  CA 99.98
MACY'S EAST #408     MOUNTAIN VIEW CA   99.99
MARSHALLS # 821      SUNNYVALE     CA 99.98
MCDONALD'S F20253    SUNNYVALE     CA   99.98
MCDONALD'S F26393    SUNNYVALE     CA   99.88
MCDONALD'S F33506    MOUNTAIN VIEW CA 99.94
MCDONALD'S F5447     SUNNYVALE     CA   99.97
MEG*LEGOLANDCALIFORNIA 760-918-5346 CA    99.96
MEMBERSHIP FEE AUG 12-JUL 13  99.91
PETSMART INC 54      SUNNYVALE     CA 99.94
PRETZEL TIME SUNRISE  CUPERTINO CA   99.97
ROSS STORE #483      SUNNYVALE     CA 99.99
RUE21 # 384 SUNNYVALE    SUNNYVALE     CA    99.94
S F SUPERMARKET      SAN FRANCISCO CA   99.98
SAFEWAY STORE 00017947 SUNNYVALE     CA    99.94
SAMSCLUB #6620       SUNNYVALE     CA 99.99
SAVEMART 607 SUNNYVALE   SUNNYVALE     CA 99.98
SIX FLAGS DISCOVERY KI 07076444000  CA    99.99
SIX FLAGS DISCOVERY KI VALLEJO      CA    99.98
SKECHERS-USA #119    SAN FRANCISCO CA 99.99
TARGET        00010983 SUNNYVALE     CA 99.97
THAO FASHION MUSIC CTR SAN FRANCISCO   CA  99.97
TOGOS BASKIN SUNNYVALE   SUNNYVALE     CA 99.95
TOYS R US #5808   QPS CUPERTINO CA    99.96
TRICKS GYMNASTICS DANC 916-3510024  CA 99.98
TRU HOLIDAY EXPRESSQPS SUNNYVALE     CA    99.98
WAL-MART #1760       SUNNYVALE     CA    99.96
mc815ll:MyHadoop-1.0.3 henry$
```

Listing 1.13 shows the Hadoop job progress report output on the console for the above job. Note that if you care about the message of

"Unable to load realm info from SCDynamicStore"

from the output shown in Listing 1.13, you can add (all in one line) the following line to your hadoop-env.sh file in the conf directory

export HADOOP_OPTS="-Djava.security.krb5.realm=OX.AC.UK - Djava.security.krb5.kdc=kdc0.ox.ac.uk:kdc1.ox.ac.uk"

as suggested by a post at https://issues.apache.org/jira/browse/HADOOP-7489.

Figure 1.22 summarizes schematically the Hadoop APIs involved in creating the console output for the above Hadoop job. The console output shown in Listing 1.13 is lengthy, but it describes exactly how a Hadoop job is executed. Here is a recap of the MapReduce sequences that occurred during that run, based on Listing 1.13:

1) One input path was identified for processing.
2) A local job with the ID of *job_local_0001* was started.
3) The map task initiated flushing map output.
4) The map task *attempt_local_0001_m_000000_0* was committed and done.
5) Merged 1 sorted segment.
6) The reduce task *attempt_local_0001_r_000000_0* completed with the output saved to the *out0* directory as specified in the job-launch command.

Also note in the counter report section of Map input records=200000 and Reduce output records=44, indicating that 200k credit card transaction records were mapped and the reduce task resulted in 44 reduce output records. These statistics are consistent with the number of 200k input records associated with 44 unique transaction descriptions indicating where those transactions occurred.

The other piece of information that can be arrived at from the job progress report is that the map task took 3 seconds, while the reduce task took 4 seconds with this specific job. In fact, I ran this same program on the same local Hadoop setup with 2M transactions, which is 10 times larger in data size than the above run. The output is given in Listing 1.14. With this 2M transaction job, the map task took 18 seconds, while the reduce task took 4 seconds. Both jobs took the same amount of time of 4 seconds for the reduce task.

In addition, you can see from Listing 1.14 that spillings began to occur when the input data size was increased from 200k to 2M. Notice the parameter io.sort.mb =100 in both Listing 1.13 and Listing 1.14. This parameter defines the size of in-memory buffer in MBs used by a map task for sorting data. Spills occur when a map task's in-memory buffer becomes insufficient for sorting all its data in memory that some must be spilled to disk. Finally, the 2M transaction job was carried out with four map tasks and one reduce task (See Figure 1.23 for the MapReduce process exhibited with this 2M credit card transaction job). We will discuss more about Hadoop MapReduce job and data flows in the next chapter when we set up a cluster to run this same Hadoop program in distributed mode.

Listing 1.13 Console output for the first MapReduce example run with an input data file of 200k credit card transactions

mc815ll:MyHadoop-1.0.3 henry$ **hadoop jar spending-patterns.jar SpendingPattern in0/credit_card_tx_0_out.txt out0**
2012-08-23 22:12:08.122 java[10447:1903] Unable to load realm info from SCDynamicStore
12/08/23 22:12:08 WARN util.NativeCodeLoader: Unable to load native-hadoop library for your platform... using builtin-java classes where applicable
12/08/23 22:12:08 WARN mapred.JobClient: Use GenericOptionsParser for parsing the arguments. Applications should implement Tool for the same.
12/08/23 22:12:08 INFO input.FileInputFormat: Total input paths to process : 1
12/08/23 22:12:08 WARN snappy.LoadSnappy: Snappy native library not loaded
12/08/23 22:12:08 INFO mapred.JobClient: Running job: job_local_0001
12/08/23 22:12:08 INFO mapred.Task: Using ResourceCalculatorPlugin : null
12/08/23 22:12:08 INFO mapred.MapTask: io.sort.mb = 100
12/08/23 22:12:08 INFO mapred.MapTask: data buffer = 79691776/99614720
12/08/23 22:12:08 INFO mapred.MapTask: record buffer = 262144/327680
12/08/23 22:12:09 INFO mapred.JobClient: map 0% reduce 0%
12/08/23 22:12:09 INFO mapred.MapTask: **Starting flush of map output**
12/08/23 22:12:09 INFO mapred.MapTask: Finished spill 0
12/08/23 22:12:09 INFO mapred.Task: Task:attempt_local_0001_m_000000_0 is done. And is in the process of commiting
12/08/23 22:12:11 INFO mapred.Task: Task 'attempt_local_0001_m_000000_0' done.
12/08/23 22:12:11 INFO mapred.Task: Using ResourceCalculatorPlugin : null
12/08/23 22:12:11 INFO mapred.LocalJobRunner:
12/08/23 22:12:11 INFO mapred.Merger: **Merging 1 sorted segments**
12/08/23 22:12:11 INFO mapred.Merger: Down to the last merge-pass, with 1 segments left of total size: 9309163 bytes
12/08/23 22:12:11 INFO mapred.Task: Task:attempt_local_0001_r_000000_0 is done. And is in the process of commiting
12/08/23 22:12:11 INFO mapred.Task: Task attempt_local_0001_r_000000_0 is allowed to commit now
12/08/23 22:12:11 INFO output.FileOutputCommitter: Saved output of task 'attempt_local_0001_r_000000_0' to out0
12/08/23 22:12:12 INFO mapred.JobClient: **map 100% reduce 0%**
12/08/23 22:12:14 INFO mapred.LocalJobRunner: reduce > reduce
12/08/23 22:12:14 INFO mapred.Task: Task **'attempt_local_0001_r_000000_0' done**.
12/08/23 22:12:15 INFO mapred.JobClient: map 100% reduce 100%
12/08/23 22:12:15 INFO mapred.JobClient: **Job complete: job_local_0001**
12/08/23 22:12:15 INFO mapred.JobClient: **Counters: 17**
12/08/23 22:12:15 INFO mapred.JobClient: File Output Format Counters
12/08/23 22:12:15 INFO mapred.JobClient: Bytes Written=2122
12/08/23 22:12:15 INFO mapred.JobClient: FileSystemCounters
12/08/23 22:12:15 INFO mapred.JobClient: FILE_BYTES_READ=32784765
12/08/23 22:12:15 INFO mapred.JobClient: FILE_BYTES_WRITTEN=18698124
12/08/23 22:12:15 INFO mapred.JobClient: File Input Format Counters
12/08/23 22:12:15 INFO mapred.JobClient: Bytes Read=11730880
12/08/23 22:12:15 INFO mapred.JobClient: Map-Reduce Framework
12/08/23 22:12:15 INFO mapred.JobClient: Map output materialized bytes=9309167
12/08/23 22:12:15 INFO mapred.JobClient: **Map input records=200000**
12/08/23 22:12:15 INFO mapred.JobClient: Reduce shuffle bytes=0
12/08/23 22:12:15 INFO mapred.JobClient: Spilled Records=391180

```
12/08/23 22:12:15 INFO mapred.JobClient:    Map output bytes=8917981
12/08/23 22:12:15 INFO mapred.JobClient:    Total committed heap usage (bytes)=392667136
12/08/23 22:12:15 INFO mapred.JobClient:    SPLIT_RAW_BYTES=141
12/08/23 22:12:15 INFO mapred.JobClient:    Combine input records=0
12/08/23 22:12:15 INFO mapred.JobClient:    Reduce input records=195590
12/08/23 22:12:15 INFO mapred.JobClient:    Reduce input groups=44
12/08/23 22:12:15 INFO mapred.JobClient:    Combine output records=0
12/08/23 22:12:15 INFO mapred.JobClient:    Reduce output records=44
12/08/23 22:12:15 INFO mapred.JobClient:    Map output records=195590
mc815ll:MyHadoop-1.0.3 henry$
```

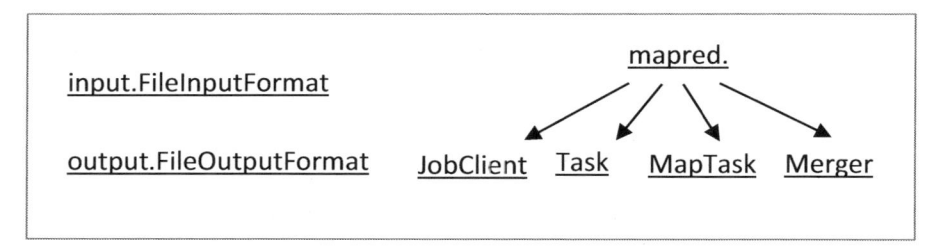

Figure 1.22 Hadoop job control APIs

Listing 1.14 Console output for the first MapReduce example run with an input data file of 2M credit card transactions

```
mc815ll:MyHadoop-1.0.3 henry$ hadoop jar spending-patterns.jar SpendingPattern
in0/credit_card_tx_0_out.txt out0
2012-08-23 19:34:57.971 java[10071:1903] Unable to load realm info from SCDynamicStore
12/08/23 19:34:58 WARN util.NativeCodeLoader: Unable to load native-hadoop library for your
platform... using builtin-java classes where applicable
12/08/23 19:34:58 WARN mapred.JobClient: Use GenericOptionsParser for parsing the arguments.
Applications should implement Tool for the same.
12/08/23 19:34:58 INFO input.FileInputFormat: Total input paths to process : 1
12/08/23 19:34:58 WARN snappy.LoadSnappy: Snappy native library not loaded
12/08/23 19:34:58 INFO mapred.JobClient: Running job: job_local_0001
12/08/23 19:34:58 INFO mapred.Task:  Using ResourceCalculatorPlugin : null
12/08/23 19:34:58 INFO mapred.MapTask: io.sort.mb = 100
12/08/23 19:34:58 INFO mapred.MapTask: data buffer = 79691776/99614720
12/08/23 19:34:58 INFO mapred.MapTask: record buffer = 262144/327680
12/08/23 19:34:59 INFO mapred.JobClient:  map 0% reduce 0%
12/08/23 19:34:59 INFO mapred.MapTask: Spilling map output: record full = true
12/08/23 19:34:59 INFO mapred.MapTask: bufstart = 0; bufend = 11950965; bufvoid = 99614720
12/08/23 19:34:59 INFO mapred.MapTask: kvstart = 0; kvend = 262144; length = 327680
12/08/23 19:35:00 INFO mapred.MapTask: Finished spill 0
12/08/23 19:35:00 INFO mapred.MapTask: Spilling map output: record full = true
12/08/23 19:35:00 INFO mapred.MapTask: bufstart = 11950965; bufend = 23902476; bufvoid =
99614720
```

12/08/23 19:35:00 INFO mapred.MapTask: kvstart = 262144; kvend = 196607; length = 327680
12/08/23 19:35:01 INFO mapred.MapTask: Starting flush of map output
12/08/23 19:35:01 INFO mapred.MapTask: Finished spill 1
12/08/23 19:35:01 INFO mapred.MapTask: Finished spill 2
12/08/23 19:35:01 INFO mapred.Merger: Merging 3 sorted segments
12/08/23 19:35:01 INFO mapred.Merger: Down to the last merge-pass, with 3 segments left of total
size: 26625462 bytes
12/08/23 19:35:02 INFO mapred.Task: Task:attempt_local_0001_m_000000_0 is done. And is in the
process of commiting
12/08/23 19:35:04 INFO mapred.Task: Task 'attempt_local_0001_m_000000_0' done.
12/08/23 19:35:04 INFO mapred.Task: Using ResourceCalculatorPlugin : null
12/08/23 19:35:04 INFO mapred.MapTask: io.sort.mb = 100
12/08/23 19:35:04 INFO mapred.MapTask: data buffer = 79691776/99614720
12/08/23 19:35:04 INFO mapred.MapTask: record buffer = 262144/327680
12/08/23 19:35:05 INFO mapred.MapTask: Spilling map output: record full = true
12/08/23 19:35:05 INFO mapred.MapTask: bufstart = 0; bufend = 11952473; bufvoid = 99614720
12/08/23 19:35:05 INFO mapred.MapTask: kvstart = 0; kvend = 262144; length = 327680
12/08/23 19:35:05 INFO mapred.JobClient: **map 100% reduce 0%**
12/08/23 19:35:05 INFO mapred.MapTask: Finished spill 0
12/08/23 19:35:06 INFO mapred.MapTask: Spilling map output: record full = true
12/08/23 19:35:06 INFO mapred.MapTask: bufstart = 11952473; bufend = 23902724; bufvoid =
99614720
12/08/23 19:35:06 INFO mapred.MapTask: kvstart = 262144; kvend = 196607; length = 327680
12/08/23 19:35:06 INFO mapred.MapTask: Starting flush of map output
12/08/23 19:35:06 INFO mapred.MapTask: Finished spill 1
12/08/23 19:35:06 INFO mapred.MapTask: Finished spill 2
12/08/23 19:35:06 INFO mapred.Merger: Merging 3 sorted segments
12/08/23 19:35:06 INFO mapred.Merger: Down to the last merge-pass, with 3 segments left of total
size: 26623561 bytes
12/08/23 19:35:07 INFO mapred.Task: Task:attempt_local_0001_m_000001_0 is done. And is in the
process of commiting
12/08/23 19:35:10 INFO mapred.Task: Task 'attempt_local_0001_m_000001_0' done.
12/08/23 19:35:10 INFO mapred.Task: Using ResourceCalculatorPlugin : null
12/08/23 19:35:10 INFO mapred.MapTask: io.sort.mb = 100
12/08/23 19:35:10 INFO mapred.MapTask: data buffer = 79691776/99614720
12/08/23 19:35:10 INFO mapred.MapTask: record buffer = 262144/327680
12/08/23 19:35:11 INFO mapred.MapTask: Spilling map output: record full = true
12/08/23 19:35:11 INFO mapred.MapTask: bufstart = 0; bufend = 11950574; bufvoid = 99614720
12/08/23 19:35:11 INFO mapred.MapTask: kvstart = 0; kvend = 262144; length = 327680
12/08/23 19:35:11 INFO mapred.MapTask: Finished spill 0
12/08/23 19:35:12 INFO mapred.MapTask: Spilling map output: record full = true
12/08/23 19:35:12 INFO mapred.MapTask: bufstart = 11950574; bufend = 23903880; bufvoid =
99614720
12/08/23 19:35:12 INFO mapred.MapTask: kvstart = 262144; kvend = 196607; length = 327680
12/08/23 19:35:12 INFO mapred.MapTask: Starting flush of map output
12/08/23 19:35:12 INFO mapred.MapTask: Finished spill 1
12/08/23 19:35:12 INFO mapred.MapTask: Finished spill 2
12/08/23 19:35:12 INFO mapred.Merger: Merging 3 sorted segments

12/08/23 19:35:12 INFO mapred.Merger: Down to the last merge-pass, with 3 segments left of total size: 26621953 bytes
12/08/23 19:35:13 INFO mapred.Task: Task:attempt_local_0001_m_000002_0 is done. And is in the process of commiting
12/08/23 19:35:13 INFO mapred.Task: Task 'attempt_local_0001_m_000002_0' done.
12/08/23 19:35:13 INFO mapred.Task: Using ResourceCalculatorPlugin : null
12/08/23 19:35:13 INFO mapred.MapTask: io.sort.mb = 100
12/08/23 19:35:13 INFO mapred.MapTask: data buffer = 79691776/99614720
12/08/23 19:35:13 INFO mapred.MapTask: record buffer = 262144/327680
12/08/23 19:35:14 INFO mapred.MapTask: Spilling map output: record full = true
12/08/23 19:35:14 INFO mapred.MapTask: bufstart = 0; bufend = 11952081; bufvoid = 99614720
12/08/23 19:35:14 INFO mapred.MapTask: kvstart = 0; kvend = 262144; length = 327680
12/08/23 19:35:14 INFO mapred.MapTask: Starting flush of map output
12/08/23 19:35:14 INFO mapred.MapTask: Finished spill 0
12/08/23 19:35:14 INFO mapred.MapTask: Finished spill 1
12/08/23 19:35:14 INFO mapred.Merger: Merging 2 sorted segments
12/08/23 19:35:14 INFO mapred.Merger: Down to the last merge-pass, with 2 segments left of total size: 13197224 bytes
12/08/23 19:35:15 INFO mapred.Task: Task:attempt_local_0001_m_000003_0 is done. And is in the process of commiting
12/08/23 19:35:16 INFO mapred.Task: Task 'attempt_local_0001_m_000003_0' done.
12/08/23 19:35:16 INFO mapred.Task: Using ResourceCalculatorPlugin : null
12/08/23 19:35:16 INFO mapred.LocalJobRunner:
12/08/23 19:35:16 INFO mapred.Merger: Merging 4 sorted segments
12/08/23 19:35:16 INFO mapred.Merger: Down to the last merge-pass, with 4 segments left of total size: 93068186 bytes
12/08/23 19:35:18 INFO mapred.Task: Task:attempt_local_0001_r_000000_0 is done. And is in the process of commiting
12/08/23 19:35:18 INFO mapred.Task: Task attempt_local_0001_r_000000_0 is allowed to commit now
12/08/23 19:35:18 INFO output.FileOutputCommitter: Saved output of task 'attempt_local_0001_r_000000_0' to out0
12/08/23 19:35:19 INFO mapred.LocalJobRunner: **reduce > reduce**
12/08/23 19:35:19 INFO mapred.Task: Task 'attempt_local_0001_r_000000_0' done.
12/08/23 19:35:20 INFO mapred.JobClient: **map 100% reduce 100%**
12/08/23 19:35:20 INFO mapred.JobClient: Job complete: job_local_0001
12/08/23 19:35:20 INFO mapred.JobClient: **Counters: 17**
12/08/23 19:35:20 INFO mapred.JobClient: **File Output Format Counters**
12/08/23 19:35:20 INFO mapred.JobClient: Bytes Written=2122
12/08/23 19:35:20 INFO mapred.JobClient: **FileSystemCounters**
12/08/23 19:35:20 INFO mapred.JobClient: FILE_BYTES_READ=874960600
12/08/23 19:35:20 INFO mapred.JobClient: FILE_BYTES_WRITTEN=691962881
12/08/23 19:35:20 INFO mapred.JobClient: **File Input Format Counters**
12/08/23 19:35:20 INFO mapred.JobClient: Bytes Read=117308458
12/08/23 19:35:20 INFO mapred.JobClient: **Map-Reduce Framework**
12/08/23 19:35:20 INFO mapred.JobClient: Map output materialized bytes=93068202
12/08/23 19:35:20 INFO mapred.JobClient: Map input records=2000000
12/08/23 19:35:20 INFO mapred.JobClient: Reduce shuffle bytes=0

```
12/08/23 19:35:20 INFO mapred.JobClient:    Spilled Records=5866632
12/08/23 19:35:20 INFO mapred.JobClient:    Map output bytes=89157090
12/08/23 19:35:20 INFO mapred.JobClient:    Total committed heap usage (bytes)=998510592
12/08/23 19:35:20 INFO mapred.JobClient:    SPLIT_RAW_BYTES=564
12/08/23 19:35:20 INFO mapred.JobClient:    Combine input records=0
12/08/23 19:35:20 INFO mapred.JobClient:    Reduce input records=1955544
12/08/23 19:35:20 INFO mapred.JobClient:    Reduce input groups=44
12/08/23 19:35:20 INFO mapred.JobClient:    Combine output records=0
12/08/23 19:35:20 INFO mapred.JobClient:    Reduce output records=44
12/08/23 19:35:20 INFO mapred.JobClient:    Map output records=1955544
mc815ll:MyHadoop-1.0.3 henry$
```

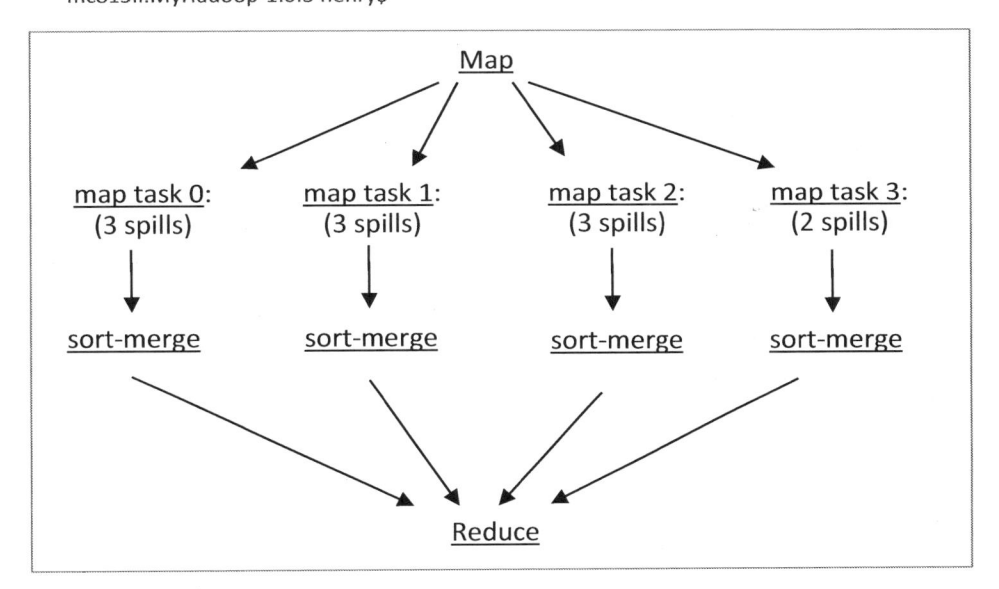

Figure 1.23 Hadoop job and data flows in a standalone environment.

1.2.6 Running Hadoop in Pseudo-Distributed Mode

Running Hadoop in a standalone environment is recommended only for development and debugging Hadoop code. The next step is to run Hadoop in pseudo-distributed mode. Arguably, even running Hadoop in pseudo-distributed environment should be avoided as much as possible, simply because it's so easy to find a few cheap PCs, put up Linux on to them, and set up a Linux cluster to run Hadoop. This is our focus in Chapter 2. For the sake of completeness, let's see how we can set up a pseudo-distributed Hadoop environment in this section. One benefit of doing so is that after you learn how to set a pseudo-distributed Hadoop environment, most of the procedures actually apply to setting up a real cluster.

SSH Configuration

If you are on Mac OS X, it's necessary to first enable remote login as shown in Figure 1.24 (you can access this Dialog from System Preferences → Sharing). Note that File Sharing and Printer Sharing are not related to Hadoop.

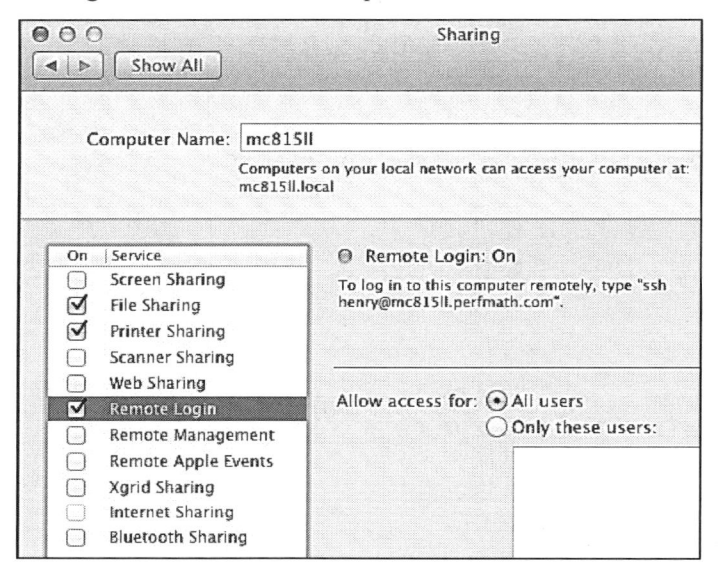

Figure 1.24 Enabling remote login on Mac OS X

Mac OS X has SSH bundled out of the box. However, Hadoop requires passphrase-less SSH login, so execute the following commands to make sure passphrase-less SSH connection is enabled on your Mac OS X (note the two single quotes with no space in between following the option "-P" in the first command).

```
$ ssh-keygen –t rsa –P '' –f ~/.ssh/id_rsa
$ cat ~/.ssh/id_rsa.pub >> ~/.ssh/authorized_keys
$ ssh localhost
```

If your "ssh localhost" command is successful, namely, you can log in without requiring a password, it means that it's all set. Otherwise, you need to figure out how to fix it before proceeding further.

Formatting Hadoop HDFS

Standalone mode uses local OS filesystem, whereas distributed mode requires using the HDFS (Hadoop Distributed FileSystem). To format the HDFS, execute the following command:

```
$ hadoop namenode -format
```

Note the entity "namenode" in the above command. In case you are wondering what a *namenode* is, here is what the Apache Hadoop API doc has to say about it (http://hadoop.apache.org/common/docs/r0.15.2/api/org/apache/hadoop/dfs/NameNode.html   ) with some minor reformatting (this is very good technical reading and it's worthwhile to spend a few minutes to read it):

NameNode serves as both directory namespace manager and "inode table" for the Hadoop DFS. There is a single NameNode running in any DFS deployment. (Well, except when there is a second backup/failover NameNode.)

The NameNode controls two critical tables:

1) filename->blocksequence (namespace)

2) block->machinelist ("inodes")

The first table is stored on disk and is very precious. The second table is rebuilt every time the NameNode comes up. 'NameNode' refers to both this class as well as the 'NameNode server'. The 'FSNamesystem' class actually performs most of the filesystem management. The majority of the 'NameNode' class itself is concerned with exposing the IPC interface to the outside world, plus some configuration management. NameNode implements the ClientProtocol interface, which allows clients to ask for DFS services. ClientProtocol is not designed for direct use by authors of DFS client code. End-users should instead use the org.apache.nutch.hadoop.fs.FileSystem class. NameNode also implements the DatanodeProtocol interface, used by DataNode programs that actually store DFS data blocks. These methods are invoked repeatedly and automatically by all the DataNodes in a DFS deployment. NameNode also implements the NamenodeProtocol interface, used by secondary namenodes or rebalancing processes to get partial namenode's state, for example partial blocksMap etc.

Configuring Hadoop for Pseudo-Distributed mode

Configuring Hadoop for pseudo-distributed mode involves modifying the files *core-site.xml, hdfs-site.xml, mapred-site.xml, masters,* and *slaves* in Hadoop's *conf* directory and make sure they are configured as shown in Listings 1.15 (a) through (e). Although you can do so in Hadoop's `conf` directory, here is what I did:

```
$ mkdir conf_pseudo
$ cd conf_pseudo
$ cp ../conf/*.xml .
$ cp ../conf/masters .
$ cp ../conf/slaves .
$ edit core-sit.xml, hdfs-sit.xml, mapred-site.xml, masters, and slaves as shown in Listings
1.15 (a) through (e)
```

The intention was to place those files in a separate directory so that we can have multiple configurations for various experimentations. Otherwise, we would have to keep modifying these files all the time whenever when we want to change to a different mode or configuration.

Listing 1.15 (a) Pseudo-distributed mode: core-site.xml

```
<?xml version="1.0"?>
```

```
<?xml-stylesheet type="text/xsl" href="configuration.xsl"?>
<configuration>
<property>
<name>fs.default.name</name>
<value>hdfs://localhost:8020</value>
</property>
</configuration>
```

Listing 1.15 (b) Pseudo-distributed mode: hdfs-site.xml

```
<?xml version="1.0"?>
<?xml-stylesheet type="text/xsl" href="configuration.xsl"?>
<configuration>
<property>
<name>dfs.replication</name>
<value>1</value>
</property>
</configuration>
```

Listing 1.15 (c) Pseudo-distributed mode: mapred-site.xml

```
<?xml version="1.0"?>
<?xml-stylesheet type="text/xsl" href="configuration.xsl"?>
<configuration>
<property>
<name>mapred.job.tracker</name>
<value>localhost:8021</value>
</property>
</configuration>
```

Listing 1.15 (d) Pseudo-distributed mode: masters

```
localhost
```

Listing 1.15 (e) Pseudo-distributed mode: slaves

```
localhost
```

You may also need to copy your *hadoop-env.sh* file from *conf* to *conf_pseudo* directory to avoid getting a "*JAVA_HOME is not set*" error when you start up the *dfs* and *mapred* daemons (refer to Section 1.2.1 about how to set JAVA_HOME environment variable in hadoop-env.sh file). When you are ready, cd to Hadoop's install directory and execute the following commands (use two consecutive dashes "--" before *config*):

```
$ bin/start-dfs.sh --config conf_pseudo
```

```
$ bin/start-mapred.sh --config conf_pseudo
```

You can verify by executing the following *jps* command to make sure that all daemons of *Namenode*, *Datanode*, *SecondaryNameNode*, *JobTracker* and *TaskTracker* have been started up properly. See Figure 1.25 as a reference on what to expect after you execute the *jps* command. We discuss more about these daemons in the next chapter when we explain how to run Hadoop on a cluster.

```
$ $JAVA_HOME/bin/jps
```

```
mc81511:hadoop-1.0.3 henry$ bin/start-dfs.sh --config conf_pseudo
starting namenode, logging to /Users/henry/dev/hadoop-1.0.3/libexec/../logs/hadoop
localhost: starting datanode, logging to /Users/henry/dev/hadoop-1.0.3/libexec/../
localhost: starting secondarynamenode, logging to /Users/henry/dev/hadoop-1.0.3/li
mc81511:hadoop-1.0.3 henry$ $JAVA_HOME/bin/jps
12972 Jps
2021
12860 DataNode
12772 NameNode
12948 SecondaryNameNode
mc81511:hadoop-1.0.3 henry$ bin/start-mapred.sh --config conf_pseudo
starting jobtracker, logging to /Users/henry/dev/hadoop-1.0.3/libexec/../logs/hado
localhost: starting tasktracker, logging to /Users/henry/dev/hadoop-1.0.3/libexec/
mc81511:hadoop-1.0.3 henry$ $JAVA_HOME/bin/jps
13017 JobTracker
2021
13105 TaskTracker
12860 DataNode
12772 NameNode
12948 SecondaryNameNode
13133 Jps
mc81511:hadoop-1.0.3 henry$
```

Figure 1.25 Verifying Hadoop running in pseudo-distributed mode using the Java jps command

You can also verify that your Hadoop is running in pseudo-distributed mode by accessing your NameNode admin console at http://localhost:50070 and MapReduce admin console at http://localhost:50037, as shown in Figures 1.26 and 1.27, respectively. On the NameNode admin console, it has two sections: one under *Cluster Summary* and the other under *NameNode Storage*. The Cluster Summary section reports statistics about the DFS (distributed filesystem), while the NameNode Storage section reports the state of the temporary storage. Since Hadoop map tasks need to do a lot of sorting and merging work, it requires temporary disk storage set up *a priori* when the allocated in-memory space becomes insufficient (recall the concept of spills we explained earlier). The NameNode admin console also reports the number of Live Nodes, Dead Nodes, Decommissioning Nodes, which would be more interesting to look at when you have a large cluster.

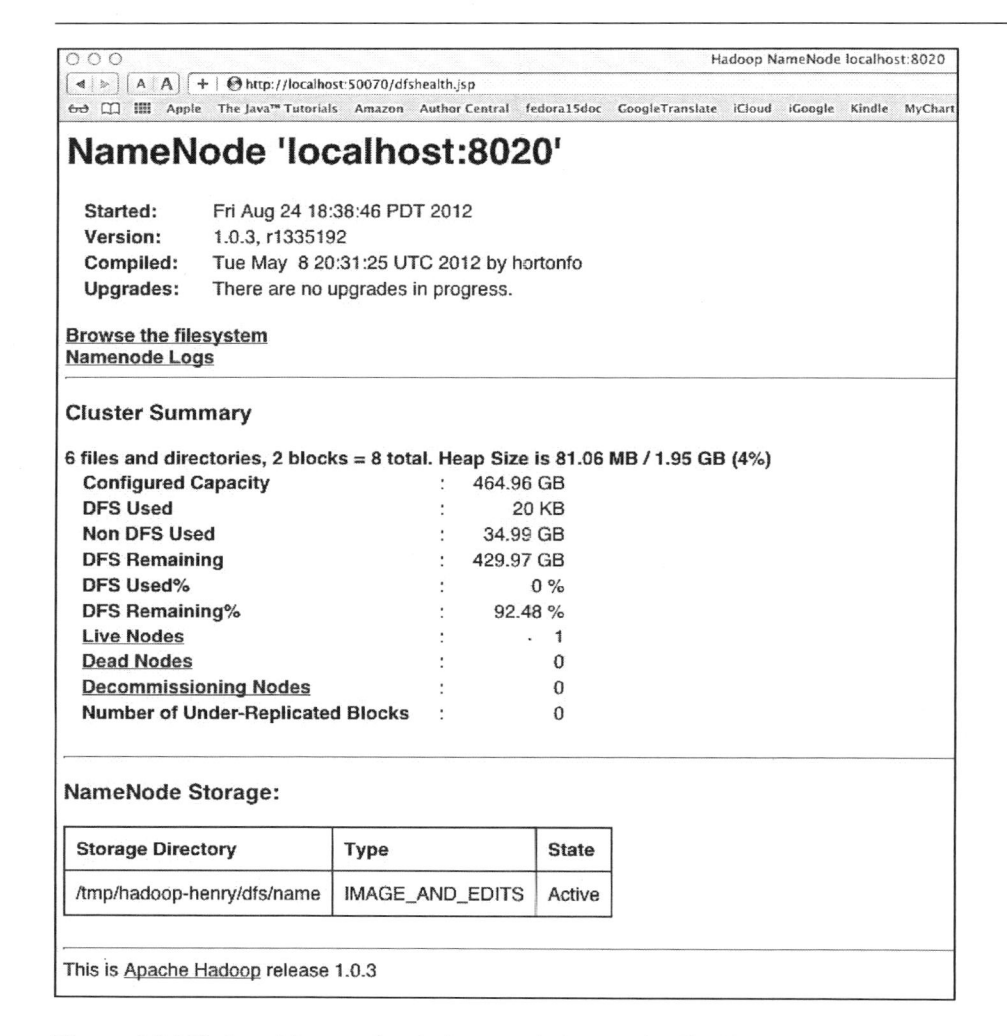

Figure 1.26 Hadoop Namenode admin console in pseudo-distributed mode

The Map/Reduce admin console has the following sections:

- **Cluster Summary**: Reports details about running map and reduce tasks, and so on.
- **Scheduling Information**: Reports queues for scheduled jobs. By default, there is only one queue named *default*.
- Running/Retired Jobs/Local Logs: We don't have a lot to look at here. We will see more later.

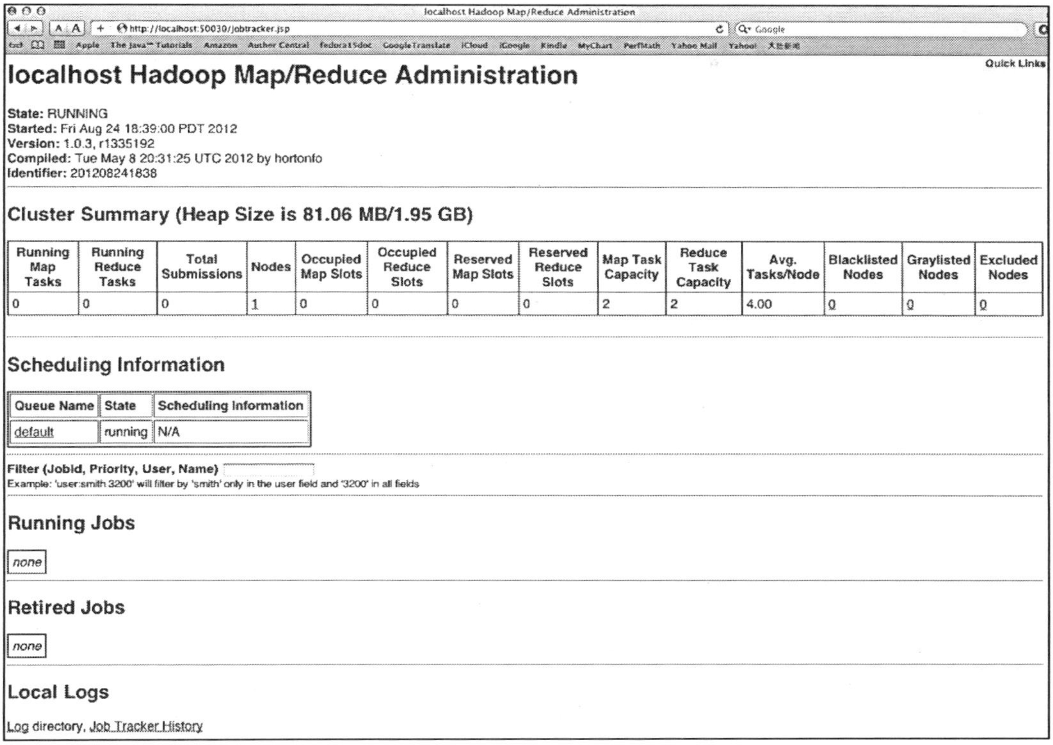

Figure 1.27 Hadoop Namenode admin console in pseudo-distributed mode

To stop those daemons, execute "*stop-dfs.sh*" and "*stop-mapred.sh*" instead.

I ran the same 2M job as described previously and saw no difference than running Hadoop in local mode. Since pseudo-distributed mode is not *real* distributed mode, it may not be worthwhile to spend too much time on it. My recommendation is either run Hadoop in local mode or in real distributed mode on a Linux cluster.

1.2.7 Running Hadoop on a Cluster in Fully Distributed Mode

Running Hadoop on a cluster in fully distributed mode requires more than one machine. It's actually not so difficult to set up a cluster using a few Linux machines that you can easily make with your used or new PCs as I did. I set up a Linux cluster in a home office environment easily by installing OpenSuse 12.1 on three used Windows XP laptops in 32-bit mode and on one newer Windows 7 PC in 64-bit mode. My point is that if you have a computer job, it's very likely that you have quite a few used PCs, so you can set up a Linux cluster easily by following the precise procedures I will share with you in the next chapter.

1.3 SUMMARY

I hope that this chapter has given you a clear idea on what Hadoop is about. If you have followed the instructions, tried out the simple SpendingPattern MapReduce program, and ran it in a local Hadoop environment successfully, you have already established a solid start point in learning Hadoop, because the remainder of the book would just keep expanding on what we introduced in this chapter about Hadoop MapReduce programming model and execution environment. Since I am anxious to help you set up a Linux cluster for Hadoop, let's wrap up this chapter and move to the next chapter to learn more about Hadoop running on a cluster in fully-distributed mode.

RECOMMENDED READING

One of the best ways to learn about a subject is to learn from the creators of the original ideas and implementations. The following two papers are highly recommended:

1. S. Ghemawat, H. Gobioff, and S. Leung, *The Google File System*, available at

http://static.googleusercontent.com/external_content/untrusted_dlcp/research.google.com/en/us/archive/gfs-sosp2003.pdf

2. J. Dean and S. Ghemawat, *MapReduce: Simplified Data Processing on Large Clusters*, available at

http://static.googleusercontent.com/external_content/untrusted_dlcp/research.google.com/en/us/archive/mapreduce-osdi04.pdf

To learn more about Maven, check out the following URL:

http://maven.apache.org/guides/mini/guide-ide-eclipse.html

EXERCISES

1.1 Explain what computing problems Hadoop solves. Give three challenging use scenarios that Hadoop would be the ideal choice to help resolve.

1.2 Explain why the *reduce* phase took the same amount of time with the 200k and 2M credit card transaction jobs described in §1.2.5 of this chapter.

1.3 Study the two Google papers listed in the preceding *Recommended Reading* section and formulate your own version of *what Hadoop is about*.

2 Setting up a Linux Hadoop Cluster

In this chapter, we focus on setting up a Linux Hadoop cluster. We choose Linux for two reasons. First, Hadoop runs on Linux in production; and secondly, it's much easier to have more Linux machines than to have the same number of Mac OS X machines. I happen to have many personal PCs (three 64-bit Windows 7, four 32-bit Windows XP, and one Mac OS X Mac Mini). Although some of them are old, I easily installed the 32-bit Linux on three Windows XP machines and the 64-bit Linux on one 64-bit Windows 7 for a 4-node Linux cluster for Hadoop.

Although this setup uses only four Linux machines, it's a real, fully distributed Hadoop environment. It resembles a production Linux Hadoop environment in many aspects except that we have only two rather than hundreds to tens of thousands of datanodes that is typical in production environment. This is less an issue, as a Linux cluster can be defined with a network topology of 1 (namenode) + 1 (secondary namenode) + n (datanodes), where n can go from 1 to any number. We choose a "1 + 1 + 2" topology, because we want to see more than one datanode for parallel, distributed computing with Hadoop. Of course, if you have more than four Linux machines, you can have more than two datanodes, or if you have only three Linux machines, you can have a "1 + 1 + 1" cluster topology.

First, I'd like to begin with how to provision your Linux machines so that you don't have to step into the same traps as I did and spend a lot of your time to figure out how to install Linux properly. One of my objectives with this book is to help you save time and learn Hadoop quickly.

2.1 PROVISIONING LINUX MACHINES

As many different flavors of Linux are available, you need to decide which flavor you would use. Out of my own experiences and judgment, I decided to stick to one flavor for all my Linux machines: The latest OpenSuse 12.1 as of this writing. I have tried Ubuntu and Fedora, and I had experiences with Red Hat, but I decided that I would choose SuSe. Let's not start up a religious war about which Linux is better, because that's not the point here. Even with OpenSuse, it is said that the KDE desktop is a lot smoother than the GNOME desktop, so I started with Open SuSe + KDE desktop. But I really had enough with the KDE's KWallet credential management service always popping up asking me to enter my password, so I had to format all my Linux machines and reinstalled OpenSuSe 12.1 with the GNOME desktop, and it has gotten much better ever since.

Some readers may feel that this book is about Hadoop, not Linux, but if you don't have a reliable Linux environment, your Hadoop learning would be affected. So please bear with me with such nuances that I feel I need to share. Of course, you could choose whatever flavor of Linux you like, as long as you feel that you could deal with it comfortably in setting up and running Hadoop on it.

Here are some lessons I learnt in provisioning my Linux machines with OpenSuSe 12.1 and GNOME desktop:

- **Fresh install or dual boot with Windows**: Somehow on my older 32-bit Windows XPs, I had to use the entire drive for Linux, which means that Windows XP would be gone and so would my data. That's fine with me because I already moved off my data and did not plan to run those PCs on Windows XP again. However, I successfully installed 64-bit OpenSuse 12.1 on one of my newer 64-bit Windows 7 with the dual boot option, although I moved off my data as well and prepared for possible data loss.
- **User account:** Since Hadoop requires that all nodes of a cluster use the same login username and password, I used the same user name of "henry" and same password for all my Linux machines.
- **Firewall and SSH**: By default, OpenSuse 12.1 enables Firewall and disables SSH. After an initial install, I found that I could not enable SSH and open up the SSH port of 22 successfully, despite applying many fixes. Eventually, I had to choose *disable firewall* and *enable SSH/open SSH port* during a fresh install in the first place before clicking on the button to kick off the installation process. It worked trouble free after I took this precaution. However, since this is a security feature, you need to decide whether you want do so as well.
- **Hostname.domain**: An OpenSuSe 12.1 installation assigns a hostname to a freshly installed instance. However, since all nodes of a cluster need to be able to communicate with each other by hostnames rather than IP's, I had to modify the domain for each Linux machine with one common domain of *perfmath.com* of my own on my home network.
- **DHCP**: Since I use DSL at home with a WRT54G wireless router, all IP's are configured dynamically. This had turned out to be a huge issue for Hadoop, since I don't have a dedicated DNS server in my home office. This issue was eventually worked out and I'll describe what needs to be done when we get there later.

Despite these issues, I had four Linux machines provisioned successfully for setting up a cluster to run Hadoop, attempting to emulate a production Hadoop environment on Linux. All machines have local IPs in the form of 192.168.1.1xx where the last two digits vary dynamically. In order to avoid IPs changing dynamically in the middle of a Hadoop MapReduce job run, all four Linux machines are connected with a 5-port switch.

Table 2.1 summarizes the specs of those Linux machines with their intended use for the Hadoop cluster. As you see, this is a "1 (*NameNode*) + 1 (*SecondaryNameNode*) + 2 (*DataNodes*)" Hadoop cluster topology. If I need to scale out for larger Hadoop jobs, I would simply add more datanodes with similarly configured Linux machines. In a production environment, if one needs to scale down, then remove some of the datanodes. This kind of elasticity has made Hadoop particularly suitable for scalable, distributed computing.

Table 2.1 Four Linux machines with their specs and intended use for a Hadoop cluster (all hosts run on OpenSuse 12.1 and have the same domain of perfmath.com)

Hostname	Specs	Use
linux-1fsw	64-bit quad-core Phenom II X4 @2.8 GHz, 8 GB RAM, 1 TB disk storage	NameNode
linux-vg5i	32-bit Intel Pentium M @ 1.86 GHz, 1 GB RAM, 77 GB disk storage.	SecondaryNameNode
linux-w9ms	Intel Core 2 Duo T9600 @ 2.8 GHz, 4 GB RAM, 155 GB disk storage.	DataNode
linux-sgpx	32-bit Intel Pentium M @ 1.86 GHz, 1.5 GB RAM, 77 GB disk storage.	DataNode

2.2 CONFIGURING A LINUX CLUSTER FOR HADOOP

To configure a Linux cluster for Hadoop, you perform most of the tasks on the NameNode machine. With my Linux machines provisioned as shown in Table 2.1 in the previous section, that means I would perform most of the cluster configuration tasks on the Linux machine linux-1fsw.perfmath.com. Figure 2.1 shows the blueprint for setting up a Linux cluster for Hadoop. Note that the left most desktop would be the NameNode, whereas the three laptops on the right side would be the SecondaryNameNode and two DataNodes. In the following sections, I will describe the steps I took to set up this Linux cluster. We start with setting up SSH connections first.

2.2.1   Checking SSH Enabling

On the NameNode Linux machine, execute the following commands to verify if SSH is enabled and running first:

```
$ which ssh
$ sudo which sshd
$ which ssh-keygen
```

Note that the second command needs to be executed with "sudo" preceded; otherwise, you might get an output of "which: no sshd in …," which would mistakenly tell you that sshd was not running, but actually it was a false indication.

Next, verify that ssh and sshd are enabled and running on all other Linux machines using the first two commands as described above. If you encounter any issues, you need to fix them before proceeding to the next step.

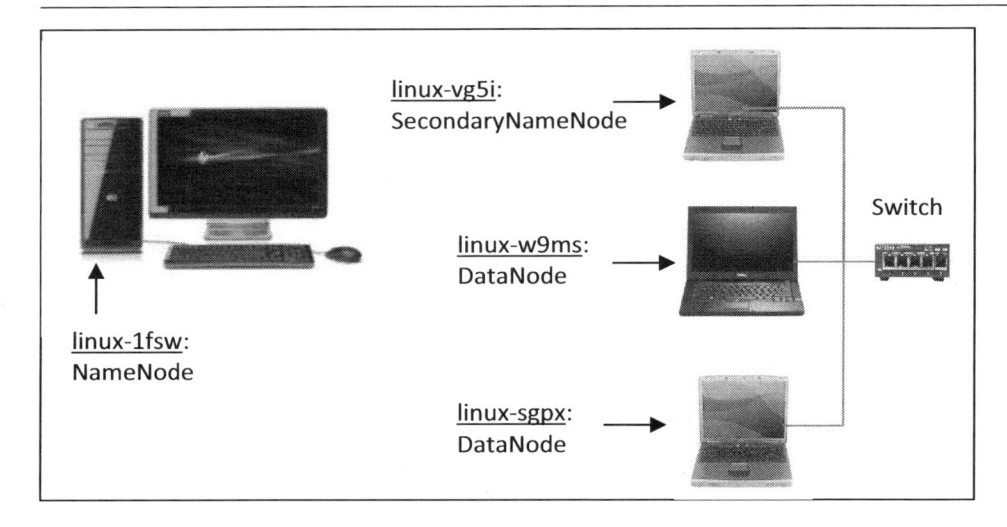

Figure 2.1 The blueprint for setting up a cluster for running Hadoop with four Linux machines shown in Table 2.1

2.2.1 Generating SSH RSA Keys

This step generates an *ssh* RSA public-private key-pair on the NameNode Linux machine, with the public key to be distributed to all other Linux machines in the cluster. Here, we only describe the mechanics of SSH key generation and distribution. Refer to other documentations if you are interested in how SSH works.

On the NameNode, execute the following command and make sure you enter an empty passphrase (which means you just hit Enter when you are asked for a passphrase):

```
$ ssh-keygen –t rsa
```

You can verify your public key on your NameNode by executing the following command:

```
$ cat ~/.ssh/id_rsa.pub
```

This is what I got after I executed the above command on my NameNode linux-1fsw:

```
henry@linux-1fsw:~/myapp/hadoop-1.0.3> cat ~/.ssh/id_rsa.pub
ssh-rsa AAAAB3NzaC1yc2EAAAADAQABAAABAQDRgvDJOOnWFzGYORLgrT/
6RZJqBWnNGA+GhZL15HDUHXqPJptwg5Kww/NIkMwzOt6Q1aFniP001Spp3
TW8yB1F4l5wjZ4fwNRylwGzw7oLUcyxpUg2+iU7AyFh1D7d55pqo2Nv2idFBa
P+kh9ggrEy6e/Cby6pQu0g4ken8lZSmUF+511J/mXDVjuRmCPHKiaqLwOqVSn
wsUvnFU/0Ser+gaQMPG8Zzc3P8h6fRVqGdoe3CpfbFS2/lIX5P1iqczwBmtJ3Tu
iY0OyTmoYpgGK50y+MZ1A07Mv/vqDHkNS93o6hVGoSkr1BZ1I4mtXnCXfQha
BQVrDRH4iawNXAayiL henry@linux-1fsw
```

Note the following with the above output:

- The first line in bold is the command for displaying the public ssh key.
- The key is preceded with ssh-rsa followed by a space and then the encrypted key and ended with a space followed by the login username and machine name.

2.2.2 Distributing the Public RSA Key

In this section, we describe how to distribute the RSA public key generated on the NameNode Linux machine to all other Linux machines of the cluster for Hadoop. I'd like to repeat that all Linux boxes should have the same username/password and should have SSH enabled and running properly. This step should be performed on the NameNode using the scp utility against every other Linux node of the cluster. For example, I executed the following command against every other Linux machine I set up for my cluster:

```
$ scp ~/.ssh/id_rsa.pub henry@linux-w9ms.perfmath.com:~/namenode_key
$ scp ~/.ssh/id_rsa.pub henry@linux-sgpx.perfmath.com:~/namenode_key
$ scp ~/.ssh/id_rsa.pub henry@linux-vg5i.perfmath.com:~/namenode_key
```

Note that if your Linux *hostname* does not work, you might need to enter the IP and hostname entries for all Linux machines in each node's */etc/hosts* file and try again. This would not be a problem in production where a DNS server is generally available, but it could be troublesome in a home office environment with DHCP where there is no dedicated DNS running. Anyway, the above scp command needs to succeed from the NameNode to every other node, one way or the other. I added the following entries in the /etc/hosts file of each Linux node of my cluster (note the IP may change after a reboot due to DHCP):

```
192.168.1.103    linux-1fsw.perfmath.com
192.168.1.108    linux-w9ms.perfmath.com
192.168.1.107    linux-sgpx.perfmath.com
192.168.1.112    linux-vg5i.perfmath.com
```

And I have to keep updating this file whenever the IPs of these Linux machines have changed. You can check the IP of your Linux machine, for example, by using the ifconfig utility as *root* as follows:

```
$ su –
linux-1fsw:~ # ifconfig
eth0     Link encap:Ethernet  HWaddr D4:85:64:C4:B4:74
         inet addr:192.168.1.103 Bcast:192.168.1.255  Mask:255.255.255.0
      ......
linux-1fsw:~ #
```

Following the successful executions of the above commands, login to each node, and execute the following command:

```
$ mv ~/namenode_key ~/.ssh/authorized_keys
```

Then, go back to the NameNode, and verify that you can login to each node via ssh successfully. The following is the output on each of my Linux machines in my environment for your reference:

```
henry@linux-1fsw:~> ssh linux-w9ms.perfmath.com
Last login: Mon Aug 20 17:54:46 2012 from linux-1fsw.perfmath.com
Have a lot of fun...
henry@linux-w9ms:~> logout
Connection to linux-w9ms.perfmath.com closed.
henry@linux-1fsw:~> ssh linux-sgpx.perfmath.com
Last login: Fri Aug 24 23:00:48 2012 from console
Have a lot of fun...
henry@linux-sgpx:~> logout
Connection to linux-sgpx.perfmath.com closed.
henry@linux-1fsw:~> ssh linux-vg5i.perfmath.com
Last login: Mon Aug 20 17:54:09 2012 from linux-1fsw.perfmath.com
Have a lot of fun...
henry@linux-vg5i:~>
```

If at a later point, you need to repeat the above procedure, for example, when the IPs of your Linux machines have changed due to DHCP, you need to overwrite your *authorized_keys* file in the *~/.ssh* directory first before you repeat the above procedure.

2.2.3 Configuring Hadoop for Distributed Mode

At this point, if you have not installed Hadoop on your NameNode, follow the instructions given in Section 1.2.1 and install Hadoop. You need to follow the same procedure and install the same version of Hadoop on every other node of your Linux cluster.

Configuring Hadoop to run in fully distributed mode requires modifying the following five files in the `conf` directory:

- **core-site.xml**: Defines the HDFS on the NameNode.
- **hdfs-site.xml**: Defines the # of replicas of the input data, which is 3 by default.
- **mapred-site.xml**: Defines the Job Tracker on the NameNode
- **masters**: Defines the SecondaryNameNode for fail-over in case the primary NameNode goes down.
- **slaves**: Defines the DataNodes.

For your reference, see Listings 2.1 (a) through (e) for the contents of these files for my cluster. You can compare and match the entities defined in these files with the cluster blueprint shown in Figure 2.1.

Listing 2.1 (a) core-site.xml

```
<?xml version="1.0"?>
<?xml-stylesheet type="text/xsl" href="configuration.xsl"?>
<configuration>
<property>
 <name>fs.default.name</name>
```

```
<value>hdfs://linux-1fsw.perfmath.com</value>
<description>fs default name. </description>
</property>
</configuration>
```

Listing 2.1 (b) hdfs-site.xml

```
<?xml version="1.0"?>
<?xml-stylesheet type="text/xsl" href="configuration.xsl"?>
<configuration>
<property>
 <name>dfs.replication</name>
 <value>3</value>
 <description>dfs replication</description>
</property></configuration>
```

Listing 2.1 (c) mapred-site.xml

```
<?xml version="1.0"?>
<?xml-stylesheet type="text/xsl" href="configuration.xsl"?>
<configuration>
<property>
 <name>mapred.job.tracker</name>
 <value>linux-1fsw.perfmath.com:7001</value>
 <description>map reduce definition </description>
</property></configuration>
```

Listing 2.1 (d) masters

```
linux-vg5i.perfmath.com
```

Listing 2.1 (e) slaves

```
linux-w9ms.perfmath.com
linux-sgpx.perfmath.com
```

Next, you need to copy all these files from your NameNode to all other nodes, for example, by using the *scp* utility on the NameNode as follows:

```
$ cd $HADOOP_INSTALL/conf
$ scp core-site.xml hdfs-site.xml mapred-site.xml masters slaves < target>/conf/
```

where <target> specifies the target Hadoop installation directory, for example, on one of my Linux nodes named linux-w9ms.perfmath.com, it is:

```
linux-w9ms.perfmath.com:~/myapp/hadoop-1.0.3
```

We are ready to start up all Hadoop daemons in a fully distributed environment.

2.2.4 Starting up Hadoop in Fully Distributed Mode

Before starting up Hadoop in fully distributed mode, execute the following command to format the HDFS first on the NameNode:

```
$ hadoop namenode -format
```

Now, to start up Hadoop in fully distributed mode on a Linux cluster, perform the following steps on the NameNode:

```
$ cd $HADOOP_INSTALL
$ bin/start-all.sh
```

Then, verify that all Hadoop daemons have been started up on their respective nodes using the Java jps utility as shown previously. Listings 2.2 (a) through (d) show Hadoop daemon processes on the NameNode, SecondaryNameNode and DataNodes running on my Linux cluster. Figure 2.2 shows all daemons from an entire cluster point of view.

To stop Hadoop running on a Linux cluster, perform the following steps on the NameNode:

```
$ cd $HADOOP_INSTALL
$ bin/stop-all.sh
```

We are ready to submit a Hadoop MapReduce job in fully distributed mode next.

Listing 2.2 (a) Hadoop daemons on the NameNode (linux-1fsw.perfmath.com)

```
henry@linux-1fsw:~/myapp/hadoop-1.0.3> bin/start-all.sh
namenode running as process 12950. Stop it first.
linux-w9ms.perfmath.com: datanode running as process 10588. Stop it first.
linux-sgpx.perfmath.com: starting datanode, logging to /home/henry/myapp/hadoop-
1.0.3/libexec/../logs/hadoop-henry-datanode-linux-sgpx.perfmath.com.out
linux-vg5i.perfmath.com: starting secondarynamenode, logging to
/home/henry/myapp/hadoop-1.0.3/libexec/../logs/hadoop-henry-secondarynamenode-
linux-vg5i.perfmath.com.out
starting jobtracker, logging to /home/henry/myapp/hadoop-1.0.3/libexec/../logs/hadoop-
henry-jobtracker-linux-1fsw.out
linux-w9ms.perfmath.com: starting tasktracker, logging to /home/henry/myapp/hadoop-
1.0.3/libexec/../logs/hadoop-henry-tasktracker-linux-w9ms.perfmath.com.out
linux-sgpx.perfmath.com: starting tasktracker, logging to /home/henry/myapp/hadoop-
1.0.3/libexec/../logs/hadoop-henry-tasktracker-linux-sgpx.perfmath.com.out
henry@linux-1fsw:~/myapp/hadoop-1.0.3> $JAVA_HOME/bin/jps
13928 JobTracker
12950 NameNode
14063 Jps
```

```
henry@linux-1fsw:~/myapp/hadoop-1.0.3>
```

Listing 2.2 (b) Hadoop Daemons on the SecondaryNameNode (linux-vg5i.perfmath.com)

```
henry@linux-vg5i:~> $JAVA_HOME/bin/jps
408 SecondaryNameNode
494 Jps
henry@linux-vg5i:~>
```

Listing 2.2 (c) Hadoop Daemons on the DataNode (linux-w9ms.perfmath.com)

```
henry@linux-w9ms:~> $JAVA_HOME/bin/jps
11110 TaskTracker
10588 DataNode
11218 Jps
henry@linux-w9ms:~>
```

Listing 2.2 (d) Hadoop Daemons on the DataNode (linux-sgpx.perfmath.com)

```
henry@linux-sgpx:~> $JAVA_HOME/bin/jps
5663 DataNode
5762 TaskTracker
5930 Jps
henry@linux-sgpx:~>
```

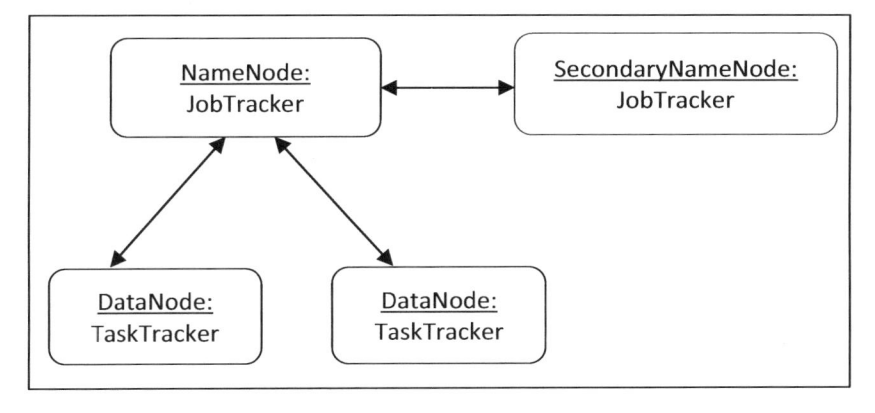

Figure 2.2 All Hadoop daemons on a Linux cluster

2.2.5 Submitting a Job to Hadoop in Fully Distributed Mode

To submit a job to Hadoop running in fully distributed mode, for example, using our spending-patterns.jar file and input data created in the previous chapter, perform the steps below:

1) If the `spending-patterns.jar` file and the `in0` folder are not on your NameNode, copy them to a folder on your NameNode (in my case: the ~henry/mydev/MyHadoop-1.0.3 folder).

2) cd to the MyHadoop-1.0.3 folder

3) Run "*hadoop fs –copyFromLocal in0/* /user/henry/in0*" to copy the input data files from local to HDFS (this is a HDFS command and we will explain later. If it complains that the directory in0 does not exist, run the command "*hadoop fs –mkdir in0*" to create it first before running the *copy* command).

4) Run the command "*$ Hadoop jar spending-patterns.jar SpendingPattern in0/credit_card_tx_0_out.txt out9*" to submit the job to Hadoop running in fully distributed mode.

Note that we do not need to copy Hadoop MapReduce programs and input data to every other node of the cluster. After a job is launched on the NameNode with the MapReduce program and input data copied onto it, Hadoop replicates all MapReduce classes and all data required to run the job to other nodes automatically as needed by itself.

Listings 2.3 and 2.4 show the console output from running the 200k and 2M credit card transaction job on this Linux cluster, respectively. Figure 2.3 shows the statistical details of a running job when it was completed, taken from the Job Tracker admin console shown in Figure 2.4, from which you can see another 2M credit card transaction SpendingPattern job still running. Those statistics are helpful in providing us with insights into some of the performance characteristics associated with that job.

Listing 2.3 Output from running a 200k credit card transaction job on a Hadoop Linux cluster

```
henry@linux-1fsw:~/mydev/MyHadoop-1.0.3> hadoop fs -copyFromLocal in0/* /user/henry/in0
henry@linux-1fsw:~/mydev/MyHadoop-1.0.3> hadoop jar spending-patterns.jar SpendingPattern
in0/credit_card_tx_0_out.txt out9
12/08/25 19:39:40 WARN mapred.JobClient: Use GenericOptionsParser for parsing the arguments.
Applications should implement Tool for the same.
12/08/25 19:39:40 INFO input.FileInputFormat: Total input paths to process : 1
12/08/25 19:39:40 INFO util.NativeCodeLoader: Loaded the native-hadoop library
12/08/25 19:39:40 WARN snappy.LoadSnappy: Snappy native library not loaded
12/08/25 19:39:41 INFO mapred.JobClient: Running job: job_201208251838_0001
12/08/25 19:39:42 INFO mapred.JobClient:  map 0% reduce 0%
12/08/25 19:39:57 INFO mapred.JobClient:  map 100% reduce 0%
12/08/25 19:40:09 INFO mapred.JobClient:  map 100% reduce 100%
12/08/25 19:40:14 INFO mapred.JobClient: Job complete: job_201208251838_0001
12/08/25 19:40:14 INFO mapred.JobClient: Counters: 29
12/08/25 19:40:14 INFO mapred.JobClient:   Job Counters
12/08/25 19:40:14 INFO mapred.JobClient:    Launched reduce tasks=1
12/08/25 19:40:14 INFO mapred.JobClient:    SLOTS_MILLIS_MAPS=12430
12/08/25 19:40:14 INFO mapred.JobClient:    Total time spent by all reduces waiting after reserving
slots (ms)=0
```

```
12/08/25 19:40:14 INFO mapred.JobClient:     Total time spent by all maps waiting after reserving slots
(ms)=0
12/08/25 19:40:14 INFO mapred.JobClient:     Launched map tasks=1
12/08/25 19:40:14 INFO mapred.JobClient:     Data-local map tasks=1
12/08/25 19:40:14 INFO mapred.JobClient:     SLOTS_MILLIS_REDUCES=10195
12/08/25 19:40:14 INFO mapred.JobClient:   File Output Format Counters
12/08/25 19:40:14 INFO mapred.JobClient:     Bytes Written=2094
12/08/25 19:40:14 INFO mapred.JobClient:   FileSystemCounters
12/08/25 19:40:14 INFO mapred.JobClient:     FILE_BYTES_READ=9309167
12/08/25 19:40:14 INFO mapred.JobClient:     HDFS_BYTES_READ=11731020
12/08/25 19:40:14 INFO mapred.JobClient:     FILE_BYTES_WRITTEN=18661131
12/08/25 19:40:14 INFO mapred.JobClient:     HDFS_BYTES_WRITTEN=2094
12/08/25 19:40:14 INFO mapred.JobClient:   File Input Format Counters
12/08/25 19:40:14 INFO mapred.JobClient:     Bytes Read=11730880
12/08/25 19:40:14 INFO mapred.JobClient:   Map-Reduce Framework
12/08/25 19:40:14 INFO mapred.JobClient:     Map output materialized bytes=9309167
12/08/25 19:40:14 INFO mapred.JobClient:     Map input records=200000
12/08/25 19:40:14 INFO mapred.JobClient:     Reduce shuffle bytes=0
12/08/25 19:40:14 INFO mapred.JobClient:     Spilled Records=391180
12/08/25 19:40:14 INFO mapred.JobClient:     Map output bytes=8917981
12/08/25 19:40:14 INFO mapred.JobClient:     CPU time spent (ms)=7200
12/08/25 19:40:14 INFO mapred.JobClient:     Total committed heap usage (bytes)=247660544
12/08/25 19:40:14 INFO mapred.JobClient:     Combine input records=0
12/08/25 19:40:14 INFO mapred.JobClient:     SPLIT_RAW_BYTES=140
12/08/25 19:40:14 INFO mapred.JobClient:     Reduce input records=195590
12/08/25 19:40:14 INFO mapred.JobClient:     Reduce input groups=44
12/08/25 19:40:14 INFO mapred.JobClient:     Combine output records=0
12/08/25 19:40:14 INFO mapred.JobClient:     Physical memory (bytes) snapshot=277852160
12/08/25 19:40:14 INFO mapred.JobClient:     Reduce output records=44
12/08/25 19:40:14 INFO mapred.JobClient:     Virtual memory (bytes) snapshot=749789184
12/08/25 19:40:14 INFO mapred.JobClient:     Map output records=195590
henry@linux-1fsw:~/mydev/MyHadoop-1.0.3>
```

Listing 2.4 Output from running a 2M credit card transaction job on a Hadoop Linux cluster

```
henry@linux-1fsw:~/mydev/MyHadoop-1.0.3> hadoop jar spending-patterns.jar SpendingPattern
in0/credit_card_tx_1_out.txt  out15
12/08/25 20:38:48 WARN mapred.JobClient: Use GenericOptionsParser for parsing the arguments.
Applications should implement Tool for the same.
12/08/25 20:38:49 INFO input.FileInputFormat: Total input paths to process : 1
12/08/25 20:38:49 INFO util.NativeCodeLoader: Loaded the native-hadoop library
12/08/25 20:38:49 WARN snappy.LoadSnappy: Snappy native library not loaded
12/08/25 20:38:49 INFO mapred.JobClient: Running job: job_201208252015_0005
12/08/25 20:38:50 INFO mapred.JobClient:  map 0% reduce 0%
12/08/25 20:39:08 INFO mapred.JobClient:  map 87% reduce 0%
12/08/25 20:39:11 INFO mapred.JobClient:  map 99% reduce 0%
12/08/25 20:39:14 INFO mapred.JobClient:  map 100% reduce 0%
```

```
12/08/25 20:39:26 INFO mapred.JobClient:  map 100% reduce 100%
12/08/25 20:39:31 INFO mapred.JobClient: Job complete: job_201208252015_0005
12/08/25 20:39:31 INFO mapred.JobClient: Counters: 29
12/08/25 20:39:31 INFO mapred.JobClient:  Job Counters
12/08/25 20:39:31 INFO mapred.JobClient:   Launched reduce tasks=1
12/08/25 20:39:31 INFO mapred.JobClient:   SLOTS_MILLIS_MAPS=32613
12/08/25 20:39:31 INFO mapred.JobClient:   Total time spent by all reduces waiting after reserving
slots (ms)=0
12/08/25 20:39:31 INFO mapred.JobClient:   Total time spent by all maps waiting after reserving slots
(ms)=0
12/08/25 20:39:31 INFO mapred.JobClient:   Launched map tasks=2
12/08/25 20:39:31 INFO mapred.JobClient:   Data-local map tasks=2
12/08/25 20:39:31 INFO mapred.JobClient:   SLOTS_MILLIS_REDUCES=13327
12/08/25 20:39:31 INFO mapred.JobClient:  File Output Format Counters
12/08/25 20:39:31 INFO mapred.JobClient:   Bytes Written=2094
12/08/25 20:39:31 INFO mapred.JobClient:  FileSystemCounters
12/08/25 20:39:31 INFO mapred.JobClient:   FILE_BYTES_READ=186136422
12/08/25 20:39:31 INFO mapred.JobClient:   HDFS_BYTES_READ=117300546
12/08/25 20:39:31 INFO mapred.JobClient:   FILE_BYTES_WRITTEN=279268826
12/08/25 20:39:31 INFO mapred.JobClient:   HDFS_BYTES_WRITTEN=2094
12/08/25 20:39:31 INFO mapred.JobClient:  File Input Format Counters
12/08/25 20:39:31 INFO mapred.JobClient:   Bytes Read=117300266
12/08/25 20:39:31 INFO mapred.JobClient:  Map-Reduce Framework
12/08/25 20:39:31 INFO mapred.JobClient:   Map output materialized bytes=93068190
12/08/25 20:39:31 INFO mapred.JobClient:   Map input records=2000000
12/08/25 20:39:31 INFO mapred.JobClient:   Reduce shuffle bytes=93068190
12/08/25 20:39:31 INFO mapred.JobClient:   Spilled Records=5866632
12/08/25 20:39:31 INFO mapred.JobClient:   Map output bytes=89157090
12/08/25 20:39:31 INFO mapred.JobClient:   CPU time spent (ms)=29420
12/08/25 20:39:31 INFO mapred.JobClient:   Total committed heap usage (bytes)=450891776
12/08/25 20:39:31 INFO mapred.JobClient:   Combine input records=0
12/08/25 20:39:31 INFO mapred.JobClient:   SPLIT_RAW_BYTES=280
12/08/25 20:39:31 INFO mapred.JobClient:   Reduce input records=1955544
12/08/25 20:39:31 INFO mapred.JobClient:   Reduce input groups=44
12/08/25 20:39:31 INFO mapred.JobClient:   Combine output records=0
12/08/25 20:39:31 INFO mapred.JobClient:   Physical memory (bytes) snapshot=515399680
12/08/25 20:39:31 INFO mapred.JobClient:   Reduce output records=44
12/08/25 20:39:31 INFO mapred.JobClient:   Virtual memory (bytes) snapshot=1101799424
12/08/25 20:39:31 INFO mapred.JobClient:   Map output records=1955544
henry@linux-1fsw:~/mydev/MyHadoop-1.0.3>
```

Kind	% Complete	Num Tasks	Pending	Running	Complete	Killed	Failed/Killed Task Attempts
map	100.00%	2	0	0	2	0	0 / 0
reduce	100.00%	1	0	0	1	0	0 / 0

	Counter	Map	Reduce	Total
Job Counters	SLOTS_MILLIS_MAPS	0	0	32,613
	Launched reduce tasks	0	0	1
	Total time spent by all reduces waiting after reserving slots (ms)	0	0	0
	Total time spent by all maps waiting after reserving slots (ms)	0	0	0
	Launched map tasks	0	0	2
	Data-local map tasks	0	0	2
	SLOTS_MILLIS_REDUCES	0	0	13,327
File Output Format Counters	Bytes Written	0	2,094	2,094
File Input Format Counters	Bytes Read	117,300,266	0	117,300,266
FileSystemCounters	FILE_BYTES_READ	93,068,232	93,068,190	186,136,422
	HDFS_BYTES_READ	117,300,546	0	117,300,546
	FILE_BYTES_WRITTEN	186,179,252	93,089,574	279,268,826
	HDFS_BYTES_WRITTEN	0	2,094	2,094
Map-Reduce Framework	Map output materialized bytes	93,068,190	0	93,068,190
	Map input records	2,000,000	0	2,000,000
	Reduce shuffle bytes	0	93,068,190	93,068,190
	Spilled Records	3,911,088	1,955,544	5,866,632
	Map output bytes	89,157,090	0	89,157,090
	CPU time spent (ms)	19,760	9,660	29,420
	Total committed heap usage (bytes)	347,803,648	103,088,128	450,891,776
	Combine input records	0	0	0
	SPLIT_RAW_BYTES	280	0	280
	Reduce input records	0	1,955,544	1,955,544
	Reduce input groups	0	44	44
	Combine output records	0	0	0
	Physical memory (bytes) snapshot	397,033,472	118,366,208	515,399,680
	Reduce output records	0	44	44
	Virtual memory (bytes) snapshot	720,232,448	381,566,976	1,101,799,424
	Map output records	1,955,544	0	1,955,544

Figure 2.3 Statistics with a completed Hadoop MapReduce job

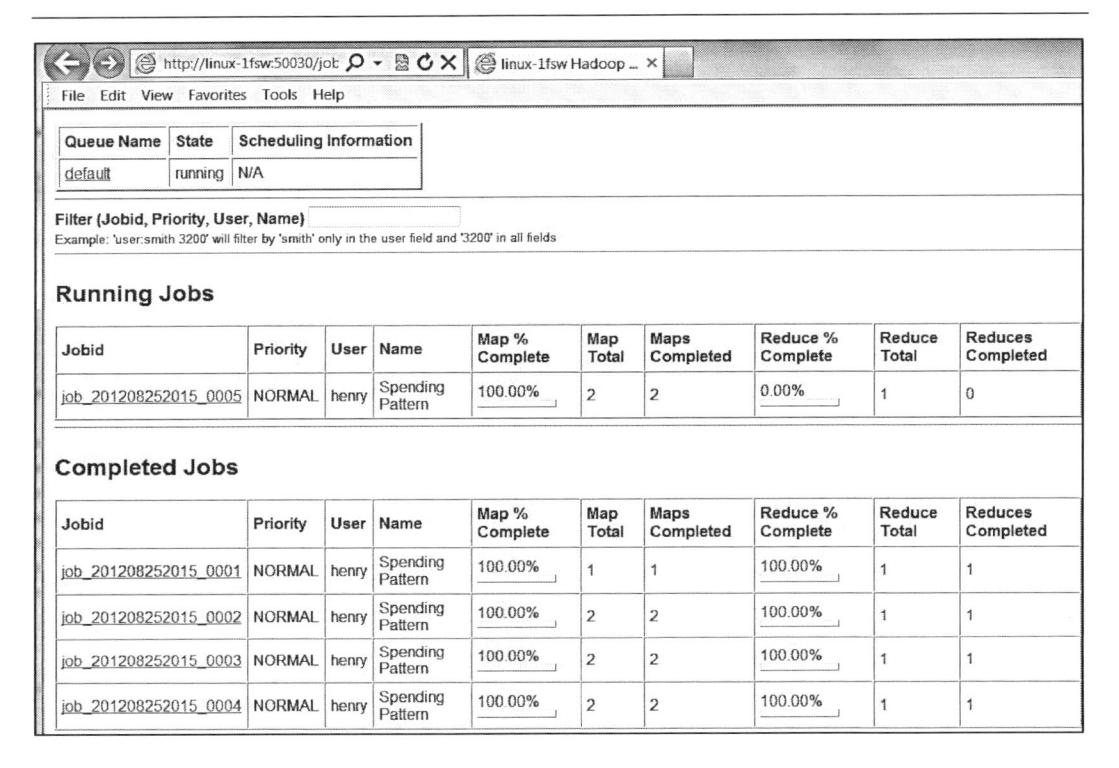

Figure 2.4 Hadoop Job Tracker admin console on a Linux cluster

2.3 SUMMARY

In this chapter, we focused on setting up a Linux cluster for running Hadoop in fully distributed mode. We re-ran the 200k and 2M credit card transaction jobs we ran with Hadoop running in pseudo-distributed mode as described in Chapter 1. If you have followed the steps presented in this chapter and actually set up a Linux cluster for running Hadoop in fully distributed mode, you certainly have gotten a much deeper understanding of how a Hadoop cluster works than just reading a verbose description about it. Starting from the next chapter, we will focus on how to develop Hadoop MapReduce programs.

RECOMMENDED READING

You can learn more about how to set up a Hadoop cluster from the Apache Hadoop's own website at http://hadoop.apache.org/common/docs/stable/cluster_setup.html. Although it is a little bit outdated (for 0.20), all concepts still apply.

EXERCISES

2.1 Where do Hadoop JobTracker and TaskTracker reside? What are their basic functions?

2.2 Can you install the SecondaryNameNode on a DataNode?

2.3 How do you submit a MapReduce job to Hadoop running in a fully distributed mode on a real cluster? Do you need to copy the MapReduce program and all its input data to every node as you would do with all configuration files?

2.4 How come the same SpendingPattern MapReduce job with 2M credit card transactions was divided into four map tasks in standalone mode as discussed in Chapter 1, while it was run with one map task on the Linux cluster discussed in this chapter?

2.5 How would you find out how a completed MapReduce job distributed its load on the datanodes of the cluster?

2.6 Where is a reduce task performed and how come?

2.7 How would you demonstrate the claimed linear scalability of Hadoop using the SpendingPattern sample introduced in Chapter 1?

Part II The Hadoop MapReduce Framework

In this second part, I will help you understand how to write Hadoop MapReduce programs. Based on the high-level overview of Hadoop and the SpendingPattern sample application developed and illustrated both in Hadoop standalone mode and cluster mode in Part I, we cover the following topics in this part:

- The Hadoop Distributed Filesystem (HDFS)
- MapReduce Job Orchestration and Workflows
- Basic MapReduce Programming
- Advanced MapReduce Programming
- Hadoop Streaming
- Hadoop Administration

Let's begin with the HDFS next.

3 The Hadoop Distributed Filesystem

Hadoop has two most basic elements: one is the Hadoop Distributed FileSystem (HDFS), and the other is the MapReduce framework. The HDFS is an indispensable part of Hadoop MapReduce framework, since Hadoop is a framework for processing large datasets after all (note the terms of *HDSF* and *DFS* are interchangeable). In this chapter, we focus on gaining a solid understanding of the Hadoop Distributed Filesystem (HDFS). In order to get as concrete as possible, we use the SpendingPattern sample and Linux cluster we set up and tested in Chapter 2 to demonstrate the HDFS concepts and features we cover.

3.1 HDFS FUNDAMENTALS

Let's start with why Hadoop needs its own distributed filesystem for its MapReduce framework on top of the already existing local filesystems. We also need to understand the specific considerations designed into the HDFS in order to support the Hadoop MapReduce framework more effectively and efficiently.

3.1.1 Why HDFS?

In a standalone Hadoop environment, an entire Hadoop job runs on the local filesystem without having to configure an HDFS. However, it's impractical to have many standalone nodes and operate all nodes on their respective local filesystems. Data retrieval and storing operations need to be coordinated in a distributed fashion. In fact, in large Hadoop production environments, working datasets and their replicas are stored on nodes divided into racks at each data center.

Figure 3.1 shows a typical Hadoop production environment. A data center hosts a number of racks, and each rack contains multiple (ideally identical physical Linux machines) nodes. The NameNode and SecondaryNameNode are hosted on the first and second racks, respectively. All remaining racks host datanodes. As you see, how would it be possible to operate each node on its local filesystem? The pioneers at Google foresaw the needs for a distributed filesystem to run massive MapReduce jobs, and hence developed the DFS to support Google operations. That is where HDFS or DFS originated.

In addition to common requirements for a distributed filesystem, an HDFS needs to have the following specific concerns taken into account from the ground up:

- **Reliability**: The HDFS is designed to operate on commodity hardware. On a cluster with tens of thousands of nodes, any node may go down at any time. The HDFS should tolerate such common failures without enduring data loss and should continue with the normal operation of the cluster without noticeable interruptions to the client.
- **Scalability**: The HDFS should be able to scale to process large datasets that are not commonly seen in the conventional relational database field. It is not uncommon that these datasets might be measured in terabytes or petabytes in large deployments.
- **Performance**: Data operations performed on an HDFS possess a pattern of *write-once, read-many*. This pattern is commonly seen with conventional batch jobs that it's more important to have high throughput with fetching blocks of data at a time rather than the first few records of a dataset. On the other hand, OLTP applications tend to modify data frequently and care more about how to fetch a few records of a table quickly to minimize response times.

Next, let's review some of the HDFS concepts that are necessary for us to understand how the Hadoop MapReduce framework works in general.

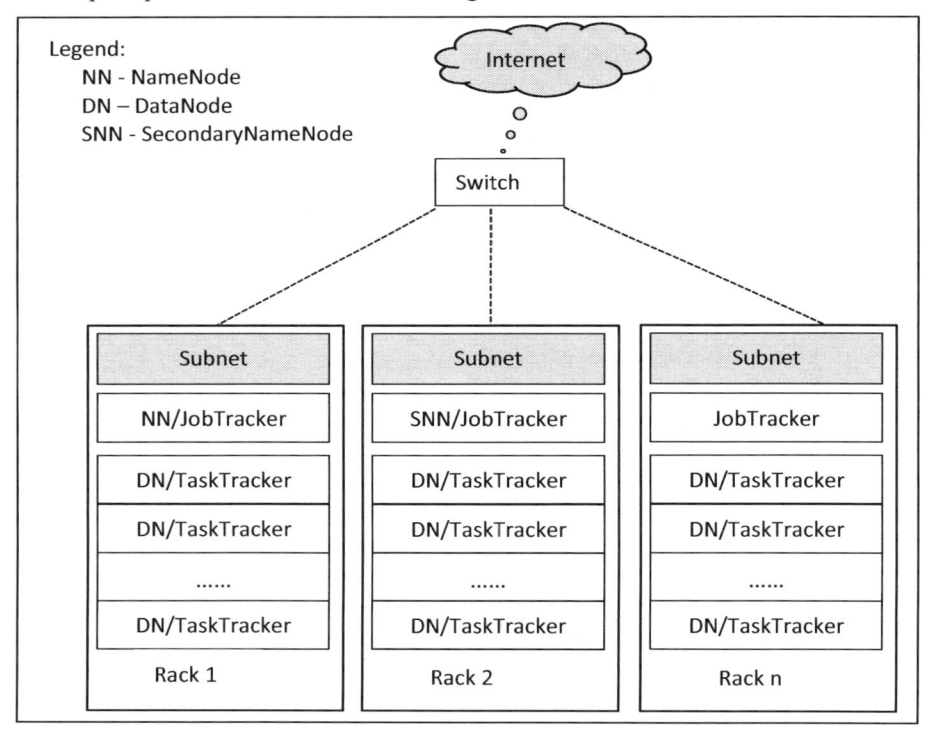

Figure 3.1 A typical Hadoop production environment with distributed data centers, racks, and nodes

3.1.2 NameNode and DataNodes

You might recall a few things from the previous chapters. One is that we used a command as follows to create a namenode:

```
$hadoop namenode -format
```

And the other is that when configuring a Linux cluster, we put the hostname of the SecondaryNameNode into a file named *masters* and the hostnames of datanodes into a file named *slaves*.

The namenode-format command essentially creates an empty HDFS to start with, while configuring masters/slaves files sets up a master/slave architecture for the HDFS to work with. To make things easier, let's revisit the concepts of NameNode and DataNode in Hadoop's context next.

If you already read enough about Hadoop, you might have seen or remember to have seen a chart as shown in Figure 3.2 (FYI: this actually is a standard chart from Hadoop's website at http://hadoop.apache.org/common/docs/r0.20.2/hdfs_design.html). As is shown, a NameNode is essentially:

- An HDFS manager that manages filesystem metadata.
- A coordinator that coordinates a client's access to data stored on datanodes.
- A coordinator that coordinates data operations in blocks on datanodes (we will explain what a block is in HDFS context next).

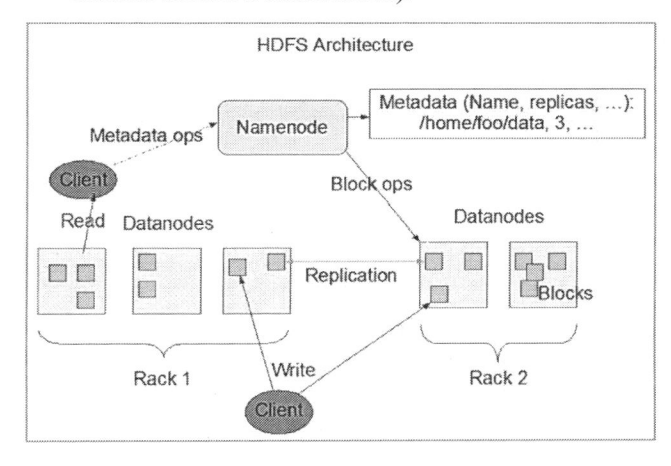

Figure 3.2 HDFS architecture

A more formal term is that a NameNode manages the HDFS namespace and metadata operations. You might wonder what a *namespace* is. The definition available on Wikipedia (http://en.wikipedia.org/wiki/Namespace) defines that:

- A namespace is a container for a set of identifiers (names), and allows the disambiguation of homonym identifiers residing in different namespaces.

- A name in a namespace consists of a namespace identifier and a local name. The namespace name is usually applied as a prefix to the local name.

The above description is the clearest definition about what a namespace is. It further summarizes its definition of a namespace more precisely in *Augmented Backus-Naur Form*:

    name = <namespace identifier> separator <local name>

For example, let's say we have a file named *readme.txt* that can be accessed in HDFS with an absolute path of */user/me/readme.txt*. In this case, Table 3.1 shows various parts associated with the terms mentioned above.

Table 3.1 A namespace example

Context	Identifier	Namespace identifier	Local name
path	/user/me/readme.txt	/user/me	readme.txt

In a filesystem, two questions often need to be answered:

- If a file is requested, where is that file located?
- If a client requests data and it's known which file contains the data, then which blocks in that file contain the data that is being requested?

With the HDFS, the NameNode keeps track of and manages such metadata. The actual data is stored on DataNodes, and it's the NameNode that actually performs filesystem namespace operations such as opening, closing, and renaming files and directories. The NameNode determines the mapping of blocks to files stored on DataNodes. The role of a DataNode is limited to fulfilling read and write requests from the filesystem's clients. When requested from the NameNode, DataNodes also create, replicate and delete data blocks. In summary, a NameNode is the house-keeper and repository for all HDFS metadata, but client data never lands on it. Client data is stored as data blocks on DataNodes (see the pointers from clients to data blocks in Figure 3.2).

3.1.3 The Concept of Blocks

As we all know, data is represented as bits of 0's and 1's, which are grouped into *bytes*, which are further grouped into *words*. At the next level, the concept of blocks is introduced at the filesystem level to simplify data access from clients or applications. The first question one might ask is what's the size of an HDFS block. The answer is that it's 64 MB by default, but can be configured to 128 MB, 256 MB, or 512 MB, and so on. This is considerably larger than the block sizes of various database systems and regular local file systems. For example, Oracle's default *db_block_size* is 8092 bytes, which can be configured to be smaller for OLTP applications or larger for batch jobs. To put it into perspective, Table 3.2 shows the block size, file size limit, and filesystem size limit on SuSe Linux (http://www.suse.de/~aj/linux_lfs.html). It is seen that the filesystem block size is limited to the range of 512 Bytes to 8092 KB on SuSe, whereas the file size and filesystem size can go up to GB, TB, PB, and even EB levels. But these filesystems do not possess the characteristics of the HDFS we described earlier, so they could not replace the role of an HDFS for Hadoop MapReduce framework no matter how big they could be.

Table 3.2 Typical block sizes, file size limits and filesystem size limits on SuSe

Filesystem	File Size Limit	Filesystem Size Limit
ext2/ext3 with 1 KiB blocksize	16448 MiB (~ 16 GiB)	2048 GiB (= 2 TiB)
ext2/3 with 2 KiB blocksize	256 GiB	8192 GiB (= 8 TiB)
ext2/3 with 4 KiB blocksize	2048 GiB (= 2 TiB)	8192 GiB (= 8 TiB)
ext2/3 with 8 KiB blocksize (Systems with 8 KiB pages like Alpha only)	65568 GiB (~ 64 TiB)	32768 GiB (= 32 TiB)
ReiserFS 3.5	2 GiB	16384 GiB (= 16 TiB)
ReiserFS 3.6 (as in Linux 2.4)	1 EiB	16384 GiB (= 16 TiB)
XFS	8 EiB	8 EiB
JFS with 512 Bytes blocksize	8 EiB	512 TiB
JFS with 4KiB blocksize	8 EiB	4 PiB
NFSv2 (client side)	2 GiB	8 EiB
NFSv3 (client side)	8 EiB	8 EiB

The next question is how the blocks are stored in an HDFS. This brings up the subject of data replication, as discussed next.

3.1.4 Data Replication

One stringent requirement on an HDFS is that files must be stored reliably on a cluster so that the normal operation of Hadoop MapReduce would not be interrupted due to sudden unavailability of data that a MapReduce job is working on. This is achieved with data replication. Recall that when configuring the Linux cluster in Chapter 2, we needed to specify how many replicas to co-exist in a Hadoop cluster. Assume that we configured to have three replicas. Then each file would be stored as a sequence of blocks with all blocks having the same size except the last block; and each block would be replicated with a replication factor of three, which means that that file would have three identical copies stored on the data nodes of the cluster (the NameNode and SecondaryNameNode only store *metadata*). Therefore, if a data node goes down, the NameNode would redirect client requests for the same block or blocks to one of the other replicas. This kind of block switching is managed by the NameNode and is transparent to the client.

How data blocks are spread on various DataNodes is governed by reliability and performance considerations. In the default case of a replication factor of three, the first replica is stored on a DataNode in a rack, whereas the other two are stored on two separate DataNodes in a separate rack remote to the first rack. It might be better to store the first two replicas on two separate DataNodes in the same rack while having the third replica stored on a DataNode in a remote rack, but this is not the case according to Hadoop's HDFS documentation. This is called *Hadoop Rack Awareness*, which requires the NameNode to store the rack _ids of all data blocks.

For large clusters with more than three replicas, there are many variations, and one has to start with something, tune and experiment until an optimal replication scheme is proven and arrived at. There is no simple guideline or panacea for a complicated matter like this other than experimenting diligently.

To check out how data is replicated, use the *fsck* command. For example, on the Linux cluster we set up in Chapter 2, we can execute the following command:

```
$ hadoop fsck / -files –blocks –locations
```

If you get a "*Connection timed out*" error, follow the below instructions to get it fixed (it worked on my Linux cluster setup):

- Stop all Hadoop daemons
- Add the following property element in your *hdfs-site.xml* file on the NameNode and copy it to all other nodes, that is, specify the NameNode host and port number explicitly:

```
<property>
    <name>dfs.http.address</name>
    <value>linux-1fsw.perfmath.com:50070</value>
</property>
```

- Start all Hadoop demons

Listing 3.1 shows the output obtained by executing the above command on my Linux cluster described in Chapter 2. Let's take a look at some of the interesting reports from this output as follows:

1) First, with the */tmp* directory, note the two reports of "`Target Replicas is ... but found 2 replicas.`" It reported "found 2 replicas," which is because we have only two DataNodes to replicate data on.
2) Second, with the */user/henry/in0* directory, note the reports on the 200k and 2M credit card transaction input data files we used in the previous chapters. The detailed information such as the # of blocks, block location and where the replicas reside is given. Since the default block size is 64 MB, the first file is contained in one block only, while the second file is divided into two blocks.
3) Third, with the */user/henry/out15* directory, it reports how the output data of one of those 2M credit card transaction MapReduce job was stored in the HDFS.
4) Finally, it reports the overall status of HDFS. Pay particular attention to the following two lines (this should be clear based on how the cluster was configured as described in Chapter 2):

```
Default replication factor: 3
Average block replication: 2.0
```

Listing 3.1 Console output from executing the command "hadoop fsck / -files –blocks – locations" on a Linux cluster

```
FSCK started by henry from /192.168.1.103 for path / at Tue Aug 28 12:20:27 PDT 2012
/ <dir>
/tmp <dir>
/tmp/hadoop-henry <dir>
/tmp/hadoop-henry/mapred <dir>
/tmp/hadoop-henry/mapred/staging <dir>
/tmp/hadoop-henry/mapred/staging/henry <dir>
/tmp/hadoop-henry/mapred/staging/henry/.staging <dir>
```

/tmp/hadoop-henry/mapred/staging/henry/.staging/job_201208162123_0001 <dir>
/tmp/hadoop-henry/mapred/staging/henry/.staging/job_201208162123_0001/job.jar 10766 bytes, 1
block(s): Under replicated blk_-4430023189985325589_1008. **Target Replicas is 10 but found 2
replica(s)**.
0. blk_-4430023189985325589_1008 len=10766 repl=2 [192.168.1.108:50010, 192.168.1.107:50010]

<... omitted to save space ...>

/user <dir>
/user/henry <dir>
/user/henry/in0 <dir>
/user/henry/in0/credit_card_tx_0_out.txt 11730880 bytes, 1 block(s): OK
0. blk_-3060698239508737898_1181 len=11730880 repl=2 [192.168.1.108:50010,
192.168.1.107:50010]

/user/henry/in0/credit_card_tx_1_out.txt 117296169 bytes, 2 block(s): OK
0. blk_-1338040152695105445_1182 len=67108864 repl=2 [192.168.1.108:50010,
192.168.1.107:50010]
1. blk_-2536563900553843259_1182 len=50187305 repl=2 [192.168.1.108:50010,
192.168.1.107:50010]

/user/henry/out15 <dir>
/user/henry/out15/_SUCCESS 0 bytes, 0 block(s): OK

/user/henry/out15/_logs <dir>
/user/henry/out15/_logs/history <dir>
/user/henry/out15/_logs/history/job_201208252015_0005_1345952329302_henry_Spending+Pattern
16980 bytes, 1 block(s): Under replicated blk_-6462168465037323946_1237. Target Replicas is 3 but
found 2 replica(s).
0. blk_-6462168465037323946_1237 len=16980 repl=2 [192.168.1.108:50010, 192.168.1.107:50010]

/user/henry/out15/_logs/history/job_201208252015_0005_conf.xml 20209 bytes, 1 block(s): Under
replicated blk_6706260074689819806_1234. Target Replicas is 3 but found 2 replica(s).
0. blk_6706260074689819806_1234 len=20209 repl=2 [192.168.1.108:50010, 192.168.1.107:50010]

/user/henry/out15/part-r-00000 2094 bytes, 1 block(s): Under replicated
blk_874266885995797314_1236. Target Replicas is 3 but found 2 replica(s).
0. blk_874266885995797314_1236 len=2094 repl=2 [192.168.1.108:50010, 192.168.1.107:50010]

Status: HEALTHY
 Total size: 250414316 B
 Total dirs: 112
 Total files: 170
 Total blocks (validated):   157 (avg. block size 1594995 B)
 Minimally replicated blocks: 157 (100.0 %)
 Over-replicated blocks: 0 (0.0 %)
 Under-replicated blocks: 30 (19.10828 %)
 Mis-replicated blocks: 0 (0.0 %)
 Default replication factor: 3

```
Average block replication:2.0
Corrupt blocks:       0
Missing replicas:       128 (40.76433 %)
Number of data-nodes:    2
Number of racks:      1
FSCK ended at Tue Aug 28 12:20:27 PDT 2012 in 42 milliseconds
The filesystem under path '/' is HEALTHY
```

If you just enter "*hadoop fsck*" at a shell prompt, it will display the usage of the command, as is shown in Listing 3.2. Note especially the options such as *–files, -blocks, -locations, -racks,* which give pertinent information on the metadata associated with a file, as we tried out above.

Listing 3.2 Usage of the fsck command

```
henry@linux-1fsw:~/myapp/hadoop-1.0.3> hadoop fsck
Usage: DFSck <path> [-move | -delete | -openforwrite] [-files [-blocks [-locations | -racks]]]
    <path> start checking from this path
    -move   move corrupted files to /lost+found
    -delete delete corrupted files
    -files    print out files being checked
    -openforwrite   print out files opened for write
    -blocks print out block report
    -locations   print out locations for every block
    -racks   print out network topology for data-node locations
       · By default fsck ignores files opened for write, use -openforwrite to report such files. They are
usually  tagged CORRUPT or HEALTHY depending on their block allocation status
Generic options supported are
-conf <configuration file>     specify an application configuration file
-D <property=value>           use value for given property
-fs <local|namenode:port>     specify a namenode
-jt <local|jobtracker:port>    specify a job tracker
-files <comma separated list of files>   specify comma separated files to be copied to the map reduce
cluster
-libjars <comma separated list of jars>   specify comma separated jar files to include in the classpath.
-archives <comma separated list of archives>   specify comma separated archives to be unarchived on
the compute machines.

The general command line syntax is
bin/hadoop command [genericOptions] [commandOptions]

henry@linux-1fsw:~/myapp/hadoop-1.0.3>
```

3.1.5 HDFS Federation

In most common cases, there is only one NameNode, which becomes a single point of failure, because if the NameNode goes down, all metadata about the entire cluster is lost. To overcome this potential risk, Hadoop has made attempt to support HDFS Federation, which introduces multiple *independent* NameNodes/namespaces without requiring coordination among federated

NameNodes. All the NameNodes use the same datanodes as common storage for blocks, which requires that each DataNode register itself with all the NameNodes in the cluster. Datanodes are also required to send periodic heartbeats and block reports to all NameNodes and handle commands from all NameNodes.

The other alternative to achieve NameNode high-availability is to use the conventional active-passive clustering technology. In such a scenario, if the active NameNode goes down, the passive NameNode can take over. Obviously, such advanced subjects are beyond the scope of this book.

3.2 BASIC HDFS COMMANDS

In this section, we introduce the HDFS command line interface, which is a convenient utility for us to interact with the HDFS both for understanding the HDFS and for performing some basic tasks when needed to make a MapReduce program work.

HDFS commands are similar to Linux native filesystem commands in many aspects but differ in syntax. In general, an HDFS command takes the form of

    $ hadoop fs –cmd <args>

A complete list of HDFS file commands can be found at the official Hadoop website (http://hadoop.apache.org/common/docs/r0.20.0/hdfs_shell.html). See Figure 3.3 for this complete list of HDFS commands.

Next, we show how to use these commands on the Linux cluster we set up in Chapter 2. Before we start, we need to understand the concept of URI for specifying the exact location of a file or directory, as all HDFS shell commands take path URIs as arguments.

The URI format is *scheme://authority/path*. For the HDFS the scheme is *hdfs*, whereas for the local filesystem it is *file*. The scheme and authority are optional. If not specified, the default scheme specified in the configuration file *core-site.xml* is used (See Listing 2.1 (a) for the Linux cluster described in Chapter 2). The full URI for an HDFS file or directory such as */user/henry/in0* can be specified as *hdfs://namenodehost/user/henry/in0* or simply as */user/henry/in0* if the configuration is set to point to *hdfs://namenodehost*. In addition, the part */user/henry* is called *home directory* for the Hadoop user account *henry,* which can be omitted as well. For example, the path URI *hdfs://linux-1fsw.perfmath/user/henry/in0* would be equivalent to *in0*.

To look up the usage of an HDFS command, enter the following command at a shell prompt:

    $ hadoop fs –help <command>

For example, enter the following command and you would get the output as shown following the command:

    henry@linux-1fsw:~/myapp/hadoop-1.0.3> **hadoop fs -help text**
    -text <src>:   Takes a source file and outputs the file in text format.
                   The allowed formats are zip and TextRecordInputStream.

Next, let's try out some typical HDFS command examples. To make it easier to identify, all commands are highlighted in bold.

HDFS File System Shell Guide

- ▣ Overview
  - ▣ cat
  - ▣ chgrp
  - ▣ chmod
  - ▣ chown
  - ▣ copyFromLocal
  - ▣ copyToLocal
  - ▣ count
  - ▣ cp
  - ▣ du
  - ▣ dus
  - ▣ expunge
  - ▣ get
  - ▣ getmerge
  - ▣ ls
  - ▣ lsr
  - ▣ mkdir
  - ▣ moveFromLocal
  - ▣ moveToLocal
  - ▣ mv
  - ▣ put
  - ▣ rm
  - ▣ rmr
  - ▣ setrep
  - ▣ stat
  - ▣ tail
  - ▣ test
  - ▣ text
  - ▣ touchz

Figure 3.3 A complete list of HDFS commands

3.2.1 mkdir /touchz /ls /copyFromLocal/ moveFromLocal

To create a directory, for example, a directory named *junk* in the user's home directory, execute the following command:

```
$ hadoop fs –mkdir junk
```

To create a zero-length file in a directory, for example, *junk0.txt* in the *junk* directory created above, execute the following command:

```
$ hadoop fs –touchz junk/junk0.txt
```

You can verify the directory and file created above by executing the following command:

```
$ hadoop fs –ls junk
```

To copy files from the local filesystem to the HDFS, execute the following command (you can perform the reverse copy from the HDFS to local with the –**copyToLocal** command):

> $ hadoop fs -**copyFromLocal** ~henry/mydev/MyHadoop-1.0.3/in0/* junk

In this case, I have two input files in the *in0* local directory for the *SpendingPattern* MapReduce program we demonstrated in the previous chapters: the 200k and 2M credit card transaction files named *credit_card_tx_0_out.txt* (11.73 MB) and *credit_card_tx_1_out.txt* (117.3 MB), respectively. Since they are large, it might take some time to copy them. After copying is done, execute the following command:

> $ hadoop **fsck** /user/henry/junk -files -blocks -locations

My output is shown in Listing 3.3. As you can see, the files copied from local to the HDFS have been replicated to the two DataNodes immediately.

Listing 3.3 Output of copying files from local to HDFS

```
$ hadoop fsck /user/henry/junk -files -blocks -locations
FSCK started by henry from /192.168.1.103 for path /user/henry/junk at Tue Aug 28 16:48:17 PDT 2012
/user/henry/junk <dir>
/user/henry/junk/credit_card_tx_0_out.txt 11730880 bytes, 1 block(s):  Under replicated blk_-
8344846552734141786_1242. Target Replicas is 3 but found 2 replica(s).
0. blk_-8344846552734141786_1242 len=11730880 repl=2 [192.168.1.107:50010,
192.168.1.108:50010]

/user/henry/junk/credit_card_tx_1_out.txt 117296169 bytes, 2 block(s):  Under replicated
blk_804601264657908161_1243. Target Replicas is 3 but found 2 replica(s).
 Under replicated blk_-7074015450267367441_1243. Target Replicas is 3 but found 2 replica(s).
0. blk_804601264657908161_1243 len=67108864 repl=2 [192.168.1.107:50010, 192.168.1.108:50010]
1. blk_-7074015450267367441_1243 len=50187305 repl=2 [192.168.1.108:50010,
192.168.1.107:50010]

/user/henry/junk/junk0.txt 0 bytes, 0 block(s):  OK

Status: HEALTHY
Total size: 129027049 B
Total dirs: 1
Total files:     3
Total blocks (validated):    3 (avg. block size 43009016 B)
Minimally replicated blocks:   3 (100.0 %)
Over-replicated blocks:    0 (0.0 %)
Under-replicated blocks:   3 (100.0 %)
Mis-replicated blocks:      0 (0.0 %)
Default replication factor: 3
Average block replication: 2.0
Corrupt blocks:         0
Missing replicas:       3 (50.0 %)
Number of data-nodes:       2
```

Number of racks: 1
FSCK ended at Tue Aug 28 16:48:17 PDT 2012 in 1 milliseconds

The filesystem under path '/user/henry/junk' is HEALTHY
henry@linux-1fsw:~/myapp/hadoop-1.0.3>

You can perform ***moveFromLocal*** and ***moveToLocal*** actions similar to ***copyFromLocal*** and ***copyToLocal*** except that it's a move rather than a copy action.

3.2.2 cp/lsr/mv/rm/rmr

In order to show the *lsr* command that lists contents of a directory recursively, create another directory in the *junk* directory, for example:

$ hadoop fs –**mkdir** junk/junk1

Now copy the junk0.txt file from HDFS to HDFS (*junk* directory to its sub-directory of *junk1*) as follows:

$ hadoop fs -**cp** junk/junk0.txt junk/junk1

Then, use the **lsr** command to list the contents of the *junk* directory recursively.

$ hadoop fs -**lsr** junk

Listing 3.4 shows the output of the *lsr* command executed above. To compare, the output of executing the *ls* command against the same *junk* directory is shown as well.

Listing 3.4 Output of the command lsr

```
henry@linux-1fsw:~/myapp/hadoop-1.0.3> hadoop fs -cp junk/junk0.txt junk/junk1
henry@linux-1fsw:~/myapp/hadoop-1.0.3> hadoop fs -lsr junk
-rw-r--r--   3 henry supergroup   11730880 2012-08-28 16:47
/user/henry/junk/credit_card_tx_0_out.txt
-rw-r--r--   3 henry supergroup  117296169 2012-08-28 16:47
/user/henry/junk/credit_card_tx_1_out.txt
-rw-r--r--   3 henry supergroup          0 2012-08-28 16:42 /user/henry/junk/junk0.txt
drwxr-xr-x   - henry supergroup          0 2012-08-28 17:47 /user/henry/junk/junk1
-rw-r--r--   3 henry supergroup          0 2012-08-28 17:47 /user/henry/junk/junk1/junk0.txt
henry@linux-1fsw:~/myapp/hadoop-1.0.3> hadoop fs -ls junk
Found 4 items
-rw-r--r--   3 henry supergroup   11730880 2012-08-28 16:47
/user/henry/junk/credit_card_tx_0_out.txt
-rw-r--r--   3 henry supergroup  117296169 2012-08-28 16:47
/user/henry/junk/credit_card_tx_1_out.txt
-rw-r--r--   3 henry supergroup          0 2012-08-28 16:42 /user/henry/junk/junk0.txt
drwxr-xr-x   - henry supergroup          0 2012-08-28 17:47 /user/henry/junk/junk1
henry@linux-1fsw:~/myapp/hadoop-1.0.3>
```

To move files from HDFS to HDFS, use the *mv* command instead:

```
$ hadoop fs –mv junk/credit_card_tx_0_out.txt junk/junk1
```

Now if you do an "*lsr*" against the *junk* directory, you would find that the above file has been moved from the *junk* directory to its sub-directory *junk1*.

Finally, to remove a file or remove a directory and its contents recursively, use the *rm* and *rmr* commands, respectively, as follows:

```
$ hadoop fs –rm junk/junk0.txt
$ hadoop fs –rmr junk
```

How do you create a new file like executing a "*vi*" command or modify a non-empty file in HDFS? Doing that directly is not supported by HDFS. However, you can use the HDFS API to interact with the HDFS programmatically, as is discussed next.

3.3   INTERACTING WITH HDFS PROGRAMMATICALLY

There might be times when you want to interact with the HDFS directly using a program rather than the manual commands as demonstrated in the preceding section. For example, if you have many small files on a local filesystem for a MapReduce program to process, you might want to use a program to combine them into a single file and then store it onto the HDFS as one big file. Another scenario, for example, is that we might want to produce test data directly onto the HDFS rather than take multiple steps of creating it on the local filesystem first and then copying it to the HDFS as we illustrated in the preceding chapters with the MapIncrease program. In this section, we use this scenario as an exercise to show how to interact with the HDFS directly through calling its API.

First, let's try out a HelloHDFS program based on an article posted at Yahoo's website at http://developer.yahoo.com/hadoop/tutorial/module2.html#programmatically. Then, we build our MapIncrease1 program that reads an input file from a directory in the HDFS and writes a synthetic credit card transaction file in the HDFS based on the # of total transactions specified at the command line.

3.3.1 HelloHDFS.java

Listing 3.5 shows the *HelloHDFS.java* program we mentioned in the preceding section. The noteworthy statements in this program are listed as follows:

- First, note the HDFS specific import statements as highlighted in bold, which shows what HDFS classes we would need for this program.
- Next, the `Configuration` and `FileSystem` classes are used to construct a FileSystem object with the following two statements:

```
Configuration conf = new Configuration ();
FileSystem fs = FileSystem.get (conf);
```

- The HDFS `Path` class is used to construct a Path object for the file to be created in HDFS with the following statement:

Path fileNamePath = new Path (theFileName);

- The `FSDataOutputStream` class is used to create a file in the HDFS for writing the hello message. The message is written with the `writeUTF` method and then the writer object is closed. These three statements are:

```
FSDataOutputStream out = fs.create (fileNamePath);
out.writeUTF (message);
out.close ();
```

- The *hello.txt* file written to HDFS is read back and displayed with the following statements:

```
FSDataInputStream in = fs.open (fileNamePath);
String messageIn= in.readUTF ();
System.out.print(messageIn);
in.close ();
```

This program is contained in *module1* in the Hadoop project we created earlier in Chapter 1. To try it out, first package it with the following command:

```
$ mvn clean package –DskipTests –Dhadoop.version=1.0.3
```

Then, move the `spending-patterns.jar` file to your Linux cluster and execute it as follows (if you have set up your own cluster):

```
$ hadoop jar spending-patterns.jar HelloHDFS
```

You should see the "Hello, HDFS" message output at the command prompt. You can also check the *hello.txt* file created in the HDFS using the commands we introduced in the previous section.

Next, let's migrate the *MapIncrease.java* program shown in Listing 1.8 from local filesystem based to HDFS based.

Listing 3.5 HelloHDFS.java

```
// import non-Hadoop java packages omitted to save space

import org.apache.hadoop.conf.Configuration;
import org.apache.hadoop.fs.FileSystem;
import org.apache.hadoop.fs.FSDataInputStream;
import org.apache.hadoop.fs.FSDataOutputStream;
import org.apache.hadoop.fs.Path;

public class HelloHDFS {

public static final String theFileName = "hello.txt";
public static final String message ="Hello, HDFS!\n";
    public static void main(String[] args) throws IOException {
        Configuration conf = new Configuration ();
```

```
        FileSystem fs = FileSystem.get (conf);

        Path fileNamePath = new Path (theFileName);

        try {
            if (fs.exists (fileNamePath)) {
                fs.delete (fileNamePath);
            }
            FSDataOutputStream out = fs.create (fileNamePath);
            out.writeUTF (message);
            out.close ();

            FSDataInputStream in = fs.open (fileNamePath);
            String messageIn= in.readUTF ();
            System.out.print(messageIn);
            in.close ();
        } catch (IOException ioe) {
            System.err.println ("IOException during operation: " + ioe.toString ());
            System.exit(1);
        }
    }
}
```

3.3.2 MapIncrease1.java

Although we cannot use the FSDataInputStream and FSDataOutputStream objects shown in the previous *HelloHDFS.java* program to read and write credit card transaction records line by line, the initial parts of creating a FileSystem object, Path object, and FSDataInputStream and FSDataOutputStream are re-usable. Especially noteworthy in Listing 3.6 (MapIncrease1.java) is that we created a BufferedReader object with an InputStreamReader object that is based on an FSDataInputStream object. Note the following sequence leading to the creation of a BufferedReader object:

FSDataInputStream → InputStreamReader → BufferedReader

Similarly, a PrintWriter object is created with an OutputStreamWriter object that is based on an FSDataOutputStream object with a similar sequence of

FSDataoutputStream → OutputStreamWriter → PrintWriter

As is seen, compared with the local filesystem based MapIncrease.java program shown in Listing 1.8, we applied several changes in the HDFS based *MapIncrease1.java* file so that BufferedReader and PrintWriter objects would be constructed using the HDFS Java API classes as noted above. The rest of the program remains the same.

To use the new, HDFS-based `MapIncrease1.java` program to generate synthetic credit card transaction data to test MapReduce on a Linux cluster as described in Chapter 2, follow the below procedure:

- Move the *credit_card_tx_0.txt* file to the HDFS *input* directory:

  $ hadoop fs -moveFromLocal credit_card_tx_0.txt input

- Produce the 200k credit card transaction synthetic data file as follows:

  $ hadoop jar spending-patterns.jar MapIncrease1 input/credit_card_tx_0.txt 200000

- Check the *input* directory to confirm the output file created:

  $ hadoop fs -ls input

- Copy the *credit_card_tx_0.txt* file to the *credit_card_tx_1.txt* file

  $ hadoop fs -cp input/credit_card_tx_0.txt input/credit_card_tx_1.txt

- Produce the 2M credit card transaction synthetic data file as follows:

  $ hadoop jar spending-patterns.jar MapIncrease1 input/credit_card_tx_1.txt 2000000

- Check the *input* directory to confirm the output file created:

  $ hadoop fs -ls input

The output should look similar to the following:

```
henry@linux-1fsw:~/mydev/MyHadoop-1.0.3> hadoop fs -ls input
Found 4 items
-rw-r--r--  3 henry supergroup    8258 2012-08-28 22:28 /user/henry/input/credit_card_tx_0.txt
-rw-r--r--  3 henry supergroup  11531480 2012-08-28 22:29
/user/henry/input/credit_card_tx_0_out.txt
-rw-r--r--  3 henry supergroup    8258 2012-08-28 22:30 /user/henry/input/credit_card_tx_1.txt
-rw-r--r--  3 henry supergroup 115297149 2012-08-28 22:30
/user/henry/input/credit_card_tx_1_out.txt
```

You can also run the following command to check how the output data files are replicated:

  $ hadoop fsck input –files –blocks -locations

As such, from this point on, we can just create synthetic credit card transaction data of arbitrary sizes in the HDFS directly to test the Hadoop MapReduce framework on a cluster setup without having to repeat the same procedure of creating data in the local filesystem first and then copy from local to HDFS.

Listing 3.6 MapIncrease1.java

```
// import non-Hadoop java packages omitted to save space
```

```java
import org.apache.hadoop.conf.Configuration;
import org.apache.hadoop.fs.FileSystem;
import org.apache.hadoop.fs.FSDataInputStream;
import org.apache.hadoop.fs.FSDataOutputStream;
import org.apache.hadoop.fs.Path;

public class MapIncrease1 {
    public static PrintWriter writer = null;
    public static BufferedReader reader = null;
    public static String dataFileIn = "credit_card_tx_0.txt";
    public static String dataFileOut;
    public static ArrayList<String> keys = new ArrayList<String>();
    public static int numOfKeys = 0;

    public static void main(String[] args) throws IOException {
        Configuration conf = new Configuration();
        FileSystem fs = FileSystem.get(conf);

        String line = "";
        dataFileIn = args[0];
        dataFileOut = dataFileIn.substring(0, dataFileIn.lastIndexOf("."))
                + "_out.txt";
        long numOfTxs = Long.parseLong(args[1]);

        Path inputFilePath = new Path(dataFileIn);
        Path outputFilePath = new Path(dataFileOut);

        try {
            FSDataInputStream in = fs.open(inputFilePath);
            reader = new BufferedReader(new InputStreamReader(in));
            while ((line = reader.readLine()) != null) {
                if (line.trim().contains("/") && !line.trim().isEmpty()
                        && !line.trim().startsWith("//")) {
                    addKeys(line);
                }
            }
        } catch (IOException ioe) {
            System.out.println(dataFileIn + " not found");
        }
        FSDataOutputStream out = fs.create(outputFilePath, true);
        writer = createWriter(out);
        long startTime = System.currentTimeMillis();

        numOfKeys = keys.size();
```

```java
        System.out.println("number of keys: " + numOfKeys);
        for (long i = 0; i < numOfTxs; i++) {
            String key = getKey();
            writeTx(key);
            if (i % 100000 == 0) {
                System.out.println("number of Txs written: " + i);
            }
        }
        writer.close();
        out.close();
        long totalTimeInSec = (System.currentTimeMillis() - startTime) / 1000;
        System.out.println("Total time in seconds: " + totalTimeInSec);
        if (totalTimeInSec > 60) {
            long totalTimeInMin = totalTimeInSec / 60;
            System.out.println("Total time in minutes: " + totalTimeInMin);
        }
        if (totalTimeInSec > 0) {
            System.out.println("Tx writing rate = "
                    + (numOfTxs / totalTimeInSec) + "/sec");
        }
    }

    public static PrintWriter createWriter(FSDataOutputStream out) {
        PrintWriter writer = null;
        writer = new PrintWriter(new OutputStreamWriter(out));
        return writer;
    }

    public static String getKey() {
        int index = (int) (Math.random() * numOfKeys);
        return keys.get(index);
    }

    public static void writeTx(String key) {
        DateFormat df = new SimpleDateFormat("MM/dd/yyyy");
        DecimalFormat myFormatter = new DecimalFormat("###.##");

        long offset = (long) (1000 * 3600 * Math.random()) * 24 * 365 * 5;
        long currTime = System.currentTimeMillis();
        String txDate = df.format(new Date(currTime - offset));
        float amount = (float) (99.99 * Math.random());
        if (key.contains("PAYMENT"))
            amount = -amount;
        writer.println(txDate + "\t" + key + "\t" + myFormatter.format(amount));
```

```
    }

    public static void addKeys(String line) {
        StringTokenizer st = new StringTokenizer(line, "\t");
        String txDate = st.nextToken();
        String description = st.nextToken();
        String amount = st.nextToken();
        if (!keys.contains(description)) {
            System.out.println("added key: " + description);
            keys.add(description);
        }
    }
}
```

3.4 SUMMARY

In this chapter, we focused on understanding the Hadoop Distributed Filesystem (HDFS). We explained why an HDFS is needed, their respective functions of a NameNode and DataNodes in a Hadoop cluster, the concept of blocks, how data replication and HDFS federation work, and so on. We listed and illustrated some of the most frequently used HDFS commands using the cluster we set up in Chapter 2.

We then demonstrated how to interact with HDFS programmatically with a *HelloHDFS* sample, which writes a "Hello, HDFS!" message to a file in HDFS and reads it back from HDFS and outputs it to the console. We migrated the local filesystem based *MapIncrease.java* program to an HDFS-based program named *MapIncrease1.java,* which reads the initial sample file and writes the synthetic credit card transactions of arbitrary sizes all from and to HDFS.

To summarize it, hierarchically, an HDFS has a simple structure of only two levels: A single instance of NameNode and any number of DataNodes in a master/slaves architecture. This simple structure enables unlimited horizontal scaling with an arbitrary number of DataNodes that can be adjusted (added or removed) dynamically on an as-needed basis. It's important that:

- A NameNode manages a namespace consisting of directories, files and blocks. It supports all basic file system operations such as file and directory creation, modification, deletion, listing, file replication, and so on. It also takes care of block management by maintaining the membership of DataNodes in a cluster. It supports block-related operations such as creation, deletion, modification and querying the location of a block, but it does not manage block storage. It also takes care of replica placement and replication.
- DataNodes are more dedicated to block storage, for example, storing the blocks on physical storage devices and providing read/write access to blocks.

You will gain more knowledge about HDFS as we move along, since whatever we do with Hadoop's MapReduce framework, we cannot do it without HDFS.

RECOMMENDED READING

The following document describes the HDFS architecture in general.

http://hadoop.apache.org/common/docs/r0.20.2/hdfs_design.html

Information about the more latest HDFS is available at

http://hadoop.apache.org/common/docs/current/hadoop-yarn/hadoop-yarn-site/HDFSHighAvailability.html

The following document describes how to set up NameNode Federation:

http://hadoop.apache.org/common/docs/r0.23.0/hadoop-yarn/hadoop-yarn-site/Federation.html

For more information on HDFS API, check out the complete JavaDoc for the HDFS API at http://hadoop.apache.org/common/docs/r0.20.2/api/index.html .

EXERCISES

3.1 Explain why Hadoop needs its own file system. What design considerations have been taken into account with the HDFS?

3.2 Since a single instance of a NameNode manages all metadata of a Hadoop cluster, it potentially could be a single point of failure. What options are available to help remedy this situation?

3.3 Try out some of the HDFS commands on your Linux cluster for Hadoop. How do you modify a file in HDFS? Can you use "*vi*" to edit a file in the HDFS?

3.4 Compile and run the HelloHDFS sample and verify that it works on your Linux cluster for Hadoop.

3.5 Run a MapIncearse1 job directly on the HDFS. Then figure out how you can probe how data is replicated in your HDFS.

4 MapReduce Job Orchestration and Workflows

In Chapter 1, we illustrated how MapReduce works with a SpendingPattern program to help you get a quick perception on what a MapReduce program looks like. We ran the SpendingPattern MapReduce program both in local mode and in pseudo-distributed mode. In Chapter 2, we focused on setting up a Linux cluster and demonstrated how MapReduce jobs run in fully distributed cluster mode. We also analyzed two MapReduce job runs with two different datasets: one with 200k and the other with 2M credit card transactions. We learnt what map tasks and reduce tasks deal with, but we really didn't get deep, as in order to be able to truly understand the MapReduce framework, it's necessary to understand how the HDFS supports it, which was covered in Chapter 3.

Now we are ready to take a deep-dive on how MapReduce jobs run so that you will understand not only how MapReduce programs work programmatically, but also how various MapReduce jobs are orchestrated in a Hadoop environment and how a MapReduce program is executed.

The following topics are covered in this chapter:

- MapReduce job orchestrators
- MapReduce workflows
- Running MapReduce jobs with multiple reduce tasks

Let's start with MapReduce job orchestrators first next.

4.1 MapReduce Job Orchestrators

One can easily imagine that there would not be only one job or a few running on a cluster with thousands or even tens of thousands of nodes. It might be fair to say that writing a piece of MapReduce program is not too complicated as long as you know how to use the MapReduce API. However, how to get massive MapReduce jobs running smoothly on a large cluster requires significant efforts not only in designing the relevant orchestrators but also in learning how to work with them properly.

In this section, we introduce two Hadoop MapReduce job orchestrators: MapReduce 1 (MR1) that works up to and includes Hadoop 1.x, and MapReduce 2 (MR2 – also known as YARN) for Hadoop 2.x and beyond. However, note that MR2 or YARN is for managing large clusters with thousands of nodes and more. Therefore, MR1 would continue to work for small to mid-size clusters. Note that the term *orchestrator* is not a formal one in Hadoop's literature – it's just my way of making it more convenient.

Let's start with the MR1 orchestrator next.

4.1.1 Hadoop MapReduce 1 Orchestrator

Figure 4.1 illustrates the structure of a Hadoop MapReduce 1 orchestrator. It consists of a JobTracker residing on a NameNode and TaskTrackers on DataNodes, typically one task tracker per DataNode. Real production Hadoop deployments have proved that a simple structure like this can handle at most several thousand nodes. However, knowing how MR1 works is beneficial for understanding how MR2 or YARN works.

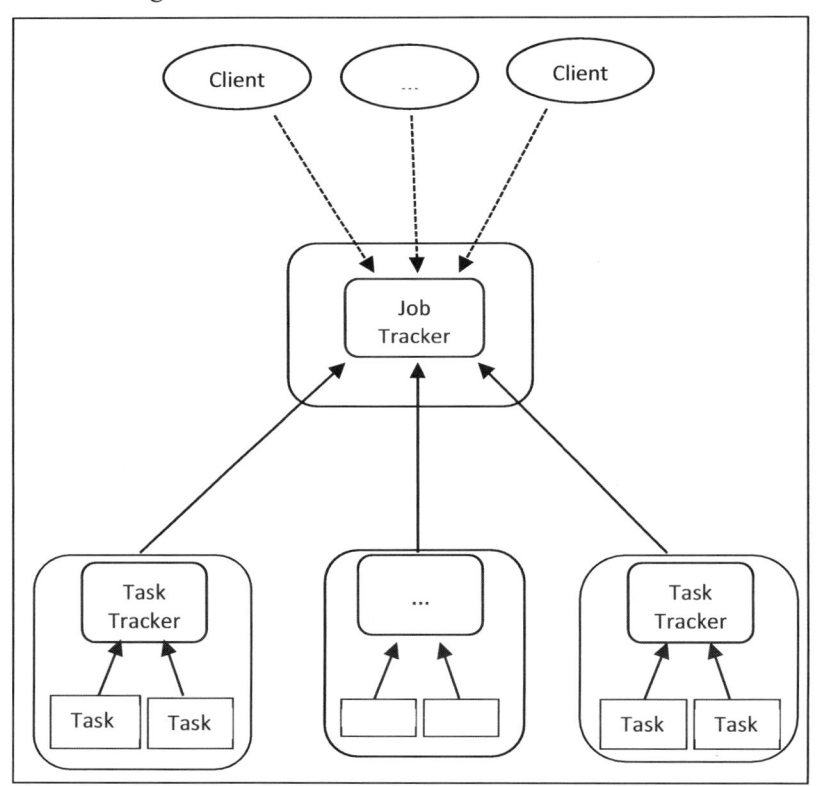

Figure 4.1 The structure of a Hadoop MapReduce 1 orchestrator

A JobTracker is a Hadoop daemon coded in Java, with its main class named *JobTracker*. A TaskTracker is also a Hadoop daemon coded in Java, with its main class named *TaskTracker*. The major responsibility of a JobTracker is to farm out MapReduce tasks to chosen nodes in the cluster, while the major responsibility of a TaskTracker is to accept tasks such as map, reduce and shuffle operations from a JobTracker and update the JobTracker with the status of the tasks that it is assigned to. More specifically:

- A JobTracker receives job submissions from clients (refer to Chapters 1 and 2 on how to submit MapReduce jobs).
- A JobTracker checks and assigns resources to jobs. The JobTracker also tracks resource utilizations so that it would know what and which resources to assign to a job, as is explained next.
- A JobTracker *splits* a job into *tasks*, and then sends tasks to chosen TaskTrackers. Every TaskTracker is configured with a set of slots for the number of map and reduce tasks that it can accept. When the JobTracker tries to find somewhere to schedule a task for carrying out the MapReduce operations, it first looks for an empty slot on the same server that hosts the DataNode containing the data, and if not, it looks for an empty slot on a machine in the same rack.
- In order to execute a task, a TaskTracker first localizes the job jar by copying it from the HDFS. It may also copy necessary files from the distributed cache to the local filesystem. It then creates a local working directory to un-jar the jar file the client submitted to the local filesystem.
- The TaskTracker is now ready to launch the task and spawns a separate, child JVM process for the task it is assigned to, namely, it does not perform the task in its own JVM. This is to ensure that a task failure would not take down the TaskTracker itself.
- TaskTrackers report the task status to the JobTracker periodically. If the JobTracker does not receive heartbeats from a TaskTracker, it schedules the task sent to that TaskTracker to another TaskTracker for execution.
- If a task is reported to have failed by a TaskTracker, the JobTracker may submit the same task to another TaskTracker while blacklisting the current TaskTracker as unavailable.
- TaskTrackers also inform the JobTracker of the number of available slots, so the JobTracker can stay up to date with to which nodes future tasks can be submitted .

Table 4.1 lists some of the methods of a JobTracker, while Table 4.2 lists of the methods of a TaskTracker, both of which give you a glimpse of what they do specifically. These methods confirm that a JobTracker manages MapReduce jobs as well as TaskTrackers. It can init/fail/kill/submit a job. It can also start/stop/kill a TaskTracker. One challenging issue with Hadoop is that the JobTracker is a single point of failure for a Hadoop environment that has only one JobTracker. If it goes down, all running MapReduce jobs are stopped. For development and testing environments, this is not a huge issue, but it would affect the normal operation of a production environment if it happens. If this is a concern for you due to your job role, you should check out other Apache projects for advices on how to avoid and recover from a JobTracker failure to resume the normal operation of your Hadoop production environment.

Table 4.1 A partial list of the methods of a JobTracker

Method	Comment (when needed)
activeTaskTrackers ()	Get the active task tracker statuses in the cluster

blacklistedTaskTrackers ()	Get the blacklisted task tracker statuses in the cluster
completedJobs() / failedJobs()	
failJob	Fail a job and inform the listeners.
getAssignedTracker ()	Get tracker name for a given task id.
getJobsFromQueue	Gets all the jobs submitted to the Queue
getMapTaskReports (JobID jobid)	
getQueueManager()	Return the QueueManager associated with the JobTracker.
getReduceTaskReports (JobID jobid)	
getRunningJobs ()	
getTaskTracker (String trackerID)	
getTotalSubmissions ()	
initJob (…)	
killJob (JobID jobid)	
killTask (TaskAttemptID taskid, …)	
setJobPriority (JobID jobid, String priority)	
startTracker (JobConf conf)	
stopTracker ()	
submitJob (JobID jobId)	Kicks off a new job

Table 4.2 A partial list of the methods of a TaskTracker

Method	Comment (when needed)
canCommit (…)	Task process checking whether it can commit.
cleanupStorage ()	Empties temporary storage directories
done (…)	Reports the task is done.
getJobJarFile (…)	
getMapCompletionEvents (…)	Called by a reduce task to get the map output locations for finished maps.

getTask (…)	Called upon startup by the child process to fetch Task data.
launchTaskForJob (…)	
shuffleError (..)	A reduce-task failed to shuffle the map-outputs
statusUpdate (…)	Called periodically to report Task progress, from 0.0 to 1.0

Before moving to the next section about YARN, let's summarize some of the important configuration parameters related to a cluster managed with the MapReduce 1 orchestrator as discussed above. Table 4.3 summarizes these parameters, some of which will be discussed later in the Hadoop performance tuning section of Chapter 8 of this book.

Table 4.3 (a) Some interesting configuration parameters related to a Hadoop cluster set in mapred-site.xml

Parameter	Comment
mapred.child.java.opts	Heap-size for a child JVM of a map/reduce task (default –Mxm200m)
mapred.tasktracker.map.tasks.maximum	The maximum number of map tasks that will be run simultaneously by a task tracker (default: 2).
mapred.tasktracker.reduce.tasks.maximum	The maximum number of reduce tasks that will be run simultaneously by a task tracker (default: 2).
mapred.reduce.parallel.copies	The default number of parallel transfers run by reduce during the copy (shuffle) phase (default: 5).
tasktracker.http.threads	The number of worker threads for the http server. This is used for map output fetching (default: 40)

Table 4.3 (b) Some interesting configuration parameters related to a Hadoop cluster set in hdfs-site.xml

Parameter	Comment
dfs.block.size	The default block size for new files (default: 67108864).
dfs.heartbeat.interval	Determines datanode heartbeat interval in seconds.
dfs.namenode.handle.count	# of NameNode threads to handle RPCs from large # of DataNodes

Table 4.3 (c) Some interesting configuration parameters related to a Hadoop cluster set in core-site.xml

Parameter	Comment
fs.inmemory.size.mb	Amount of memory for merging map outputs before reducing.
io.sort.factor	# of streams merged at once while sorting files.
io.sort.mb	The number of streams to merge at once while sorting files. This determines the number of open file handles (default: 10)
io.file.buffer.size	The size of buffer for use in sequence files. The size of this buffer should probably be a multiple of hardware page size (4096 on Intel x86), and it determines how much data is buffered during read and write operations (default: 4096).

4.1.2 Hadoop MapReduce 2 Orchestrator - YARN

The Hadoop MapReduce 2 orchestrator named YARN is for managing large clusters with thousands of or more nodes. In this section, we provide a brief coverage about YARN to help gain some insights into how different it is from the MapReduce 1 orchestrator introduced in the previous section.

Comparing Figure 4.1 and Figure 4.2, we see that the previous JobTracker is replaced with a ResourceManager, and the previous TaskTracker is replaced with a NodeManager. However, this subtle difference is over-shadowed with the introduction of two extra entities: a container and an application master on a node. Each new entity has its responsibilities as described below

- **Resource Manager**: According to Apache, a ResourceManager is primarily a pure scheduler now. Its role is strictly limited to arbitrating available resources among the competing applications. It strives for optimizing cluster efficiency while managing various constraints such as SLAs associated with each application.
- **Node Manager**: Responsible for managing resources on a node based on the policies set by the ResourceManager.
- **Application Master**: Responsible for negotiating appropriate resource containers from the ResourceManager, including tracking their status and monitoring progress as well.
- **Container**: Grants rights to an application to use a specific amount of resources such as memory and CPU on a specific host.

Since a ResourceManager is a pure scheduler now, the responsibilities of a traditional resource manager are now shifted to the AppMaster, which is also responsible for managing fault tolerance. As you can see, all the complexities associated with the NodeName in MapReduce 1 orchestrator now lie with the AppMaster. According to tests conducted at Yahoo, this has helped extend Hadoop's scalability drastically.

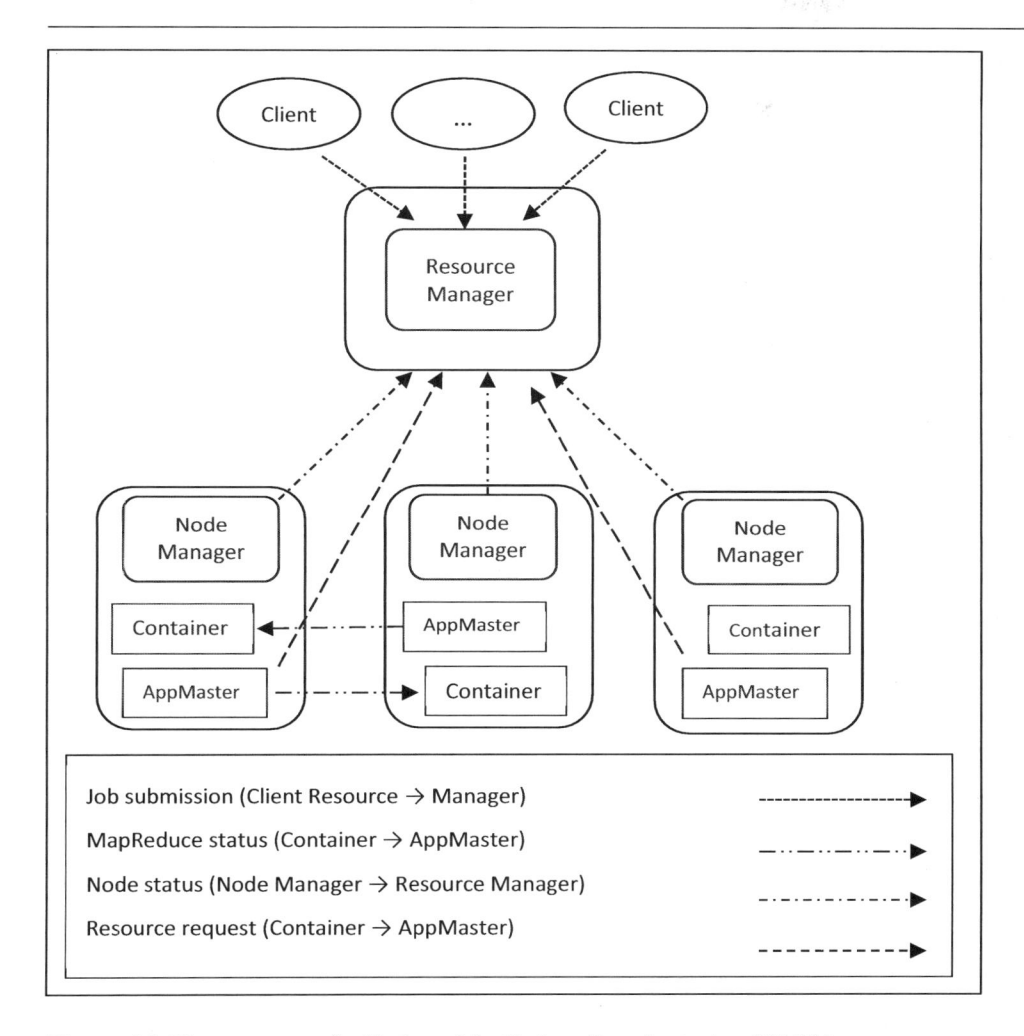

Figure 4.2 The structure of a Hadoop MapReduce 2 orchestrator -YARN

If you are interested in learning more about YARN, refer to Apache's YARN website at http://hadoop.apache.org/common/docs/r0.23.0/hadoop-yarn/hadoop-yarn-site/YARN.html.

4.2 MAPREDUCE WORKFLOWS

In this section, we focus on understanding typical MapReduce workflows in local mode, in pseudo-distributed mode, and in fully distributed mode. Since YARN typically is used with thousands of or more nodes in large cluster environments, the workflows we explore here apply to MR1 only. This is sufficient for us, because our purposes here are for knowing more about the intricacies involved with typical MapReduce workflows so that we can develop high performance, scalable MapReduce programs.

Let's start with MapReduce workflows in local mode next.

4.2.1 MapReduce Workflows in Local Mode

We take a unique approach to exploring the MapReduce workflow with a given Hadoop running mode by examining the verbose output messages from a MapReduce job run rather than by going with what the Hadoop MapReduce documents have to say. This approach can help avoid the version-applicability issue.

In order to have as many output lines as possible from a MapReduce job run, we need to change the default log4j level from INFO to DEBUG. There might be multiple options to accomplish this, but the easiest way is to make the following changes in the `log4j.properties` file located in Hadoop's *conf* directory, as shown is Listing 4.1 (if you are not familiar with log4j, visit http://logging.apache.org/log4j/1.2/ for a quick brush-up):

```
# lof4j.rootLogger=${hadoop.root.logger}, console, EventCounter
lof4j.rootLogger=DEBUG, console, EventCounter
```

Since this is only a temporary expedient, we would need to change it back by commenting out the newly-added DEBUG line and uncommenting the original line. If you are familiar with log4j, take a cursory look at Listing 4.1 and it may help enhance your Hadoop learning further just by knowing what items can be logged and how they are logged. You can change the default logging levels for the items that you need to debug or understand more.

With the above change, I re-ran the 2M credit card transaction MapReduce job as described in chapter 2 with all output lines collected into a text file. Since there are many DEBUG lines like

```
12/08/31 10:41:07 DEBUG mapred.Counters: Adding MAP_OUTPUT_BYTES
12/08/31 10:41:07 DEBUG mapred.Counters: Adding MAP_OUTPUT_RECORDS
12/08/31 10:41:07 DEBUG mapred.Counters: Adding COMBINE_INPUT_RECORDS
12/08/31 10:41:07 DEBUG mapred.Counters: Adding COMBINE_OUTPUT_RECORDS
12/08/31 10:41:07 DEBUG mapred.Counters: Adding
MAP_OUTPUT_MATERIALIZED_BYTES
```

I had to apply "/V" option to the "*find*" MS-DOS command to eliminate them so that the output would not be too verbose and take too much space. I also applied the "/N" option to add the line numbers to the output. See Listing 4.1 for the trimmed-down output lines that we would use to reconstruct the MapReduce workflow in local mode.

So here is a replay of the events that occurred during that MapReduce job run (we go by line numbers for the sake of unambiguity):

1) Line #1: The SpendingPattern MapReduce job is submitted to Hadoop.
2) Line #2: Creating splits in the local staging directory.
3) Line #3: One total input path was identified (note that this run had only one input file. More complicated MapReduce jobs could have more input paths).

4) Line 7: The TaskRunner did some house-cleaning work by deleting some contents in the */tmp* directory.

5) Line 27: JobClient queried that both map and reduce tasks just started with 0% progress for both.

6) Line 28: The MapTask reported that it had record full so it started spilling map output to disk.

7) Line 31: The MapTask reported that it had finished spill 0.

8) Line 32: The MapTask reported that it started another round of spilling map output.

9) Line 35: The MapTask reported starting flush of map output.

10) Lines 36 – 37: The MapTask reported that it had finished spill 1 and spill 2.

11) Lines 38 – 40: The MapTask reported the details of those three spills with this first map task.

12) Line 41: The Merger reported that it started merging those 3 sorted segments (or those 3 spills). Apparently those 3 spills had been sorted before merging.

13) Line 43: The Task reported that the first map task was done and it was in the process of committing (or flushing the memory buffer to disk).

14) Line 80: The Task reported that 'attempt_local_0001_m_000000_0' (the first map task) was done completely.

15) Lines 99 – 151: The second map task experienced the same sequence of events as the first map task did.

16) Lines 156 -208: The third map task experienced the same sequence of events as the previous two map tasks.

17) Lines 213 -260: The fourth map task experienced the same sequence of events as the previous three map tasks except that it had 2 instead of 3 spills, since this last map task had less than 1 block of data to process.

18) Line 291: The Merger reported that it was merging 4 sorted segments (as the results of those 4 map tasks). Note that that was the second time the Merger kicked in: The first merge merged the spills of each map task, and the second merge merged the map outputs of all map tasks).

19) Line 317: The Task reported that the reduce job (…r_...0) was done and was in the process of committing reduce output to disk.

20) Line 344: The Task reported that the reduce job got permission to commit.

21) Line 345: The FileOutputCommitter reported that it moved the file from the temp directory to the designated directory.

22) Line 369: The Task reported that the reduce job was done.

23) Lines 376 – 377: The JobClient queried that both map and reduce tasks had been 100% complete.

24) Lines 400 – 403: The FileSystem cleared the cache.

25) Line 404: the entire job was completed and the normal shell prompt appeared.

The above counting is tedious, but it indisputably recounted what had occurred with that MapReduce work. Figure 4.3 further illustrates the above MapReduce workflow graphically. One thing you might have noticed is that very little was told about the reduce task. I suspect that it was a local job so there was no need to copy the map output data from one node to another. We will double check this when we explore the MapReduce workflow in fully distributed mode next.

Listing 4.1 Hadoop log4j.properties (default)

```
# Define some default values that can be overridden by system properties
hadoop.root.logger=INFO,console
hadoop.log.dir=.
hadoop.log.file=hadoop.log
#
# Job Summary Appender
#
# Use following logger to send summary to separate file defined by
# hadoop.mapreduce.jobsummary.log.file rolled daily:
# hadoop.mapreduce.jobsummary.logger=INFO,JSA
#
hadoop.mapreduce.jobsummary.logger=${hadoop.root.logger}
hadoop.mapreduce.jobsummary.log.file=hadoop-mapreduce.jobsummary.log

# Define the root logger to the system property "hadoop.root.logger".
log4j.rootLogger=${hadoop.root.logger}, EventCounter

# Logging Threshold
log4j.threshhold=ALL

#
# Daily Rolling File Appender
#

log4j.appender.DRFA=org.apache.log4j.DailyRollingFileAppender
log4j.appender.DRFA.File=${hadoop.log.dir}/${hadoop.log.file}

# Rollver at midnight
log4j.appender.DRFA.DatePattern=.yyyy-MM-dd

# 30-day backup
#log4j.appender.DRFA.MaxBackupIndex=30
log4j.appender.DRFA.layout=org.apache.log4j.PatternLayout

# Pattern format: Date LogLevel LoggerName LogMessage
log4j.appender.DRFA.layout.ConversionPattern=%d{ISO8601} %p %c: %m%n
# Debugging Pattern format
#log4j.appender.DRFA.layout.ConversionPattern=%d{ISO8601} %-5p %c{2} (%F:%M(%L)) - %m%n

#
# console
# Add "console" to rootlogger above if you want to use this
#

log4j.appender.console=org.apache.log4j.ConsoleAppender
log4j.appender.console.target=System.err
```

```
log4j.appender.console.layout=org.apache.log4j.PatternLayout
log4j.appender.console.layout.ConversionPattern=%d{yy/MM/dd HH:mm:ss} %p %c{2}: %m%n

#
# TaskLog Appender
#

#Default values
hadoop.tasklog.taskid=null
hadoop.tasklog.iscleanup=false
hadoop.tasklog.noKeepSplits=4
hadoop.tasklog.totalLogFileSize=100
hadoop.tasklog.purgeLogSplits=true
hadoop.tasklog.logsRetainHours=12

log4j.appender.TLA=org.apache.hadoop.mapred.TaskLogAppender
log4j.appender.TLA.taskId=${hadoop.tasklog.taskid}
log4j.appender.TLA.isCleanup=${hadoop.tasklog.iscleanup}
log4j.appender.TLA.totalLogFileSize=${hadoop.tasklog.totalLogFileSize}

log4j.appender.TLA.layout=org.apache.log4j.PatternLayout
log4j.appender.TLA.layout.ConversionPattern=%d{ISO8601} %p %c: %m%n

#
#Security audit appender
#
hadoop.security.log.file=SecurityAuth.audit
log4j.appender.DRFAS=org.apache.log4j.DailyRollingFileAppender
log4j.appender.DRFAS.File=${hadoop.log.dir}/${hadoop.security.log.file}

log4j.appender.DRFAS.layout=org.apache.log4j.PatternLayout
log4j.appender.DRFAS.layout.ConversionPattern=%d{ISO8601} %p %c: %m%n
#new logger
log4j.logger.SecurityLogger=OFF,console
log4j.logger.SecurityLogger.additivity=false

#
# Rolling File Appender
#

#log4j.appender.RFA=org.apache.log4j.RollingFileAppender
#log4j.appender.RFA.File=${hadoop.log.dir}/${hadoop.log.file}

# Logfile size and and 30-day backups
#log4j.appender.RFA.MaxFileSize=1MB
#log4j.appender.RFA.MaxBackupIndex=30

#log4j.appender.RFA.layout=org.apache.log4j.PatternLayout
#log4j.appender.RFA.layout.ConversionPattern=%d{ISO8601} %-5p %c{2} - %m%n
```

```
#log4j.appender.RFA.layout.ConversionPattern=%d{ISO8601} %-5p %c{2} (%F:%M(%L)) - %m%n

#
# FSNamesystem Audit logging
# All audit events are logged at INFO level
#
log4j.logger.org.apache.hadoop.hdfs.server.namenode.FSNamesystem.audit=WARN

# Custom Logging levels

hadoop.metrics.log.level=INFO
#log4j.logger.org.apache.hadoop.mapred.JobTracker=DEBUG
#log4j.logger.org.apache.hadoop.mapred.TaskTracker=DEBUG
#log4j.logger.org.apache.hadoop.fs.FSNamesystem=DEBUG
log4j.logger.org.apache.hadoop.metrics2=${hadoop.metrics.log.level}

# Jets3t library
log4j.logger.org.jets3t.service.impl.rest.httpclient.RestS3Service=ERROR

#
# Null Appender
# Trap security logger on the hadoop client side
#
log4j.appender.NullAppender=org.apache.log4j.varia.NullAppender

#
# Event Counter Appender
# Sends counts of logging messages at different severity levels to Hadoop Metrics.
#
log4j.appender.EventCounter=org.apache.hadoop.log.metrics.EventCounter

#
# Job Summary Appender
#
log4j.appender.JSA=org.apache.log4j.DailyRollingFileAppender
log4j.appender.JSA.File=${hadoop.log.dir}/${hadoop.mapreduce.jobsummary.log.file}
log4j.appender.JSA.layout=org.apache.log4j.PatternLayout
log4j.appender.JSA.layout.ConversionPattern=%d{yy/MM/dd HH:mm:ss} %p %c{2}: %m%n
log4j.appender.JSA.DatePattern=.yyyy-MM-dd
log4j.logger.org.apache.hadoop.mapred.JobInProgress$JobSummary=${hadoop.mapreduce.jobsumma
ry.logger}
log4j.additivity.org.apache.hadoop.mapred.JobInProgress$JobSummary=false
```

Listing 4.2 Console output of a MapReduce local run with DEBUG on

```
[1]mc815ll:MyHadoop-1.0.3 henry$ hadoop jar spending-patterns.jar SpendingPattern
in0/credit_card_tx_1_out.txt out13
```

[2]12/08/31 10:41:07 DEBUG mapred.JobClient: Creating splits at file:/tmp/hadoop-henry/mapred/staging/henry167431850/.staging/job_local_0001
[3]12/08/31 10:41:07 INFO input.FileInputFormat: Total input paths to process : 1
[4]12/08/31 10:41:07 WARN snappy.LoadSnappy: Snappy native library not loaded
[5]12/08/31 10:41:07 DEBUG input.FileInputFormat: Total # of splits: 4
[6]12/08/31 10:41:07 DEBUG mapred.JobClient: Printing tokens for job: job_local_0001
[7]12/08/31 10:41:07 DEBUG mapred.TaskRunner: Fully deleting contents of /tmp/hadoop-henry/mapred/local/localRunner
[8]12/08/31 10:41:07 INFO mapred.JobClient: Running job: job_local_0001
[9]12/08/31 10:41:07 DEBUG mapred.SortedRanges: currentIndex 0   0:0
[12]12/08/31 10:41:07 DEBUG mapred.TaskRunner: mapred.local.dir for child : /tmp/hadoop-henry/mapred/local/taskTracker/henry/jobcache/job_local_0001/attempt_local_0001_m_000000_0
[13]12/08/31 10:41:07 DEBUG mapred.Task: using new api for output committer
[14]12/08/31 10:41:07 INFO mapred.Task: Using ResourceCalculatorPlugin : null
[19]12/08/31 10:41:07 INFO mapred.MapTask: io.sort.mb = 100
[20]12/08/31 10:41:07 INFO mapred.MapTask: data buffer = 79691776/99614720
[21]12/08/31 10:41:07 INFO mapred.MapTask: record buffer = 262144/327680
[27]12/08/31 10:41:08 INFO mapred.JobClient: map 0% reduce 0%
[28]12/08/31 10:41:08 INFO mapred.MapTask: Spilling map output: record full = true
[29]12/08/31 10:41:08 INFO mapred.MapTask: bufstart = 0; bufend = 11950965; bufvoid = 99614720
[30]12/08/31 10:41:08 INFO mapred.MapTask: kvstart = 0; kvend = 262144; length = 327680
[31]12/08/31 10:41:09 INFO mapred.MapTask: Finished spill 0
[32]12/08/31 10:41:09 INFO mapred.MapTask: Spilling map output: record full = true
[33]12/08/31 10:41:09 INFO mapred.MapTask: bufstart = 11950965; bufend = 23902476; bufvoid = 99614720
[34]12/08/31 10:41:09 INFO mapred.MapTask: kvstart = 262144; kvend = 196607; length = 327680
[35]12/08/31 10:41:09 INFO mapred.MapTask: Starting flush of map output
[36]12/08/31 10:41:10 INFO mapred.MapTask: Finished spill 1
[37]12/08/31 10:41:10 INFO mapred.MapTask: Finished spill 2
[38]12/08/31 10:41:10 DEBUG mapred.MapTask: MapId=attempt_local_0001_m_000000_0 Reducer=0Spill =0(0,12475255, 12475259)
[39]12/08/31 10:41:10 DEBUG mapred.MapTask: MapId=attempt_local_0001_m_000000_0 Reducer=0Spill =1(0,12475799, 12475803)
[40]12/08/31 10:41:10 DEBUG mapred.MapTask: MapId=attempt_local_0001_m_000000_0 Reducer=0Spill =2(0,1674408, 1674412)
[41]12/08/31 10:41:10 INFO mapred.Merger: Merging 3 sorted segments
[42]12/08/31 10:41:10 INFO mapred.Merger: Down to the last merge-pass, with 3 segments left of total size: 26625462 bytes
[43]12/08/31 10:41:11 INFO mapred.Task: Task:attempt_local_0001_m_000000_0 is done. And is in the process of commiting
[80]12/08/31 10:41:13 INFO mapred.Task: Task 'attempt_local_0001_m_000000_0' done.
[96]12/08/31 10:41:13 DEBUG mapred.SortedRanges: currentIndex 0   0:0
[99]12/08/31 10:41:13 DEBUG mapred.TaskRunner: mapred.local.dir for child : /tmp/hadoop-henry/mapred/local/taskTracker/henry/jobcache/job_local_0001/attempt_local_0001_m_000001_0
[100]12/08/31 10:41:13 DEBUG mapred.Task: using new api for output committer
...... removed lines 99 - 135 to save space
[151]12/08/31 10:41:16 INFO mapred.Task: Task 'attempt_local_0001_m_000001_0' done.
[152]12/08/31 10:41:16 DEBUG mapred.SortedRanges: currentIndex 0   0:0
[155]

[156]12/08/31 10:41:16 DEBUG mapred.TaskRunner: mapred.local.dir for child : /tmp/hadoop-henry/mapred/local/taskTracker/henry/jobcache/job_local_0001/attempt_local_0001_m_000002_0
[157]
[158]12/08/31 10:41:16 DEBUG mapred.Task: using new api for output committer
...... removed lines 159 - 192 to save space
 [208]12/08/31 10:41:19 INFO mapred.Task: Task 'attempt_local_0001_m_000002_0' done.
[209]12/08/31 10:41:19 DEBUG mapred.SortedRanges: currentIndex 0   0:0
[212]
[213]12/08/31 10:41:19 DEBUG mapred.TaskRunner: mapred.local.dir for child : /tmp/hadoop-henry/mapred/local/taskTracker/henry/jobcache/job_local_0001/attempt_local_0001_m_000003_0
[214]12/08/31 10:41:19 DEBUG mapred.Task: using new api for output committer
[215]12/08/31 10:41:19 INFO mapred.Task: Using ResourceCalculatorPlugin : null
[220]12/08/31 10:41:19 INFO mapred.MapTask: io.sort.mb = 100
[221]12/08/31 10:41:19 INFO mapred.MapTask: data buffer = 79691776/99614720
[222]12/08/31 10:41:19 INFO mapred.MapTask: record buffer = 262144/327680
[228]
[229]12/08/31 10:41:20 INFO mapred.MapTask: Spilling map output: record full = true
[232]12/08/31 10:41:20 INFO mapred.MapTask: Starting flush of map output
[233]12/08/31 10:41:20 INFO mapred.MapTask: Finished spill 0
[234]12/08/31 10:41:20 INFO mapred.MapTask: Finished spill 1
[235]12/08/31 10:41:20 DEBUG mapred.MapTask: MapId=attempt_local_0001_m_000003_0
Reducer=0Spill =0(0,12476371, 12476375)
[236]12/08/31 10:41:20 DEBUG mapred.MapTask: MapId=attempt_local_0001_m_000003_0
Reducer=0Spill =1(0,720853, 720857)
[237]12/08/31 10:41:20 INFO mapred.Merger: Merging 2 sorted segments
[238]12/08/31 10:41:20 INFO mapred.Merger: Down to the last merge-pass, with 2 segments left of total size: 13197224 bytes
[239]12/08/31 10:41:20 INFO mapred.Task: Task:attempt_local_0001_m_000003_0 is done. And is in the process of commiting
[260]12/08/31 10:41:22 INFO mapred.Task: Task 'attempt_local_0001_m_000003_0' done.
[261]12/08/31 10:41:22 DEBUG mapred.SortedRanges: currentIndex 0   0:0
[269]12/08/31 10:41:22 DEBUG mapred.Task: using new api for output committer
[270]12/08/31 10:41:22 INFO mapred.Task: Using ResourceCalculatorPlugin : null
[291]12/08/31 10:41:22 INFO mapred.Merger: Merging 4 sorted segments
[292]12/08/31 10:41:22 INFO mapred.Merger: Down to the last merge-pass, with 4 segments left of total size: 93068186 bytes
[317]12/08/31 10:41:24 INFO mapred.Task: Task:attempt_local_0001_r_000000_0 is done. And is in the process of commiting
[344]12/08/31 10:41:24 INFO mapred.Task: Task attempt_local_0001_r_000000_0 is allowed to commit now
[345]12/08/31 10:41:24 DEBUG output.FileOutputCommitter: Moved
file:/Users/henry/dev2/workspace/MyHadoop-1.0.3/out13/_temporary/_attempt_local_0001_r_000000_0/part-r-00000 to out13/part-r-00000
[346]12/08/31 10:41:24 INFO output.FileOutputCommitter: Saved output of task 'attempt_local_0001_r_000000_0' to out13
[347]12/08/31 10:41:25 INFO mapred.LocalJobRunner: reduce > reduce
[369]12/08/31 10:41:25 INFO mapred.Task: Task 'attempt_local_0001_r_000000_0' done.
[376]12/08/31 10:41:26 INFO mapred.JobClient: map 100% reduce 100%

```
[377]12/08/31 10:41:26 INFO mapred.JobClient: Job complete: job_local_0001
[378]12/08/31 10:41:26 INFO mapred.JobClient: Counters: 17
...... Counters removed to save space
 [396]12/08/31 10:41:26 INFO mapred.JobClient:    Reduce input groups=44
[397]12/08/31 10:41:26 INFO mapred.JobClient:    Combine output records=0
[398]12/08/31 10:41:26 INFO mapred.JobClient:    Reduce output records=44
[399]12/08/31 10:41:26 INFO mapred.JobClient:    Map output records=1955544
[400]12/08/31 10:41:26 DEBUG fs.FileSystem: Starting clear of FileSystem cache with 1 elements.
[401]12/08/31 10:41:26 DEBUG fs.FileSystem: Removing filesystem for file:///
[402]12/08/31 10:41:26 DEBUG fs.FileSystem: Removing filesystem for file:///
[403]12/08/31 10:41:26 DEBUG fs.FileSystem: Done clearing cache
[404]mc815ll:MyHadoop-1.0.3 henry$
```

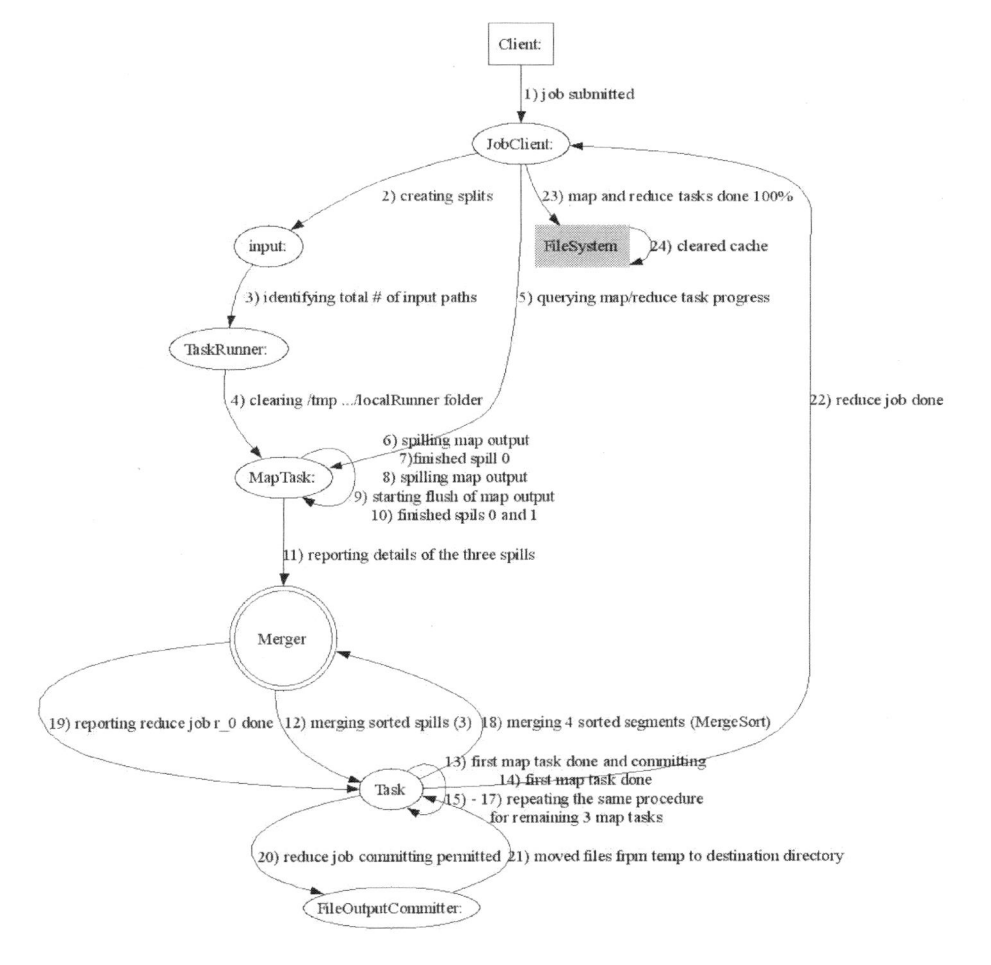

Figure 4.3 MapReduce workflow with Hadoop running in local mode

4.2.2 MapReduce Workflow in Fully Distributed Mode

In this section, we analyze how a MapReduce job is run with Hadoop running in fully distributed mode. Since it's too verbose to have DEBUG turned on for logging via log4j, the default logging level of INFO would be used. The other factor is that there were multiple Linux nodes involved and timing was not synchronized across all nodes, so we would not attempt to construct the sequence of events that occurred on multiple nodes. Instead, we would take a look at the events that occurred on each node with the following two jobs:

- Job 1: A 2M credit card transaction job as was run in local mode discussed in the previous section.
- Job 2: A 10M credit card transaction job to compare with the 2M credit card transaction job.

The Linux cluster on which we would run Hadoop in fully distributed mode was the same as described in Figure 2.1. As was introduced there, there were four Linux nodes with this cluster, each of which was named as *linux-<unique_string>.perfmath.com* with the part *<unique_string>* identifying a unique node as follows:

- *1fsw*: NameNode
- *w9ms*: 1st DataNode
- *sgpx*: 2nd DataNode
- *vg5i*: SecondaryNameNode

Each MapReduce job was submitted on the NameNode (*1fsw*). Let's take a look at how the first SpendingPattern MapReduce job was carried out on this cluster based on the job configuration file, job result output, and logs on various nodes.

Hadoop MapReduce Job Configuration File

First, there was a job configuration file located in Hadoop's *logs* folder on the NameNode (1fsw) and named *job_201209021930_0001_conf.xml* for the 2M credit card transaction job (note that timestamp in the format of *year-month-date-hour-minute* is part of the file name). This file is given in Appendix B as Table B.1 for convenience, which will be referenced later. Although this job configuration file is lengthy, it's worthwhile to spend a few minutes and take a cursory look at it, because it encompasses almost all Hadoop concepts we covered so far and beyond. It's especially worthwhile to take a look at those parameters highlighted in bold, as they are very useful for helping us understand not only a Hadoop MapReduce workflow but also the entire Hadoop MapReduce framework. It might not be exaggerating to say that if anybody understands most of the parameters listed in Table B.1, his knowledge level of Hadoop can be rated to at least eight or higher, although one can make safe guesses on the meanings of many parameters just based on what their names suggest.

MapReduce Result Output from the 2M Credit Card Transaction Job

Next, let's take a look at the MapReduce result output from the 2M credit card transaction job displayed on the console where the job was submitted. All output lines from this job were pipelined to a text file, which is shown in Listing 4.3. As is seen, it's much less lengthy than its local run counterpart shown in Listing 4.2, because when a MapReduce job is run on a cluster in fully-distributed mode, logs are scattered on various nodes rather than on one node only. It's interesting to note that the job execution output reports mostly the progress of the map and reduce tasks without intermediate steps as was the case with the standalone mode. Finally, note the line of *"Reduce output records = 44"* at the end of the report, which serves as the proof that the job completed with the expected # of records as we have 44 unique keys no matter how large the synthetic credit card transaction data file is.

Listing 4.3 MapReduce result output from the 2M credit card transaction job

```
henry@linux-1fsw:~/mydev/MyHadoop-1.0.3> hadoop jar spending-patterns.jar SpendingPattern
input/credit_card_tx_1_out.txt out30
12/09/02 19:33:59 INFO input.FileInputFormat: Total input paths to process : 1
12/09/02 19:33:59 INFO util.NativeCodeLoader: Loaded the native-hadoop library
12/09/02 19:33:59 WARN snappy.LoadSnappy: Snappy native library not loaded
12/09/02 19:33:59 INFO mapred.JobClient: Running job: job_201209021930_0001
12/09/02 19:34:00 INFO mapred.JobClient:  map 0% reduce 0%
12/09/02 19:34:18 INFO mapred.JobClient:  map 45% reduce 0%
12/09/02 19:34:21 INFO mapred.JobClient:  map 90% reduce 0%
12/09/02 19:34:24 INFO mapred.JobClient:  map 100% reduce 0%
12/09/02 19:34:33 INFO mapred.JobClient:  map 100% reduce 16%
12/09/02 19:34:39 INFO mapred.JobClient:  map 100% reduce 100%
12/09/02 19:34:44 INFO mapred.JobClient: Job complete: job_201209021930_0001
12/09/02 19:34:45 INFO mapred.JobClient: Counters: 29
12/09/02 19:34:45 INFO mapred.JobClient:   Job Counters
12/09/02 19:34:45 INFO mapred.JobClient:     Launched reduce tasks=1
12/09/02 19:34:45 INFO mapred.JobClient:     SLOTS_MILLIS_MAPS=31889
12/09/02 19:34:45 INFO mapred.JobClient:     Launched map tasks=2
12/09/02 19:34:45 INFO mapred.JobClient:     Data-local map tasks=2
12/09/02 19:34:45 INFO mapred.JobClient:     SLOTS_MILLIS_REDUCES=16277
12/09/02 19:34:45 INFO mapred.JobClient:   File Output Format Counters
12/09/02 19:34:45 INFO mapred.JobClient:     Bytes Written=2094
12/09/02 19:34:45 INFO mapred.JobClient:   FileSystemCounters
12/09/02 19:34:45 INFO mapred.JobClient:     FILE_BYTES_READ=186135834
12/09/02 19:34:45 INFO mapred.JobClient:     HDFS_BYTES_READ=115301520
12/09/02 19:34:45 INFO mapred.JobClient:     FILE_BYTES_WRITTEN=279267938
12/09/02 19:34:45 INFO mapred.JobClient:     HDFS_BYTES_WRITTEN=2094
12/09/02 19:34:45 INFO mapred.JobClient:   File Input Format Counters
12/09/02 19:34:45 INFO mapred.JobClient:     Bytes Read=115301246
12/09/02 19:34:45 INFO mapred.JobClient:   Map-Reduce Framework
12/09/02 19:34:45 INFO mapred.JobClient:     Map output materialized bytes=93067896
12/09/02 19:34:45 INFO mapred.JobClient:     Map input records=2000000
12/09/02 19:34:45 INFO mapred.JobClient:     Reduce shuffle bytes=93067896
12/09/02 19:34:45 INFO mapred.JobClient:     Spilled Records=5866200
12/09/02 19:34:45 INFO mapred.JobClient:     Map output bytes=89157084
12/09/02 19:34:45 INFO mapred.JobClient:     CPU time spent (ms)=33000
12/09/02 19:34:45 INFO mapred.JobClient:     Total committed heap usage (bytes)=408621056
12/09/02 19:34:45 INFO mapred.JobClient:     Combine input records=0
12/09/02 19:34:45 INFO mapred.JobClient:     SPLIT_RAW_BYTES=274
```

```
12/09/02 19:34:45 INFO mapred.JobClient:    Reduce input records=1955400
12/09/02 19:34:45 INFO mapred.JobClient:    Reduce input groups=44
12/09/02 19:34:45 INFO mapred.JobClient:    Combine output records=0
12/09/02 19:34:45 INFO mapred.JobClient:    Physical memory (bytes) snapshot=486535168
12/09/02 19:34:45 INFO mapred.JobClient:    Reduce output records=44
12/09/02 19:34:45 INFO mapred.JobClient:    Virtual memory (bytes) snapshot=1099612160
12/09/02 19:34:45 INFO mapred.JobClient:    Map output records=1955400
```

NameNode Log File for the 2M Credit Card Transaction Job

In order to see the activities on the NameNode, Listing 4.4 shows the NameNode log file located in Hadoop's *logs* folder on the NameNode (*1fsw*) and named *hadoop-henry-namenode-linux-1fsw.log* for the 2M credit card transaction job. As is seen, most of the lines were from *org.apache.hadoop.hdfs.StateChange* class and the *org.apache.hadoop.hdfs.server.namenode.FSNamesystem* class, reporting file and block management activities. Note the following two lines as highlighted:

```
2012-09-02 19:33:59,475 INFO org.apache.hadoop.hdfs.StateChange: BLOCK*
NameSystem.addStoredBlock: blockMap updated: 192.168.1.107:50010 is added to
blk_3644556054527339756_1300 size 10933
2012-09-02 19:33:59,477 INFO org.apache.hadoop.hdfs.StateChange: BLOCK*
NameSystem.addStoredBlock: blockMap updated: 192.168.1.108:50010 is added to
blk_3644556054527339756_1300 size 10933
```

In the above case, the same block was replicated on the two DataNodes, one with the IP of 192.168.1.107 for the DataNode named *linux-sgpx* and the other with the IP of 192.168.1.108 for the DataNode named *linux-w9ms*. At the end, the two DataNodes were asked to delete a same block as shown below:

```
2012-09-02 19:34:46,798 INFO org.apache.hadoop.hdfs.StateChange: BLOCK* ask
192.168.1.107:50010 to delete  blk_-6378875809667677080_1306
2012-09-02 19:34:49,799 INFO org.apache.hadoop.hdfs.StateChange: BLOCK* ask
192.168.1.108:50010 to delete  blk_-6378875809667677080_1306
```

You can also identify other HDFS activities such as *increasing replication for files*, etc. The main point is that the NameNode oversees file and block management chores.

Listing 4.4 NameNode log file for the 2M credit card transaction job (hadoop-henry-namenode-linux-1fsw.log)

```
2012-09-02 19:33:59,372 INFO org.apache.hadoop.hdfs.server.namenode.FSNamesystem: Number of
transactions: 8 Total time for transactions(ms): 1Number of transactions batched in Syncs: 0 Number
of syncs: 6 SyncTimes(ms): 66
2012-09-02 19:33:59,430 INFO org.apache.hadoop.hdfs.StateChange: BLOCK*
NameSystem.allocateBlock: /tmp/hadoop-
henry/mapred/staging/henry/.staging/job_201209021930_0001/job.jar.
blk_3644556054527339756_1300
2012-09-02 19:33:59,475 INFO org.apache.hadoop.hdfs.StateChange: BLOCK*
NameSystem.addStoredBlock: blockMap updated: 192.168.1.107:50010 is added to
blk_3644556054527339756_1300 size 10933
```

```
2012-09-02 19:33:59,477 INFO org.apache.hadoop.hdfs.StateChange: BLOCK*
NameSystem.addStoredBlock: blockMap updated: 192.168.1.108:50010 is added to
blk_3644556054527339756_1300 size 10933
2012-09-02 19:33:59,479 INFO org.apache.hadoop.hdfs.StateChange: Removing lease on  file
/tmp/hadoop-henry/mapred/staging/henry/.staging/job_201209021930_0001/job.jar from client
DFSClient_1928806363
2012-09-02 19:33:59,480 INFO org.apache.hadoop.hdfs.StateChange: DIR* NameSystem.completeFile:
file /tmp/hadoop-henry/mapred/staging/henry/.staging/job_201209021930_0001/job.jar is closed by
DFSClient_1928806363
2012-09-02 19:33:59,488 INFO org.apache.hadoop.hdfs.server.namenode.FSNamesystem: Increasing
replication for file /tmp/hadoop-
henry/mapred/staging/henry/.staging/job_201209021930_0001/job.jar. New replication is 10
2012-09-02 19:33:59,554 INFO org.apache.hadoop.hdfs.server.namenode.FSNamesystem: Increasing
replication for file /tmp/hadoop-
henry/mapred/staging/henry/.staging/job_201209021930_0001/job.split. New replication is 10
2012-09-02 19:33:59,572 INFO org.apache.hadoop.hdfs.StateChange: BLOCK*
NameSystem.allocateBlock: /tmp/hadoop-
henry/mapred/staging/henry/.staging/job_201209021930_0001/job.split. blk_-
2355765291382363343_1301
2012-09-02 19:33:59,582 INFO org.apache.hadoop.hdfs.StateChange: BLOCK*
NameSystem.addStoredBlock: blockMap updated: 192.168.1.107:50010 is added to blk_-
2355765291382363343_ 1301 size 281
2012-09-02 19:33:59,585 INFO org.apache.hadoop.hdfs.StateChange: BLOCK*
NameSystem.addStoredBlock: blockMap updated: 192.168.1.108:50010 is added to blk_-
2355765291382363343_1301 size 281
...... (redundant lines deleted) .....
2012-09-02 19:34:44,125 INFO org.apache.hadoop.hdfs.StateChange: Removing lease on  file
/user/henry/out30/_logs/history/job_201209021930_0001_1346639639732_henry_Spending+Pattern
from client DFSClient_784408489
2012-09-02 19:34:44,125 INFO org.apache.hadoop.hdfs.StateChange: DIR* NameSystem.completeFile:
file
/user/henry/out30/_logs/history/job_201209021930_0001_1346639639732_henry_Spending+Pattern
is closed by DFSClient_784408489
2012-09-02 19:34:44,155 INFO org.apache.hadoop.hdfs.StateChange: BLOCK*
NameSystem.addToInvalidates: blk_-6378875809667677080 is added to invalidSet of
192.168.1.107:50010
2012-09-02 19:34:44,155 INFO org.apache.hadoop.hdfs.StateChange: BLOCK*
NameSystem.addToInvalidates: blk_-6378875809667677080 is added to invalidSet of
192.168.1.108:50010
2012-09-02 19:34:46,798 INFO org.apache.hadoop.hdfs.StateChange: BLOCK* ask
192.168.1.107:50010 to delete  blk_-6378875809667677080_1306
2012-09-02 19:34:49,799 INFO org.apache.hadoop.hdfs.StateChange: BLOCK* ask
192.168.1.108:50010 to delete  blk_-6378875809667677080_1306
```

JobTracker Log File for the 2M Credit Card Transaction Job

Another interesting log file to look at is the job tracker log file. Figure 4.4 shows the sequence of the events that occurred as reported by the JobTracker, based on Listing 4.5, which shows the JobTracker log file for the 2M credit card transaction job located in Hadoop's *logs* folder and named *hadoop-henry-jobtracker-linux-1fsw.log*. Note that the job was split into two splits, which were made available on both DataNodes (*w9ms* and *sgpx*). The first map task was executed on *w9ms* while the second map task was executed on *sgpx*. The reduce job was executed on *w9ms*, which probably was because the Job Scheduler *knew* that *w9ms* had more capacity in terms of CPU and RAM than *sgpx*.

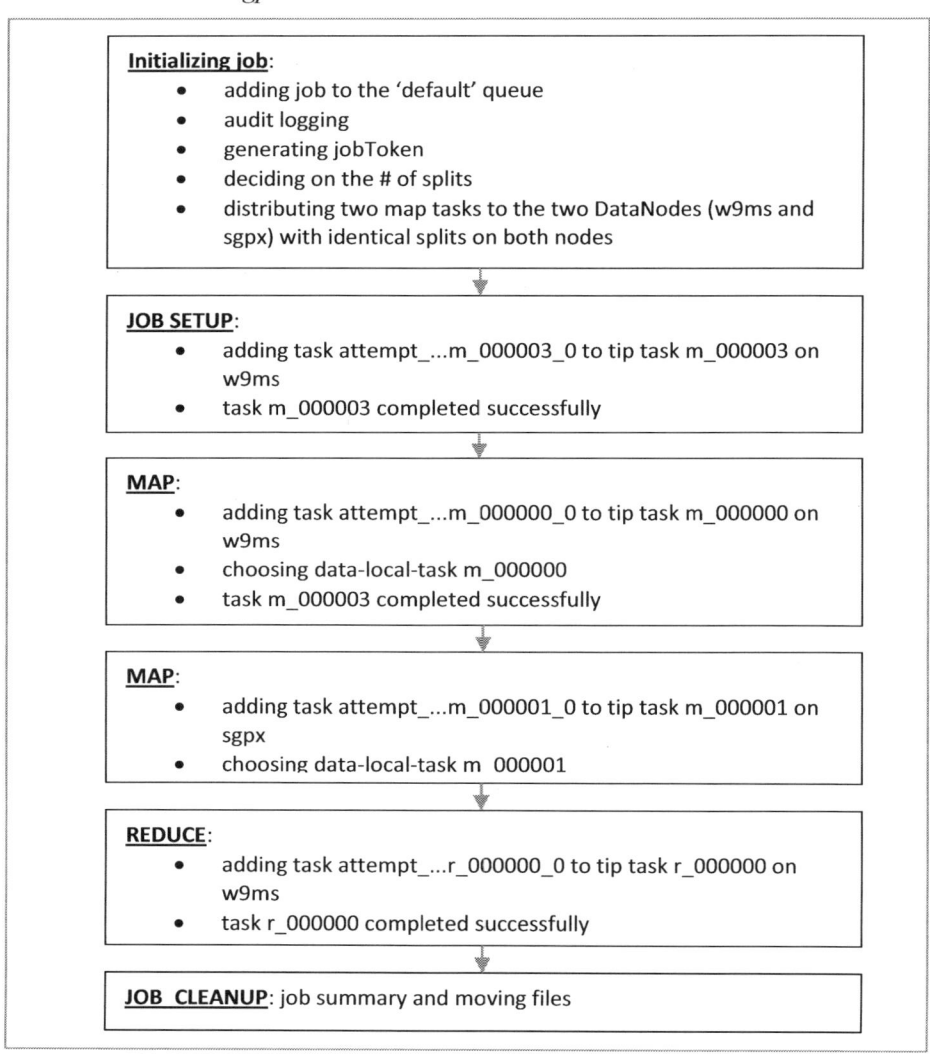

Figure 4.4 Sequence of events reported by the job tracker for the 2M credit card transaction MapReduce job

Listing 4.5 JobTracker log file for the 2M credit card transaction job named hadoop-henry-jobtracker-linux-1fsw.log

2012-09-02 19:33:59,751 INFO org.apache.hadoop.util.NativeCodeLoader: Loaded the native-hadoop library

2012-09-02 19:33:59,797 INFO org.apache.hadoop.mapred.JobInProgress: job_201209021930_0001: nMaps=2 nReduces=1 max=-1

2012-09-02 19:33:59,799 INFO org.apache.hadoop.mapred.JobTracker: Job job_201209021930_0001 **added successfully for user 'henry' to queue 'default'**

2012-09-02 19:33:59,801 INFO org.apache.hadoop.mapred.JobTracker: **Initializing job**_201209021930_0001

2012-09-02 19:33:59,801 INFO org.apache.hadoop.mapred.JobInProgress: Initializing job_201209021930_0001

2012-09-02 19:33:59,801 INFO org.apache.hadoop.mapred.**AuditLogger:** USER=henry
     IP=192.168.1.103   OPERATION=SUBMIT_JOB   TARGET=job_201209021930_0001 RESULT=SUCCESS

2012-09-02 19:33:59,962 INFO org.apache.hadoop.mapred.JobInProgress: **jobToken** generated and stored with users keys in /tmp/hadoop-henry/mapred/system/job_201209021930_0001/jobToken

2012-09-02 19:33:59,975 INFO org.apache.hadoop.mapred.JobInProgress: **Input size for job job**_201209021930_0001 = 115297149. **Number of splits = 2**

2012-09-02 19:33:59,976 INFO org.apache.hadoop.mapred.JobInProgress:
tip:task_201209021930_0001_m_000000 has split on node:/default-rack/linux-w9ms.perfmath.com

2012-09-02 19:33:59,976 INFO org.apache.hadoop.mapred.JobInProgress:
tip:task_201209021930_0001_m_000000 **has split on node:/default-rack/linux-sgpx.perfmath.com**

2012-09-02 19:33:59,976 INFO org.apache.hadoop.mapred.JobInProgress:
tip:task_201209021930_0001_m_000001 **has split on node:/default-rack/linux-sgpx.perfmath.com**

2012-09-02 19:33:59,976 INFO org.apache.hadoop.mapred.JobInProgress:
tip:task_201209021930_0001_m_000001 **has split on node:/default-rack/linux-w9ms.perfmath.com**

2012-09-02 19:33:59,976 INFO org.apache.hadoop.mapred.JobInProgress: job_201209021930_0001 LOCALITY_WAIT_FACTOR=1.0

2012-09-02 19:33:59,977 INFO org.apache.hadoop.mapred.JobInProgress: Job job_201209021930_0001 initialized successfully with 2 map tasks and 1 reduce tasks.

2012-09-02 19:34:01,934 INFO org.apache.hadoop.mapred.JobTracker: Adding task (JOB_SETUP) 'attempt_201209021930_0001_m_000003_0' to tip task_201209021930_0001_m_000003, for tracker 'tracker_linux-w9ms.perfmath.com:localhost/127.0.0.1:56663'

2012-09-02 19:34:07,989 INFO org.apache.hadoop.mapred.JobInProgress: Task 'attempt_201209021930_0001_m_000003_0' has completed **task_201209021930_0001_m_000003 successfully**.

2012-09-02 19:34:07,994 INFO org.apache.hadoop.mapred.JobTracker: Adding task (MAP) 'attempt_201209021930_0001_m_000000_0' to tip task_201209021930_0001_m_000000, for tracker 'tracker_linux-w9ms.perfmath.com:localhost/127.0.0.1:56663'

2012-09-02 19:34:07,995 INFO org.apache.hadoop.mapred.JobTracker: **Choosing data-local task task_201209021930_0001_m_000000**

2012-09-02 19:34:10,981 INFO org.apache.hadoop.mapred.JobTracker: Adding task (MAP) 'attempt_201209021930_0001_m_000001_0' to tip task_201209021930_0001_m_000001, for tracker 'tracker_linux-sgpx.perfmath.com:localhost/127.0.0.1:53282'

2012-09-02 19:34:10,982 INFO org.apache.hadoop.mapred.JobInProgress: Choosing data-local task task_201209021930_0001_m_000001

2012-09-02 19:34:20,018 INFO org.apache.hadoop.mapred.JobInProgress: Task
'attempt_201209021930_0001_m_000000_0' has completed task_201209021930_0001_m_000000
successfully.
2012-09-02 19:34:20,025 INFO org.apache.hadoop.mapred.JobTracker: Adding task (REDUCE)
'attempt_201209021930_0001_r_000000_0' to tip task_201209021930_0001_r_000000, for tracker
'tracker_linux-w9ms.perfmath.com:localhost/127.0.0.1:56663'
2012-09-02 19:34:26,050 INFO org.apache.hadoop.mapred.JobInProgress: Task
'attempt_201209021930_0001_m_000001_0' has completed task_201209021930_0001_m_000001
successfully.
2012-09-02 19:34:38,075 INFO org.apache.hadoop.mapred.JobInProgress: Task
'attempt_201209021930_0001_r_000000_0' has completed task_201209021930_0001_r_000000
successfully.
2012-09-02 19:34:38,083 INFO org.apache.hadoop.mapred.JobTracker: Adding task (JOB_CLEANUP)
'attempt_201209021930_0001_m_000002_0' to tip task_201209021930_0001_m_000002, for tracker
'tracker_linux-w9ms.perfmath.com:localhost/127.0.0.1:56663'
2012-09-02 19:34:44,097 INFO org.apache.hadoop.mapred.JobInProgress: Task
'attempt_201209021930_0001_m_000002_0' has completed task_201209021930_0001_m_000002
successfully.
2012-09-02 19:34:44,099 INFO org.apache.hadoop.mapred.JobInProgress: **Job
job_201209021930_0001 has completed successfully.**
2012-09-02 19:34:44,101 INFO org.apache.hadoop.mapred.JobInProgress$**JobSummary**:
jobId=job_201209021930_0001,submitTime=1346639639732,launchTime=1346639639976,firstMapTa
skLaunchTime=1346639647994,firstReduceTaskLaunchTime=1346639660021,firstJobSetupTaskLaunch
Time=1346639641911,firstJobCleanupTaskLaunchTime=1346639678083,finishTime=1346639684099,n
umMaps=2,numSlotsPerMap=1,numReduces=1,numSlotsPerReduce=1,user=henry,queue=default,stat
us=SUCCEEDED,mapSlotSeconds=31,reduceSlotsSeconds=16,clusterMapCapacity=4,clusterReduceCapa
city=4,jobName=Spending Pattern
2012-09-02 19:34:44,143 INFO org.apache.hadoop.mapred.JobHistory: **Creating** DONE subfolder at
file:/home/henry/myapp/hadoop-1.0.3/logs/history/done/version-1/linux-
1fsw.perfmath.com_1346639432209_/2012/09/02/000000
2012-09-02 19:34:44,150 INFO org.apache.hadoop.mapred.JobHistory: **Moving**
file:/home/henry/myapp/hadoop-
1.0.3/logs/history/job_201209021930_0001_1346639639732_henry_Spending+Pattern to
file:/home/henry/myapp/hadoop-1.0.3/logs/history/done/version-1/linux-
1fsw.perfmath.com_1346639432209_/2012/09/02/000000
2012-09-02 19:34:44,153 INFO org.apache.hadoop.mapred.JobTracker: **Removing** task
'attempt_201209021930_0001_m_000000_0'
2012-09-02 19:34:44,153 INFO org.apache.hadoop.mapred.JobTracker: **Removing** task
'attempt_201209021930_0001_m_000002_0'
2012-09-02 19:34:44,153 INFO org.apache.hadoop.mapred.JobTracker: **Removing** task
'attempt_201209021930_0001_m_000003_0'
2012-09-02 19:34:44,153 INFO org.apache.hadoop.mapred.JobTracker: **Removing** task
'attempt_201209021930_0001_r_000000_0'
2012-09-02 19:34:44,153 INFO org.apache.hadoop.mapred.JobTracker: **Removing** task
'attempt_201209021930_0001_m_000001_0'
2012-09-02 19:34:44,159 INFO org.apache.hadoop.mapred.JobHistory: Moving
file:/home/henry/myapp/hadoop-1.0.3/logs/history/job_201209021930_0001_conf.xml to

file:/home/henry/myapp/hadoop-1.0.3/logs/history/done/version-1/linux-1fsw.perfmath.com_1346639432209_/2012/09/02/000000

DataNode Log File for the 2M Credit Card Transaction Job

Listing 4.6 shows the activities that occurred on one of the DataNode (*w9ms* with the IP of 192.168.1.08). This is about 1/3 of the entire log file, since the remaining 2/3 do not add new information and waste space, and hence deleted. The following types of activities were reported form this DataNode's log file:

- MBean registration for jvm, DataNode, SocketReader, etc. Note the following line showing that this DataNode was registered:

  2012-09-02 19:29:20,721 INFO org.apache.hadoop.hdfs.server.datanode.**DataNode**: dnRegistration = **DatanodeRegistration**(linux-**w9ms**.perfmath.com:50010, storageID=DS-35359591-68.180.151.96-50010-1345171471181, infoPort=50075, ipcPort=50020)

- Reporting block scanning as indicated by the following line:

  2012-09-02 19:29:20,742 INFO org.apache.hadoop.hdfs.server.datanode.DataNode: **Starting asynchronous block report scan**

- Reporting receiving blocks as indicated by the following line (note that 192.168.1.103 designated as *src* is the NameNode's IP):

  2012-09-02 19:30:03,207 INFO org.apache.hadoop.hdfs.server.datanode.DataNode: **Receiving block** blk_-8493118710276832678_1299 src: /192.168.1.103:43488 dest: /192.168.1.108:50010

- Reporting *clienttrace* as indicated by the following line (note *src* and *dest*):

  org.apache.hadoop.hdfs.server.datanode.DataNode.clienttrace: src: /192.168.1.103:43488, dest: /192.168.1.108:50010, bytes: 4, op: HDFS_WRITE, cliID: DFSClient_-1574902968, offset: 0, srvID: DS-35359591-68.180.151.96-50010-1345171471181, blockid: blk_-8493118710276832678_1299, duration: 12838432

- Scheduling block for deletion as indicated by the following line:

  Scheduling block blk_-914839810111907020_1298 file /tmp/hadoop-henry/dfs/data/current/blk_-914839810111907020 for deletion
  2012-09-02 19:30:05,784 INFO org.apache.hadoop.hdfs.server.datanode.DataNode: **Deleted block blk**_-914839810111907020_1298 at file /tmp/hadoop-henry/dfs/data/current/blk_-914839810111907020

The remaining 2/3 of the log files were mostly receiving blocks, scheduling block for deletion, and deleting blocks. Next, we take a look at the task tracker's log file.

Listing 4.6 DataNode log file located on the DataNode's *logs* folder and named *hadoop-henry-datanode-linux-w9ms.perfmath.com.log* for the 2M credit card transaction job

2012-09-02 19:29:19,633 INFO org.apache.hadoop.metrics2.impl.MetricsSystemImpl: Scheduled snapshot period at 10 second(s).

2012-09-02 19:29:19,696 INFO org.apache.hadoop.metrics2.impl.MetricsSourceAdapter: MBean for source ugi registered.

2012-09-02 19:29:19,948 INFO org.apache.hadoop.hdfs.server.datanode.DataNode: Registered FSDatasetStatusMBean

2012-09-02 19:29:19,955 INFO org.apache.hadoop.hdfs.server.datanode.DataNode: Opened info server at 50010

2012-09-02 19:29:19,957 INFO org.apache.hadoop.hdfs.server.datanode.DataNode: Balancing bandwith is 1048576 bytes/s

2012-09-02 19:29:20,041 INFO org.mortbay.log: Logging to org.slf4j.impl.Log4jLoggerAdapter(org.mortbay.log) via org.mortbay.log.**Slf4jLog**

2012-09-02 19:29:20,113 INFO org.apache.hadoop.http.HttpServer: Added global filtersafety (class=org.apache.hadoop.http.HttpServer$QuotingInputFilter)

2012-09-02 19:29:20,123 INFO org.apache.hadoop.hdfs.server.datanode.DataNode: dfs.webhdfs.enabled = false

2012-09-02 19:29:20,123 INFO org.apache.hadoop.http.HttpServer: Port returned by webServer.getConnectors()[0].getLocalPort() before open() is -1. Opening the listener on 50075

2012-09-02 19:29:20,123 INFO org.apache.hadoop.http.HttpServer: listener.getLocalPort() returned 50075 webServer.getConnectors()[0].getLocalPort() returned 50075

2012-09-02 19:29:20,123 INFO org.apache.hadoop.http.HttpServer: Jetty bound to port 50075

2012-09-02 19:29:20,490 INFO org.apache.hadoop.metrics2.impl.MetricsSourceAdapter: MBean for source **jvm** registered.

2012-09-02 19:29:20,491 INFO org.apache.hadoop.metrics2.impl.MetricsSourceAdapter: MBean for source **DataNode** registered.

2012-09-02 19:29:20,716 INFO org.apache.hadoop.ipc.Server: Starting **SocketReader**

2012-09-02 19:29:20,718 INFO org.apache.hadoop.metrics2.impl.MetricsSourceAdapter: MBean for source RpcDetailedActivityForPort50020 registered.

2012-09-02 19:29:20,718 INFO org.apache.hadoop.metrics2.impl.MetricsSourceAdapter: MBean for source RpcActivityForPort50020 registered.

2012-09-02 19:29:20,721 INFO org.apache.hadoop.hdfs.server.datanode.DataNode: dnRegistration = **DatanodeRegistration**(linux-**w9ms**.perfmath.com:50010, storageID=DS-35359591-68.180.151.96-50010-1345171471181, infoPort=50075, ipcPort=50020)

2012-09-02 19:29:20,742 INFO org.apache.hadoop.hdfs.server.datanode.DataNode: **Starting asynchronous block report scan**

2012-09-02 19:29:20,742 INFO org.apache.hadoop.hdfs.server.datanode.DataNode: **DatanodeRegistration**(192.168.1.108:50010, storageID=DS-35359591-68.180.151.96-50010-1345171471181, infoPort=50075, ipcPort=50020)In DataNode.run, data = FSDataset{dirpath='/tmp/hadoop-henry/dfs/data/current'}

2012-09-02 19:29:20,742 INFO org.apache.hadoop.ipc.Server: **IPC Server Responder**: starting

2012-09-02 19:29:20,743 INFO org.apache.hadoop.ipc.Server: **IPC Server listener** on 50020: starting

2012-09-02 19:29:20,743 INFO org.apache.hadoop.ipc.Server: **IPC Server handler 0** on 50020: starting

2012-09-02 19:29:20,744 INFO org.apache.hadoop.ipc.Server: **IPC Server handler 1** on 50020: starting

2012-09-02 19:29:20,744 INFO org.apache.hadoop.hdfs.server.datanode.DataNode: using BLOCKREPORT_INTERVAL of 3600000msec Initial delay: 0msec

2012-09-02 19:29:20,744 INFO org.apache.hadoop.ipc.Server: IPC Server handler 2 on 50020: starting

2012-09-02 19:29:20,746 INFO org.apache.hadoop.hdfs.server.datanode.DataNode: **Starting Periodic block scanner**.

2012-09-02 19:29:20,750 INFO org.apache.hadoop.hdfs.server.datanode.DataNode: Finished asynchronous block report scan in 8ms

```
2012-09-02 19:29:20,764 INFO org.apache.hadoop.hdfs.server.datanode.DataNode: Generated rough
(lockless) block report in 11 ms
2012-09-02 19:29:20,766 INFO org.apache.hadoop.hdfs.server.datanode.DataNode: Reconciled
asynchronous block report against current state in 2 ms
2012-09-02 19:29:23,745 INFO org.apache.hadoop.hdfs.server.datanode.DataNode: Reconciled
asynchronous block report against current state in 1 ms
2012-09-02 19:29:23,764 INFO org.apache.hadoop.hdfs.server.datanode.DataNode: BlockReport of
109 blocks took 1 msec to generate and 19 msecs for RPC and NN processing
2012-09-02 19:30:03,207 INFO org.apache.hadoop.hdfs.server.datanode.DataNode: Receiving block
blk_-8493118710276832678_1299 src: /192.168.1.103:43488 dest: /192.168.1.108:50010
2012-09-02 19:30:03,373 INFO org.apache.hadoop.hdfs.server.datanode.DataNode.clienttrace: src:
/192.168.1.103:43488, dest: /192.168.1.108:50010, bytes: 4, op: HDFS_WRITE, cliID: DFSClient_-
1574902968, offset: 0, srvID: DS-35359591-68.180.151.96-50010-1345171471181, blockid: blk_-
8493118710276832678_1299, duration: 12838432
2012-09-02 19:30:03,373 INFO org.apache.hadoop.hdfs.server.datanode.DataNode: PacketResponder
1 for block blk_-8493118710276832678_1299 terminating
2012-09-02 19:30:05,783 INFO org.apache.hadoop.hdfs.server.datanode.DataNode: Scheduling block
blk_-914839810111907020_1298 file /tmp/hadoop-henry/dfs/data/current/blk_-
914839810111907020 for deletion
2012-09-02 19:30:05,784 INFO org.apache.hadoop.hdfs.server.datanode.DataNode: Deleted block
blk_-914839810111907020_1298 at file /tmp/hadoop-henry/dfs/data/current/blk_-
914839810111907020
2012-09-02 19:32:49,771 INFO org.apache.hadoop.hdfs.server.datanode.DataNode: Receiving block
blk_3644556054527339756_1300 src: /192.168.1.103:43493 dest: /192.168.1.108:50010
2012-09-02 19:32:49,785 INFO org.apache.hadoop.hdfs.server.datanode.DataNode.clienttrace: src:
/192.168.1.103:43493, dest: /192.168.1.108:50010, bytes: 10933, op: HDFS_WRITE, cliID:
DFSClient_1928806363, offset: 0, srvID: DS-35359591-68.180.151.96-50010-1345171471181, blockid:
blk_3644556054527339756_1300, duration: 7657456
2012-09-02 19:32:49,785 INFO org.apache.hadoop.hdfs.server.datanode.DataNode: PacketResponder
1 for block blk_3644556054527339756_1300 terminating
2012-09-02 19:32:49,883 INFO org.apache.hadoop.hdfs.server.datanode.DataNode: Receiving block
blk_-2355765291382363343_1301 src: /192.168.1.103:43494 dest: /192.168.1.108:50010
< more lines from this point on deleted to save space>
```

TaskTracker's log file on one of the DataNode (w9ms – 192.168.1.108)

Listing 4.7 shows the task tracker log file located in Hadoop's *logs* folder and named *hadoop-henry-tasktracker-linux-w9ms.perfmath.com.log*. This is the same DataNode whose DataNode log file is shown in Listing 4.6. Typically, we are more interested in job tracker and task tracker log files than NameNode and DataNode log files, because the former contains more detailed information about how a MapReduce job and task were executed.

In Listing 4.7, the first part is similar to what we saw in the DataNode log file shown in Listing 4.6, namely, MBean source registrations. Let's jump to the line time-stamped 2012-09-02 19:30:03,740 (this DataNode of *w9ms* was about 1m11s ahead of the NameNode of *1fsw* in timing or add 1m11s to this timestamp to compensate for the time difference between the two nodes). This line indicates that the parameter *FILE_CACHE_SIZE* for the *mapOutputServlet* was set to 2000. Nevertheless, what we are most interested in are those lines containing *LaunchTaskAction* (*registerTask*), each of which tells us that a new task was started at the given timestamp. Four such lines can be identified as follows:

1) Timestamp 19:32:52,278: LaunchTaskAction attempt_...m_000003_0
2) Timestamp 19:32:58,305: LaunchTaskAction attempt_...m_000000_0
3) Timestamp 19:33:10,341: LaunchTaskAction attempt_...r_000000_0
4) Timestamp 19:33:28,395: LaunchTaskAction attempt_...m_000002_0

This means that four tasks (three map tasks and one reduce task) were launched on this DataNode. Next, let's analyze the events that occurred with the first map task attempt, as presented after Listing 4.7.

Listing 4.7 TaskTracker's log file on one of the DataNode (w9ms – 192.168.1.108)

```
2012-09-02 19:29:23,148 INFO org.apache.hadoop.mapred.TaskTracker: STARTUP_MSG:
/************************************************************
STARTUP_MSG: Starting TaskTracker
STARTUP_MSG:   host = linux-w9ms.perfmath.com/192.168.1.108
STARTUP_MSG:   args = []
STARTUP_MSG:   version = 1.0.3
STARTUP_MSG:   build = https://svn.apache.org/repos/asf/hadoop/common/branches/branch-1.0 -r
1335192; compiled by 'hortonfo' on Tue May  8 20:31:25 UTC 2012
************************************************************/
2012-09-02 19:29:23,421 INFO org.apache.hadoop.metrics2.impl.MetricsSystemImpl: Scheduled
snapshot period at 10 second(s).
2012-09-02 19:29:23,422 INFO org.apache.hadoop.metrics2.impl.MetricsSystemImpl: TaskTracker
metrics system started
2012-09-02 19:29:23,671 INFO org.apache.hadoop.metrics2.impl.MetricsSourceAdapter: MBean for
source ugi registered.
2012-09-02 19:29:23,862 INFO org.mortbay.log: Logging to
org.slf4j.impl.Log4jLoggerAdapter(org.mortbay.log) via org.mortbay.log.Slf4jLog
2012-09-02 19:29:23,926 INFO org.apache.hadoop.http.HttpServer: Added global filtersafety
(class=org.apache.hadoop.http.HttpServer$QuotingInputFilter)
2012-09-02 19:29:23,948 INFO org.apache.hadoop.mapred.TaskLogsTruncater: Initializing logs'
truncater with mapRetainSize=-1 and reduceRetainSize=-1
2012-09-02 19:29:23,951 INFO org.apache.hadoop.mapred.TaskTracker: Starting tasktracker with
owner as henry
2012-09-02 19:29:23,952 INFO org.apache.hadoop.mapred.TaskTracker: Good mapred local directories
are: /tmp/hadoop-henry/mapred/local
2012-09-02 19:29:23,957 INFO org.apache.hadoop.util.NativeCodeLoader: Loaded the native-hadoop
library
2012-09-02 19:29:23,972 INFO org.apache.hadoop.metrics2.impl.MetricsSourceAdapter: **MBean for
source jvm registered**.
2012-09-02 19:29:23,973 INFO org.apache.hadoop.metrics2.impl.MetricsSourceAdapter: MBean for
source TaskTrackerMetrics registered.
2012-09-02 19:29:24,027 INFO org.apache.hadoop.metrics2.impl.MetricsSourceAdapter: MBean for
source RpcDetailedActivityForPort56663 registered.
```

2012-09-02 19:29:24,027 INFO org.apache.hadoop.metrics2.impl.MetricsSourceAdapter: MBean for source RpcActivityForPort56663 registered.
2012-09-02 19:29:24,027 INFO org.apache.hadoop.ipc.Server: Starting SocketReader
2012-09-02 19:29:24,040 INFO org.apache.hadoop.ipc.Server: IPC Server Responder: starting
2012-09-02 19:29:24,048 INFO org.apache.hadoop.ipc.Server: IPC Server listener on 56663: starting
2012-09-02 19:29:24,048 INFO org.apache.hadoop.ipc.Server: IPC Server handler 0 on 56663: starting
2012-09-02 19:29:24,048 INFO org.apache.hadoop.ipc.Server: IPC Server handler 1 on 56663: starting
2012-09-02 19:29:24,048 INFO org.apache.hadoop.ipc.Server: IPC Server handler 2 on 56663: starting
2012-09-02 19:29:24,048 INFO org.apache.hadoop.mapred.TaskTracker: TaskTracker up at: localhost/127.0.0.1:56663
2012-09-02 19:29:24,048 INFO org.apache.hadoop.mapred.TaskTracker: Starting tracker tracker_linux-w9ms.perfmath.com:localhost/127.0.0.1:56663
2012-09-02 19:29:24,049 INFO org.apache.hadoop.ipc.Server: IPC Server handler 3 on 56663: starting
2012-09-02 19:30:03,418 INFO org.apache.hadoop.mapred.TaskTracker: Starting thread: Map-events fetcher for all reduce tasks on tracker_linux-w9ms.perfmath.com:localhost/127.0.0.1:56663
2012-09-02 19:30:03,428 INFO org.apache.hadoop.util.ProcessTree: setsid exited with exit code 0
2012-09-02 19:30:03,431 INFO org.apache.hadoop.mapred.TaskTracker: Using ResourceCalculatorPlugin : org.apache.hadoop.util.LinuxResourceCalculatorPlugin@3afb99
2012-09-02 19:30:03,433 WARN org.apache.hadoop.mapred.TaskTracker: TaskTracker's totalMemoryAllottedForTasks is -1. TaskMemoryManager is disabled.
2012-09-02 19:30:03,435 INFO org.apache.hadoop.mapred.IndexCache: IndexCache created with max memory = 10485760
2012-09-02 19:30:03,441 INFO org.apache.hadoop.metrics2.impl.MetricsSourceAdapter: MBean for source ShuffleServerMetrics registered.
2012-09-02 19:30:03,443 INFO org.apache.hadoop.http.HttpServer: Port returned by webServer.getConnectors()[0].getLocalPort() before open() is -1. Opening the listener on 50060
2012-09-02 19:30:03,443 INFO org.apache.hadoop.http.HttpServer: listener.getLocalPort() returned 50060 webServer.getConnectors()[0].getLocalPort() returned 50060
2012-09-02 19:30:03,443 INFO org.apache.hadoop.http.HttpServer: Jetty bound to port 50060
2012-09-02 19:30:03,443 INFO org.mortbay.log: jetty-6.1.26
2012-09-02 19:30:03,740 INFO org.mortbay.log: Started SelectChannelConnector@0.0.0.0:50060
2012-09-02 19:30:03,740 INFO org.apache.hadoop.mapred.TaskTracker: FILE_CACHE_SIZE for mapOutputServlet set to : 2000
2012-09-02 19:32:52,278 INFO org.apache.hadoop.mapred.TaskTracker: **LaunchTaskAction** (registerTask): attempt_201209021930_0001_**m_000003_0** task's state:UNASSIGNED
2012-09-02 19:32:52,281 INFO org.apache.hadoop.mapred.TaskTracker: Trying to launch : attempt_201209021930_0001_m_000003_0 which needs 1 slots
2012-09-02 19:32:52,281 INFO org.apache.hadoop.mapred.TaskTracker: In TaskLauncher, current free slots : 2 and trying to launch attempt_201209021930_0001_m_000003_0 which needs 1 slots
2012-09-02 19:32:52,454 INFO org.apache.hadoop.mapred.JobLocalizer: Initializing user henry on this TT.
2012-09-02 19:32:52,662 INFO org.apache.hadoop.mapred.JvmManager: In JvmRunner constructed JVM ID: jvm_201209021930_0001_m_1308056117
2012-09-02 19:32:52,662 INFO org.apache.hadoop.mapred.JvmManager: JVM Runner jvm_201209021930_0001_m_1308056117 spawned.
2012-09-02 19:32:52,663 INFO org.apache.hadoop.mapred.TaskController: Writing commands to /tmp/hadoop-henry/mapred/local/ttprivate/taskTracker/henry/jobcache/job_201209021930_0001/attempt_201209021930_0001_m_000003_0/taskjvm.sh

2012-09-02 19:32:53,236 INFO org.apache.hadoop.mapred.TaskTracker: JVM with ID:
jvm_201209021930_0001_m_1308056117 given task: attempt_201209021930_0001_m_000003_0
2012-09-02 19:32:56,817 INFO org.apache.hadoop.mapred.TaskTracker:
attempt_201209021930_0001_m_000003_0 0.0% setup
2012-09-02 19:32:56,819 INFO org.apache.hadoop.mapred.TaskTracker: Task
attempt_201209021930_0001_m_000003_0 is done.
2012-09-02 19:32:56,819 INFO org.apache.hadoop.mapred.TaskTracker: reported output size for
attempt_201209021930_0001_m_000003_0 was -1
2012-09-02 19:32:56,827 INFO org.apache.hadoop.mapred.TaskTracker: addFreeSlot : current free
slots : 2
2012-09-02 19:32:56,974 INFO org.apache.hadoop.mapred.JvmManager: JVM :
jvm_201209021930_0001_m_1308056117 exited with exit code 0. Number of tasks it ran: 1
2012-09-02 19:32:57,023 INFO org.apache.hadoop.io.nativeio.NativeIO: Initialized cache for UID to
User mapping with a cache timeout of 14400 seconds.
2012-09-02 19:32:57,023 INFO org.apache.hadoop.io.nativeio.NativeIO: Got UserName henry for UID
1000 from the native implementation
2012-09-02 19:32:58,305 INFO org.apache.hadoop.mapred.TaskTracker: **LaunchTaskAction**
(registerTask): attempt_201209021930_0001_**m_000000_0** task's state:UNASSIGNED
2012-09-02 19:32:58,305 INFO org.apache.hadoop.mapred.TaskTracker: Trying to launch :
attempt_201209021930_0001_m_000000_0 which needs 1 slots
2012-09-02 19:32:58,305 INFO org.apache.hadoop.mapred.TaskTracker: In TaskLauncher, current free
slots : 2 and trying to launch attempt_201209021930_0001_m_000000_0 which needs 1 slots
2012-09-02 19:32:58,306 INFO org.apache.hadoop.mapred.TaskTracker: Received KillTaskAction for
task: attempt_201209021930_0001_m_000003_0
2012-09-02 19:32:58,306 INFO org.apache.hadoop.mapred.TaskTracker: About to purge task:
attempt_201209021930_0001_m_000003_0
2012-09-02 19:32:58,307 INFO org.apache.hadoop.mapred.IndexCache: Map ID
attempt_201209021930_0001_m_000003_0 not found in cache
2012-09-02 19:32:58,318 INFO org.apache.hadoop.mapred.JvmManager: In JvmRunner constructed
JVM ID: jvm_201209021930_0001_m_979671452
2012-09-02 19:32:58,318 INFO org.apache.hadoop.mapred.JvmManager: JVM Runner
jvm_201209021930_0001_m_979671452 spawned.
2012-09-02 19:32:58,319 INFO org.apache.hadoop.mapred.TaskController: Writing commands to
/tmp/hadoop-
henry/mapred/local/ttprivate/taskTracker/henry/jobcache/job_201209021930_0001/attempt_201209
021930_0001_m_000000_0/taskjvm.sh
2012-09-02 19:32:58,841 INFO org.apache.hadoop.mapred.TaskTracker: JVM with ID:
jvm_201209021930_0001_m_979671452 given task: attempt_201209021930_0001_m_000000_0
2012-09-02 19:33:05,452 INFO org.apache.hadoop.mapred.TaskTracker:
attempt_201209021930_0001_m_000000_0 0.9131682%
2012-09-02 19:33:08,476 INFO org.apache.hadoop.mapred.TaskTracker:
attempt_201209021930_0001_m_000000_0 1.0%
2012-09-02 19:33:08,479 INFO org.apache.hadoop.mapred.TaskTracker:
attempt_201209021930_0001_m_000000_0 1.0%
2012-09-02 19:33:08,481 INFO org.apache.hadoop.mapred.TaskTracker: Task
attempt_201209021930_0001_m_000000_0 is done.
2012-09-02 19:33:08,481 INFO org.apache.hadoop.mapred.TaskTracker: reported output size for
attempt_201209021930_0001_m_000000_0 was 54169578

2012-09-02 19:33:08,481 INFO org.apache.hadoop.mapred.TaskTracker: addFreeSlot : current free slots : 2

2012-09-02 19:33:08,548 INFO org.apache.hadoop.mapred.JvmManager: JVM : jvm_201209021930_0001_m_979671452 exited with exit code 0. Number of tasks it ran: 1

2012-09-02 19:33:10,341 INFO org.apache.hadoop.mapred.TaskTracker: **LaunchTaskAction** (registerTask): attempt_201209021930_0001_**r_000000_0** task's state:UNASSIGNED

2012-09-02 19:33:10,341 INFO org.apache.hadoop.mapred.TaskTracker: Trying to launch : attempt_201209021930_0001_r_000000_0 which needs 1 slots

2012-09-02 19:33:10,341 INFO org.apache.hadoop.mapred.TaskTracker: In TaskLauncher, current free slots : 2 and trying to launch attempt_201209021930_0001_r_000000_0 which needs 1 slots

2012-09-02 19:33:10,346 INFO org.apache.hadoop.mapred.JvmManager: In JvmRunner constructed JVM ID: jvm_201209021930_0001_r_1308056117

2012-09-02 19:33:10,346 INFO org.apache.hadoop.mapred.JvmManager: JVM Runner jvm_201209021930_0001_r_1308056117 spawned.

2012-09-02 19:33:10,347 INFO org.apache.hadoop.mapred.TaskController: Writing commands to /tmp/hadoop-henry/mapred/local/ttprivate/taskTracker/henry/jobcache/job_201209021930_0001/attempt_201209 021930_0001_r_000000_0/taskjvm.sh

2012-09-02 19:33:10,884 INFO org.apache.hadoop.mapred.TaskTracker: JVM with ID: jvm_201209021930_0001_r_1308056117 given task: attempt_201209021930_0001_r_000000_0

2012-09-02 19:33:17,520 INFO org.apache.hadoop.mapred.TaskTracker: attempt_201209021930_0001_**r_000000_0 0.0% reduce > copy** >

2012-09-02 19:33:18,261 INFO org.apache.hadoop.mapred.TaskTracker.**clienttrace**: src: 192.168.1.108:50060, dest: 192.168.1.108:47632, bytes: 54169578, op: **MAPRED_SHUFFLE**, cliID: attempt_201209021930_0001_**m_000000_0**, duration: 1205870871

2012-09-02 19:33:20,562 INFO org.apache.hadoop.mapred.TaskTracker: attempt_201209021930_0001_r_000000_0 0.16666667% reduce > copy (1 of 2 at 6.46 MB/s) >

2012-09-02 19:33:22,570 INFO org.apache.hadoop.mapred.TaskTracker: attempt_201209021930_0001_r_000000_0 0.16666667% reduce > copy (1 of 2 at 6.46 MB/s) >

2012-09-02 19:33:22,580 INFO org.apache.hadoop.mapred.TaskTracker: attempt_201209021930_0001_r_000000_0 0.16666667% reduce > copy (1 of 2 at 6.46 MB/s) >

2012-09-02 19:33:23,601 INFO org.apache.hadoop.mapred.TaskTracker: attempt_201209021930_0001_r_000000_0 0.8882711% reduce > reduce

2012-09-02 19:33:24,040 INFO org.apache.hadoop.mapred.TaskTracker: Task attempt_201209021930_0001_r_000000_0 is in commit-pending, task state:COMMIT_PENDING

2012-09-02 19:33:24,040 INFO org.apache.hadoop.mapred.TaskTracker: attempt_201209021930_0001_r_000000_0 0.8882711% reduce > reduce

2012-09-02 19:33:25,376 INFO org.apache.hadoop.mapred.TaskTracker: Received commit task action for attempt_201209021930_0001_r_000000_0

2012-09-02 19:33:26,618 INFO org.apache.hadoop.mapred.TaskTracker: attempt_201209021930_0001_r_000000_0 1.0% reduce > reduce

2012-09-02 19:33:26,620 INFO org.apache.hadoop.mapred.TaskTracker: attempt_201209021930_0001_r_000000_0 1.0% reduce > reduce

2012-09-02 19:33:26,620 INFO org.apache.hadoop.mapred.TaskTracker: Task attempt_201209021930_0001_**r_000000_0 is done**.

2012-09-02 19:33:26,620 INFO org.apache.hadoop.mapred.TaskTracker: reported output size for attempt_201209021930_0001_r_000000_0 was -1

2012-09-02 19:33:26,621 INFO org.apache.hadoop.mapred.TaskTracker: addFreeSlot : current free slots : 2

2012-09-02 19:33:26,798 INFO org.apache.hadoop.mapred.JvmManager: JVM :
jvm_201209021930_0001_r_1308056117 exited with exit code 0. Number of tasks it ran: 1
2012-09-02 19:33:28,395 INFO org.apache.hadoop.mapred.TaskTracker: **LaunchTaskAction**
(registerTask): attempt_201209021930_0001_**m_000002_0** task's state:UNASSIGNED
2012-09-02 19:33:28,395 INFO org.apache.hadoop.mapred.TaskTracker: Received KillTaskAction for
task: attempt_201209021930_0001_r_000000_0
2012-09-02 19:33:28,395 INFO org.apache.hadoop.mapred.TaskTracker: About to purge task:
attempt_201209021930_0001_r_000000_0
2012-09-02 19:33:28,396 INFO org.apache.hadoop.mapred.TaskTracker: Trying to launch :
attempt_201209021930_0001_m_000002_0 which needs 1 slots
2012-09-02 19:33:28,396 INFO org.apache.hadoop.mapred.TaskTracker: In TaskLauncher, current free
slots : 2 and trying to launch attempt_201209021930_0001_m_000002_0 which needs 1 slots
2012-09-02 19:33:28,403 INFO org.apache.hadoop.mapred.JvmManager: In JvmRunner constructed
JVM ID: jvm_201209021930_0001_m_1726003901
2012-09-02 19:33:28,403 INFO org.apache.hadoop.mapred.JvmManager: JVM Runner
jvm_201209021930_0001_m_1726003901 spawned.
2012-09-02 19:33:28,405 INFO org.apache.hadoop.mapred.TaskController: Writing commands to
/tmp/hadoop-
henry/mapred/local/ttprivate/taskTracker/henry/jobcache/job_201209021930_0001/attempt_201209
021930_0001_m_000002_0/taskjvm.sh
2012-09-02 19:33:28,920 INFO org.apache.hadoop.mapred.TaskTracker: JVM with ID:
jvm_201209021930_0001_m_1726003901 given task: attempt_201209021930_0001_m_000002_0
2012-09-02 19:33:29,493 INFO org.apache.hadoop.mapred.TaskTracker:
attempt_201209021930_0001_m_000002_0 0.0%
2012-09-02 19:33:32,343 INFO org.apache.hadoop.mapred.TaskTracker:
attempt_201209021930_0001_m_000002_0 0.0% cleanup
2012-09-02 19:33:32,346 INFO org.apache.hadoop.mapred.TaskTracker: Task
attempt_201209021930_0001_m_000002_0 is done.
2012-09-02 19:33:32,346 INFO org.apache.hadoop.mapred.TaskTracker: reported output size for
attempt_201209021930_0001_m_000002_0 was -1
2012-09-02 19:33:32,346 INFO org.apache.hadoop.mapred.TaskTracker: addFreeSlot : current free
slots : 2
2012-09-02 19:33:32,397 INFO org.apache.hadoop.mapred.JvmManager: JVM :
jvm_201209021930_0001_m_1726003901 exited with exit code 0. Number of tasks it ran: 1
2012-09-02 19:33:34,462 INFO org.apache.hadoop.mapred.TaskTracker: Received 'KillJobAction' for
job: job_201209021930_0001
2012-09-02 19:33:34,462 INFO org.apache.hadoop.mapred.IndexCache: Map ID
attempt_201209021930_0001_m_000002_0 not found in cache
2012-09-02 19:33:34,462 INFO org.apache.hadoop.mapred.UserLogCleaner: Adding
job_201209021930_0001 for user-log deletion with retainTimeStamp:1346726014462
2012-09-02 19:34:04,650 INFO org.mortbay.log:
org.mortbay.io.nio.SelectorManager$SelectSet@1f7896f JVM BUG(s) - injecting delay1 times
2012-09-02 19:34:04,650 INFO org.mortbay.log:
org.mortbay.io.nio.SelectorManager$SelectSet@1f7896f JVM BUG(s) - recreating selector 1 times,
canceled keys 26 times

The events of the first map task occurred between 19:32:52,278 and 19:32:56,974, with the recorded sequence as shown in Figure 4.5. This map task workflow is self-explanatory and needs no more explanation.

```
1)   Checking if the required # of slots for the task are available
2)   Initializing user
3)   Constructing JVM ID
4)   Spawning JVM
5)   Writing commands to file .../taskvm.sh
6)   Assigning task to JVM
7)   Reporting task done
8)   Returning the slot(s)
9)   JVM shutdown (exited).
```

Figure 4.5 Map task workflow in fully distributed mode

Next, let's take a look at the events of the reduce task bound by the timestamps of 19:33:10,341 – 19:33:26:798, which lasted 16s457ms. By careful examination, it is seen that the reduce task events are similar to map task events that all steps listed in Figure 4.5 for the map task workflow apply to a reduce task as well except that there are more detailed recordings about the events during a reduce task execution. Without renumbering the steps, we can copy the 9 steps for a map task and add several intermediate steps between step 6 and step 7 to construct the workflow for a reduce task as shown in Figure 4.6. We can summarize those intermediate steps as *shuffle* → *copy* → *reduce*, with the # of copy actions depending on the local IO bandwidth, which was 6.46 MB/s in this case. Pay particular attention to the shuffling action as noted below:

```
2012-09-02 19:33:18,261 INFO org.apache.hadoop.mapred.TaskTracker.clienttrace: src:
192.168.1.108:50060, dest: 192.168.1.108:47632, bytes: 54169578, op: MAPRED_SHUFFLE, cliID:
attempt_201209021930_0001_m_000000_0, duration: 1205870871
```

To put it into proper context, compare the above log with the shuffling operation recorded by the task tracker on another DataNode (*linux-sgpx*/192.168.1.107) as shown below:

```
2012-09-02 19:32:34,788 INFO org.apache.hadoop.mapred.TaskTracker.clienttrace: src:
192.168.1.107:50060, dest: 192.168.1.108:35638, bytes: 38898318, op: MAPRED_SHUFFLE, cliID:
attempt_201209021930_0001_m_000001_0, duration: 3935870755
```

See Table 4.4 for a shuffle operation comparison between the two DataNodes.

1) Checking if the required # of slots for the task are available
2) Initializing user
3) Constructing JVM ID
4) Spawning JVM
5) Writing commands to file …/taskvm.sh
6) Assigning task to JVM
   copy → **MAPRED_SHUFFLE** → **copy** …→**reduce**
7) Reporting task done
8) Returning the slot(s)
9) JVM shutdown (exited).

Figure 4.6 Reduce task workflow in fully distributed mode

Table 4.4 Shuffle (MAPRED_SHUFFLE) operation comparison between the two DataNodes

Entry/DataNode	linux-w9ms (192.168.1.108)	linux-sgpx (192.168.1.107)
src	192.168.1.108	192.168.1.107
dest	192.168.1.108	192.168.1.108
bytes	54,169,578	38,898,318
cliID	attempt_...m_000000_0	attempt_...m_000001_0

Since the reducer was assigned to the DataNode named *linux-w9ms*, it' clear that the operation of shuffling merely means copying map task output data from various source DataNodes to destination DataNodes on which reducers run. In this case, since we had only one reducer on the DataNode named linux-w9ms, the map output datum on both DataNodes were copied to the reducer DataNode named *linux-w9ms*. If there were multiple reducers, the map output datum from all map tasks would be partitioned first and then shuffled among the assigned reducers.

10M Credit Card Transaction MapReduce Job

In order to see more details about the map and reduce task workflows, the input data was increased from 2M to 10M credit card transactions. The same SpendingPattern MapReduce job was run with the 10M transaction dataset, and the output was collected into a text file as shown in Listing 4.8. As it turned out, it was not much different from the 2M transaction job except that the number of map tasks increased from 2 to 8 but the number of reduce tasks remained one. However, we did observe one difference as shown in Listing 4.8 that reduce task started even before all map tasks completed. Therefore, map and reduce tasks do not necessarily proceed in series as mistakenly noted by some other Hadoop books.

Listing 4.8 MapReduce result output from the 10M credit card transaction

jobhenry@linux-1fsw:~/mydev/MyHadoop-1.0.3> **hadoop jar spending-patterns.jar SpendingPattern input/credit_card_tx_2_out.txt out31**

12/09/02 19:39:43 WARN mapred.JobClient: Use GenericOptionsParser for parsing the arguments. Applications should implement Tool for the same.

12/09/02 19:39:43 INFO input.FileInputFormat: Total input paths to process : 1

12/09/02 19:39:43 INFO util.NativeCodeLoader: Loaded the native-hadoop library

12/09/02 19:39:43 WARN snappy.LoadSnappy: Snappy native library not loaded

12/09/02 19:39:43 INFO mapred.JobClient: Running job: job_201209021939_0001

12/09/02 19:39:44 INFO mapred.JobClient: map 0% reduce 0%

12/09/02 19:40:03 INFO mapred.JobClient: map 11% reduce 0%

12/09/02 19:40:06 INFO mapred.JobClient: map 26% reduce 0%

12/09/02 19:40:09 INFO mapred.JobClient: map 32% reduce 0%

12/09/02 19:40:12 INFO mapred.JobClient: map 33% reduce 0%

12/09/02 19:40:15 INFO mapred.JobClient: map 34% reduce 0%

12/09/02 19:40:18 INFO mapred.JobClient: map 41% reduce 0%

12/09/02 19:40:21 INFO mapred.JobClient: map 49% reduce 0%

12/09/02 19:40:24 INFO mapred.JobClient: map 58% reduce 0%

12/09/02 19:40:27 INFO mapred.JobClient: map 60% reduce 3%

12/09/02 19:40:30 INFO mapred.JobClient: map 65% reduce 7%

12/09/02 19:40:33 INFO mapred.JobClient: map 66% reduce 7%

12/09/02 19:40:36 INFO mapred.JobClient: map 69% reduce 7%

12/09/02 19:40:39 INFO mapred.JobClient: map 72% reduce 11%

12/09/02 19:40:43 INFO mapred.JobClient: map 76% reduce 14%

12/09/02 19:40:46 INFO mapred.JobClient: map 86% reduce 22%

12/09/02 19:40:49 INFO mapred.JobClient: map 92% reduce 22%

12/09/02 19:40:52 INFO mapred.JobClient: map 95% reduce 22%

12/09/02 19:40:55 INFO mapred.JobClient: map 99% reduce 25%

12/09/02 19:40:58 INFO mapred.JobClient: map 100% reduce 25%

12/09/02 19:41:10 INFO mapred.JobClient: map 100% reduce 29%

12/09/02 19:41:16 INFO mapred.JobClient: map 100% reduce 33%

12/09/02 19:41:19 INFO mapred.JobClient: map 100% reduce 74%

12/09/02 19:41:22 INFO mapred.JobClient: map 100% reduce 91%

12/09/02 19:41:28 INFO mapred.JobClient: map 100% reduce 100%

12/09/02 19:41:33 INFO mapred.JobClient: Job complete: job_201209021939_0001

12/09/02 19:41:33 INFO mapred.JobClient: Counters: 29

12/09/02 19:41:33 INFO mapred.JobClient: Job Counters

12/09/02 19:41:33 INFO mapred.JobClient: Launched reduce tasks=1

12/09/02 19:41:33 INFO mapred.JobClient: SLOTS_MILLIS_MAPS=211659

12/09/02 19:41:33 INFO mapred.JobClient: Total time spent by all reduces waiting after reserving slots (ms)=0

12/09/02 19:41:33 INFO mapred.JobClient: Total time spent by all maps waiting after reserving slots (ms)=0

12/09/02 19:41:33 INFO mapred.JobClient: Launched map tasks=10

12/09/02 19:41:33 INFO mapred.JobClient: Data-local map tasks=10

12/09/02 19:41:33 INFO mapred.JobClient: SLOTS_MILLIS_REDUCES=74442

12/09/02 19:41:33 INFO mapred.JobClient: File Output Format Counters

12/09/02 19:41:33 INFO mapred.JobClient: Bytes Written=2094

12/09/02 19:41:33 INFO mapred.JobClient: FileSystemCounters

12/09/02 19:41:33 INFO mapred.JobClient: FILE_BYTES_READ=930691746

```
12/09/02 19:41:33 INFO mapred.JobClient:    HDFS_BYTES_READ=576509434
12/09/02 19:41:33 INFO mapred.JobClient:    FILE_BYTES_WRITTEN=1396251616
12/09/02 19:41:33 INFO mapred.JobClient:    HDFS_BYTES_WRITTEN=2094
12/09/02 19:41:33 INFO mapred.JobClient:    File Input Format Counters
12/09/02 19:41:33 INFO mapred.JobClient:    Bytes Read=576508201
12/09/02 19:41:33 INFO mapred.JobClient:    Map-Reduce Framework
12/09/02 19:41:33 INFO mapred.JobClient:       Map output materialized bytes=465345771
12/09/02 19:41:33 INFO mapred.JobClient:       Map input records=10000000
12/09/02 19:41:33 INFO mapred.JobClient:       Reduce shuffle bytes=465345771
12/09/02 19:41:33 INFO mapred.JobClient:       Spilled Records=29333859
12/09/02 19:41:33 INFO mapred.JobClient:       Map output bytes=445789811
12/09/02 19:41:33 INFO mapred.JobClient:       CPU time spent (ms)=135570
12/09/02 19:41:33 INFO mapred.JobClient:       Total committed heap usage (bytes)=1686253568
12/09/02 19:41:33 INFO mapred.JobClient:       Combine input records=0
12/09/02 19:41:33 INFO mapred.JobClient:       SPLIT_RAW_BYTES=1233
12/09/02 19:41:33 INFO mapred.JobClient:       Reduce input records=9777953
12/09/02 19:41:33 INFO mapred.JobClient:       Reduce input groups=44
12/09/02 19:41:33 INFO mapred.JobClient:       Combine output records=0
12/09/02 19:41:33 INFO mapred.JobClient:       Physical memory (bytes) snapshot=1898565632
12/09/02 19:41:33 INFO mapred.JobClient:       Reduce output records=44
12/09/02 19:41:33 INFO mapred.JobClient:       Virtual memory (bytes) snapshot=3666075648
12/09/02 19:41:33 INFO mapred.JobClient:       Map output records=9777953
henry@linux-1fsw:~/mydev/MyHadoop-1.0.3>
```

Next, let's reconfigure the cluster to run with two reduce tasks and see what interesting reduce workflow steps we would find out.

4.3 RUNNING MAPREDUCE JOBS WITH MULTIPLE REDUCE TASKS

To configure for a MapReduce job to run with more than one reduce task, first, refer to Table 4.1 and note the parameter named *mapred.reduce.tasks*. This is the setting that would instruct Hadoop how many reduce tasks to use for a MapReduce job. Add this entry in the *mapred-site.xml* file as shown in Listing 4.9, and then copy it to all other nodes.

Listing 4.9 Specifying more than one reducers in mapred-site.xml file

```
<?xml version="1.0"?>
<?xml-stylesheet type="text/xsl" href="configuration.xsl"?>
<configuration>
<property>
 <name>mapred.job.tracker</name>
 <value>linux-1fsw.perfmath.com:8021</value>
 <description>map reduce definition </description>
</property>
<property>
 <name>mapred.reduce.tasks</name>
```

```
<value>2</value>
<description> number of reduce tasks </description>
</property>
</configuration>
```

The next step is to run the command "bin/start-all.sh" to start up all Hadoop daemons. After making sure all daemons are running, submit a 10M credit card transaction job as shown below:

```
$ hadoop jar spending-patterns.jar SpendingPattern input/credit_card_tx_2_out.txt out40
```

Listing 4.10 shows the job output on the console where the job was submitted. It started at 13:54:52 and finished at 13:56:56, taking a total time of 2m4s, which is 14 seconds longer than the same job executed with a single reduce task as shown in Listing 4.8. But this is not what we are concerned about. We are more interested in the reduce task events when a MapReduce job is executed with more than one reduce task. Such information is recorded in the task tracker log files, as is discussed following Listing 4.10 next.

Listing 4.10 A 10M credit card transaction MapReduce job executed with two reducers

```
henry@linux-1fsw:~/mydev/MyHadoop-1.0.3> hadoop jar spending-patterns.jar SpendingPattern
input/credit_card_tx_2_out.txt out40
12/09/06 13:54:52 WARN mapred.JobClient: Use GenericOptionsParser for parsing the arguments.
Applications should implement Tool for the same.
12/09/06 13:54:52 INFO input.FileInputFormat: Total input paths to process : 1
12/09/06 13:54:52 INFO util.NativeCodeLoader: Loaded the native-hadoop library
12/09/06 13:54:52 WARN snappy.LoadSnappy: Snappy native library not loaded
12/09/06 13:54:53 INFO mapred.JobClient: Running job: job_201209061351_0001
12/09/06 13:54:54 INFO mapred.JobClient:  map 0% reduce 0%
12/09/06 13:55:11 INFO mapred.JobClient:  map 13% reduce 0%
12/09/06 13:55:14 INFO mapred.JobClient:  map 19% reduce 0%
12/09/06 13:55:15 INFO mapred.JobClient:  map 25% reduce 0%
12/09/06 13:55:17 INFO mapred.JobClient:  map 28% reduce 0%
12/09/06 13:55:20 INFO mapred.JobClient:  map 32% reduce 0%
12/09/06 13:55:23 INFO mapred.JobClient:  map 35% reduce 0%
12/09/06 13:55:26 INFO mapred.JobClient:  map 46% reduce 0%
12/09/06 13:55:29 INFO mapred.JobClient:  map 55% reduce 0%
12/09/06 13:55:32 INFO mapred.JobClient:  map 63% reduce 3%
12/09/06 13:55:35 INFO mapred.JobClient:  map 66% reduce 3%
12/09/06 13:55:41 INFO mapred.JobClient:  map 66% reduce 5%
12/09/06 13:55:44 INFO mapred.JobClient:  map 73% reduce 11%
12/09/06 13:55:47 INFO mapred.JobClient:  map 82% reduce 11%
12/09/06 13:55:50 INFO mapred.JobClient:  map 86% reduce 12%
12/09/06 13:55:53 INFO mapred.JobClient:  map 88% reduce 14%
12/09/06 13:55:56 INFO mapred.JobClient:  map 94% reduce 20%
12/09/06 13:55:59 INFO mapred.JobClient:  map 96% reduce 20%
12/09/06 13:56:02 INFO mapred.JobClient:  map 98% reduce 20%
12/09/06 13:56:05 INFO mapred.JobClient:  map 100% reduce 20%
12/09/06 13:56:09 INFO mapred.JobClient:  map 100% reduce 22%
```

```
12/09/06 13:56:17 INFO mapred.JobClient: map 100% reduce 27%
12/09/06 13:56:24 INFO mapred.JobClient: map 100% reduce 62%
12/09/06 13:56:38 INFO mapred.JobClient: map 100% reduce 64%
12/09/06 13:56:41 INFO mapred.JobClient: map 100% reduce 66%
12/09/06 13:56:44 INFO mapred.JobClient: map 100% reduce 84%
12/09/06 13:56:47 INFO mapred.JobClient: map 100% reduce 90%
12/09/06 13:56:51 INFO mapred.JobClient: map 100% reduce 100%
12/09/06 13:56:56 INFO mapred.JobClient: Job complete: job_201209061351_0001
12/09/06 13:56:56 INFO mapred.JobClient: Counters: 29
12/09/06 13:56:56 INFO mapred.JobClient:  Job Counters
12/09/06 13:56:56 INFO mapred.JobClient:   Launched reduce tasks=3
12/09/06 13:56:56 INFO mapred.JobClient:   SLOTS_MILLIS_MAPS=216523
12/09/06 13:56:56 INFO mapred.JobClient:   Total time spent by all reduces waiting after reserving
slots (ms)=0
12/09/06 13:56:56 INFO mapred.JobClient:   Total time spent by all maps waiting after reserving slots
(ms)=0
12/09/06 13:56:56 INFO mapred.JobClient:   Launched map tasks=10
12/09/06 13:56:56 INFO mapred.JobClient:   Data-local map tasks=10
12/09/06 13:56:56 INFO mapred.JobClient:   SLOTS_MILLIS_REDUCES=186897
12/09/06 13:56:56 INFO mapred.JobClient:  File Output Format Counters
12/09/06 13:56:56 INFO mapred.JobClient:   Bytes Written=2094
12/09/06 13:56:56 INFO mapred.JobClient:  FileSystemCounters
12/09/06 13:56:56 INFO mapred.JobClient:   FILE_BYTES_READ=930781585
12/09/06 13:56:56 INFO mapred.JobClient:   HDFS_BYTES_READ=576509434
12/09/06 13:56:56 INFO mapred.JobClient:   FILE_BYTES_WRITTEN=1396273514
12/09/06 13:56:56 INFO mapred.JobClient:   HDFS_BYTES_WRITTEN=2094
12/09/06 13:56:56 INFO mapred.JobClient:  File Input Format Counters
12/09/06 13:56:56 INFO mapred.JobClient:   Bytes Read=576508201
12/09/06 13:56:56 INFO mapred.JobClient:  Map-Reduce Framework
12/09/06 13:56:56 INFO mapred.JobClient:   Map output materialized bytes=465345825
12/09/06 13:56:56 INFO mapred.JobClient:   Map input records=10000000
12/09/06 13:56:56 INFO mapred.JobClient:   Reduce shuffle bytes=451433479
12/09/06 13:56:56 INFO mapred.JobClient:   Spilled Records=29333859
12/09/06 13:56:56 INFO mapred.JobClient:   Map output bytes=445789811
12/09/06 13:56:56 INFO mapred.JobClient:   CPU time spent (ms)=143540
12/09/06 13:56:56 INFO mapred.JobClient:   Total committed heap usage (bytes)=1917329408
12/09/06 13:56:56 INFO mapred.JobClient:   Combine input records=0
12/09/06 13:56:56 INFO mapred.JobClient:   SPLIT_RAW_BYTES=1233
12/09/06 13:56:56 INFO mapred.JobClient:   Reduce input records=9777953
12/09/06 13:56:56 INFO mapred.JobClient:   Reduce input groups=44
12/09/06 13:56:56 INFO mapred.JobClient:   Combine output records=0
12/09/06 13:56:56 INFO mapred.JobClient:   Physical memory (bytes) snapshot=2129461248
12/09/06 13:56:56 INFO mapred.JobClient:   Reduce output records=44
12/09/06 13:56:56 INFO mapred.JobClient:   Virtual memory (bytes) snapshot=4043124736
12/09/06 13:56:56 INFO mapred.JobClient:   Map output records=9777953
henry@linux-1fsw:~/mydev/MyHadoop-1.0.3>
```

Let's check out the task tracker log files on both nodes to see how a reduce task is executed exactly.

First, Listing 4.11 displays the task tracker log file on the DataNode named *linux-w9ms,* while Listing 4.12 displays the task tracker log file on the DataNode named *linux-sgpx*, with many lines deleted to make them less verbose. The major point here is that there is a turbulent *shuffle/copy/sort* process with all these sub-processes inter-mingled with each other before data can be ready for the reduce task to take as input for the final stage of reducing in the entire lifecycle of a MapReduce job. We also see cross-node shuffling operations in Listing 4.12 where data was shuffled from the node *linux-sgpx* to the node *linux-w9ms*. Overall, this shuffle/copy/sort process is similar to what's going on in a post office where letters are sorted and sent to different next stops based on some criterion like zipcode, whereas *reduce* is similar to the final stop of delivering mails to receivers. However, there are some pieces of information missing from the task tracker log files, for example:

1) We didn't see partitioning messages from the task tracker logs (*partitioning* partitions map output among all reducers). Perhaps it's a part of shuffling operation as it's necessary to know which reduce task to shuffle data to after all.

2) We didn't see MERGER messages as we did with the logs from the local mode MapReduce job run described previously. Perhaps merging is a part of the sorting sub-process as merge and sort are inseparable entities in the merge-sort algorithm.

The final reduce output result could be queried with the command:

```
$ hadoop fs –ls out40
```

Figure 4.7 shows the result output stored in files *part-r-00000* and *part-r-00001* out of the above 2-reducer, 10 M credit card transaction Spending Pattern MapReduce job run. The reduce output result is stored in the HDFS, not necessarily on the nodes where the reduce tasks reside as mistakenly presented in some Hadoop texts.

Given what we have observed with this two reduce task, 10M credit card transaction MapReduce job as we analyzed above, we can construct a more generic workflow as shown in Figure 4.8 following Listing 4.12. Note the intermediate stage of *partitioning/shuffling/copying/sorting/merging* despite the fact that we didn't see partitioning and merging messages from the task tracker logs. Note also that mappers and reducers could be on the same node or different nodes. It's inappropriate to draw a box indicating that the left branch should be on one node and the right branch on another node.

Listing 4.11 Task tracker log file for the reduce task of processing 10M credit card transactions on the DataNode named linux-w9ms (192.168.1.108)

```
...... parts removed to save space .....

2012-09-06 13:54:14,114 INFO org.apache.hadoop.mapred.TaskTracker.clienttrace: src:
192.168.1.108:50060, dest: 192.168.1.108:47845, bytes: 23606919, op: MAPRED_SHUFFLE, cliID:
attempt_201209061351_0001_m_000001_0, duration: 1102763557
......
2012-09-06 13:54:15,794 INFO org.apache.hadoop.mapred.TaskTracker.clienttrace: src:
192.168.1.108:50060, dest: 192.168.1.108:47845, bytes: 23590093, op: MAPRED_SHUFFLE, cliID:
attempt_201209061351_0001_m_000000_0, duration: 1622794003
```

2012-09-06 13:54:28,691 INFO org.apache.hadoop.mapred.TaskTracker.clienttrace: src: 192.168.1.108:50060, dest: 192.168.1.101:35969, bytes: 30580770, op: **MAPRED_SHUFFLE**, cliID: attempt_201209061351_0001_m_000000_0, duration: 3531476873
2012-09-06 13:54:30,480 INFO org.apache.hadoop.mapred.TaskTracker: attempt_201209061351_0001_m_000006_0 0.6329426%
2012-09-06 13:54:30,785 INFO org.apache.hadoop.mapred.TaskTracker: attempt_201209061351_0001_r_000000_0 0.14814815% **reduce > copy** (4 of 9 at 4.09 MB/s) >
2012-09-06 13:54:35,773 INFO org.apache.hadoop.mapred.TaskTracker.clienttrace: src: 192.168.1.108:50060, dest: 192.168.1.101:35972, bytes: 30627775, op: **MAPRED_SHUFFLE**, cliID: attempt_201209061351_0001_m_000005_0, duration: 3384748228
2012-09-06 13:54:36,839 INFO org.apache.hadoop.mapred.TaskTracker: attempt_201209061351_0001_r_000000_0 0.14814815% **reduce > copy** (4 of 9 at 4.09 MB/s) >
2012-09-06 13:54:37,337 INFO org.apache.hadoop.mapred.TaskTracker: attempt_201209061351_0001_m_000007_0 0.8017434%
2012-09-06 13:54:39,124 INFO org.apache.hadoop.mapred.TaskTracker.clienttrace: src: 192.168.1.108:50060, dest: 192.168.1.108:47868, bytes: 23581811, op: **MAPRED_SHUFFLE**, cliID: attempt_201209061351_0001_m_000006_0, duration: 617116254
2012-09-06 13:54:42,858 INFO org.apache.hadoop.mapred.TaskTracker: attempt_201209061351_0001_r_000000_0 0.25925928% **reduce > copy** (7 of 9 at 4.37 MB/s) >
......
2012-09-06 13:54:52,047 INFO org.apache.hadoop.mapred.TaskTracker.clienttrace: src: 192.168.1.108:50060, dest: 192.168.1.108:47876, bytes: 23550408, op: **MAPRED_SHUFFLE**, cliID: attempt_201209061351_0001_m_000007_0, duration: 272019647
......
2012-09-06 13:54:55,036 INFO org.apache.hadoop.mapred.TaskTracker: attempt_201209061351_0001_r_000000_0 0.2962963% **reduce > copy** (8 of 9 at 3.91 MB/s) >
......
2012-09-06 13:55:02,182 INFO org.apache.hadoop.mapred.TaskTracker.clienttrace: src: 192.168.1.108:50060, dest: 192.168.1.108:47877, bytes: 13912346, op: **MAPRED_SHUFFLE**, cliID: attempt_201209061351_0001_m_000008_1, duration: 113511361
2012-09-06 13:55:02,224 INFO org.apache.hadoop.mapred.TaskTracker: attempt_201209061351_0001_r_000000_0 0.2962963% **reduce > copy** (8 of 9 at 3.91 MB/s) >
2012-09-06 13:55:02,441 INFO org.apache.hadoop.mapred.TaskTracker.clienttrace: src: 192.168.1.108:50060, dest: 192.168.1.101:35981, bytes: 30590207, op: **MAPRED_SHUFFLE**, cliID: attempt_201209061351_0001_m_000006_0, duration: 3108798753
2012-09-06 13:55:02,503 WARN org.apache.hadoop.mapred.TaskTracker: getMapOutput(attempt_201209061351_0001_m_000007_0,1) failed :
2012-09-06 13:55:02,503 INFO org.apache.hadoop.mapred.TaskTracker.clienttrace: src: 192.168.1.108:50060, dest: 192.168.1.101:35981, bytes: 327680, op: **MAPRED_SHUFFLE**, cliID: attempt_201209061351_0001_m_000007_0, duration: 2048655
2012-09-06 13:55:02,503 ERROR org.mortbay.log: /mapOutput
java.lang.IllegalStateException: Committed
......
2012-09-06 13:55:18,428 INFO org.apache.hadoop.mapred.TaskTracker.clienttrace: src: 192.168.1.108:50060, dest: 192.168.1.108:47885, bytes: 30566324, op: **MAPRED_SHUFFLE**, cliID: attempt_201209061351_0001_m_000001_0, duration: 509932933

```
2012-09-06 13:55:18,500 INFO org.apache.hadoop.mapred.TaskTracker:
attempt_201209061351_0001_r_000001_1 0.0% reduce > copy >
2012-09-06 13:55:20,358 WARN org.apache.hadoop.mapred.TaskTracker:
getMapOutput(attempt_201209061351_0001_m_000005_0,1) failed :
2012-09-06 13:55:20,359 INFO org.apache.hadoop.mapred.TaskTracker.clienttrace: src:
192.168.1.108:50060, dest: 192.168.1.108:47885, bytes: 262144, op: MAPRED_SHUFFLE, cliID:
attempt_201209061351_0001_m_000005_0, duration: 1787519
2012-09-06 13:55:20,359 ERROR org.mortbay.log: /mapOutput
java.lang.IllegalStateException: Committed

2012-09-06 13:55:25,386 INFO org.apache.hadoop.mapred.TaskTracker.clienttrace: src:
192.168.1.108:50060, dest: 192.168.1.108:47887, bytes: 30627775, op: MAPRED_SHUFFLE, cliID:
attempt_201209061351_0001_m_000005_0, duration: 694986073
2012-09-06 13:55:27,071 INFO org.apache.hadoop.mapred.TaskTracker.clienttrace: src:
192.168.1.108:50060, dest: 192.168.1.101:35983, bytes: 18054395, op: MAPRED_SHUFFLE, cliID:
attempt_201209061351_0001_m_000008_1, duration: 2618806275
2012-09-06 13:55:27,859 INFO org.apache.hadoop.mapred.TaskTracker:
attempt_201209061351_0001_r_000001_1 0.22222224% reduce > copy (6 of 9 at 12.51 MB/s) >
2012-09-06 13:55:29,001 INFO org.apache.hadoop.mapred.TaskTracker.clienttrace: src:
192.168.1.108:50060, dest: 192.168.1.108:47888, bytes: 30621332, op: MAPRED_SHUFFLE, cliID:
attempt_201209061351_0001_m_000007_0, duration: 426767398
2012-09-06 13:55:29,202 INFO org.apache.hadoop.mapred.TaskTracker.clienttrace: src:
192.168.1.108:50060, dest: 192.168.1.108:47888, bytes: 18054395, op: MAPRED_SHUFFLE, cliID:
attempt_201209061351_0001_m_000008_1, duration: 186957434
2012-09-06 13:55:30,508 INFO org.apache.hadoop.mapred.TaskTracker:
attempt_201209061351_0001_r_000001_1 0.22222224% reduce > copy (6 of 9 at 12.51 MB/s) >
2012-09-06 13:55:30,880 INFO org.apache.hadoop.mapred.TaskTracker:
attempt_201209061351_0001_r_000001_1 0.33333334% reduce > sort
2012-09-06 13:55:33,898 INFO org.apache.hadoop.mapred.TaskTracker:
attempt_201209061351_0001_r_000001_1 0.8844978% reduce > reduce
2012-09-06 13:55:35,117 INFO org.apache.hadoop.mapred.TaskTracker: Task
attempt_201209061351_0001_r_000001_1 is in commit-pending, task state:COMMIT_PENDING
2012-09-06 13:55:35,117 INFO org.apache.hadoop.mapred.TaskTracker:
attempt_201209061351_0001_r_000001_1 0.8844978% reduce > reduce
2012-09-06 13:55:35,383 INFO org.apache.hadoop.mapred.TaskTracker: Received commit task action
for attempt_201209061351_0001_r_000001_1
2012-09-06 13:55:36,922 INFO org.apache.hadoop.mapred.TaskTracker:
attempt_201209061351_0001_r_000001_1 1.0% reduce > reduce
2012-09-06 13:55:36,925 INFO org.apache.hadoop.mapred.TaskTracker:
attempt_201209061351_0001_r_000001_1 1.0% reduce > reduce
2012-09-06 13:55:36,925 INFO org.apache.hadoop.mapred.TaskTracker: Task
attempt_201209061351_0001_r_000001_1 is done.
......
```

Listing 4.12 Task tracker log file for the reduce task of processing 10M credit card transactions on the DataNode named *linux-sgpx* (192.168.1.101 note that this IP has changed from 192.168.107 since the last time the same job was run)

```
< ... parts deleted to save space ...>
```

```
2012-09-06 13:53:47,547 INFO org.apache.hadoop.mapred.TaskTracker.clienttrace: src:
192.168.1.101:50060, dest: 192.168.1.101:50262, bytes: 65536, op: MAPRED_SHUFFLE, cliID:
attempt_201209061351_0001_m_000002_0, duration: 95683606
2012-09-06 13:53:47,553 ERROR org.mortbay.log: /mapOutput
java.lang.IllegalStateException: Committed
2012-09-06 13:53:48,691 INFO org.apache.hadoop.mapred.TaskTracker:
attempt_201209061351_0001_r_000001_0 0.11111112% reduce > copy (3 of 9 at 4.38 MB/s) >
2012-09-06 13:53:52,090 INFO org.apache.hadoop.mapred.TaskTracker:
attempt_201209061351_0001_r_000001_0 0.14814815% reduce > copy (4 of 9 at 5.08 MB/s) >
2012-09-06 13:53:52,825 INFO org.apache.hadoop.mapred.TaskTracker.clienttrace: src:
192.168.1.101:50060, dest: 192.168.1.108:46721, bytes: 23567135, op: MAPRED_SHUFFLE, cliID:
attempt_201209061351_0001_m_000002_0, duration: 2054952799
2012-09-06 13:53:54,557 INFO org.apache.hadoop.mapred.TaskTracker:
attempt_201209061351_0001_m_000008_0 0.4878577%
2012-09-06 13:53:54,850 INFO org.apache.hadoop.mapred.TaskTracker.clienttrace: src:
192.168.1.101:50060, dest: 192.168.1.108:46721, bytes: 23546328, op: MAPRED_SHUFFLE, cliID:
attempt_201209061351_0001_m_000003_0, duration: 1956756863
2012-09-06 13:53:55,164 INFO org.apache.hadoop.mapred.TaskTracker:
attempt_201209061351_0001_r_000001_0 0.14814815% reduce > copy (4 of 9 at 5.08 MB/s) >
……
2012-09-06 13:54:14,271 INFO org.apache.hadoop.mapred.TaskTracker.clienttrace: src:
192.168.1.101:50060, dest: 192.168.1.101:50269, bytes: 30601333, op: MAPRED_SHUFFLE, cliID:
attempt_201209061351_0001_m_000002_0, duration: 1301186345
2012-09-06 13:54:15,746 INFO org.apache.hadoop.mapred.TaskTracker.clienttrace: src:
192.168.1.101:50060, dest: 192.168.1.101:50269, bytes: 30624799, op: MAPRED_SHUFFLE, cliID:
attempt_201209061351_0001_m_000003_0, duration: 1223159593
2012-09-06 13:54:16,176 INFO org.apache.hadoop.mapred.TaskTracker:
attempt_201209061351_0001_r_000001_0 0.25925928% reduce > copy (7 of 9 at 4.09 MB/s) >
……
2012-09-06 13:54:34,897 INFO org.apache.hadoop.mapred.TaskTracker.clienttrace: src:
192.168.1.101:50060, dest: 192.168.1.108:46739, bytes: 30601333, op: MAPRED_SHUFFLE, cliID:
attempt_201209061351_0001_m_000002_0, duration: 3850187323
2012-09-06 13:54:40,526 INFO org.apache.hadoop.mapred.TaskTracker:
attempt_201209061351_0001_r_000001_0 0.2962963% reduce > copy (8 of 9 at 3.24 MB/s)
2012-09-06 13:54:41,026 INFO org.apache.hadoop.mapred.TaskTracker:
attempt_201209061351_0001_r_000001_0 0.33333334% reduce > sort
2012-09-06 13:54:41,064 INFO org.apache.hadoop.mapred.TaskTracker.clienttrace: src:
192.168.1.101:50060, dest: 192.168.1.108:46741, bytes: 30624799, op: MAPRED_SHUFFLE, cliID:
attempt_201209061351_0001_m_000003_0, duration: 3397662648
2012-09-06 13:54:42,554 INFO org.apache.hadoop.mapred.TaskTracker:
attempt_201209061351_0001_r_000001_0 0.33333334% reduce > sort
2012-09-06 13:54:44,063 INFO org.apache.hadoop.mapred.TaskTracker:
attempt_201209061351_0001_r_000001_0 0.69545126% reduce > reduce
2012-09-06 13:54:52,880 INFO org.apache.hadoop.mapred.TaskTracker:
attempt_201209061351_0001_r_000001_0 0.9102739% reduce > reduce
2012-09-06 13:54:53,003 INFO org.apache.hadoop.mapred.JvmManager: JVM :
jvm_201209061351_0001_r_-1418542528 exited with exit code 0. Number of tasks it ran: 0
……
```

```
henry@linux-1fsw:~/myapp/hadoop-1.0.3> hadoop fs -ls out40
Found 4 items
-rw-r--r--   3 henry supergroup          0 2012-09-06 13:56 /user/henry/out40/_SUCCESS
drwxr-xr-x   - henry supergroup          0 2012-09-06 13:54 /user/henry/out40/_logs
-rw-r--r--   3 henry supergroup        911 2012-09-06 13:56 /user/henry/out40/part-r-00000
-rw-r--r--   3 henry supergroup       1183 2012-09-06 13:56 /user/henry/out40/part-r-00001
henry@linux-1fsw:~/myapp/hadoop-1.0.3> █
```

Figure 4.7 Reduce output result with the two reduce task, 10M credit card transaction Spending Pattern MapReduce job run

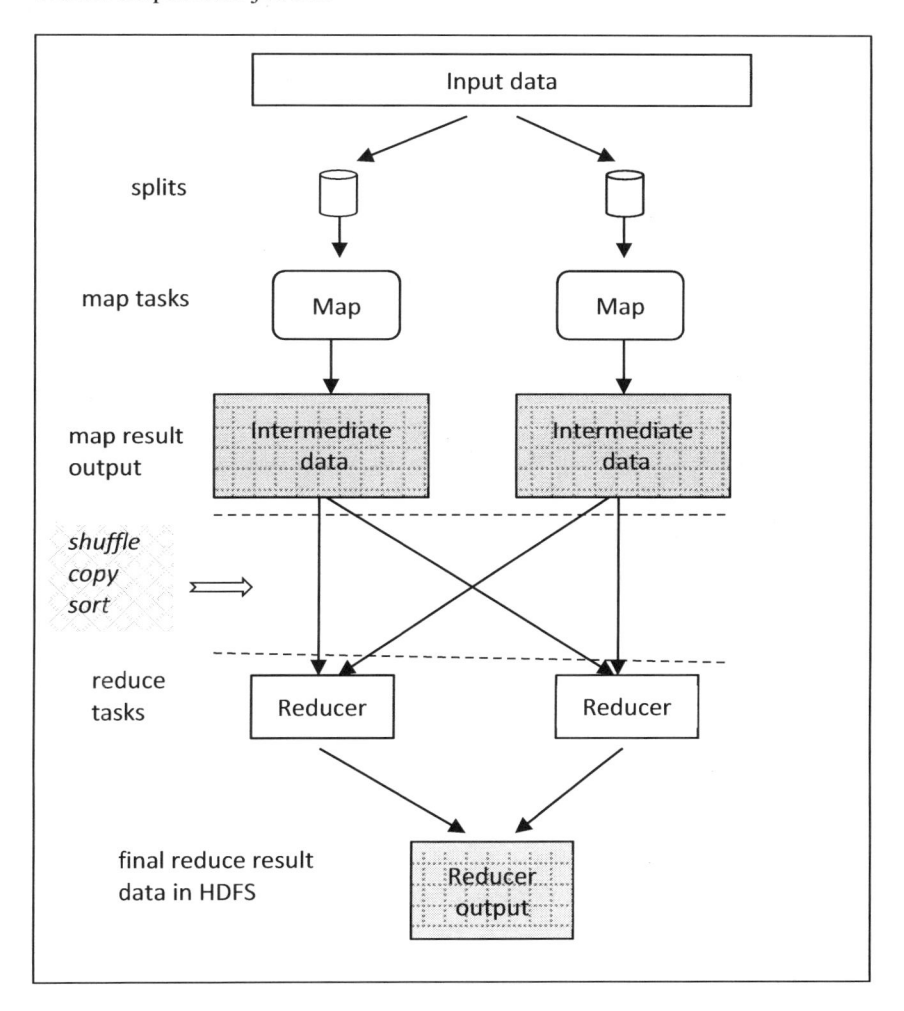

Figure 4.8 A generic MapReduce workflow with multiple reducers

4.4 SUMMARY

In this chapter, we focused on understanding Hadoop MapReduce job orchestration and workflows. First, we introduced the MapReduce 1 orchestrator that can handle up to thousands of nodes. Then, we pointed out that one needs to use the MapReduce 2 orchestrator or YARN to manage larger clusters beyond thousands of nodes.

The MapReduce workflow was presented in two different types of Hadoop running mode: local and fully distributed. In local mode, all activities occur on the same machine, whereas in fully distributed mode, activities are distributed among multiple nodes. We primarily depended upon the actual logs collected from both local and distributed mode to construct the MapReduce workflow in each case. Both job orchestration and workflow are essential subjects that one needs to understand in order to develop high performing, scalable Hadoop MapReduce applications, which is the subject of the remaining chapters of this book.

RECOMMENDED READING

The following link provides more information about Hadoop JobTracker API:

http://hadoop.apache.org/common/docs/r1.0.1/api/org/apache/hadoop/mapred/TaskTracker.html

The following link describes how a JobTracker manages a job:

http://wiki.apache.org/hadoop/JobTracker

The following link provides a brief description about a TaskTracker:

http://wiki.apache.org/hadoop/TaskTracker

The following link provides information on TaskTracker API:

http://hadoop.apache.org/common/docs/r1.0.1/api/org/apache/hadoop/mapred/TaskTracker.html

For a list of Hadoop default parameter settings, check out the following link: http://hadoop.apache.org/common/docs/r0.19.2/hadoop-default.html

EXERCISES

4.1 What is a Hadoop *client*? Does a client have to run outside a Hadoop node or cluster?

4.2 A job tracker typically runs on a NameNode, while task trackers run on DataNodes. Does it mean that a job tracker has the same responsibilities as a NameNode and a task tracker has the same responsibilities of a DataNode?

4.3 What are the major differences between the Hadoop MapReduce 1 job orchestrator and MapReduce 2 job orchestrator or YARN? Which component in YARN handles most of the complexities involved in managing a large Hadoop cluster?

4.4 How do you change the logging level to DEBUG when you debug a MapReduce program in local mode?

4.5 Explain why Hadoop attempts more map and reduce tasks than specified? How does Hadoop reconcile multiple map and reduce task results?

4.6 From where can you find the job configuration file for a MapReduce job? Use Table A.1 to identify at least five parameters that are reliability-oriented and five parameters that are performance and/or scalability oriented.

4.7 How do you estimate the # of map tasks with a given MapReduce job? What about the # of reduce tasks? Is the # of reduce tasks determined by Hadoop or by the user?

4.8 What's your opinion on what the concept of *shuffling* means in Hadoop's context? Does it mean the entire process from partitioning map output data to feeding the reducer with sorted data? How do you self-verify if your opinion is correct or incorrect?

4.9 How do you identify the events that occurred in the reduce tasks associated with a MapReduce job?

5 Basic MapReduce Programming

Having covered some of the basic Hadoop concepts, HDFS, and MapReduce job orchestration and workflows in local mode and in fully distributed mode, now we are ready to take a deeper delve into the bits of MapReduce programming. The previous preparations are necessary, as in order to be able to develop high quality MapReduce programs, the first step is that a developer needs to understand at least how a simple MapReduce program, such as the SpendingPattern MapReduce program, runs in local and a smaller real cluster environment. The next step is to understand all essential building blocks for writing a MapReduce program so that a developer would be able to solve different flavors of MapReduce problems. We would take a systematic, consistent approach to presenting these building blocks in this chapter rather than spread them into several chapters like a few other Hadoop books do.

The building blocks for building MapReduce programs are divided into the following sections in this chapter:

- Java Data Types
- Hadoop Data Types
- InputFormat
- OutputFormat
- OutputCommitter
- TaskAttemptContext and TaskInputOutputContext
- Mapper
- Reducer
- Partitioner
- Combiner

Let's start with the subject of Java data types next.

5.1 JAVA DATA TYPES

Since Hadoop data types are simply wrappers of some Java data types, it's beneficial to have a brief review on Java data types first to lay down the context for our discussions in the next section on Hadoop data types. Let's start with Java primitive types first.

5.1.1 Java Primitive Types

Java defines eight *primitive* data types (also known as simple types), which are grouped into four sets as follows:

- **Integer**: This set includes *byte*, *short*, *int*, and *long*.
- **Floating-point numbers**: This set includes *float* and *double*, which represents numbers with fractional precision.
- **Characters**: This set has only one member of *char*, which represents letters and numbers in a character set.
- **Boolean**: This set also has one member of *boolean*, which represents a special type with *true/false* values.

Primitive types are bound by explicit ranges and mathematical behaviors. Table 5.1 shows the width and range for each primitive type.

Table 5.1 Java primitive types

Type	Width (bits)	Range
byte	8	-128 to 127
short	16	-32,768 to 32,767
int	32	-2,147,483,648 to 2,147,483,647
long	64	-9,223,372,036,854,775,808 to 9,223,372,036,854,775,807
float	32	1.4e-045 to 3.4e+038
double	64	4.9e-324 to 1.8e+308
char	16 (Unicode)	0 – 65,536
boolean	1	*true* or *false*

Although Java is completely object-oriented, primitive types are not. Primitive types are used for representing quantities for the sake of performance. Besides, primitive data types form the basis for creating all other data types, for example, the Java type wrappers as discussed next.

5.1.2 Java Type Wrappers

Java primitive types are indispensable for all types of computing. However, there exist certain limitations with primitive types. For example, one can't pass a primitive type for reference to a method. In addition, many of the standard data structures implemented in Java operate on objects, which means that one can't use these data structures to store primitive types. In order to circumvent such situations, Java provides type wrappers for primitive types. Each type wrapper is simply a class that encapsulates a primitive type within an object. Here is a summary of Java type wrappers, using the primitive type *int* as an example:

- Each type wrapper has a constructor with its corresponding primitive type in the following form (this process of encapsulating a value within an object is called *boxing*) :

```
TypeWrapper tw = new TypeWrapper (PrimitiveType pt);
Integer itg = new Integer (999); // example for TypeWrapper Integer
```

- The inverse process of boxing is called unboxing, which extracts the value from its type wrapper, for example:

```
PrimitiveType pt = TypeWrapperObject.<primitiveType>Value ();
int i = itg.intValue ();  // example for primitive type int
```

5.1.3 Java Autoboxing/Auto-unboxing

It gets interesting that since JDK 5, Java added two features for boxing and unboxing operations: *autoboxing* and auto-*unboxing*. The purpose with autoboxing is that it's no longer necessary to manually construct an object in order to wrap a primitive type. One can assign a value to its corresponding type wrapper directly. Java would automatically construct the object. For example, the following two statements would be equivalent to each other:

```
Integer itg = new Integer (999);
Integer itg = 999; // autoboxing an integer
```

Similarly, auto-unboxing eliminates the <primitive>Value () call as follows:

```
int i = itg.intValue ();     // example for primitive type int
int i = itg;                 // auto-unboxing an Integer wrapper
```

5.1.4 Java Generics

In addition to Java primitive types and type wrappers, another important feature is Java *generics* introduced since JDK 5, which is also known as *parameterized types*. The concept behind generics is that it enables a programmer to create classes, interfaces, and methods that are not tied to a specific type. A class, interface, or method that has its arguments specified using *generics* is called a *generic* class, a *generic* interface, or a *generic* method. One example with generics is that you can create a stack object with any type wrappers, String, or Object, for example:

```
Stack<Integer> s = new Stack<Integer> ();
Stack<String> s = new Stack<String> ();
Stack<Object> s = new Stack<Object> ();
......
```

Java generics has solved not only the type-safety issue but also the original clumsy type cast issue (type safety means that a program cannot perform an operation on an object unless that operation is valid for that object). With generics, all casts are automatic and implicit. We have seen Hadoop using generics for Mapper and Reducer classes as shown in Listings 1.9 and 1.10 in Chapter 1.

Note that one can only use a class type for generics. In other words, primitive types cannot be passed as parameterized types. If you need to pass a primitive type, use its type wrapper as illustrated above. Java's autoboxing and auto-unboxing features have made the use of type wrappers transparent.

5.1.5 Java Bounded Types and Wildcard Arguments

Java provides bounded types. An upper bounded type is defined as:

<*T* extends *superclass*>

The above form specifies that the type parameter *T* must be a class derived from the *superclass*, or the *superclass* itself (inclusive). Similarly, a lower bounded type is defined as:

<*T* super *subclass*>

The above form specifies that the type parameter *T* must be a class above the subclass, excluding the *subclass* itself (exclusive).

The above declarations can also be replaced with a wildcard (?) argument

<?>

which means any unknown type. Thus, we would have the corresponding upper and lower bounded types of:

<? extends superclass>
<? super subclass>

We will see such examples in Chapter 6 when we discuss chained mappers and reducers.

5.1.6 Java Streams

A Java program performs I/O through streams. A stream is linked to a physical device such as a console or a disk drive through the Java I/O stream. A stream could be an input stream or an output stream, depending on which direction it flows. There are two types of Java streams:

- **Byte Streams**: Handle input and output of bytes. They are used for reading or writing binary data. There are two abstract classes associated with a byte stream: *InputStream* and *OutputStream*. All other byte stream related classes implement these two classes and override the two methods of *read ()* and *write ()* that reads and writes bytes of data. Table 5.2 shows all byte stream classes in Java's java.io package.
- **Character Streams**: Handle input and output of characters (note that underlying a character stream is still a byte stream that works at the lowest I/O level). Similar to byte streams, there are two abstract classes associated with a character stream: *Reader* and *Writer*. All other character stream related classes implement these two classes and override the two methods of read () and write () that reads and writes bytes of data. Table 5.3 shows all character stream classes in Java's java.io package.

In practice, one may need to follow a specific sequence to create a stream using the streams at lower levels.

Table 5.2 The byte stream classes in the java.io package

Stream Class	Function
InputStream	Abstract class that defines stream input
OutputStream	Abstract class that defines stream output
BufferedInputStream	Buffered input stream
BufferedOutputStream	Buffered output stream
ByteArrayInputStream	Input stream that reads from a byte array
ByteArrayOutputStream	output stream that writes to a byte array
DataInputStream	An input stream for reading standard Java data types
DataOutputStream	An output stream for writing standard Java data types
FileInputStream	Input stream that reads from a file
FileOutputStream	Output stream that writes to a file
FilterInputStream	Implements InputStream
FilterOutputStream	Implements OutputStream
ObjectInputStream	Input stream for objects
ObjectOutputStream	Output stream for objects
PipedInputStream	Input stream pipe
PipedOutputStream	Output stream pipe
PrintStream	OutputStream that implements `print ()` and `println()`
PushbackInputStream	Input stream that supports returning a byte back to the source
SquenceInputStream	Input stream that supports reading from multiple sources sequentially

Table 5.3 The character stream I/O classes in the java.io package

Stream Class	Function
Reader	Abstract class that defines character stream input
Writer	Abstract class that defines character stream output
BufferedReader	Buffered input character stream

BufferedWriter	Buffered output character stream
CharArrayReader	Input stream that reads from a character array
CharArrayWriter	Output stream that writes to a character array
FileReader	Input stream that reads from a file
FileWriter	Output stream that writes to a file
FilterReader	Filtered reader
FilterWriter	Filtered writer
InputStreamReader	Input stream that converts bytes to characters
LineNumberReader	Input stream that counts lines
OutputStreamWriter	Output stream that converts characters to bytes
PipedReader	Input pipe
PipedWriter	Output type
PrintWriter	Output stream that implements *print ()* and *println ()*
PushbackReader	Input stream that allows characters to be returned to the input stream
StringReader	Input stream that reads from a string
StringWriter	Output stream that writes to a string

Users can create their own readers and writers using either stream as discussed above. On the other hand, Java provides the following pre-defined, byte-oriented streams:

- **System.in**: An object of type *InputStream* linked to the keyboard.
- **System.err**: An object of *PrintStream* linked to the console.
- **System.out**: Also an object of *PrintStream* linked to the console.

Since these three pre-defined streams are byte oriented, they often need to be wrapped in character streams. For example, the following statement creates a reader with a *System.in* stream wrapped in an *InputStreamReader* that is in turn wrapped in a *BufferedReader* stream:

```
BufferedReader reader = new BufferedReader (new InputStreamReader (System.in));
```

Then, you can use this reader to read input from the keyboard with its *read* () method. Since Hadoop moves both data and Java class code, we will see similar examples later.

5.2   HADOOP DATA TYPES

As a distributed Java framework for processing large datasets, what data types to use is an unavoidable subject for Hadoop MapReduce framework designers. One might ask why we couldn't just use or re-use Java data types, as the Hadoop MapReduce framework is based on Java after all. The answer is 'yes' if we only run our MapReduce programs in local mode, but that would totally defeat the major objective of Hadoop MapReduce framework as a *distributed* platform for processing large datasets. As you have already learnt in Chapter 1, the Mapper and Reducer classes of a MapReduce program take a large text data file and maneuver the data records in the file in an orderly way as follows in the general <key/value> form:

map: (K1, V1) → list (K2, V2)
reduce: (K2, list(V2)) → list (K3, V3)

Table 5.4 more explicitly shows what it means by the above form (left side input, right side output). We will explain what it means by *list* later when we actually examine a Mapper and a Reducer class.

Table 5.4 Map and reduce input/output

task	input	output
map	(K1, V1)	list (K2, V2)
reduce	(K2, list (V2))	list (K3, V3)

As is seen in Table 5.4, a MapReduce operates on key/value pairs. Each key and its corresponding value must have data types for them. One might ask: Why don't we use the Java long type wrapper *Long* to represent a key and *String* to represent a value, when we need a numeric type for key and a textual type for value? In order to answer this question, let's take a look at how Java wrapper Long is defined. One convenient way to find out the most authoritative definition of Java types is that you create a statement in a Java program as follows:

Long long1 = new Long (12345);

Then, put your cursor on "Long" and you should see a pop-up window showing the definition of *Long*. You can click F2 hot key to freeze it. The following description is what we would get about *Long* with the Content Assist feature of the Eclipse IDE:

The Long class wraps a value of the primitive type long in an object. An object of type Long contains a single field whose type is long.

Next, let's take a look at what methods the Long class implements. Once again, the best place to look for is the Content Assist feature of the Eclipse IDE. Figure 5.1 shows all methods of Long obtained this way. Similarly, you can get all methods of the *java.lang.String* class this way. It's clear that neither *Long* nor *String* is serializable, since neither of them implements the public interface Serializable (*java.io.Serializable*). The term object serialization in Java is a mechanism for representing an object as a sequence of bytes that includes both the object's data and the metadata information such as the object's type and the types of data stored in the object. After a serialized object has been written to a file, it can be read from the file and de-serialized to restore the object's representation in memory by re-creating the object based on the type information and bytes that represent the object and its data. This is a feature that Hadoop must have, as it shuffles both mapper/reducer classes and data it operates upon across networks and of course across separate JVMs.

*MapIncrease2.java   HelloHDFS.java

```
long1.
Config
FileSy      byteValue() : byte – Long
            compareTo(Long anotherLong) : int – Long
String      doubleValue() : double – Long
dataFi      equals(Object obj) : boolean – Long
dataFi      floatValue() : float – Long
            getClass() : Class<?> – Object
long n      hashCode() : int – Long
            intValue() : int – Long
Path i      longValue() : long – Long
Path o      notify() : void – Object
            notifyAll() : void – Object
try {       shortValue() : short – Long
    FS      toString() : String – Long
    re      wait() : void – Object
    wh      wait(long timeout) : void – Object
            wait(long timeout, int nanos) : void – Object
            MAX_VALUE : long – Long
    }       MIN_VALUE : long – Long
} catc      SIZE : int – Long
    Sy      TYPE : Class<java.lang.Long> – Long
}           bitCount(long i) : int – Long
FSData      decode(String nm) : Long – Long
writer      getLong(String nm) : Long – Long
long s      getLong(String nm, Long val) : Long – Long
            getLong(String nm, long val) : Long – Long
numOfk      highestOneBit(long i) : long – Long
System      lowestOneBit(long i) : long – Long
for (l      numberOfLeadingZeros(long i) : int – Long
    St      numberOfTrailingZeros(long i) : int – Long
    wr      parseLong(String s) : long – Long
    if      parseLong(String s, int radix) : long – Long
            reverse(long i) : long – Long
    }       reverseBytes(long i) : long – Long
writer      rotateLeft(long i, int distance) : long – Long
out.cl      rotateRight(long i, int distance) : long – Long
long t      signum(long i) : int – Long
System      toBinaryString(long i) : String – Long
if (to      toHexString(long i) : String – Long
    lo      toOctalString(long i) : String – Long
    Sy      toString(long i) : String – Long
}           toString(long i, int radix) : String – Long
if (to      valueOf(long l) : Long – Long
    Sy      valueOf(String s) : Long – Long
            valueOf(String s, int radix) : Long – Long
    }
}                        Press '^Space' to show Template Proposals
```

Figure 5.1 Methods implemented in *java.lang.Long*

5.2.1 Java DataInput and DataOutput Interfaces

Before we discuss Hadoop data types, we need to understand two Java public interfaces: *DataInput* and *DataOutput*. Some of the Java stream classes we introduced in the previous section implement these interfaces, as is shown in Figure 5.2.

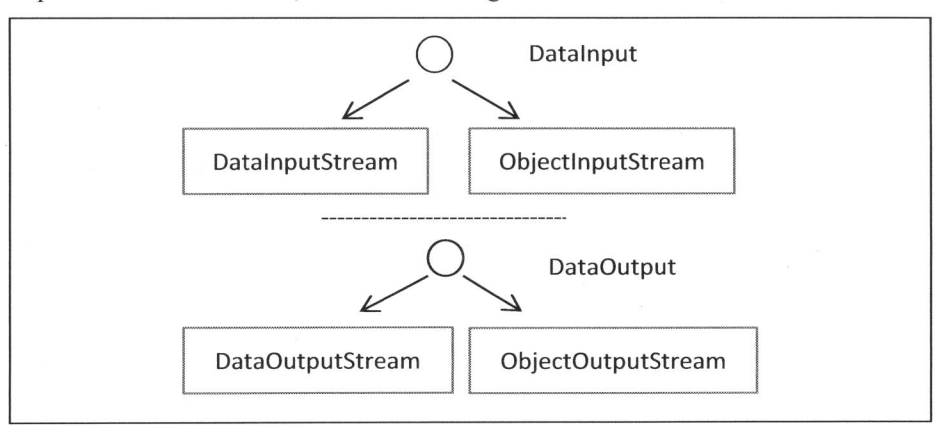

Figure 5.2 The Java DataInput and DataOutput public interfaces implemented by some Java stream classes

The DataInput interface is designed to de-serialize Java primitive types by reading bytes from a binary stream and reconstructing from them the data in any of the Java primitive types. It can also de-serialize a String in Java modified UTF-8 format.

With all the reading routines in the DataInput interface, if end of file (EOF) is reached before the desired number of bytes has been read, an EOFException is thrown. On the other hand, if for whatever reason bytes cannot be read other than end of file, an IOException is thrown, which includes the case that the input stream has been closed.

The DataOutput interface is designed for serializing data from Java primitive types to a series of bytes and writing the bytes to a binary stream. The class that impements this interface can also be used to serialize a String into Java modified UTF-8 format and write the resulting series of bytes. Similar to DataInput interface, an IOException is thrown if any errors occur during writing serialized bytes.

5.2.2 Writable and WritableComparable

Hadoop has a base class interface *Writable*. Its main purpose is for creating key and value types. All key and value types in the Hadoop Map-Reduce framework implement this interface. A writable object is a serializable object that implements a simple, efficient, serialization protocol, based on `DataInput` and `DataOutput`, as is shown in Listing 5.1. In this example, the custom Writable class named `Lucky5Writable` implements a static `read (DataInput in)` method, which creates a new instance from the input; then, it calls the `readFields (DataInput in)` method and returns the Writable instance.

Listing 5.1 A custom Writable class that implements the base class interface Writable

```java
import java.io.*;
import org.apache.hadoop.io.*;

public class Lucky5Writable implements Writable {
   private int luckyNumber;
   private long timestamp;

   public void write(DataOutput out) throws IOException {
      out.writeInt(luckyNumber);
      out.writeLong(timestamp);
   }

   public void readFields(DataInput in) throws IOException {
      luckyNumber = in.readInt();
      timestamp = in.readLong();
   }

   public static Lucky5Writable read(DataInput in) throws IOException {
      Lucky5Writable writable = new Lucky5Writable();
      writable.readFields(in);
      return writable;
   }
   public String toString () {
      return "luckyNumber = " + luckyNumber +
            " timestamp = " + timestamp ;
   }
}
```

It's insufficient to have just a Writable interface for Hadoop. Hadoop has another basic data type: *WritableComparable*, which is a sub-interface of *Writable*. The purpose for this interface is obvious: It's for *keys* which need to be sorted all the time. A *WritableComparable* combines the functions of a *Writable* and a *Comparable* so that it is not only a Writable but also a Comparable.

WritableComparables can be compared to each other, typically via Comparators. All types used for keys in the Hadoop MapReduce framework need to implement this interface. Of course, a WritableComparable can also be used for a *value* if necessary.

Similar to Listing 5.1, Listing 5.2 shows a custom WritableComparable that implements the WritableComparable interface. Note that the generics <Lucky5WritableComparable> must be there. Otherwise, the following compilation error would occur, complaining that

"*Lucky5WritableComparable is not abstract and does not override abstract method compareTo …*":

```
[INFO] ------------------------------------------------------------
[ERROR] COMPILATION ERROR :
[INFO] ------------------------------------------------------------
[ERROR] /Users/henry/dev2/workspace/MyHadoop-
1.0.3/module1/src/main/java/com/perfmath/Lucky5WritableComparable.java:[4,7]
Lucky5WritableComparable is not abstract and does not override abstract method
compareTo(org.apache.hadoop.io.WritableComparable) in java.lang.Comparable
[ERROR] /Users/henry/dev2/workspace/MyHadoop-
1.0.3/module1/src/main/java/com/perfmath/Lucky5WritableComparable.java:[21,1] method does not
override or implement a method from a supertype
......
```

In addition to the *compareTo* method, the custom `Lucky5WritableComparable` class shown in Listing 5.2 overrides the following two methods:

- **write**: Serializes the fields of this object to the output stream.
- **readFields**: Deserializes the fields of this object from the input stream. For best possible performance, storage in the existing object should be re-used if possible.

The `compareTo` method compares two instances of the same class `Lucky5WritableComparable`. It uses a ternary operator (?) for the result of the comparison operation. First, if the timestamp of the *this* object is larger than that of the object being compared with, it returns -1 immediately; otherwise, if the lucky numbers of the two objects match, it returns 1. Listing 5.3 shows a test driver for both the `Lucky5Writable` class and the `Lucky5WritableComparable` class. You can compile and run the test driver as follows:

```
$ mvn clean package –DskipTests –Dhadoop.version=1.0.3
$ hadoop jar spending-patterns.jar Lucky5WritableDriver
```

In my case, I got the following output:

```
luckyNumber = 99999 timestamp=1347944029882
luckyNumber = 99999 timestamp=1347992086007
result1 = 1
result2 = -1
```

Note that you cannot just open up a text file and put an integer number and a long number there to make up an input file. Instead, you need to use the DataOutputStream/FileOutputStream and the write method of the custom Writable or WritableComparable class to make up the input files. Also, for timestamp values, you can use the Java built-in function *System.currentTimeMillis* ().

Listing 5.2 A custom Writable class that implements the base class interface WritableComparable

```
import java.io.*;
import org.apache.hadoop.io.*;
```

```java
public class Lucky5WritableComparable implements
WritableComparable <Lucky5WritableComparable> {
   private int luckyNumber;
   private long timestamp;

   @Override
   public void write(DataOutput out) throws IOException {
      out.writeInt(luckyNumber);
      out.writeLong(timestamp);
   }

   @Override
   public void readFields(DataInput in) throws IOException {
      luckyNumber = in.readInt();
      timestamp = in.readLong();
   }

   @Override
   public int compareTo(Lucky5WritableComparable wc) {
      return (this.timestamp > wc.timestamp ? -1 :
         (this.luckyNumber != wc.luckyNumber ? 0 : 1));
   }

   public static Lucky5WritableComparable read(DataInput in) throws IOException {
      Lucky5WritableComparable wc = new Lucky5WritableComparable();
      wc.readFields(in);
      return wc;
   }
   public String toString () {
      return "luckyNumber = " + luckyNumber + " timestamp = " + timestamp ;
   }
}
```

Listing 5.3 The test driver for the Writable and WritableComparable classes

```java
import java.io.*;

public class Lucky5WritableDriver {
   public static void main(String[] args) throws IOException {
      testLucky5Writable();
      testLucky5WritableComparable();
   }
```

```java
public static void testLucky5Writable() throws FileNotFoundException {
    DataInputStream dis = new DataInputStream ( new FileInputStream (
        "writable.txt"));
    DataOutputStream dos = new DataOutputStream ( new FileOutputStream(
        "writeOut.txt"));
    try {
        Lucky5Writable writable = Lucky5Writable.read(dis);
        writable.write(dos);
    } catch (Exception e) {
        e.printStackTrace();
    } finally {
        try {
            if (dis != null)
                dis.close();
            if (dos != null)
                dos.close();
        } catch (IOException e) {
            e.printStackTrace();
        }
    }
}

public static void testLucky5WritableComparable()
        throws FileNotFoundException {
    DataInputStream dis1 = new DataInputStream (new FileInputStream(
        "writable.txt"));
    DataInputStream dis2 = new DataInputStream (new FileInputStream(
        "writeOut1.txt"));
    DataOutputStream dos = new DataOutputStream (new FileOutputStream(
        "writeOut2.txt"));
    try {
        Lucky5WritableComparable writableComparable1 =
            Lucky5WritableComparable .read(dis1);
        System.out.println(writableComparable1.toString ());
        Lucky5WritableComparable writableComparable2 =
            Lucky5WritableComparable .read(dis2);
        System.out.println(writableComparable2.toString ());

        int result1 = writableComparable1.compareTo(writableComparable1);
        int result2 = writableComparable2.compareTo(writableComparable1);
        System.out.println("result1 = " + result1);
        System.out.println("result2 = " + result2);
        writableComparable2.write(dos);
    } catch (Exception e) {
```

```
                e.printStackTrace();
        } finally {
            try {
                if (dis1 != null)
                    dis1.close();
                if (dis2 != null)
                    dis2.close();
                if (dos != null)
                    dos.close();
            } catch (IOException e) {
                e.printStackTrace();
            }
        }
    }
}
```

Similar to Java type wrappers discussed in the previous section, Hadoop pre-defines certain wrapper classes on top of the Java type wrappers. Essentially, Hadoop basic data types are wrappers of Java type wrappers (or wrappers of wrappers). See Table 5.5 for a list of Hadoop native data types for supporting MapReduce keys and values. Note that the *Text* and *NullWritable* are not wrappers of Java type wrappers, though.

As we have seen in Chapter 1, every MapReduce program driver requires to have an InputFormat class and an OutputFormat class specified. We discuss these two classes in the next two sections.

Table 5.5 Hadoop data types for MapReduce key/value pairs

Class	Function
BooleanWritable	Wrapper for a Java Boolean object
ByteWritable	Wrapper for a Java Byte object
DoubleWritable	Wrapper for a Java Double object
FloatWritable	Wrapper for a Java Float object
IntWritable	Wrapper for a Java Integer object
LongWritable	Wrapper for a Java Long object
Text	Wrapper for storing text in the UTF8 format
NullWritable	Place holder for null key or value

5.3 INPUTFORMAT

The InputFormat class is contained in the org.apache.hadoop.mapreduce package, extends the Object class and has a hierarchy of Object → InputFormat as defined below:

```
package org.apache.hadoop.mapreduce;
java.lang.Object
 ↳ org.apache.hadoop.mapreduce.InputFormat<LongWritable,T>
```

public abstract class InputFormat<K,V> extends Object

The purpose of having this class is to help check the input specification for a MapReduce job. It has two methods as defined below for fulfilling this purpose:

- **getSplits:**

  public abstract List<**InputSplit**> **getSplits** (JobContext context)

- **createRecordReader**:

  public abstract **RecordReader** <K,V> **createRecordReader** (
      InputSplit split, TaskAttemptContext context)

The getSplits method logically splits the set of input files for the job, based on the job configuration and suggested number of splits passed in as parameters. It then returns an array of InputSplits for the job. Each InputSplit is then assigned to an individual Mapper for processing. Note that splits are logical divisions rather than physical chunks. For example, a split could be defined as an <input-file-path, start, offset> tuple so that multiple readers can read different parts of one or more files simultaneously. This implementation is driven by scalability requirements.

The createRecordReader method creates a RecordReader for a given split. The framework calls RecordReader.initialize (InputSplit, TaskAttemptContext) for the given InputSplit and task before the split is used.

Next, let's take a look at the two important classes that the InputFormat class depends on: The InputSplit class and the RecordReader class.

5.3.1 InputSplit and RecordReader

The InputSplit class is contained in the package org.apache.hadoop.mapreduce, extends the Object class, and has a hierarchy of Object → InputSplit as defined below:

```
package org.apache.hadoop.mapreduce;
java.lang.Object
 ↳ org.apache.hadoop.mapreduce.InputSplit
```

public abstract class InputSplit extends Object {...}

It has only two methods: getLength () and getLocations (). An InputSplit object represents the data to be processed by an individual Mapper. The data format is byte-oriented, which is converted into record-oriented by using the RecordReader class. A RecordReader takes a byte oriented input split, breaks it into records and presents records in the form of key-value pairs to the map or reduce tasks. A subtle issue is that record boundaries must be dealt with properly.

Table 5.6 lists the methods of the RecordReader class for converting byte-oriented input data into byte-oriented. It shows how an InputFormat object creates key-value pairs for further processing through a RecordReader.

Table 5.6 Methods of the RecordReader class

Method	Comment
abstract void **initialize** (InputSplit split, TaskAttemptContext context)	Called once to initialize a record reader.
abstract boolean **nextKeyValue** ()	Read the next key/value pair from the input
abstract KEYIN **getCurrentKey** ()	Get the current key.
abstract KEYIN **getCurrentValue** ()	Get the current value.
abstract void **close** ()	Close the RecordReader.
abstract float **getProgress** ()	Return progress from 0.0 to 1.0.

For a given file, how many input splits it will be arrived at depends on the total size, in bytes, of the input file and the FileSystem block size, which is treated as an upper bound for input splits. A lower bound on the split size can be set via *mapreduce.input.fileinputformat.split.minsize.*

5.3.2 FileInputFormat

The InputFormat class has several implementation classes, two of which are the FileInputFormat class and the DBInputFormat class. In this section, we discuss the FileInputFormat class, with the DBInputFormat class left for the next section.

The FileInputFormat class is contained in the org.apache.hadoop.mapreduce package and has a hierarchy of Object → InputFormat → FileInputFormat as defined below:

```
package org.apache.hadoop.mapreduce;
java.lang.Object
 ↳ org.apache.hadoop.mapreduce.InputFormat<LongWritable,T>
    ↳ org.apache.hadoop.mapreduce.lib.input.FileInputFormat<K,V>


public abstract class FileInputFormat<K,V> extends InputFormat<K,V>
```

This class is the base class for all file-based InputFormats. It implements a generic method of getSplits (JobContext), as we discussed in the previous section when introducing the InputFormat class. It has many interesting methods that specify what operations the FileInputFormat class can perform. Table 5.7 lists all the methods of the FileInputFormat class (note that almost all Hadoop classes tend to be very compact, so one can comprehend a class better by examining its API than relying on verbose textual descriptions).

Let's take a look at some of the most interesting methods as follows:

- **add/set input path(s)**: As you seen from Table 5.7, seven methods are associated with this function. They are:

  o addInputPath
  o addInputPaths
  o getInputPathFilter
  o getInputPaths
  o setInputPathFilter
  o setInputPaths (2)

- **computeSplitSize**: This method computes the number of splits based on those parameters as specified. It is seen that block size is taken into account. It has the following methods that supports this method:

  o getSplits
  o isSplitable
  o setMinInputSplitSize

- getBlockIndex: This method gets a block based on block locations and offset parameters passed in.

Table 5.8 further explains the three sub-classes of the FileInputFormat class, all defined in the package of `org.apache.hadoop.mapreduce.lib.input`. Note that Hadoop can take either text or binary files as input. Binary files are also called *sequence files*. In general, it's more efficient to process sequence files than to process regular text files.

Table 5.7 Methods of the FileInputFormat class

Type	Method signature
static void	addInputPath(Job job, Path path) Add a Path to the list of inputs for the map-reduce job.
static void	addInputPaths(Job job, String commaSeparatedPaths) Add the given comma separated paths to the list of inputs for the map-reduce job.
protected long	computeSplitSize(long blockSize, long minSize, long maxSize)
protected int	getBlockIndex(BlockLocation[] blkLocations, long offset)
protected long	getFormatMinSplitSize()
static PathFilter	getInputPathFilter(JobContext context)
static Path[]	getInputPaths(JobContext context)
static long	getMaxSplitSize(JobContext context)
static long	getMinSplitSize(JobContext job)
List<InputSplit>	getSplits(JobContext job) Generate the list of files and make them into FileSplits.
protected	isSplitable(JobContext context, Path filename)

boolean	Check if the given file is splitable.
protected List<FileStatus>	listStatus(JobContext job) List input directories.
static void	setInputPathFilter(Job job, Class<? extends PathFilter> filter) Set a PathFilter to be applied to the input paths for the map-reduce job.
static void	setInputPaths(Job job, Path... inputPaths) Set the array of Paths as the list of inputs for the map-reduce job.
static void	setInputPaths(Job job, String commaSeparatedPaths) Set the given comma separated paths as the list of inputs for the map-reduce job.
static void	setMaxInputSplitSize(Job job, long size)
static void	setMinInputSplitSize(Job job, long size)

Table 5.8 A partial list of implementing sub-classes of FileInputFormat

Type	Class
text	**TextInputFormat**: An InputFormat for plain text files that use either line feed or carriage-return to signal end of line. Files are broken into lines. Each line number is a key and the line itself is the value. Has two methods: ■ *createRecordReader* (…) (inherited from InputFormat discussed previously) ■ *isSplitable* (…) (see Table 5.7)
text	**KeyValueTextInputFormat**: Similar to the TextInputFormat class except that each line is divided into key and value parts by a separator byte. If no such a byte exists, the key will be the entire line and value will be empty. Has the same two methods as the TextInputFormat class.
binary or text	**SequenceFileInputFormat**: Has three variations: ■ *SequenceFileAsBinaryInputFormat* <*BytesWritable, BytesWritable*>: InputFormat reading keys and values from SequenceFiles, which are files in binary (raw) rather than text format. ■ *SequenceFileAsTextInputFormat* <*Text, Text*>: similar to SequenceFileAsBinaryInputFormat except that it generates SequenceFileAsTextRecordReader with input keys and values converted to String forms by calling toString() method. ■ *SequenceFileInputFilter* <*K, V*>: A class that allows a MapReduce job to work on a sample of sequence files. The sample is decided by the filter class set by the setFilterClass (Job job, Class<?> filterClass) method.

Next, we present a KeyValueTextFileInputFormat example to help solidify what we have learnt in this section about various FileInputFormats.

5.3.3 A KeyValueTextInputFormat Example

Since Hadoop MapReduce programs operate on large datasets, it's necessary to specify the input format for input data. Table 5.8 presented in the preceding section shows five types of input format. The input format of TextInputFormat is used by default, as we have seen from the SpendingPattern MapReduce sample illustrated in Chapter 1. With this type of input format, one has to parse every input record to extract the key-value pair for the output of a map task. See Listing 1.9 *SpendingPatternMapper.java* on how each key-value pair is made out of the input records to the Mapper.

Now let's examine several input records as shown below. It is seen that the format is defined with three fields: the transaction date, the description that contains the name of a store and location, and the transaction amount.

```
04/16/2009    RUE21 # 384 SUNNYVALE    SUNNYVALE    CA    23.23
08/13/2011    MARSHALLS # 821        SUNNYVALE    CA        92.56
03/15/2011    MEG*LEGOLANDCALIFORNIA 760-918-5346 CA    35.73
06/25/2010    LORI'S GIFTS STORE#233 SAN FRANCISCO   CA 15.23
```

For our analysis, we really don't care about the transaction date. All we care about is how much was spent at a certain store with a given transaction. Therefore, we really don't need the transaction date field in the input records. If we don't have this field, we can just use the description field as the key and the amount field as the value. This is an ideal fit for the KeyValueTextInputFormat as we discussed in the preceding section.

In this section, let's see how we can make a version of the SpendingPattern MapReduce program that uses the KeyValueTextInputFormat in place of the default TextInputFormat as we did in Chapter 1.

Preparing the Input File

The first step is to eliminate the transaction date field in the input data file. This can be easily accomplished by modifying the `MapIncrease1.java` program shown in Listing 3.6. This Java class was copied to a new class file named `MapIncrease2.java` with the following two changes applied:

- The output file name was post-prefixed with "`_kv.txt`" to distinguish it from the output file to be used as the input file for the Mapper that uses the default TextInputFormat.
- The `writeTx` method was modified so that only the *description* field and the *amount* field would be output.

Then, the new input file was created by following the below procedure:

- Building *spending-patterns.jar*:

  `$ mvn clean package –DskipTests –Dhadoop.version=1.0.3`

- Copying *spending-patterns.jar* from workspace to Hadoop's installation folder
- Executing MapIncrease2 to create the synthetic credit card transaction data file based on the file *credit_card_tx_0.txt* in the folder *in0*:

    $ hadoop jar spending-patterns.jar MapIncrease2 in0/credit_card_tx_0.txt 2000000

- Verifying that the output file *credit_card_tx_0_out_kv.txt* has been created in the HDFS

    $ hadoop fs –ls in0

Creating a New Mapper Class

Since the input format has changed, the mapper class must change as well. With the default TextInputFormat, the map method of the mapper class as shown in Listing 1.9 has the following signature:

    map(LongWritable key, Text value, Context context)

In this case, the second parameter *value* represents the entire line of a transaction record that includes the fields of *transaction date*, *description*, and *amount*. Now with the KeyValueTextInputFormat for the input file, the key and value are separated by a tab (\t). Therefore, we must change the signature of the new mapper class. See Listing 5.4 for the new mapper named SpendingPattern1.java. Note that the first two parameters are the key and value fields, and the key fields with their corresponding values are written out directly in the *context.write* (…) statement.

Listing 5.4 The KeyValueTextInputFormat example: the mapper

```
import java.io.IOException;
import java.util.StringTokenizer;
import org.apache.hadoop.io.FloatWritable;
import org.apache.hadoop.io.LongWritable;
import org.apache.hadoop.io.Text;
import org.apache.hadoop.mapreduce.Mapper;

public class SpendingPatternMapper1 extends
        Mapper<Text, Text, Text, FloatWritable> {

    @Override
    public void map(Text key, Text value, Context context) throws IOException,
            InterruptedException {
        if (!key.toString().contains("PAYMENT")) {
            float amount = Float.parseFloat(value.toString());
            context.write(key, new FloatWritable(amount));
        }
    }
}
```

Creating a New MapReduce Driver Program

Since we have a new input format and a new mapper class, we must have a new MapReduce driver program to reflect these changes. This new MapReduce driver program is displayed in Listing 5.5. Note that the new input format and the new mapper class are set through the *job.setInputFormatClass* and *job.setMapperClass* statements. Compare Listing 5.5 with Listing 1.11 to see the changes caused by changing the input format.

Listing 5.5 The KeyValueTextInputFormat example: the driver

```java
import org.apache.hadoop.fs.Path;
import org.apache.hadoop.io.FloatWritable;
import org.apache.hadoop.io.Text;
import org.apache.hadoop.mapreduce.Job;
import org.apache.hadoop.mapreduce.lib.input.FileInputFormat;
import org.apache.hadoop.mapreduce.lib.input.KeyValueTextInputFormat;
import org.apache.hadoop.mapreduce.lib.output.FileOutputFormat;

public class SpendingPattern1 {

  public static void main(String[] args) throws Exception {
    if (args.length != 2) {
      System.err.println("Usage: SpendingPattern <input path> <output path>");
      System.exit(-1);
    }

    Job job = new Job();
    job.setJarByClass(SpendingPattern1.class);
    job.setJobName("Spending Pattern");
    job.setInputFormatClass (KeyValueTextInputFormat.class);

    FileInputFormat.addInputPath(job, new Path(args[0]));
    FileOutputFormat.setOutputPath(job, new Path(args[1]));

    job.setMapperClass(SpendingPatternMapper1.class);
    job.setReducerClass(SpendingPatternReducer.class);

    job.setOutputKeyClass(Text.class);
    job.setOutputValueClass(FloatWritable.class);

    System.exit(job.waitForCompletion(true) ? 0 : 1);
  }
}
```

Running the KeyValueTextInputFormat Example

With the new input data file, the new mapper class, and the new driver class built into the spending-patterns.jar file, this KeyValueTextInputFormat example was launched with the command:

$ hadoop jar spending-patterns.jar SpendingPattern1 in0/credit_card_tx_0_out_kv.txt out20

The job output is displayed in Listing 5.6. By comparing Listing 5.6 with Listing 1.14 (both processed 2M credit card transactions in local mode except that one used the KeyValueTextInputFormat and the other used the TextInputFormat), we can observe the following two major improvements by using the KeyValueTextInputFormat in place of the default TextInputFormat:

■ Merging sorted segments decreased from 4 to 3 as there was less data to process due to the input file decreased from 115 MB to 93 MB.
■ The total job execution time had decreased from 22 seconds to 16 seconds, representing a 27% performance gain.

However, changing the input format does not change the final reduce output. You can verify this by comparing the counter *Reduce output records* from both runs.

Listing 5.6 Console output of the KeyValueTextInputFormat example run

```
mc815ll:hadoop-1.0.3 henry$ hadoop jar spending-patterns.jar SpendingPattern1
in0/credit_card_tx_0_out_kv.txt out20
12/09/18 15:04:00 INFO input.FileInputFormat: Total input paths to process : 1
12/09/18 15:04:00 INFO mapred.JobClient: Running job: job_local_0001
12/09/18 15:04:00 INFO mapred.Task:  Using ResourceCalculatorPlugin : null
12/09/18 15:04:00 INFO mapred.MapTask: io.sort.mb = 100
12/09/18 15:04:00 INFO mapred.MapTask: data buffer = 79691776/99614720
12/09/18 15:04:00 INFO mapred.MapTask: record buffer = 262144/327680
12/09/18 15:04:01 INFO mapred.JobClient:  map 0% reduce 0%
12/09/18 15:04:01 INFO mapred.MapTask: Spilling map output: record full = true
12/09/18 15:04:02 INFO mapred.MapTask: Finished spill 0
12/09/18 15:04:02 INFO mapred.MapTask: Spilling map output: record full = true
12/09/18 15:04:03 INFO mapred.MapTask: Finished spill 1
12/09/18 15:04:03 INFO mapred.MapTask: Starting flush of map output
12/09/18 15:04:03 INFO mapred.MapTask: Finished spill 2
12/09/18 15:04:03 INFO mapred.Merger: Merging 3 sorted segments
12/09/18 15:04:03 INFO mapred.Merger: Down to the last merge-pass, with 3 segments left of total
size: 33471433 bytes
12/09/18 15:04:04 INFO mapred.Task: Task:attempt_local_0001_m_000000_0 is done. And is in the
process of commiting
12/09/18 15:04:06 INFO mapred.Task: Task 'attempt_local_0001_m_000000_0' done.
12/09/18 15:04:06 INFO mapred.Task:  Using ResourceCalculatorPlugin : null
12/09/18 15:04:06 INFO mapred.MapTask: io.sort.mb = 100
12/09/18 15:04:06 INFO mapred.MapTask: data buffer = 79691776/99614720
12/09/18 15:04:06 INFO mapred.MapTask: record buffer = 262144/327680
12/09/18 15:04:07 INFO mapred.MapTask: Spilling map output: record full = true
12/09/18 15:04:07 INFO mapred.MapTask: Finished spill 0
```

12/09/18 15:04:07 INFO mapred.JobClient: map 100% reduce 0%
12/09/18 15:04:07 INFO mapred.MapTask: Spilling map output: record full = true
12/09/18 15:04:08 INFO mapred.MapTask: Finished spill 1
12/09/18 15:04:08 INFO mapred.MapTask: Starting flush of map output
12/09/18 15:04:08 INFO mapred.MapTask: Finished spill 2
12/09/18 15:04:08 INFO mapred.Merger: Merging 3 sorted segments
12/09/18 15:04:08 INFO mapred.Merger: Down to the last merge-pass, with 3 segments left of total size: 33473173 bytes
12/09/18 15:04:09 INFO mapred.Task: Task:attempt_local_0001_m_000001_0 is done. And is in the process of commiting
12/09/18 15:04:09 INFO mapred.Task: **Task 'attempt_local_0001_m_000001_0' done.**
12/09/18 15:04:09 INFO mapred.Task: Using ResourceCalculatorPlugin : null
12/09/18 15:04:09 INFO mapred.MapTask: io.sort.mb = 100
12/09/18 15:04:09 INFO mapred.MapTask: data buffer = 79691776/99614720
12/09/18 15:04:09 INFO mapred.MapTask: record buffer = 262144/327680
12/09/18 15:04:10 INFO mapred.MapTask: Spilling map output: record full = true
12/09/18 15:04:10 INFO mapred.MapTask: Finished spill 0
12/09/18 15:04:10 INFO mapred.MapTask: Spilling map output: record full = true
12/09/18 15:04:10 INFO mapred.MapTask: Starting flush of map output
12/09/18 15:04:11 INFO mapred.MapTask: Finished spill 1
12/09/18 15:04:11 INFO mapred.MapTask: Finished spill 2
12/09/18 15:04:11 INFO mapred.Merger: Merging 3 sorted segments
12/09/18 15:04:11 INFO mapred.Merger: Down to the last merge-pass, with 3 segments left of total size: 26114104 bytes
12/09/18 15:04:11 INFO mapred.Task: Task:attempt_local_0001_m_000002_0 is done. And is in the process of commiting
12/09/18 15:04:12 INFO mapred.Task: **Task 'attempt_local_0001_m_000002_0' done.**
12/09/18 15:04:12 INFO mapred.Task: Using ResourceCalculatorPlugin : null
12/09/18 15:04:12 INFO mapred.LocalJobRunner:
12/09/18 15:04:12 INFO mapred.Merger: Merging 3 sorted segments
12/09/18 15:04:12 INFO mapred.Merger: Down to the last merge-pass, with 3 segments left of total size: 93058698 bytes
12/09/18 15:04:13 INFO mapred.Task: Task:attempt_local_0001_r_000000_0 is done. And is in the process of commiting
12/09/18 15:04:13 INFO mapred.Task: Task attempt_local_0001_r_000000_0 is allowed to commit now
12/09/18 15:04:13 INFO **output.FileOutputCommitter: Saved output of task 'attempt_local_0001_r_000000_0' to out20**
12/09/18 15:04:15 INFO mapred.LocalJobRunner: reduce > reduce
12/09/18 15:04:15 INFO mapred.Task: Task 'attempt_local_0001_r_000000_0' done.
12/09/18 15:04:16 INFO mapred.JobClient: map 100% reduce 100%
12/09/18 15:04:16 INFO mapred.JobClient: Job complete: job_local_0001
12/09/18 15:04:16 INFO mapred.JobClient: Counters: 17
12/09/18 15:04:16 INFO mapred.JobClient: File Output Format Counters
12/09/18 15:04:16 INFO mapred.JobClient: Bytes Written=2122
12/09/18 15:04:16 INFO mapred.JobClient: FileSystemCounters
12/09/18 15:04:16 INFO mapred.JobClient: FILE_BYTES_READ=669247027
12/09/18 15:04:16 INFO mapred.JobClient: FILE_BYTES_WRITTEN=573278584
12/09/18 15:04:16 INFO mapred.JobClient: File Input Format Counters

```
12/09/18 15:04:16 INFO mapred.JobClient:    Bytes Read=94044957
12/09/18 15:04:16 INFO mapred.JobClient:    Map-Reduce Framework
12/09/18 15:04:16 INFO mapred.JobClient:    Map output materialized bytes=93058710
12/09/18 15:04:16 INFO mapred.JobClient:    Map input records=2000000
12/09/18 15:04:16 INFO mapred.JobClient:    Reduce shuffle bytes=0
12/09/18 15:04:16 INFO mapred.JobClient:    Spilled Records=5866140
12/09/18 15:04:16 INFO mapred.JobClient:    Map output bytes=89147932
12/09/18 15:04:16 INFO mapred.JobClient:    Total committed heap usage (bytes)=797261824
12/09/18 15:04:16 INFO mapred.JobClient:    SPLIT_RAW_BYTES=393
12/09/18 15:04:16 INFO mapred.JobClient:    Combine input records=0
12/09/18 15:04:16 INFO mapred.JobClient:    Reduce input records=1955380
12/09/18 15:04:16 INFO mapred.JobClient:    Reduce input groups=44
12/09/18 15:04:16 INFO mapred.JobClient:    Combine output records=0
12/09/18 15:04:16 INFO mapred.JobClient:    Reduce output records=44
12/09/18 15:04:16 INFO mapred.JobClient:    Map output records=1955380
mc815ll:hadoop-1.0.3 henry$
```

5.3.4 DBInputFormat

Another implementation of the InputFormat class is the DBInputFormat class. This class allows a MapReduce job to take input from a database and/or dump results back to the database. It is contained in the package of org.apache.hadoop.mapreduce.lib.db, and has a hierarchy of Object → InputFormat → DBInputFormat as defined below:

```
package org.apache.hadoop.mapreduce.lib.db;
java.lang.Object
  ↳ org.apache.hadoop.mapreduce.InputFormat<LongWritable,T>
    ↳ org.apache.hadoop.mapreduce.lib.db.DBInputFormat<T>


public class DBInputFormat<T extends DBWritable>
    extends InputFormat <LongWritable,T>
        implements Configurable {...}
```

As is seen, it has a parameterized type that extends DBWritable, which implements Writable. It has methods like getDBConf (), getDBProductName (), getConnection (), createDBRecordReader (), etc., to help facilitate its interaction with a database. This is a more specialized subject and you need to consult Hadoop's Java API documentation if you have such a need for your project.

5.4 OUTPUTFORMAT

MapReduce jobs output data both in map and reduce phases. Therefore, output format is needed as much as input format. In this section, we explore how Hadoop's OutputFormat class works. In fact, it's a lot easier to understand the OutputFormat class after we have learnt about the InputFormat class, as the only major difference is that the former does not deal with *splits* as the latter does.

The OutputFormat class is contained in the `org.apache.hadoop.mapreduce` package, extends the `Object` class, and has a hierarchy of `Object` → `OutputFormat` as defined below:

```
package org.apache.hadoop.mapreduce;
java.lang.Object
 ↳ org.apache.hadoop.mapreduce.OutputFormat<K,V>
```

```
public abstract class OutputFormat<K,V>extends Object {...}
```

Its purpose is for describing the output specification for a MapReduce job. It has three methods, which are summarized in Table 5.9. The `checkOutputSpecs` methods works on the context of a given job, while the `getOutputCommitter` method works on the context of a given task attempt. The `getRecordWriter` method returns a `RecordWriter` object, which does the actual output work through its write methods. The RecordWriter class is discussed in the next section together with the SequenceFile class.

Table 5.9 The methods of the OutputFormat class

Type	Method signature
abstract void	checkOutputSpecs(JobContext context) Check for validity of the output-specification for the job.
abstract OutputCommitter	getOutputCommitter(TaskAttemptContext context) Get the output committer for this task.
abstract RecordWriter<K,V>	getRecordWriter(TaskAttemptContext context) Get the RecordWriter for the given task.

5.4.1 RecordWriter and SequenceFile

A RecordWriter object writes key-value pairs to an output file. It has only two methods:

- **void write (K key, V value):** Writes a key-value pair to a file.
- **void close (TaskAttemptContext contxt):** Close the writer to future operations.

You can think of a RecordWriter as the counterpart to a RecordReader.

A SequenceFile is a flat file for containing key-value pairs for a MapReduce job. In contrast with a plain text file, a SequenceFile is compressible, and thus potentially yields better performance when the file size is large. A SequenceFile can be operated upon with the following three classes for reading, writing, and sorting operations:

- **SequenceFile.Reader**: A static class for reading key-value pairs from a sequence-format file.
- **SequenceFile.Writer**: A static class for key-value pairs to a sequence-format file.
- **SequenceFile.Sorter**: Sorts key-value pairs in a sequence-format file. It can take multiple input files, sort them, and output the sorted results in one output file in the same sequence format as the input files.

A SequenceFile can be in one the following three formats:

1) Uncompressed: No compression is applied.
2) Record-compressed: All values are compressed while keys are not.
3) Block-compressed: Everything is compressed except the header.

We will show some sequence format output examples after discussing FileOutputFormat next.

5.4.2 FileOutputFormat

The `FileOutputFormat` class is contained in the package of `org.apache.hadoop.mapreduce.io.output`, extends the `OutputFormat` class and has a hierarchy of `Object → OutputFormat → FileOutputFormat` as shown below:

```
package org.apache.hadoop.mapreduce.io.output;
java.lang.Object
    ↳ org.apache.hadoop.mapreduce.OutputFormat<K,V>
        ↳ org.apache.hadoop.mapreduce.lib.output.FileOutputFormat<K,V>

public class FileOutputFormat<K,V> extends OutputFormat<K,V> {...}
```

Table 5.10 shows the methods of the `FileOutputFormat`. The `checkOutputSpecs` (`JobContext job`) method checks if the output-specification for the job is valid, whereas the `getRecordWriter` (`TaskAttemptContext context`) method returns a RecordWriter for writing the output for the given task.

The `checkOutputSpecs` method is invoked only during runtime. For example, the `SequenceFileAsBinaryOutputFormat` does not support Record compression. This error is not caught during the compiling phase. It's caught only during the job execution phase. The following error message occurred during a MapReduce job run that enabled compression for the SequenceFileAsBinaryOutputFormat class.

```
12/09/19 15:41:51 ERROR security.UserGroupInformation: PriviledgedActionException as:henry
cause:org.apache.hadoop.mapred.InvalidJobConfException: SequenceFileAsBinaryOutputFormat
doesn't support Record Compression
Exception in thread "main" org.apache.hadoop.mapred.InvalidJobConfException:
SequenceFileAsBinaryOutputFormat doesn't support Record Compression
    at
org.apache.hadoop.mapreduce.lib.output.SequenceFileAsBinaryOutputFormat.checkOutputSpecs(Se
quenceFileAsBinaryOutputFormat.java:194)
    at org.apache.hadoop.mapred.JobClient$2.run(JobClient.java:887)
    at org.apache.hadoop.mapred.JobClient$2.run(JobClient.java:850)
    at java.security.AccessController.doPrivileged(Native Method)
    at javax.security.auth.Subject.doAs(Subject.java:396)
    at org.apache.hadoop.security.UserGroupInformation.doAs(UserGroupInformation.java:1121)
    at org.apache.hadoop.mapred.JobClient.submitJobInternal(JobClient.java:850)
    at org.apache.hadoop.mapreduce.Job.submit(Job.java:500)
    at org.apache.hadoop.mapreduce.Job.waitForCompletion(Job.java:530)
    at SpendingPattern1b.main(SpendingPattern1b.java:36)
    ......
```

Table 5.11 summarizes the three sub-classes implementing the `FileOutputFormat` class: the `TextOutputFormat` class, the `SequenceFileOutputFormat` class, and the `SquenceFileAsBinaryOutputFormat`. Several examples using these `FileOutputFormat` classes are presented in the next section.

Table 5.10 Some methods of the FileOutputFormat class

Type	Method signature
void	checkOutputSpecs(JobContext job)
static boolean	getCompressOutput(JobContext job)
Path	getDefaultWorkFile(TaskAttemptContext context, String extension) Get the default path and filename for the output format.
OutputCommitter	getOutputCommitter(TaskAttemptContext context)
static Class<? extends CompressionCodec>	getOutputCompressorClass(JobContext job, Class<? extends CompressionCodec> defaultValue)
protected static String	getOutputName(JobContext job) Get the base output name for the output file.
static Path	getOutputPath(JobContext job) Get the Path to the output directory.
static Path	getPathForWorkFile(TaskInputOutputContext<?,?,?,?> context, String name, String extension)
abstract RecordWriter<K,V>	getRecordWriter(TaskAttemptContext job) Get the RecordWriter for the given task.
static String	getUniqueFile(TaskAttemptContext context, String name, String extension) Generate a unique filename, based on the task id
static Path	getWorkOutputPath(TaskInputOutputContext<?,?,?,?> context) Get the Path to the task's temporary output directory
static void	setCompressOutput(Job job, boolean compress) Set whether the output of the job is compressed.
static void	setOutputCompressorClass(Job job, Class<? extends CompressionCodec> codecClass)
protected static void	setOutputName(JobContext job, String name) Set the base output name for output file to be created.
static void	setOutputPath(Job job, Path outputDir) Set the Path of the output directory .

Table 5.11 A list of sub-classes of FileOutputFormat

Type	Class
text	**TextOutputFormat**: The default OutputFormat that writes plain text files using its *getRecordWriter* (…) method.
text	**SequenceFileOutputFormat**: An OutputFormat that writes SequenceFiles. In addition to the usual *getReaders* and *getRecordWriters* methods, it has a *getOutputCompressionType* method and a *setOutputCompressionType* method for compressing the output data if specified.
binary	**SequenceFileAsBinaryOutputFormat**: An OutputFormat that writes keys and values in binary (raw) format, defined with the generics of *SequenceFileAsBinaryOutputFormat <BytesWritable, BytesWritable >*. It has the following methods: ■ **checkOutputSpecs** (JobContext job) for checking the validity of the output-spec for a given job. ■ **getRecordWriter** (TaskAttemptContext context) for getting a RecordWriter for a given task. ■ **getSequenceFileOutput[Key|Value]Class** (*JobContext job*) for getting the key or value class for the given job. ■ **setSequenceFileOutput[Key|Value]Class** (Job job, Class<?> theClass*)* for setting the key or value class for the given job.

5.4.3 FileOutputFormat Examples

In this section, we present two examples associated with the OutputFormat class: One is with SequenceFileOutputFormat and the other with SequenceFileAsBinaryOutputFormat. We'll see what changes we need to make in order to use these output formats in place of the default TextOutputFormat as we have been using so far.

The SequenceFileOutputFormat Example

In the previous `KeyValueTextInputFormat` example, we created a new MapReduce program named `SpendingPattern1.java` and added one statement as follows in order to change from the default `TextInputFormat` to `KeyValueTextInputFormat` (See Listing 5.5):

```
job.setInputFormatClass (KeyValueTextInputFormat.class);
```

Now, in order to change the reduce output format from the default `TextOutputFormat` to `SequenceFileOutputFormat`, similar to what we did with the `KeyValueTextInputFormat` example, we need to add the following statement to the `SpendingPattern1.java` class:

```
job.setOutputFormatClass (SequenceFileOutputFormat.class);
```

Let's add this statement to *SpendingPattern1.java* and rename it *SpendingPattern1a.java*, as shown in Listing 5.7. Note that we'll continue using the same `SpendingPatternMapper1.java` and `SpendingPatternReducer.java` as we did with the `KeyValueTextInputFormat` example.

After re-packaging and copying the spending-patterns.jar file to Hadoop's installation directory, we can run this example with the following command:

```
$hadoop jar spending-patterns.jar SpendingPattern1a in0/credit_card_tx_0_out_kv.txt out23
```

This run took the same amount of execution time of 16 seconds as with the KeyValueTextInputFormat example, which was launched with the default output format of TextOutputFormat. However, the *File Output Format Counter* of *Bytes Written* increased from 2122 bytes with TextOutputFormat to 2439 bytes with SequenceFileOutputFormat. This is because SequenceFileOutputFormat has extra headers to write, while TextOutputFormat doesn't.

You might wonder what the output looks like from the SequenceFileOutputFormat. Figure 5.3 shows the comparison of the final reduce output between the TextOutputFormat and SequenceFileOutputFormat, which were stored in the *out20* and *out23* directories, respectively (you can identify the commands used to display the partial output for each case).

Listing 5.7 The SequenceFileOutputFormat example: the driver

```
aimport org.apache.hadoop.fs.Path;
import org.apache.hadoop.io.FloatWritable;
import org.apache.hadoop.io.Text;
import org.apache.hadoop.mapreduce.Job;
import org.apache.hadoop.mapreduce.lib.input.FileInputFormat;
import org.apache.hadoop.mapreduce.lib.input.KeyValueTextInputFormat;
import org.apache.hadoop.mapreduce.lib.output.FileOutputFormat;
import org.apache.hadoop.mapreduce.lib.output.SequenceFileOutputFormat;

public class SpendingPattern1a {
 public static void main(String[] args) throws Exception {
  if (args.length != 2) {
   System.err.println("Usage: SpendingPattern <input path> <output path>");
   System.exit(-1);
  }

  Job job = new Job();
  job.setJarByClass(SpendingPattern1.class);
  job.setJobName("Spending Pattern");
  job.setInputFormatClass (KeyValueTextInputFormat.class);
  job.setOutputFormatClass (SequenceFileOutputFormat.class);

  FileInputFormat.addInputPath(job, new Path(args[0]));
  FileOutputFormat.setOutputPath(job, new Path(args[1]));
```

```
job.setMapperClass(SpendingPatternMapper1.class);
job.setReducerClass(SpendingPatternReducer.class);

job.setOutputKeyClass(Text.class);
job.setOutputValueClass(FloatWritable.class);

System.exit(job.waitForCompletion(true) ? 0 : 1);
  }
}
```

```
mc815ll:hadoop-1.0.3 henry$ head out20/part-r-00000
76 10115095           SUNNYVALE           CA        99.98
76CR5754SUNNYVALE10080067 SUNNYVALE       CA        99.99
99 RANCH #1776        SAN FRANCISCO       CA        99.99
BABIES R US #6447   QPS SUNNYVALE         CA        99.99
BR/TOGO'S #332475   Q35 SUNNYVALE         CA        99.99
CENTURY THEATRES 41QPS SUNNYVALE          CA        99.99
CUTEGIRL.COM          CUPERTINO CA        99.99
CVS PHARMACY #9923    SUNNYVALE           CA        99.98
Chinese Gourmet Expres CUPERTINO CA       99.99
DISH NETWORK-ONE TIME  800-894-9131    CO 99.99
mc815ll:hadoop-1.0.3 henry$ head out23/part-r-00000
SEQorg.apache.hadoop.io.Text"org.apache.hadoop.io.FloatWritable???@*?M17-??0?H/+*76 101150
95          SUNNYVALE           CAB???2.-76CR5754SUNNYVALE10080067 SUNNYVALE           CAB???/
+*99 RANCH #1776         SAN FRANCISCO   CAB???/+*BABIES R US #6447   QPS SUNNYVALE
 CAB???/+*BR/TOGO'S #332475   Q35 SUNNYVALE         CAB???/+*CENTURY THEATRES 41QPS SUNNYVAL
E          CAB???{$#CUTEGIRL.COM         CUPERTINO CAB???/+*CVS PHARMACY #9923        SUNNYVA
LE          CAB???{$#Chinese Gourmet Expres CUPERTINO CAB???,{'DISH NETWORK-ONE TIME  800-89
4-9131    COB???,{'DISNEY RESORT-WDTC     ANAHEIM     CAB???/+*DOLRTREE 1228 00012286 SUNN
YVALE       CAB???/+*GROCERY OUTLET OF FO   SUNNYVALE         CAB???/+*GYMBOREE   504850050
483 SUNNYVALE         CAB???/+*IDEAL CUTS         SUNNYVALE         CAB???/+*KOHLS #0663
          SUNNYVALE           CAB???'#"KP INTERNATIONAL MARKE MILPITAS CAB???/+*LORI'S GIFT
S STORE#233 SAN FRANCISCO     CAB???,{'MACY'S EAST #408        MOUNTAIN VIEW CAB???/+*MARSHA
LLS # 821          SUNNYVALE         CAB???/+*MCDONALD'S F20253    SUNNYVALE           CAB???/
+*MCDONALD'S F26393     SUNNYVALE         CAB???,{'MCDONALD'S F33506     MOUNTAIN VIEW CA
B???/+*MCDONALD'S F5447       SUNNYVALE         CAB???,{'MEG*LEGOLANDCALIFORNIA 760-918-534
6  CAB???!MEMBERSHIP FEE AUG 12-JUL 13B???/+*PETSMART INC 54       SUNNYVALE           CAB??
?{$#PRETZEL TIME SUNRISE   CUPERTINO CAB???/+*ROSS STORE #483      SUNNYVALE           CAB?
??2.-RUE21 # 384 SUNNYVALE     SUNNYVALE         CAB???/+*S F SUPERMARKET       SAN FRANCI
SCO     CAB???/+*SAFEWAY STORE 00017947 SUNNYVALE         CAB???/+*SAMSCLUB #6620           SU
NNYVALE         CAB???2.-SAVEMART 607 SUNNYVALE     SUNNYVALE         CAB???,{'SIX FLAGS DISC
OVERY KI 07076444000   CAB???,{'SIX FLAGS DISCOVERY KI VALLEJO       CAB?????????@*?M10??
-7?H/+*SKECHERS-USA #119     SAN FRANCISCO   CAB???/+*TARGET       00010983 SUNNYVALE
     CAB???/+*THAO FASHION MUSIC CTR SAN FRANCISCO     CAB???2.-TOGOS BASKIN SUNNYVALE
SUNNYVALE         CAB???{$#TOYS R US #5808    QPS CUPERTINO CAB???,{'TRICKS GYMNASTICS DANC
 916-3510024   CAB???/+*TRU HOLIDAY EXPRESSQPS SUNNYVALE           CAB???/+*WAL-MART #1760
mc815ll:hadoop-1.0.3 henry$ ▊
```

Figure 5.3 Comparison of the reduce output between the TextOutputFormat and SequenceFileOutputFormat

The SequenceFileAsBinaryOutputFormat Example

To change the file output format from `SequenceFileOutputFormat` to `SequenceFileAsBinaryOutputFormat`, you might think all we need to do is to change the following statement for the preceding example from

```
job.setOutputFormatClass (SequenceFileOutputFormat.class);
```

to

```
job.setOutputFormatClass (SequenceFileAsBinaryOutputFormat.class);
```

Yes, it compiles with no warnings and no errors about this specific change, but when the job was executed, the following error occurred:

```
12/09/19 10:12:15 WARN mapred.LocalJobRunner: job_local_0001
java.lang.ClassCastException: org.apache.hadoop.io.Text cannot be cast to
org.apache.hadoop.io.BytesWritable at
org.apache.hadoop.mapreduce.lib.output.SequenceFileAsBinaryOutputFormat$1.write(SequenceFile
AsBinaryOutputFormat.java:146) at
org.apache.hadoop.mapred.ReduceTask$NewTrackingRecordWriter.write(ReduceTask.java:587) at
org.apache.hadoop.mapreduce.TaskInputOutputContext.write(TaskInputOutputContext.java:80)
    at SpendingPatternReducer.reduce(SpendingPatternReducer.java:20)
    at SpendingPatternReducer.reduce(SpendingPatternReducer.java:8)
    at org.apache.hadoop.mapreduce.Reducer.run(Reducer.java:176)
    ......
```

The issue was that when SequenceFileAsBinaryOutputFormat was specified, the reducer output keys and values were both expected to be the type of BytesWritable instead of Text and FloatWritable as specified in the SpendingPatternReducer.java class (See Listing 1.10). Therefore, we needed to have a new reducer class as shown in Listing 5.8. Note that the original statement

```
context.write(new Text(description), new FloatWritable(amount));
```

must be converted to

```
context.write(new BytesWritable(newKey),
new BytesWritable(newMaxValue));
```

to meet the new requirements imposed by SequenceFileAsBinaryOutputFormat. Note also how Text and FloatWritable are converted into BytesWritable. The new SpendingPattern MapReduce program, named SpendingPattern1b.java, is shown in Listing 5.9, with SequenceFileAsBinaryOutputFormat specified as the output format class.

Similar to the preceding example, this example can be run with the following command except that a different MapReduce driver program (SpendingPattern1b) and a different output directory (*out24*) should be specified:

```
$hadoop jar spending-patterns.jar SpendingPattern1b in0/credit_card_tx_0_out_kv.txt
out24
```

It took exactly the same amount of time and same amount of *file output format bytes written* as with the preceding example.

Listing 5.8 The SequenceFileAsBinaryOutputFormat example: the reducer

```
import java.io.IOException;
```

```java
import org.apache.hadoop.io.IntWritable;
import org.apache.hadoop.io.FloatWritable;
import org.apache.hadoop.io.BytesWritable;
import org.apache.hadoop.io.Text;
import org.apache.hadoop.mapreduce.Reducer;

public class SpendingPatternReducer1 extends
      Reducer<Text, FloatWritable, BytesWritable, BytesWritable> {

   @Override
   public void reduce(Text key, Iterable<FloatWritable> values,
         Context context) throws IOException, InterruptedException {

      float maxValue = Float.MIN_VALUE;
      for (FloatWritable value : values) {
         maxValue = Math.max(maxValue, value.get());
      }
      byte[] newKey = key.toString().getBytes();
      byte[] newMaxValue = Float.toString(maxValue).getBytes();
      context.write(new BytesWritable(newKey),
new BytesWritable(newMaxValue));
   }
}
```

Listing 5.9 The SequenceFileAsBinaryOutputFormat example: the driver

```java
import org.apache.hadoop.fs.Path;
import org.apache.hadoop.io.FloatWritable;
import org.apache.hadoop.io.Text;
import org.apache.hadoop.mapreduce.Job;
import org.apache.hadoop.mapreduce.lib.input.FileInputFormat;
import org.apache.hadoop.mapreduce.lib.input.KeyValueTextInputFormat;
import org.apache.hadoop.mapreduce.lib.output.FileOutputFormat;
import org.apache.hadoop.mapreduce.lib.output.SequenceFileAsBinaryOutputFormat;

public class SpendingPattern1b {

  public static void main(String[] args) throws Exception {
   if (args.length != 2) {
    System.err.println("Usage: SpendingPattern <input path> <output path>");
    System.exit(-1);
   }

   Job job = new Job();
```

```
job.setJarByClass(SpendingPattern1.class);
job.setJobName("Spending Pattern");
job.setInputFormatClass (KeyValueTextInputFormat.class);
job.setOutputFormatClass (SequenceFileAsBinaryOutputFormat.class);

FileInputFormat.addInputPath(job, new Path(args[0]));
FileOutputFormat.setOutputPath(job, new Path(args[1]));

job.setMapperClass(SpendingPatternMapper1.class);
job.setReducerClass(SpendingPatternReducer1.class);

job.setOutputKeyClass(Text.class);
job.setOutputValueClass(FloatWritable.class);

System.exit(job.waitForCompletion(true) ? 0 : 1);
  }
}
```

5.4.4 DBOutputFormat

Similar to the DBInputFormat class, there is a DBOutputFormat class for writing data to a SQL table in a database. It is contained in the package of org.apache.hadoop.mapreduce.lib.db and has a hierarchy of Object → OutputFormat DBOutputFormat as defined as follows:

```
package org.apache.hadoop.mapreduce.lib.db;
java.lang.Object
 ↪ org.apache.hadoop.mapreduce.OutputFormat<K,V>
   ↪ org.apache.hadoop.mapreduce.lib.db.DBOutputFormat<K,V>

public class DBOutputFormat<K extends DBWritable, V>
extends OutputFormat <K, V> {...}
```

As is seen, it has a parameterized type that extends DBWritable for the key, and a type for the value. It uses a nested class DBOutputFormat.DBRecordWriter to write the reduce output to a SQL table. In addition to its inherited method of checkOutputSpecs (JobContext context), It has DB operation specific methods such as:

■   **constructQuery:**

public String constructQuery (String table, String[] fieldNames)

This method constructs the query used as the prepared statement to insert data. The table parameter specifies the table to insert data into, while the fieldNames parameter specifies the fields to insert into.

■   **setOutput:**

```
public static void setOutput(Job job, String tableName,  String... fieldNames)
```

This method initializes the reduce-part of the job with the appropriate output settings for a given job. The second parameter of `tableName` specifies the table to insert data into, while the third parameter of `fieldNames` specifies the field names in the table.

- **setOutput**:

```
public static void setOutput(Job job, String tableName, int fieldCount)
```

This method initializes the reduce-part of the job with the appropriate output settings for a given job. The second parameter of `tableName` specifies the table to insert data into, while the third parameter of `fieldCount` specifies the number of fields in the table. Again, this is a more specialized subject and you need to consult Hadoop's Java API documentation if you have such a need for your project.

5.5 OUTPUTCOMMITTER

The `OutputCommitter` class handles the committing of both map task output and reduce task output for a MapReduce job. Its utilities include:

1) Setting up the job during initialization, for example, creating the temporary output directory for the job during the initialization of the job.
2) Cleaning up the job after the job completion, for example, removing the temporary output directory after the job completion.
3) Setting up the task temporary output.
4) Checking whether a task needs a commit. If a task does not need to commit, then the commit procedure can be skipped.
5) Committing of the task output.
6) Discarding the task commit.

The `FileOutputCommitter` class extends `OutputCommitter` and controls committing files specified in a job output directory. It is contained in the package of `org.apache.hadoop.mapreduce.lib.output` and has a hierarchy of `Object` → `OutputCommitter` as defined as follows:

```
package org.apache.hadoop.mapreduce.lib.output;
java.lang.Object
  ↳ org.apache.hadoop.mapreduce.OutputCommitter
```

It has a constructor defined in the form:

```
public class FileOutputCommitter extends OutputCommitter {
    FileOutputCommitter (Path outputPath, TaskAttemptContext context)
    ......
}
```

Table 5.12 shows the methods of the `FileOutputCommitter` class. It is seen that it can initiate setting up/committing/aborting/cleaning up jobs and/or tasks. These methods are used more likely in the internal implementations of controlling Hadoop job orchestration and MapReduce workflows than directly in MapReduce programs. For example, from a 2M credit card transaction job run as shown in Listing 1.14 presented in Chapter 1, we observed output lines like:

12/08/23 19:35:07 INFO mapred.Task: Task:**attempt_local_0001_m_000001_0** is done. And is **in the process of commiting**
12/08/23 19:35:10 INFO mapred.Task: Task 'attempt_local_0001_m_000001_0' done.

These messages indicate how a map task was committed. We also observed the lines like:

12/08/23 19:35:18 INFO mapred.Task: Task:**attempt_local_0001_r_000000_0** is done. And is **in the process of commiting**
12/08/23 19:35:18 INFO mapred.Task: Task attempt_local_0001_r_000000_0 is allowed to commit now
12/08/23 19:35:18 INFO output.FileOutputCommitter: Saved output of task 'attempt_local_0001_r_000000_0' to out0

These messages indicate not only how a reduce task was committed but also how FileOutputCommitter was used to save the final reduce output result to the HDFS in local storage.

Table 5.12 Methods of FileOutputCommitter

Type	Method signature
void	abortJob(JobContext context, JobStatus.State state) Delete the temporary directory, including all of the work directories.
void	abortTask(TaskAttemptContext context) Delete the work directory
void	commitJob(JobContext context) Delete the temporary directory, including all of the work directories.
void	commitTask(TaskAttemptContext context) Move the files from the work directory to the job output directory
Path	getWorkPath() Get the directory that the task should write results into
boolean	needTaskCommit(TaskAttemptContext context) Did this task write any files in the work directory?
void	setupJob(JobContext context) Create the temporary directory that is the root of all of the task work directories.
void	setupTask(TaskAttemptContext context)

5.6   TASKATTEMPTCONTEXT AND TASKINPUTOUTPUTCONTEXT

We have seen many task attempt lines in the logs we reviewed in the previous chapters. They are closely associated with the `TaskAttemptContext` class and let's take a look at this class in this section.

The `TaskAttemptContext` class is contained in the `org.apache.hadoop.mapreduce` package, extends `JobContext`, and has a hierarchy of `Object → JobContext → TaskAttemptContext` as defined as follows:

```
package org.apache.hadoop.mapreduce;
java.lang.Object
  ↳ org.apache.hadoop.mapreduce.JobContext
    ↳ org.apache.hadoop.mapreduce.TaskAttemptContext


public class TaskAttemptContext extends JobContext implements Progressable {...}
```

As is seen, it extends `JobContext`, which enables it to get access to and set/reset properties for a job context. It is extended by the `TaskInputOutputContext <KEYIN, VALUEIN, KEYOUT, VALUEOUT>` class, which makes it possible to coordinate task execution and task input/output.

Since the `TaskAttemptContext` class is used more by Hadoop job orchestration and workflow management, we focus more on the `TaskInputOutputContext` class in this section, which is contained in the `org.apache.hadoop.mapreduce` package and has a hierarchy of `Object → JobContext → TaskAttemptContext → TaskInputOutputContext` as shown below:

```
package org.apache.hadoop.mapreduce;
java.lang.Object
  ↳ org.apache.hadoop.mapreduce.JobContext
    ↳ org.apache.hadoop.mapreduce.TaskAttemptContext
      ↳ org.apache.hadoop.mapreduce.TaskInputOutputContext
          <KEYIN,VALUEIN,KEYOUT,VALUEOUT>
```

The constructor for the TaskInputOutputContext class is defined as follows:

```
public abstract class askInputOutputContext <KEYIN,VALUEIN,KEYOUT,VALUEOUT>
  extends TaskAttemptContext implements Progressable {
      TaskInputOutputContext (
      Configuration conf,
      TaskAttemptID taskid,
      RecordWriter<KEYOUT,VALUEOUT> output,
      OutputCommitter committer,
      StatusReporter reporter)
}
```

It is seen that it has access to the job configuration and a specific task being attempted as identified with the `taskid` parameter. Besides, it can manipulate output with the help of `OutputCommitter`, as we have seen in the preceding section.

Table 5.13 summarizes the methods of `TaskInputOutputContext`. Once again, it is seen that it gets `Counter`, `CurrentKey`, `CurrentValue`, `OutputCommitter` for the attempted task. It can also advance to the next key-value pair with its `nextKeyValue` () method. It sets status and reports progress of the task. Finally, it can generate output key-value pair with its `write` method. We have seen two such examples, one in Listing 5.4 for the `KeyValueTextInputOutputFormat` example:

context.write (key, new FloatWritable(amount));

and the other in Listing 5.8 for the `SequenceFileAsBinaryOutputFormat` example:

context.write (new BytesWritable(newKey),
new BytesWritable(newMaxValue));

These are examples of `TaskInputOutputContext` in coordinating and accomplishing task output operations.

Table 5.13 Methods of TaskInputOutputContext

Type	Method signature
Counter	getCounter(Enum<?> counterName)
Counter	getCounter(String groupName, String counterName)
abstract KEYIN	getCurrentKey()
abstract VALUEIN	getCurrentValue()
OutputCommitter	getOutputCommitter()
abstract boolean	nextKeyValue()
void	progress()
void	setStatus(String status)
void	write(KEYOUT key, VALUEOUT value) Generates an output key/value pair.

5.7 MAPPER

Before discussing the classes of Mapper, Reducer, Partitioner and Combiner in the remainder of this chapter, let's take a look at how a Hadoop job is configured in the next section. This part is common to all MapReduce programs, and let's spend a little bit more time in this section so that we can comprehend it once and for all.

5.7.1 Configuration, JobConf, JobContext and Job

Hadoop has made its MapReduce framework easy to program by shifting all complexities to configuring a MapReduce job. Therefore, it's crucial to understand how configuration works in order to be able to program MapReduce better. For this purpose, we explore four classes: `Configuration`, `JobConf`, `JobContext`, and `Job` next.

Configuration

The `Configuration` class is contained in the package of `org.apache.hadoop.conf`, extends the Object class, implements the Iterable and Writable interfaces, and has a hierarchy of `Object → Configuration` as is shown below:

```
package org.apache.hadoop.conf;
public class Configuration extends Object implements Iterable <Map.Entry<String,String>>, Writable {...}
```

```
java.lang.Object
  ↳ org.apache.hadoop.conf.Configuration
```

Its major functionality is to organize resources. A resource contains a set of name/value pairs as XML data. It can be named by either a *String* or a *Path*. A resource represented by a String as a file name is passed in via classpath, whereas a resource represented by a Path is accessed directly from the local filesystem.

When a MapReduce job is initiated, Hadoop by default looks for two resources and loads them in-order from the classpath:

■ **core-default.xml**: This XML file defines all default configuration settings for Hadoop. You might think that this file is located in the *conf* directory, but actually, it was packaged into the hadoop-core-<version>.jar file, as is shown in Figure 5.4. See Table A.1 for all default job configuration parameters loaded from the core-default.xml file for a job we ran. Since this file is located in the `hadoop-core-<version>.jar` file, it is available via classpath when a Hadoop job is launched.

■ **core-site.xml**: This XML file defines site (or environment) specific configuration for a given Hadoop environment. In this file, admins can add an entry of <final>true</final> in a <property> element to make the named property immutable.

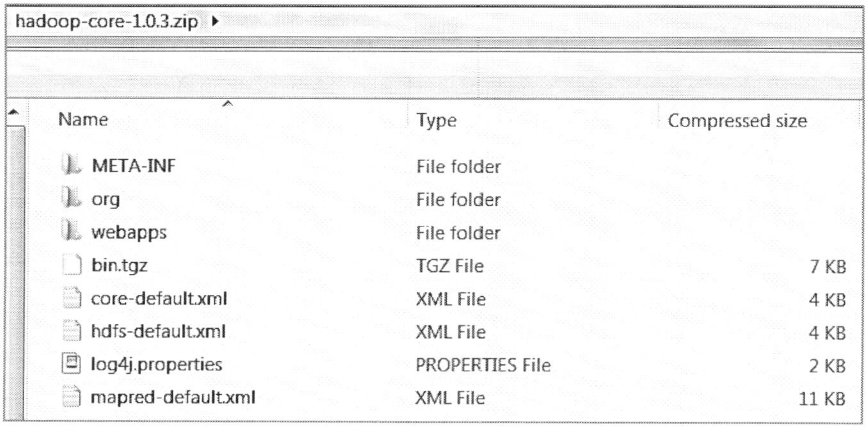

hadoop-core-1.0.3.zip ▸		
Name ⌃	Type	Compressed size
META-INF	File folder	
org	File folder	
webapps	File folder	
bin.tgz	TGZ File	7 KB
core-default.xml	XML File	4 KB
hdfs-default.xml	XML File	4 KB
log4j.properties	PROPERTIES File	2 KB
mapred-default.xml	XML File	11 KB

Figure 5.4 Contents of the hadoop-core-1.0.3.jar (this screenshot was obtained by renaming it from .jar to .zip)

Applications may add additional resources, which are loaded subsequent to the resources in the order they are loaded.

The Configuration class has as many as over 50 methods, most of which are getters and setters. The following methods are directly related to adding a resource, showing how resources are represented:

■ *addDefaultResource (String name)*: Adds a default resource.
■ *addResource (InputStream in)*: Adds a configuration read from an *InputStream*.
■ *addResource (Path file)*: Adds a configuration resource as specified by a Path parameter.
■ *addResource (String name)*: Adds a configuration resource represented by a String variable.
■ *addResource (URL url)*: Adds a configuration resource as specified by a URL passed in.

JobConf

The JobConf class is contained in the package of org.apache.hadoop.mapred, extends the Configuration class, and has a hierarchy of Object → Configuration → JobConf as is shown below:

```
package org.apache.hadoop.mapred;
public class JobConf extends Configuration {...}
```

```
java.lang.Object
  └ org.apache.hadoop.conf.Configuration
    └ org.apache.hadoop.mapred.JobConf
```

It is the primary interface for a user to specify a MapReduce job to the Hadoop framework for execution. However, Hadoop may not execute a job as exactly as specified by the user for two reasons:

1) If a parameter is marked as final by an admin as described above, it cannot be honored.
2) Settings specified by the user are only hints, meaning that they may or may not be taken by Hadoop. For example, the job parameter set by the setNumReduceTasks (int numReduceTasks) method is generally taken by Hadoop, but the job parameter set by the setNumMapTasks (int numMapTasks) method may not be taken, since Hadoop has its own algorithms to determine the optimal number of map tasks. The examples in the previous chapter illustrated this.

JobConf typically specifies Mapper, Partitioner (if any), Combiner (if any), Reducer, InputFormat, and OutputFormat, and so on. It may also specify the following features:

■ Comparators to help sort input and/or output data.

■ Files to be put in the DistributedCache, which boosts an application's performance by caching application-specific files in the forms of text, archives, and jars, etc.

■ Whether or not intermediate and/or job outputs are to be compressed and how if to be compressed.

JobContext

The JobContext class provides a read-only view of a MapReduce job at runtime. It is contained in the package mapreduce and has the hierarchy of Object → JobContext as follows:

```
package org.apache.hadoop.mapreduce;
java.lang.Object
  ↳ org.apache.hadoop.mapreduce.JobContext
```

It has a constructor as shown below with a Configuration parameter and a JobID parameter.

```
public class JobContext extends Object {
    JobContext(Configuration conf, JobID jobId) {...}
    ...
}
```

Table 5.14 (a) shows the fields of this class. Note the following three interesting fields:

- protected JobConf conf: This is the job configuration object we discussed above.
- protected Credentials credentials: This is a field for reading and writing secret keys and Tokens.
- protected UserGroupInformation ugi: This is a UserGroupInformation object that has a reference to the current user (we have seen this from the logs in the previous chapter).

Table 5.14 (b) lists the methods of this class. They are all getters as all the fields are read-only. Given what we have covered, most of the getters should be easily comprehensible by now.

Table 5.14 (a) Some of the fields of the JobContext class

Type	Field name
protected static String	COMBINE_CLASS_ATTR
protected JobConf	conf
protected Credentials	credentials
protected static String	INPUT_FORMAT_CLASS_ATTR
static String	JOB_NAMENODES
protected static String	MAP_CLASS_ATTR
protected static String	OUTPUT_FORMAT_CLASS_ATTR
protected static String	PARTITIONER_CLASS_ATTR
protected static String	REDUCE_CLASS_ATTR
protected UserGroupInformation	ugi The UserGroupInformation object that has a reference to the current user

Table 5.14 (b) Methods of the JobContext class

Type	Method signature

Class<? extends Reducer<?,?,?,?>>	getCombinerClass()
Configuration	getConfiguration()
Credentials	getCredentials() Get credentials for the job.
RawComparator<?>	getGroupingComparator()
Class<? extends InputFormat<?,?>>	getInputFormatClass()
String	getJar()
JobID	getJobID()
String	getJobName()
Class<?>	getMapOutputKeyClass()
Class<?>	getMapOutputValueClass()
Class<? extends Mapper<?,?,?,?>>	getMapperClass()
int	getNumReduceTasks()
Class<? extends OutputFormat <?,?>>	getOutputFormatClass()
Class<?>	getOutputKeyClass()
Class<?>	getOutputValueClass()
Class<? extends Partitioner<?,?>>	getPartitionerClass()
Class<? extends Reducer<?,?,?,?>>	getReducerClass()
RawComparator<?>	getSortComparator()
Path	getWorkingDirectory()

Job

The Job class extends the JobContext class so that all setters for JobContext can be found in this class. It is contained in the package of `org.apache.hadoop.mapreduce` and has the hierarchy of `Object → JobContext → Job` as follows:

```
package org.apache.hadoop.mapreduce;
java.lang.Object
  ↪ org.apache.hadoop.mapreduce.JobContext
      ↪ org.apache.hadoop.mapreduce.Job
```

The Job class has three constructors as shown below:

```
public class Job extends JobContext {
    Job () {...}
    Job (Configuration conf) {...}
    Job (Configuration conf, String jobName) {...}
    ...
}
```

The user can configure a job with one of the three constructors as shown above, submit it, control its execution, and query its state. Table 5.15 further shows the methods of the Job class. Again, given what we have covered and the logs we reviewed in the previous chapters, all these methods should be easily comprehensible. Actually, if you can take a cursory look at these methods, you would be able to immediately understand what this class does and what it can do.

In the next section, we present an example to help illustrate how the classes presented above and their methods are used to set up a typical Hadoop MapReduce job.

Table 5.15 Methods of the Job class

Type	Method signature
void	failTask(TaskAttemptID taskId)
Counters	getCounters()
String	getJar()
TaskCompletionEvent[]	getTaskCompletionEvents(int startFrom)
String	getTrackingURL()
boolean	isComplete()
boolean	isSuccessful()
void	killJob()
void	killTask(TaskAttemptID taskId)
float	mapProgress()
float	reduceProgress()
void	setCombinerClass(Class<? extends Reducer> cls)
void	setGroupingComparatorClass(Class<? extends RawComparator> cls)
void	setInputFormatClass(Class<? extends InputFormat> cls)
void	setJarByClass(Class<?> cls)
void	setJobName(String name)
void	setMapOutputKeyClass(Class<?> theClass)
void	setMapOutputValueClass(Class<?> theClass)
void	setMapperClass(Class<? extends Mapper> cls)
void	setMapSpeculativeExecution(boolean speculativeExecution)
void	setNumReduceTasks(int tasks)
void	setOutputFormatClass(Class<? extends OutputFormat> cls)
void	setOutputKeyClass(Class<?> theClass)
void	setOutputValueClass(Class<?> theClass)

void	setPartitionerClass(Class<? extends Partitioner> cls)
void	setReducerClass(Class<? extends Reducer> cls)
void	setReduceSpeculativeExecution(boolean speculativeExecution)
void	setSortComparatorClass(Class<? extends RawComparator> cls)
void	setSpeculativeExecution(boolean speculativeExecution)
float	setupProgress()
void	setWorkingDirectory(Path dir)
void	submit() Submit the job to the cluster and returns immediately.
boolean	waitForCompletion(boolean verbose) Submit the job to the cluster and wait for it to finish.

5.7.2 A Hadoop Job Configuration Example

If you take a look at Listing 5.6 obtained with the KeyValueTextInputFormat example, you would notice the following WARNINGs at the beginning of the job execution console output:

12/09/18 15:04:00 **WARN** util.NativeCodeLoader: **Unable to load native-hadoop library for your platform**... using builtin-java classes where applicable
12/09/18 15:04:00 WARN mapred.JobClient: Use GenericOptionsParser for parsing the arguments. Applications should implement Tool for the same.

The first warning occurred due to the fact the Hadoop native library was not installed on the Mac OS X machine on which the sample was run. This did not affect any samples we ran so far, but it would prevent certain Hadoop features from working. For example, using GzipCodec to compress output would not work, and one has to use the DefaultCodec or install the Hadoop native library to make it work (we'll get back to this issue later when we discuss *Compression*).

The issue we would resolve next is the second warning about Hadoop's GenericOptionsParser. Let's pause for a moment and understand what GenericOptionsParser is about.

GenericOptionsParser is a class contained in the package of org.apache.hadoop.util. It parses command line arguments generic to the Hadoop framework. It recognizes certain standard command line arguments, enabling Hadoop job submitters to conveniently specify a namenode, a jobtracker, and some additional configuration resources. Generic command line arguments might modify Configuration objects. The general command line syntax is:

$ bin/hadoop command [genericOptions] [commandOptions]

The supported *genericOptions* include:

-conf <configuration file>   specify a configuration file
-D <property=value>   use value for given property
-fs <local|namenode:port>   specify a namenode

-jt <local|jobtracker:port>	specify a job tracker
-files <comma separated list of files>	specify comma separated files to be copied to the nodes in a cluster
-libjars <comma separated list of jars>	specify comma separated jar files to include in the classpath.
-archives <comma separated list of archives>	specify comma separated archives to be unarchived on the compute machines.

Let's use our most recent MapReduce program SpendingPattern1b.java, shown in Listing 5.9, to explain further what generic options are. We once ran this program with the following command:

```
$hadoop jar spending-patterns.jar SpendingPattern1b in0/credit_card_tx_0_out_kv.txt
out24
```

In this case, the command part is *jar spending-patterns.jar SpendingPattern1b* and the commandOptions part is *in0/credit_card_tx_0_out_kv.txt out24*. Suppose we ran this program with the following command using the generic option of *–D mapred.reduce.tasks=1* (note the position the generic option is inserted):

```
$hadoop jar spending-patterns.jar SpendingPattern1b –D mapred.reduce.tasks=1
↪in0/credit_card_tx_0_out_kv.txt out24
```

It would not recognize this generic option. That's because the SpendingPattern1b.java program shown in Listing 5.9 does not extend/implement certain Hadoop class/interface. To make it work, we have to modify the SpendingPattern1b.java program to make it look like SpendingPattern1c.java as is shown in Listing 5.10 (a) below, which uses a utility program JobInit.java as shown in Listing 5.10 (b) to take care of the part of initializing a job with command options. Note that we have to add the following *import* statements:

```
import org.apache.hadoop.conf.Configured;
import org.apache.hadoop.util.Tool;
import org.apache.hadoop.util.ToolRunner;
import org.apache.hadoop.util.GenericOptionsParser;
import org.apache.hadoop.conf.*;
```

In addition, the SpendingPattern1c class must extend Configured and implement Tool, both of which are contained in the package of org.apache.hadoop.util. Now, if you try the above generic option of *–D mapred.reduce.tasks=1*, it would recognize this generic option. However, the second warning related to the *GenericOptionsParser* as described above would still appear unless the following two statements are added:

```
Configuration conf = new Configuration();
String remainingArgs[] = new GenericOptionsParser(conf,
            args).getRemainingArgs();
```

Listing 5.10 (c) shows the partial output of a run with the modified SpendingPattern driver (SpendingPattern1c) to help confirm that the warning related to the *GenericOptionsParser* had been indeed resolved.

Before we conclude this section, you may want to examine Listings 5.10 (a) and (b) and cross-check with Table 5.15 to see what methods of the Job class have been used in this example. You can use some other methods of the Job class to customize your own MapReduce driver as needed.

Listing 5.10 (a) The Job Configuration example: the driver

```java
import org.apache.hadoop.fs.Path;
import org.apache.hadoop.io.FloatWritable;
import org.apache.hadoop.io.Text;
import org.apache.hadoop.io.BytesWritable;
import org.apache.hadoop.mapreduce.Job;
import org.apache.hadoop.mapreduce.lib.input.FileInputFormat;
import org.apache.hadoop.mapreduce.lib.input.KeyValueTextInputFormat;
import org.apache.hadoop.mapreduce.lib.output.FileOutputFormat;
import org.apache.hadoop.mapreduce.lib.output.SequenceFileAsBinaryOutputFormat;

import org.apache.hadoop.conf.Configured;
import org.apache.hadoop.util.Tool;
import org.apache.hadoop.util.ToolRunner;
import org.apache.hadoop.util.GenericOptionsParser;
import org.apache.hadoop.conf.*;

public class SpendingPattern1c extends Configured implements Tool {

    @Override
    public int run(String[] args) throws Exception {
        Configuration conf = new Configuration();
        String remainingArgs[] = new GenericOptionsParser(conf,
            args).getRemainingArgs();
        Job job = JobInit.init (this, getConf (), args);
        if (job == null) {
            return -1;
        }
        job.setJobName("Spending Pattern");
        job.setInputFormatClass(KeyValueTextInputFormat.class);
        job.setOutputFormatClass(SequenceFileAsBinaryOutputFormat.class);

        job.setMapperClass(SpendingPatternMapper1.class);
        job.setReducerClass(SpendingPatternReducer1.class);
```

```java
            job.setOutputKeyClass(Text.class);
            job.setOutputValueClass(FloatWritable.class);
            return job.waitForCompletion(true) ? 0 : 1;
    }

    public static void main(String[] args) throws Exception {
        int exitCode = ToolRunner.run(new SpendingPattern1c(), args);
        System.exit(exitCode);
    }
}
```

Listing 5.10 (b) JobInit.java

```java
import java.io.IOException;

import org.apache.hadoop.conf.Configuration;
import org.apache.hadoop.fs.Path;
import org.apache.hadoop.mapreduce.Job;
import org.apache.hadoop.mapreduce.lib.input.FileInputFormat;
import org.apache.hadoop.mapreduce.lib.output.FileOutputFormat;
import org.apache.hadoop.util.GenericOptionsParser;
import org.apache.hadoop.util.Tool;

public class JobInit {

  public static Job init (Tool tool, Configuration conf,
     String[] args) throws IOException {

   if (args.length != 2) {
    printUsage(tool, "<input> <output>");
    return null;
   }
   Job job = new Job(conf);
   job.setJarByClass(tool.getClass());
   FileInputFormat.addInputPath(job, new Path(args[0]));
   FileOutputFormat.setOutputPath(job, new Path(args[1]));
   return job;
  }

  public static void printUsage(Tool tool, String commandOptions) {
    System.err.printf("Usage: %s [genericOptions] %s\n\n",
       tool.getClass().getSimpleName(), commandOptions);
    GenericOptionsParser.printGenericCommandUsage(System.err);
  }
```

```
}
```

Listing 5.10 (c) Partial output of the job configuration example

```
mc815ll:hadoop-1.0.3 henry$ hadoop jar spending-patterns.jar SpendingPattern1c -D
mapred.reduce.tasks=1 in0/credit_card_tx_0_out_kv.txt out46
12/09/20 14:36:36 WARN util.NativeCodeLoader: Unable to load native-hadoop library for your
platform... using builtin-java classes where applicable
12/09/20 14:36:36 INFO input.FileInputFormat: Total input paths to process : 1
12/09/20 14:36:36 WARN snappy.LoadSnappy: Snappy native library not loaded
12/09/20 14:36:36 INFO mapred.JobClient: Running job: job_local_0001
12/09/20 14:36:36 INFO mapred.Task:  Using ResourceCalculatorPlugin : null
12/09/20 14:36:36 INFO mapred.MapTask: io.sort.mb = 100
.................... < omitted to save space > .........................
12/09/20 14:36:49 INFO mapred.Task: Task:attempt_local_0001_r_000000_0 is done. And is in the
process of commiting
12/09/20 14:36:49 INFO mapred.Task: Task attempt_local_0001_r_000000_0 is allowed to commit
now
12/09/20 14:36:49 INFO output.FileOutputCommitter: Saved output of task
'attempt_local_0001_r_000000_0' to out46
12/09/20 14:36:51 INFO mapred.LocalJobRunner: reduce > reduce
12/09/20 14:36:51 INFO mapred.Task: Task 'attempt_local_0001_r_000000_0' done.
12/09/20 14:36:52 INFO mapred.JobClient:  map 100% reduce 100%
12/09/20 14:36:52 INFO mapred.JobClient: Job complete: job_local_0001
12/09/20 14:36:52 INFO mapred.JobClient: Counters: 17
.................... < omitted to save space > .........................
12/09/20 14:36:52 INFO mapred.JobClient:     Reduce input groups=44
12/09/20 14:36:52 INFO mapred.JobClient:     Reduce output records=44
12/09/20 14:36:52 INFO mapred.JobClient:     Map output records=1955380
mc815ll:hadoop-1.0.3 henry$
```

5.7.3 MapContext, Mapper.Context and Mapper

The Mapper class depends on the Mapper.Context class, which extends the MapContext class. These classes are presented in reverse order next.

MapContext

In order to execute a map task, it is necessary to have a proper context. This required context is provided by the MapContext class. This class is contained in the mapreduce package and has the hierarchy of Object → JobContext → TaskAttemptContext → TaskInputOutputContext as follows:

```
package org.apache.hadoop.mapreduce;

java.lang.Object
 ↳ org.apache.hadoop.mapreduce.JobContext
   ↳ org.apache.hadoop.mapreduce.TaskAttemptContext
```

```
        ↳ org.apache.hadoop.mapreduce.TaskInputOutputContext
    <KEYIN,VALUEIN,KEYOUT,VALUEOUT>
            ↳ org.apache.hadoop.mapreduce.MapContext
    <KEYIN,VALUEIN,KEYOUT,VALUEOUT>
```

It has four typed parameters: an input key-value pair and an output key-value pair. It has the following constructor and methods:

```
public class MapContext<KEYIN,VALUEIN,KEYOUT,VALUEOUT> extends
    TaskInputOutputContext<KEYIN,VALUEIN,KEYOUT,VALUEOUT> {
        /* constructor */
        MapContext (
        Configuration conf,
        TaskAttemptID taskid,
        RecordReader<KEYIN,VALUEIN> reader,
        RecordWriter<KEYOUT,VALUEOUT> writer,
        OutputCommitter committer,
        StatusReporter reporter,
        InputSplit split)

        /* methods */
        public InputSplit getInputSplit() {...}    // Get the input split for this map.
        public KEYIN getCurrentKey() {...}         // Get the current key.
        public VALUEIN getCurrentValue() {...} // Get the current value.
        public boolean nextKeyValue() {...}        //Advance to the next key, value pair
}
```

The four methods shown above operates on input splits, keys and values for a given map task. In fact, we need to go down one level deeper, because a Mapper object depends directly on a Mapper.Context object, as discussed next.

Mapper.Context

The Mapper.Context class extends the MapContext class directly. This class is contained in the mapreduce package and has the hierarchy of Object → JobContext → TaskAttemptContext → TaskInputOutputContext → MapContext as follows:

```
package org.apache.hadoop.mapreduce;

java.lang.Object
    ↳ org.apache.hadoop.mapreduce.JobContext
        ↳ org.apache.hadoop.mapreduce.TaskAttemptContext
            ↳ org.apache.hadoop.mapreduce.TaskInputOutputContext
                <KEYIN,VALUEIN,KEYOUT,VALUEOUT>
                ↳ org.apache.hadoop.mapreduce.MapContext
                    <KEYIN,VALUEIN,KEYOUT,VALUEOUT>
```

↳ **org.apache.hadoop.mapreduce.Mapper.Context**

It has a constructor as shown below, which is identical with the constructor for the `MapContext` class that we have just illustrated:

```
public class Mapper.Context extends
    MapContext<KEYIN,VALUEIN,KEYOUT,VALUEOUT> {
        Mapper.Context (
        Configuration conf,
        TaskAttemptID taskid,
        RecordReader<KEYIN,VALUEIN> reader,
        RecordWriter<KEYOUT,VALUEOUT> writer,
        OutputCommitter committer,
        StatusReporter reporter,
        InputSplit split)
}
```

The `Mapper.Context` class does not have its own methods, though. All its methods are inherited from its super classes.

Next, we discuss the Mapper class, which is the main subject for this section.

Mapper

Given the preparation work we have done in the previous sections, it's now easy to describe the Mapper class.

The Mapper class extends the Object class directly. It is contained in the `mapreduce` package and has the hierarchy of `Object → Mapper` as follows:

```
package org.apache.hadoop.mapreduce;
java.lang.Object
    ↳ org.apache.hadoop.mapreduce.Mapper <KEYIN,VALUEIN,KEYOUT,VALUEOUT>
```

It has a default constructor and four methods as shown below:

```
public class Mapper<KEYIN,VALUEIN,KEYOUT,VALUEOUT> extends Object {
    /* constructor */
    public Mapper ();

    /* methods */
     protected void    setup (Mapper.Context context) {...}
     protected void    cleanup(Mapper.Context context) {...}
     protected void    map (KEYIN key, VALUEIN value, Mapper.Context context) {...}
     public void       run (Mapper.Context context) { ...}
}
```

The `setup` method and the `cleanup` method are called once at the beginning and end of a map task, respectively. The map method is called once for each key/value pair in the input split. Users can override the `run` method for more complete control over the execution of the map task.

The function of a mapper (or map task) is to map (or transform) input key/value pairs contained in the given input splits to a set of intermediate key/value pairs. Specifically, a Mapper goes through the following execution logic during the mapping phase:

- The Hadoop MapReduce framework spawns one map task for each InputSplit generated by the InputFormat for the job. Mapper implementations can access the `Configuration` for the job via the `JobContext.getConfiguration()` method.
- The framework first calls the `setup (Mapper.Context)` method, as described above, to initialize the task.
- The framework then calls the `map (Object, Object, Context)` method for each key/value pair in the InputSplit.
- Finally, the framework calls the `cleanup (Context)` method to clean up the task.

Note that there are additional steps for processing intermediate map output results. Specific steps depend on what are specified following the mapper. Typical situations include:

- **No Reducers?**: If the job has zero Reducers, the output of the Mapper is directly written to the `OutputFormat` without performing key-sorting operations.
- **Grouping**: First, all intermediate values associated with a given output *key* are subsequently grouped by the framework. Users can control the sorting and grouping processes by specifying two key `RawComparator` classes.
- **Partitioning**: The Mapper outputs are partitioned per Reducer if the user implements a custom Partitioner. Partitioning is a process to control which keys (and hence records) go to which Reducer. We will talk more about partitioning later in this chapter.
- **Combining**: Users can optionally specify a combiner, via `Job.setCombinerClass(Class)`, to perform local aggregation of the intermediate outputs, which helps to cut down the amount of data transferred from the Mapper to the Reducer. We will talk more about combining later in this chapter.
- **Compressing**: Applications can specify if and how the intermediate outputs should be compressed and which `CompressionCodec` (compression scheme) is to be used via the `Configuration`. Compression is a more advanced topic and we will talk more about it in the next chapter.
- **Shuffling**: After going through all above steps, the map output results are shuffled to a reducer or multiple reducers for the next phase of MapReduce.

Next, let's take a look at the Mapper's sub-classes.

5.7.4 Mapper's Sub-Classes

The Mapper class has the following sub-classes for handling various special mapping requirements:

- **DelegatingMapper <K1, V1, K2, V2>**: This mapper is contained in the package of `org.apache.hadoop.mapreduce.lib.input`. As its name suggests, this class delegates mapping tasks to other mappers. It is called mostly internally by the MapReduce framework itself to delegate mapping tasks to the mappers specified in a MapReduce job.

- **FieldSelectionMapper <K, V>**: This mapper is contained in the package of org.apache.hadoop.mapreduce.lib.fieldsel. It can be used to perform field selections in a manner similar to the UNIX utility *cut*, which selects specific fields of a record using a spec expression. An input record is treated as fields separated by a user specified separator, or if no user specified separator is given, the default tab separator ("\t") would be used. The user can specify a list of fields that form the map output keys, and a list of fields that form the map output values. If the input format is TextInputFormat, the mapper will ignore the key to the map function, and the fields are for the value only. The field separator can be overwritten with the attribute "mapreduce.data.field.separator", and the map output field list spec is under the attribute "mapreduce.fieldsel.map.output.key.value.fields.spec". These attributes can be set with Hadoop generic options, for example:

    - D mapreduce.data.field.separator=\t
    - D mapreduce.fieldsel.map.output.key.value.fields.spec =4,3,0,1:6,5,1-3,7-

    Note that the value is expected to be in the form of "*keyFieldsSpec:valueFieldsSpec*" with comma (,) separating fields and colon (:) separating the key and the value parts. The rules for specifying the key and value specs are:

    o   If a single number (e.g., 4) is given, it represents a specific field.
    o   If a range (e.g., 1-3) is given, it represents a range of fields, inclusive on both ends.
    o   If an open range (e.g., 3-) is given, it represents all the fields starting from that field (in this case 3 and above). The open range field spec applies to value fields only, and they have no effect on the key fields. The above example specifies to use fields 4,3,0 and 1 for keys, and fields 6,5,1,2,3,7 and above for values.

    The reduce output field list spec is under the attribute "mapreduce.fieldsel .reduce.output.key.value.fields.spec". The reducer extracts output key/value pairs in a similar manner, except that the key is never ignored.
- **InverseMapper**: This mapper is contained in the package of org.apache.hadoop.mapreduce.lib.map. As its name suggests, it swaps keys and values when there is such a need.
- **MultithreadedMapper <K1, V1, K2, V2>**: This mapper is contained in the package of org.apache.hadoop.mapreduce.lib.map as well. It has two of its own methods of setNumberOfThreads (Job job, int threads) and getNumberOfThreads (JobContext job) to make a map task multithreaded. By default, a map task is executed in single threaded mode and parallelism is achieved with splitting inputs and spawning one map task per split.
- **TokenCounterMapper**: This mapper is contained in the package of org.apache.hadoop.mapreduce.lib.map as well. It tokenizes the input values and emits each word with a count of one.

In the next section, we present an example to demonstrate how a Mapper works.

5.7.5 An Mapper Example

So far, we have been using one MapReduce program that finds the maximum amount spent at each store out of millions of credit card transactions. Let's change it a little bit, as that's not all the Hadoop MapReduce framework is for. Let's say that we want to find out the number of times that credit card transactions occurred at each store. This is another typical type of problems that the Hadoop MapReduce framework can solve. It is similar to the ubiquitous word-counting Hadoop sample, but not exactly the same.

To achieve the above objective, we need three pieces of MapReduce programs: a mapper, a reducer and a driver. To make it simple, we impose three requirements;

1) The input format needs to be `KeyValueTextInputFormat`.
2) The output format needs to be `TextOutputFormat` so that we can view the final output results conveniently.
3) The driver should allow the use of Hadoop generic options when needed.

And that's all our requirements for now. We are free to use any programs we have developed so far as templates, and we can just start with a proper template and adapt it. You can actually start doing this yourself and compare with the mapper, reducer and driver provided here. The Mapper is presented in Listing 5.11. As is seen, the most relevant statement is the `context.write` statement:

```
context.write(key, new IntWritable (1));
```

which *counts* "1" for each key. We will run this example after presenting the Reducer and the driver in the next section.

Listing 5.11 The mapper example: the driver

```java
import java.io.IOException;
import java.util.StringTokenizer;
import org.apache.hadoop.io.IntWritable;
import org.apache.hadoop.io.LongWritable;
import org.apache.hadoop.io.Text;
import org.apache.hadoop.mapreduce.Mapper;

public class SpendingPatternMapper1d extends
    Mapper<Text, Text, Text, IntWritable> {

  @Override
  public void map(Text key, Text value, Context context) throws IOException,
      InterruptedException {
    if (!key.toString().contains("PAYMENT")) {
      context.write(key, new IntWritable (1));
    }
  }
}
```

5.8 REDUCER

Similar to the Mapper class, the Reducer class requires proper context as well. Let's follow the similar sequence to presenting the Mapper class to present the Reducer class and start with the ReduceContext class next.

5.8.1 ReduceContext, Reducer.Context and Iterable

Similar to the Mapper class, the Reducer class depends on the Reducer.Context class, which depends on the ReduceContext class. These classes are presented in reverse order next.

ReduceContext

In order to execute a reduce task, it is necessary to have a proper context. The ReduceContext class provides this required context. Similar to the MapperContext class, this class is contained in the mapreduce package and has the hierarchy of Object → JobContext → TaskAttemptContext → TaskInputOutputContext as follows:

```
package org.apache.hadoop.mapreduce;
java.lang.Object
 ↳ org.apache.hadoop.mapreduce.JobContext
   ↳ org.apache.hadoop.mapreduce.TaskAttemptContext
     ↳ org.apache.hadoop.mapreduce.TaskInputOutputContext
        <KEYIN,VALUEIN,KEYOUT,VALUEOUT>
       ↳ org.apache.hadoop.mapreduce.ReduceContext
          <KEYIN,VALUEIN,KEYOUT,VALUEOUT>
```

It has four typed parameters: an input key-value pair and an output key-value pair. It has the following constructor and methods:

```
public class ReduceContext<KEYIN,VALUEIN,KEYOUT,VALUEOUT> extends
   TaskInputOutputContext<KEYIN,VALUEIN,KEYOUT,VALUEOUT> {
      /* constructor */
      public ReduceContext (Configuration conf,
             TaskAttemptID taskid,
             RawKeyValueIterator input,
             Counter inputKeyCounter,
             Counter inputValueCounter,
             RecordWriter<KEYOUT,VALUEOUT> output,
             OutputCommitter committer,
             StatusReporter reporter,
             RawComparator<KEYIN> comparator,
             Class<KEYIN> keyClass,
             Class<VALUEIN> valueClass) throws InterruptedException,
                IOException
      /* methods */
```

```
public boolean nextKey()              {...}
public boolean nextKeyValue()      {...}
public KEYIN getCurrentKey()        {...}
public VALUEIN getCurrentValue()  {...}
public Iterable<VALUEIN> getValues() {...}
}
```

Compared with the MapContext class, the ReduceContext class has a few extra parameters such as RawKeyValueIterator, Counters for inputKey and inputValue, RawComparator, and Class for keyClass and valueClass. That's because the main job of a Mapper is to form key-value pairs on a record by record basis, whereas the main job of a Reducer is to process the large number of values for a given key, oftentimes from multiple map sources.

As far as the methods of the ReduceContext are concerned, the first four methods are self-explanatory according to their names. The last method getValues () iterates through the values for the current key for performing the actual reducing task.

Similar to the relationship between the MapContext class and the Mapper.Context class as we introduced in the previous section, the Reducer.Context class extends the ReduceContext class, as discussed next.

Reducer.Context

The Reducer.Context class extends the ReduceContext class directly. It is contained in the mapreduce package and has the hierarchy of Object → JobContext → TaskAttemptContext → TaskInputOutputContext → ReduceContext as follows:

```
package org.apache.hadoop.mapreduce;
java.lang.Object
 ↪ org.apache.hadoop.mapreduce.JobContext
   ↪ org.apache.hadoop.mapreduce.TaskAttemptContext
     ↪ org.apache.hadoop.mapreduce.TaskInputOutputContext
         <KEYIN,VALUEIN,KEYOUT,VALUEOUT>
       ↪ org.apache.hadoop.mapreduce.ReduceContext
           <KEYIN,VALUEIN,KEYOUT,VALUEOUT>
         ↪ org.apache.hadoop.mapreduce.Reducer.Context
```

It has a constructor as shown below, which is identical with the constructor for the ReduceContext class that we have just illustrated:

```
public class Reducer.Context extends
   ReduceContext<KEYIN,VALUEIN,KEYOUT,VALUEOUT> {
       public Reducer.Context(Configuration conf,
               TaskAttemptID taskid,
               RawKeyValueIterator input,
               Counter inputKeyCounter,
               Counter inputValueCounter,
               RecordWriter<KEYOUT,VALUEOUT> output,
```

```
                    OutputCommitter committer,
                    StatusReporter reporter,
                    RawComparator<KEYIN> comparator,
                    Class<KEYIN> keyClass,
                    Class<VALUEIN> valueClass)
}
```

The `Reducer.Context` class does not have its own methods, though. It inherits all its methods from its super classes.

Interface Iterable <T>

Reducer requires the set of values to be the Java type Iterable. Any class that implements this interface allows an object to be the target of the "foreach" statement. This interface has only one method of

```
Iterator<T> iterator ()
```

which returns an iterator over a set of elements of type T. The interface Iterator is another Java utility class in the package *java.util* that it facilitates iterating over a collection. An iterator has three methods:

- `hasNext ()`: Returns true if the iteration has more elements.
- `next ()`: Returns the next element in the iteration.
- `remove ()`: Removes from the underlying collection the last element returned by the iterator.

We will see how these classes are used by Reducer next.

5.8.2 Reducer

Similar to the Mapper class, the Reducer class extends the Object class directly. It is contained in the `mapreduce` package and has the hierarchy of Object → Mapper as follows:

```
package org.apache.hadoop.mapreduce;
java.lang.Object
  ↳ org.apache.hadoop.mapreduce.Reducer <KEYIN,VALUEIN,KEYOUT,VALUEOUT>
```

It has a default constructor and four methods as shown below:

```
public class Reducer<KEYIN,VALUEIN,KEYOUT,VALUEOUT> extends Object {
    /* constructor */
    public Reducer ();

    /* methods */
    protected void    setup (Reducer.Context context) {...}
    protected void    cleanup(Reducer.Context context) {...}
    protected void    reduce (KEYIN key, VALUEIN value, Reducer.Context context) {...}
    public void       run (Reducer.Context context) { ...}
}
```

The `setup` method and the `cleanup` method are called once at the beginning and end of a reduce task, respectively. The `reduce` method is called once for each key in the input split. Users can override the `run` method for more complete control over the execution of the reduce task.

As we have stated repeatedly, the function of a reducer is to reduce a set of intermediate values associated with the same key to a smaller set of values or even one oftentimes. Classes implementing Reducer can access the Configuration for the job via the `Job.getConfiguration ()` method and initialize themselves. After being initialized, a Reducer goes through the following three primary phases with the reduce task:

1) **Shuffle**: The term of "shuffle" might be a misnomer as *shuffling* typically means random permutation of a collection of objects. What it really means here in Hadoop's context is that the Reducer copies the grouped (sorted or partitioned) output from Mappers to Reducers using the HTTP protocol. How destinations of copying operation are determined will be discussed in the next section when we introduce the Partitioner class.

2) **Sort**: The framework merge-sorts Reducer inputs by keys generated from multiple Mappers. As we observed from the logs presented in Chapter 4, the shuffle and sort operations occur simultaneously, that is, the pre-sorted input key-value pairs to a reducer are merged while they are being fetched. Note that one can also set it up to perform a secondary sort (sorting based on composite keys). Refer to the Hadoop MapReduce API documentation for more information if you have a need for secondary sort your project.

3) **Reduce**: In this phase, the `reduce (Object, Iterable, Context)` method is called for each key- values pair (note the plural) in the sorted inputs. The output of the reduce task is typically written to a `RecordWriter` via `TaskInputOutputContext.write (Object, Object)` as we discussed previously. Note that the output of the Reducer is not re-sorted and may not be sorted.

In the next section, we discuss a few implementers of the Reducer class.

5.8.3 Reducer Implementers

Similar to the `FieldSelectionMapper` class, there is a `FieldSelectionReducer` class, which can be used to perform field selections in a manner similar to the UNIX utility `cut` as we described previously. The input data is assumed to be separated as fields with the default tab separator of "\t" or a user specified separator. The field separator is under the attribute "`mapreduce.fieldsel.data.field.separator`". The user can specify a list of fields that form the reduce output keys, and a list of fields that form the reduce output values. The fields are the union of those from the key and those from the value. The reduce output field list spec is under the attribute "`mapreduce.fieldsel.reduce.output.key.value.fields.spec`". All other discussions we had with the `FieldSelectionMapper` class apply to the `FieldSelectionReducer` class as well.

In addition to the above class, a few additional classes such as `IntSumReducer`, `LongSumReducer`, `SecondarySort.Reducer`, and `WordCount.IntSumReducer` implement the Reducer class. Actually, you can easily extend the Reducer class and come up with your own reducers comparable to those extended "sum" reducers except the `SecondarySort.Reducer`, which might require some extra thoughts.

With the `SecondarySort.Reducer`, you achieve a secondary sort on the values returned by the value iterator by extending the key with the secondary key and defining a grouping comparator. The keys will be sorted using the entire key, but will be grouped using the grouping comparator to decide which keys and values are sent in the same call to reduce. The grouping comparator is specified via `Job.setGroupingComparatorClass(Class)`. The sort order is controlled by `Job.setSortComparatorClass(Class)`.

The Hadoop API documentation gives an example on `SecondarySort.Reducer`. The use case is to find duplicate web pages and tag them all with the url of the "best" known example. The suggested implementation is like:

- Map Input Key: url
- Map Input Value: document
- Map Output Key: document checksum, url pagerank
- Map Output Value: url
- Partitioner: by checksum
- OutputKeyComparator: by checksum and then decreasing pagerank
- OutputValueGroupingComparator: by checksum

With this example, the map output key has two parts: the document checksum and the url pagerank. This composite key sets the stage for secondary sort reducing. The Partitioner partitions using the first part of the composite key. The OutputKeyComparator specifies that key comparison should be first based on checksum and then pagerank. The OutputValueGroupingComparator specifies that output value grouping comparison should be based on checksum.

5.8.4 A Reducer Example

In the preceding section, we stated that we would develop a new MapReduce program that would count the number of times customers had shopped at a store for a given period covering the credit card transactions contained in the input file. You were asked to come up with the mapper by yourself with the given requirements or you could examine the version of the Mapper provided in Listing 5.11 for the changes made relative to the mapper from the KeyValueTextInputFormat example. In this section, I would ask you to do the same. First, you can try to develop a reducer and a driver that would work with the mapper provided in the preceding section, because you would learn more by trying it out yourself. Alternatively, you can study the reducer and the driver provided in this section as shown in Listings 5.12 (a) and (b), and try to identify the crucial changes we have made in order to turn our previous MapReduce sample into a new sample that counts the number of times customers shopped at each store.

For your reference, Listing 5.13 shows the abridged console output obtained from the following job submission:

```
$ hadoop jar spending-patterns.jar SpendingPattern1d in0/credit_card_tx_0_out_kv.txt out50
```

The final reduce output contains the following contents in the *part-r-00000* file:

```
mc815ll:hadoop-1.0.3 henry$ hadoop fs -cat out50/part-r-00000
76 10115095        SUNNYVALE    CA    44990
76CR5754SUNNYVALE10080067 SUNNYVALE    CA    44637
99 RANCH #1776      SAN FRANCISCO   CA    44307
...... <ommited to save space> ......
WAL-MART #1760      SUNNYVALE    CA    44187
mc815ll:hadoop-1.0.3 henry$
```

Each line as shown above represents the description field (store name and city), whereas the last integer represents the number of times that credit card transactions occurred at that store. If your implementation works, you should get similar results.

Listing 5.12 (a) The Reducer example: the Reducer

```
import java.io.IOException;

import org.apache.hadoop.io.IntWritable;
import org.apache.hadoop.io.Text;
import org.apache.hadoop.mapreduce.Reducer;

public class SpendingPatternReducer1d extends
        Reducer<Text, IntWritable, Text, IntWritable> {

    @Override
    public void reduce(Text key, Iterable<IntWritable> values,
            Context context) throws IOException, InterruptedException {

        int sum = 0;
        for (IntWritable value : values) {
            sum = sum + value.get();
        }
        context.write(key, new IntWritable(sum));
    }
}
```

Listing 5.12 (b) The Reducer example: the driver

```
import org.apache.hadoop.fs.Path;
import org.apache.hadoop.io.IntWritable;
import org.apache.hadoop.io.Text;
import org.apache.hadoop.mapreduce.Job;
import org.apache.hadoop.mapreduce.lib.input.FileInputFormat;
import org.apache.hadoop.mapreduce.lib.input.KeyValueTextInputFormat;
```

```java
import org.apache.hadoop.mapreduce.lib.output.FileOutputFormat;
import org.apache.hadoop.mapreduce.lib.output.TextOutputFormat;

import org.apache.hadoop.conf.Configured;
import org.apache.hadoop.util.Tool;
import org.apache.hadoop.util.ToolRunner;
import org.apache.hadoop.util.GenericOptionsParser;
import org.apache.hadoop.conf.*;

public class SpendingPattern1d extends Configured implements Tool {

    @Override
    public int run(String[] args) throws Exception {
        Configuration conf = new Configuration();
        String remainingArgs[] = new GenericOptionsParser(conf,
            args).getRemainingArgs();
        Job job = JobInit.init (this, getConf (), args);
        if (job == null) {
            return -1;
        }

        job.setJobName("Spending Pattern");
        job.setInputFormatClass(KeyValueTextInputFormat.class);
        job.setOutputFormatClass(TextOutputFormat.class);

        job.setMapperClass(SpendingPatternMapper1d.class);
        job.setReducerClass(SpendingPatternReducer1d.class);

        job.setOutputKeyClass(Text.class);
        job.setOutputValueClass(IntWritable.class);
        return job.waitForCompletion(true) ? 0 : 1;
    }

    public static void main(String[] args) throws Exception {
        int exitCode = ToolRunner.run(new SpendingPattern1d(), args);
        System.exit(exitCode);
    }
}
```

Listing 5.13 Console output of the MapReduce program that counts the number of times customers shopped at a store for a given period

```
mc815ll:hadoop-1.0.3 henry$ hadoop jar spending-patterns.jar SpendingPattern1d
in0/credit_card_tx_0_out_kv.txt out50
```

```
12/09/21 12:56:27 WARN util.NativeCodeLoader: Unable to load native-hadoop library for your
platform... using builtin-java classes where applicable
12/09/21 12:56:27 INFO input.FileInputFormat: Total input paths to process : 1
12/09/21 12:56:27 WARN snappy.LoadSnappy: Snappy native library not loaded
12/09/21 12:56:27 INFO mapred.JobClient: Running job: job_local_0001
12/09/21 12:56:27 INFO mapred.Task:  Using ResourceCalculatorPlugin : null
...
12/09/21 12:56:28 INFO mapred.MapTask: Spilling map output: record full = true
12/09/21 12:56:28 INFO mapred.JobClient:  map 0% reduce 0%
......
12/09/21 12:56:41 INFO mapred.Task: Task attempt_local_0001_r_000000_0 is allowed to commit
now
12/09/21 12:56:41 INFO output.FileOutputCommitter: Saved output of task
'attempt_local_0001_r_000000_0' to out50
12/09/21 12:56:43 INFO mapred.Task: Task 'attempt_local_0001_r_000000_0' done.
12/09/21 12:56:43 INFO mapred.JobClient:  map 100% reduce 100%
12/09/21 12:56:43 INFO mapred.JobClient: Job complete: job_local_0001
......
12/09/21 12:56:43 INFO mapred.JobClient:    Map input records=2000000
......
12/09/21 12:56:43 INFO mapred.JobClient:    Combine input records=0
12/09/21 12:56:43 INFO mapred.JobClient:    Reduce input records=1955380
12/09/21 12:56:43 INFO mapred.JobClient:    Reduce input groups=44
12/09/21 12:56:43 INFO mapred.JobClient:    Combine output records=0
12/09/21 12:56:43 INFO mapred.JobClient:    Reduce output records=44
12/09/21 12:56:43 INFO mapred.JobClient:    Map output records=1955380
mc815ll:hadoop-1.0.3 henry$
```

5.9 PARTITIONER

A *Partitioner*, if specified, partitions the keys of the intermediate map outputs from map tasks. The number of partitions matches the number of reduce tasks, and therefore if there is only one reduce task, then partitioning does not apply. When there are more than one reduce task, the map outputs from multiple map tasks are partitioned and directed to multiple reduce tasks.

In this section, we discuss the Partitioner and its implementers.

5.9.1 Partitioner

The Partitioner class is contained in the package of org.apache.hadoop.mapreduce and has the hierarchy of Object → Partitioner as follows:

```
package org.apache.hadoop.mapreduce;
java.lang.Object
  ↳ org.apache.hadoop.mapreduce.Partitioner<KEY,VALUE>
```

It has a default constructor and one method as shown below:

```
public abstract class Partitioner <KEY,VALUE> extends Object {
    public Partitioner ();
    int getPartition (K2 key, V2 value, int numPartitions) { ...}
}
```

The `getPartition` method creates and returns the partitioning number within the range of the total number of partitions for a given key. Typically, the partitioning scheme is based on hashing on the keys. There are other ways to alter the partitioning scheme, as is discussed in the next section.

5.9.2 Implementers of the Partitioner Class

The implementers of the Partitioner class include the following:

- `BinaryPartitioner`
- `HashPartitioner`
- `KeyFieldBasedPartitioner`
- `SecondarySort.FirstPartitioner.`

The `BinaryPartitioner` partitions `BinaryComparable` keys using a configurable part of the bytes array returned by `BinaryComparable.getBytes()`, whereas the `HashPartitioner` partitions keys by their `Object.hashCode()`. The `KeyFieldBasedPartitioner` provides a mechanism for partitioning keys based on certain key fields. The `SecondarySort.FirstPartitioner` partitions keys based on the first part of the composite key (see §5.8.3 on the concept of a composite key in the context of secondary sort).

Next, we present a Partitioner example to wrap up our discussion on Partitioner.

5.9.3 A Partitioner Example

We know that Hadoop uses the HashPartitioner by default if no custom Partitioner is specified. In this section, we present a custom Partitioner that partitions every map key using the hashCode of a store name prefix, which is arbitrarily defined as the part from the first character to the first subsequent space of the store name. This way, all records associated with the same store would go to the same Reducer. After going through this example, you would have a better understanding of how Hadoop partitioning works and how to implement your own custom Partitioner.

Let's re-use our previous MapReduce sample of counting the number of times customers shopped at a store during a given period that covers the credit card transactions contained in the input file. We can re-use the same Mapper and Reducer, but we need a Partitioner class and a new driver. Listing 5.14 shows the new Partitioner class named `StorePartitioner.java`. It appears to be very simple and compact. It *extends Partitioner* and *overrides* only one method of *getPartition* with the parameters given. It extracts the storeNamePrefix as we described above. Then it returns the partition number represented as a non-negative integer. Note that we have to apply `Math.abs` (...) function to the hashCode; otherwise it may return invalid negative partition numbers. In fact, when the `Math.abs` (...) function was not applied at first, a test run resulted in the following errors (note the "-1" partition number returned for these two keys):

java.io.IOException: Illegal partition for **MEG*LEGOLANDCALIFORNIA 760-918-5346 CA (-1)**
    at org.apache.hadoop.mapred.MapTask$MapOutputBuffer.collect(MapTask.java:1073)
    at org.apache.hadoop.mapred.MapTask$NewOutputCollector.write(MapTask.java:691)
    at org.apache.hadoop.mapreduce.
TaskInputOutputContext.write(TaskInputOutputContext.java:80)
    at SpendingPatternMapper1d.map(SpendingPatternMapper1d.java:15)
    at SpendingPatternMapper1d.map(SpendingPatternMapper1d.java:8)
    at org.apache.hadoop.mapreduce.Mapper.run(Mapper.java:144)
    at org.apache.hadoop.mapred.MapTask.runNewMapper(MapTask.java:764)
    at org.apache.hadoop.mapred.MapTask.run(MapTask.java:370)
    at org.apache.hadoop.mapred.Child$4.run(Child.java:255)
    at **java.security.AccessController.doPrivileged**(Native Method)
    at **javax.security.auth.Subject.doAs**(Subject.java:396)
    at org.apache.hadoop.security.UserGroupInformation.
doAs(UserGroupInformation.java:1121)
    at org.apache.hadoop.**mapred.Child.main**(Child.java:249)

12/09/21 22:13:32 INFO mapred.JobClient: Task Id : attempt_201209212204_0002_m_000001_0,
Status : FAILED
java.io.IOException: Illegal partition for **Chinese Gourmet Expres CUPERTINO CA (-1)**
    ......

Next, we need a new driver that has the custom *StorePartitioner* taken into account. Listing 5.15 shows this new driver named SpendingPattern1e.java. Note that the job.setPartitionerClass (StorePartitioner.class) is placed between the job.setMapperClass and job.setReducerClass statements. We continue our discussion after Listing 5.15.

Listing 5.14 The Partitioner example: the StorePartitioner

```
import org.apache.hadoop.io.IntWritable;
import org.apache.hadoop.io.Text;
import org.apache.hadoop.mapreduce.Partitioner;

public class StorePartitioner extends Partitioner <Text, IntWritable>{
  @Override
  public int getPartition (Text key, IntWritable count, int numPartitions) {
    int index = key.toString ().indexOf (" ");
    String storeNamePrefix = key.toString ();
    if ( index > 0) {
        storeNamePrefix = storeNamePrefix.substring (0, index);
    }
    return Math.abs(storeNamePrefix.hashCode ()) % numPartitions;
  }
}
```

Listing 5.15 The Partitioner example: the driver

```
import org.apache.hadoop.fs.Path;
import org.apache.hadoop.io.IntWritable;
import org.apache.hadoop.io.Text;
import org.apache.hadoop.io.BytesWritable;
import org.apache.hadoop.mapreduce.Job;
import org.apache.hadoop.mapreduce.lib.input.FileInputFormat;
import org.apache.hadoop.mapreduce.lib.input.KeyValueTextInputFormat;
import org.apache.hadoop.mapreduce.lib.output.FileOutputFormat;
import org.apache.hadoop.mapreduce.lib.output.TextOutputFormat;

import org.apache.hadoop.conf.Configured;
import org.apache.hadoop.util.Tool;
import org.apache.hadoop.util.ToolRunner;
import org.apache.hadoop.util.GenericOptionsParser;
import org.apache.hadoop.conf.*;

public class SpendingPattern1e extends Configured implements Tool {

    @Override
    public int run(String[] args) throws Exception {
        Configuration conf = new Configuration();
        String remainingArgs[] = new GenericOptionsParser(conf,
            args).getRemainingArgs();
        Job job = JobInit.init (this, getConf (), args);
        if (job == null) {
            return -1;
        }

        job.setJobName("Spending Pattern");
        job.setInputFormatClass(KeyValueTextInputFormat.class);
        job.setOutputFormatClass(TextOutputFormat.class);

        job.setMapperClass(SpendingPatternMapper1d.class);
        job.setPartitionerClass(StorePartitioner.class);
        job.setReducerClass(SpendingPatternReducer1d.class);

        job.setOutputKeyClass(Text.class);
        job.setOutputValueClass(IntWritable.class);
        return job.waitForCompletion(true) ? 0 : 1;
    }

    public static void main(String[] args) throws Exception {
```

```
        int exitCode = ToolRunner.run(new SpendingPattern1e(), args);
        System.exit(exitCode);
    }
}
```

Baseline

Now in order to demonstrate the new Partitioner in play, we need to run this example on the Linux cluster described in Chapter 2, as there is only one Reducer when running Hadoop in local mode. Also, we needed to establish a baseline first without involving the custom StorePartitioner. Such a run was carried out and the output results are shown in Listing 5.16. Note the following:

- The driver SpendingPattern1d was used with the *credit_card_tx_0_out_kv.txt* as the input file, and the output folder was *out1d*.
- The run took 43 seconds end-to-end.
- Partition 0 contains three transactions at MCDONALD'S and one transaction at SIX FLAGS, while partition 1 contains one transaction at MCDONALD'S and one transaction at SIX FLAGS.

Next, a test run was carried out with the custom StorePartitioner applied. Listing 5.17 shows the results. Note the following:

- The driver SpendingPattern1e was used with the same *credit_card_tx_0_out_kv.txt* as the input file, and the output folder was *out1e*.

- The run took 52 seconds end-to-end, which was nine seconds longer than the baseline run as described above.

- Partition 0 contains all four transactions for MCDONALD'S and all two transactions at SIX FLAGS, which was what we expected.

This wraps up our discussion on Partitioner. We proceed to discussing Combiner next.

Listing 5.16 Baseline run without the custom StorePartitioner on the four-node Linux cluster

```
henry@linux-1fsw:~/myapp/hadoop-1.0.3> hadoop jar spending-patterns.jar SpendingPattern1d
in0/credit_card_tx_0_out_kv.txt out1d
12/09/21 22:11:35 INFO input.FileInputFormat: Total input paths to process : 1
12/09/21 22:11:35 INFO util.NativeCodeLoader: Loaded the native-hadoop library
12/09/21 22:11:35 WARN snappy.LoadSnappy: Snappy native library not loaded
12/09/21 22:11:36 INFO mapred.JobClient: Running job: job_201209212204_0001
12/09/21 22:11:37 INFO mapred.JobClient:  map 0% reduce 0%
12/09/21 22:11:54 INFO mapred.JobClient:  map 49% reduce 0%
12/09/21 22:11:55 INFO mapred.JobClient:  map 99% reduce 0%
12/09/21 22:11:57 INFO mapred.JobClient:  map 100% reduce 0%
12/09/21 22:12:07 INFO mapred.JobClient:  map 100% reduce 16%
12/09/21 22:12:12 INFO mapred.JobClient:  map 100% reduce 66%
12/09/21 22:12:13 INFO mapred.JobClient:  map 100% reduce 100%
12/09/21 22:12:18 INFO mapred.JobClient: Job complete: job_201209212204_0001
```

```
12/09/21 22:12:18 INFO mapred.JobClient: Counters: 29
12/09/21 22:12:18 INFO mapred.JobClient:   Job Counters
12/09/21 22:12:18 INFO mapred.JobClient:     Launched reduce tasks=2
12/09/21 22:12:18 INFO mapred.JobClient:     SLOTS_MILLIS_MAPS=26363
12/09/21 22:12:18 INFO mapred.JobClient:     Launched map tasks=2
12/09/21 22:12:18 INFO mapred.JobClient:     Data-local map tasks=2
12/09/21 22:12:18 INFO mapred.JobClient:     SLOTS_MILLIS_REDUCES=30054
12/09/21 22:12:18 INFO mapred.JobClient:   File Output Format Counters
12/09/21 22:12:18 INFO mapred.JobClient:     Bytes Written=2094
12/09/21 22:12:18 INFO mapred.JobClient:   FileSystemCounters
12/09/21 22:12:18 INFO mapred.JobClient:     FILE_BYTES_READ=186129753
12/09/21 22:12:18 INFO mapred.JobClient:     HDFS_BYTES_READ=93291334
12/09/21 22:12:18 INFO mapred.JobClient:     FILE_BYTES_WRITTEN=279263320
12/09/21 22:12:18 INFO mapred.JobClient:     HDFS_BYTES_WRITTEN=2094
12/09/21 22:12:18 INFO mapred.JobClient:   File Input Format Counters
12/09/21 22:12:18 INFO mapred.JobClient:     Bytes Read=93291058
12/09/21 22:12:18 INFO mapred.JobClient:   Map-Reduce Framework
12/09/21 22:12:18 INFO mapred.JobClient:     Map output materialized bytes=93058716
12/09/21 22:12:18 INFO mapred.JobClient:     Map input records=2000000
12/09/21 22:12:18 INFO mapred.JobClient:     Reduce shuffle bytes=93058716
12/09/21 22:12:18 INFO mapred.JobClient:     Spilled Records=5866140
12/09/21 22:12:18 INFO mapred.JobClient:     Map output bytes=89147932
12/09/21 22:12:18 INFO mapred.JobClient:     CPU time spent (ms)=27860
12/09/21 22:12:18 INFO mapred.JobClient:     Total committed heap usage (bytes)=517255168
12/09/21 22:12:18 INFO mapred.JobClient:     Combine input records=0
12/09/21 22:12:18 INFO mapred.JobClient:     SPLIT_RAW_BYTES=276
12/09/21 22:12:18 INFO mapred.JobClient:     Reduce input records=1955380
12/09/21 22:12:18 INFO mapred.JobClient:     Reduce input groups=44
12/09/21 22:12:18 INFO mapred.JobClient:     Combine output records=0
12/09/21 22:12:18 INFO mapred.JobClient:     Physical memory (bytes) snapshot=599420928
12/09/21 22:12:18 INFO mapred.JobClient:     Reduce output records=44
12/09/21 22:12:18 INFO mapred.JobClient:     Virtual memory (bytes) snapshot=1433640960
12/09/21 22:12:18 INFO mapred.JobClient:     Map output records=1955380
henry@linux-1fsw:~/myapp/hadoop-1.0.3> hadoop fs -ls out1d
-rw-r--r--  3 henry supergroup     911 2012-09-21 22:12 /user/henry/out1d/part-r-00000
-rw-r--r--  3 henry supergroup    1183 2012-09-21 22:12 /user/henry/out1d/part-r-00001
henry@linux-1fsw:~/myapp/hadoop-1.0.3> hadoop fs -cat out1d/part-r-00000
76CR5754SUNNYVALE10080067 SUNNYVALE    CA  44637
BABIES R US #6447 QPS SUNNYVALE    CA  44272
BR/TOGO'S #332475 Q35 SUNNYVALE    CA 44531
CUTEGIRL.COM       CUPERTINO CA  44248
DISH NETWORK-ONE TIME  800-894-9131 CO 44521
DISNEY RESORT-WDTC    ANAHEIM     CA 44195
GROCERY OUTLET OF FO  SUNNYVALE      CA 44313
GYMBOREE 504850050483 SUNNYVALE    CA    44268
IDEAL CUTS       SUNNYVALE     CA 44420
LORI'S GIFTS STORE#233 SAN FRANCISCO   CA44249
MCDONALD'S F20253    SUNNYVALE    CA  44382
MCDONALD'S F33506    MOUNTAIN VIEW CA44631
```

```
MCDONALD'S F5447      SUNNYVALE      CA    44508
PRETZEL TIME SUNRISE   CUPERTINO CA    44410
ROSS STORE #483        SUNNYVALE      CA 44690
RUE21 # 384 SUNNYVALE    SUNNYVALE      CA    44319
SIX FLAGS DISCOVERY KI 07076444000  CA    44492
TARGET      00010983 SUNNYVALE      CA44805
WAL-MART #1760        SUNNYVALE      CA    44187
henry@linux-1fsw:~/myapp/hadoop-1.0.3> hadoop fs -cat out1d/part-r-00001
76 10115095        SUNNYVALE      CA    44990
99 RANCH #1776        SAN FRANCISCO  CA    44307
CENTURY THEATRES 41QPS SUNNYVALE      CA    44470
CVS PHARMACY #9923    SUNNYVALE      CA 44670
Chinese Gourmet Expres CUPERTINO CA    44577
DOLRTREE 1228 00012286 SUNNYVALE      CA    44260
KOHLS #0663        SUNNYVALE      CA    44502
KP INTERNATIONAL MARKE MILPITAS CA    44138
MACY'S EAST #408      MOUNTAIN VIEW CA    44720
MARSHALLS # 821      SUNNYVALE      CA 44491
MCDONALD'S F26393    SUNNYVALE      CA 44118
MEG*LEGOLANDCALIFORNIA 760-918-5346 CA    44445
MEMBERSHIP FEE AUG 12-JUL 13  44527
PETSMART INC 54      SUNNYVALE      CA 44522
S F SUPERMARKET      SAN FRANCISCO  CA  44532
SAFEWAY STORE 00017947 SUNNYVALE      CA    44406
SAMSCLUB #6620        SUNNYVALE      CA44629
SAVEMART 607 SUNNYVALE    SUNNYVALE      CA 44281
SIX FLAGS DISCOVERY KI VALLEJO      CA    44638
SKECHERS-USA #119    SAN FRANCISCO  CA 44266
THAO FASHION MUSIC CTR SAN FRANCISCO  CA 44791
TOGOS BASKIN SUNNYVALE    SUNNYVALE      CA 44094
TOYS R US #5808    QPS CUPERTINO CA    44288
TRICKS GYMNASTICS DANC 916-3510024  CA 44284
TRU HOLIDAY EXPRESSQPS SUNNYVALE      CA    44356
henry@linux-1fsw:~/myapp/hadoop-1.0.3>
```

Listing 5.17 A test run with the custom StorePartitioner applied.

```
henry@linux-1fsw:~/myapp/hadoop-1.0.3> hadoop jar spending-patterns.jar SpendingPattern1e
in0/credit_card_tx_0_out_kv.txt out1e
12/09/21 22:40:43 INFO input.FileInputFormat: Total input paths to process : 1
12/09/21 22:40:43 INFO util.NativeCodeLoader: Loaded the native-hadoop library
12/09/21 22:40:43 WARN snappy.LoadSnappy: Snappy native library not loaded
12/09/21 22:40:43 INFO mapred.JobClient: Running job: job_201209212204_0004
12/09/21 22:40:44 INFO mapred.JobClient:  map 0% reduce 0%
12/09/21 22:41:01 INFO mapred.JobClient:  map 29% reduce 0%
12/09/21 22:41:02 INFO mapred.JobClient:  map 79% reduce 0%
12/09/21 22:41:04 INFO mapred.JobClient:  map 89% reduce 0%
12/09/21 22:41:07 INFO mapred.JobClient:  map 98% reduce 0%
```

```
12/09/21 22:41:11 INFO mapred.JobClient:  map 98% reduce 8%
12/09/21 22:41:13 INFO mapred.JobClient:  map 100% reduce 8%
12/09/21 22:41:22 INFO mapred.JobClient:  map 100% reduce 16%
12/09/21 22:41:28 INFO mapred.JobClient:  map 100% reduce 58%
12/09/21 22:41:29 INFO mapred.JobClient:  map 100% reduce 100%
12/09/21 22:41:34 INFO mapred.JobClient: Job complete: job_201209212204_0004
12/09/21 22:41:34 INFO mapred.JobClient: Counters: 29
12/09/21 22:41:34 INFO mapred.JobClient:  Job Counters
12/09/21 22:41:34 INFO mapred.JobClient:    Launched reduce tasks=2
12/09/21 22:41:34 INFO mapred.JobClient:    SLOTS_MILLIS_MAPS=36757
12/09/21 22:41:34 INFO mapred.JobClient:    Launched map tasks=2
12/09/21 22:41:34 INFO mapred.JobClient:    Data-local map tasks=2
12/09/21 22:41:34 INFO mapred.JobClient:    SLOTS_MILLIS_REDUCES=46619
12/09/21 22:41:34 INFO mapred.JobClient:  File Output Format Counters
12/09/21 22:41:34 INFO mapred.JobClient:    Bytes Written=2094
12/09/21 22:41:34 INFO mapred.JobClient:  FileSystemCounters
12/09/21 22:41:34 INFO mapred.JobClient:    FILE_BYTES_READ=186141808
12/09/21 22:41:34 INFO mapred.JobClient:    HDFS_BYTES_READ=93291334
12/09/21 22:41:34 INFO mapred.JobClient:    FILE_BYTES_WRITTEN=279263692
12/09/21 22:41:35 INFO mapred.JobClient:    HDFS_BYTES_WRITTEN=2094
12/09/21 22:41:35 INFO mapred.JobClient:  File Input Format Counters
12/09/21 22:41:35 INFO mapred.JobClient:    Bytes Read=93291058
12/09/21 22:41:35 INFO mapred.JobClient:  Map-Reduce Framework
12/09/21 22:41:35 INFO mapred.JobClient:    Map output materialized bytes=93058716
12/09/21 22:41:35 INFO mapred.JobClient:    Map input records=2000000
12/09/21 22:41:35 INFO mapred.JobClient:    Reduce shuffle bytes=93058716
12/09/21 22:41:35 INFO mapred.JobClient:    Spilled Records=5866140
12/09/21 22:41:35 INFO mapred.JobClient:    Map output bytes=89147932
12/09/21 22:41:35 INFO mapred.JobClient:    CPU time spent (ms)=37100
12/09/21 22:41:35 INFO mapred.JobClient:    Total committed heap usage (bytes)=414003200
12/09/21 22:41:35 INFO mapred.JobClient:    Combine input records=0
12/09/21 22:41:35 INFO mapred.JobClient:    SPLIT_RAW_BYTES=276
12/09/21 22:41:35 INFO mapred.JobClient:    Reduce input records=1955380
12/09/21 22:41:35 INFO mapred.JobClient:    Reduce input groups=44
12/09/21 22:41:35 INFO mapred.JobClient:    Combine output records=0
12/09/21 22:41:35 INFO mapred.JobClient:    Physical memory (bytes) snapshot=544260096
12/09/21 22:41:35 INFO mapred.JobClient:    Reduce output records=44
12/09/21 22:41:35 INFO mapred.JobClient:    Virtual memory (bytes) snapshot=1433722880
12/09/21 22:41:35 INFO mapred.JobClient:    Map output records=1955380
henry@linux-1fsw:~/myapp/hadoop-1.0.3> hadoop fs -ls out1e
-rw-r--r--  3 henry supergroup     1280 2012-09-21 22:41 /user/henry/out1e/part-r-00000
-rw-r--r--  3 henry supergroup      814 2012-09-21 22:41 /user/henry/out1e/part-r-00001
henry@linux-1fsw:~/myapp/hadoop-1.0.3> hadoop fs -cat out1e/part-r-00000
76CR5754SUNNYVALE10080067 SUNNYVALE     CA  44637
99 RANCH #1776      SAN FRANCISCO   CA    44307
BABIES R US #6447  QPS SUNNYVALE     CA  44272
BR/TOGO'S #332475 Q35 SUNNYVALE      CA 44531
CENTURY THEATRES 41QPS SUNNYVALE     CA   44470
CUTEGIRL.COM        CUPERTINO CA  44248
```

```
CVS PHARMACY #9923    SUNNYVALE      CA  44670
DISH NETWORK-ONE TIME  800-894-9131  CO 44521
DISNEY RESORT-WDTC    ANAHEIM      CA 44195
GYMBOREE 504850050483 SUNNYVALE      CA   44268
LORI'S GIFTS STORE#233 SAN FRANCISCO   CA44249
MACY'S EAST #408     MOUNTAIN VIEW CA   44720
MCDONALD'S F20253     SUNNYVALE      CA  44382
MCDONALD'S F26393     SUNNYVALE      CA  44118
MCDONALD'S F33506     MOUNTAIN VIEW CA44631
MCDONALD'S F5447     SUNNYVALE      CA  44508
MEMBERSHIP FEE AUG 12-JUL 13  44527
PETSMART INC 54     SUNNYVALE      CA 44522
PRETZEL TIME SUNRISE  CUPERTINO CA   44410
SAFEWAY STORE 00017947 SUNNYVALE      CA   44406
SAMSCLUB #6620     SUNNYVALE      CA44629
SIX FLAGS DISCOVERY KI 07076444000  CA    44492
SIX FLAGS DISCOVERY KI VALLEJO     CA   44638
SKECHERS-USA #119     SAN FRANCISCO  CA  44266
THAO FASHION MUSIC CTR SAN FRANCISCO   CA 44791
TOGOS BASKIN SUNNYVALE   SUNNYVALE      CA 44094
TRICKS GYMNASTICS DANC 916-3510024  CA 44284
henry@linux-1fsw:~/myapp/hadoop-1.0.3> hadoop fs -cat out1e/part-r-00001
76 10115095        SUNNYVALE      CA   44990
Chinese Gourmet Expres CUPERTINO CA   44577
DOLRTREE 1228 00012286 SUNNYVALE      CA   44260
GROCERY OUTLET OF FO   SUNNYVALE      CA 44313
IDEAL CUTS        SUNNYVALE      CA44420
KOHLS #0663        SUNNYVALE      CA   44502
KP INTERNATIONAL MARKE MILPITAS CA  44138
MARSHALLS # 821     SUNNYVALE      CA44491
MEG*LEGOLANDCALIFORNIA 760-918-5346 CA   44445
ROSS STORE #483     SUNNYVALE      CA 44690
RUE21 # 384 SUNNYVALE    SUNNYVALE      CA   44319
S F SUPERMARKET     SAN FRANCISCO  CA   44532
SAVEMART 607 SUNNYVALE   SUNNYVALE      CA 44281
TARGET     00010983 SUNNYVALE      CA44805
TOYS R US #5808   QPS CUPERTINO CA   44288
TRU HOLIDAY EXPRESSQPS SUNNYVALE      CA   44356
WAL-MART #1760     SUNNYVALE      CA   44187
henry@linux-1fsw:~/myapp/hadoop-1.0.3>
```

5.10 COMBINER

Very surprisingly, Hadoop does not have a class or interface named *Combiner*. Instead, the user has two choices:

- Using the same Reducer class as the Combiner when applicable. For example, if the function of the Reducer is to find the max value for a given key, then the Combiner can be applied to each map output so that the number of values corresponding to a key can be reduced to one, thus avoiding sending all values across the network to one or more reducers.

■ Creating a custom combiner to combine the intermediate output results from map tasks with a similar reduce function but not exactly the same as the final reducer function.

The purpose of using a combiner class is to pre-process map task intermediate output results without having to send all of them to reducers across a network. Therefore, creating a combiner for a MapReduce job is purely performance-driven. Next, we use two examples to help illustrate how a combiner can help cut the volume of data that would have to be sent across a network to reducers otherwise.

Let's take a look at how to use a combiner to help reduce the map output results before they are sent to the reducers. Essentially, you can consider a combiner a *local reducer*. It's interesting to note that you can just add one line in the driver program to invoke a combiner. Listing 5.18 shows how this is done in the driver `SpendingPattern1f.java`. Note the sequence of Mapper → Combiner → Partitioner → Reducer as shown below:

```
job.setMapperClass(SpendingPatternMapper1d.class);
job.setCombinerClass(SpendingPatternReducer1d.class);
job.setPartitionerClass(StorePartitioner.class);
job.setReducerClass(SpendingPatternReducer1d.class);
```

To see how the mapper, the combiner, the partitioner and the reducer work together with this example, a test run was carried out on the same Linux cluster with the following command:

```
$ hadoop jar spending-patterns.jar SpendingPattern1f in0/credit_card_tx_0_out_kv.txt out1f
```

The output is presented in Listing 5.19. It is seen that:

■ The run took 38 seconds end-to-end.

■ Partition 0 contains all four transactions at MCDONALD'S and all two transaction at SIX FLAGS.

More importantly, we now see the following counters from the counter:

```
12/09/21 22:44:17 INFO mapred.JobClient:    Combine input records=1955776
12/09/21 22:44:17 INFO mapred.JobClient:    SPLIT_RAW_BYTES=276
12/09/21 22:44:17 INFO mapred.JobClient:    Reduce input records=88
12/09/21 22:44:17 INFO mapred.JobClient:    Reduce input groups=44
12/09/21 22:44:17 INFO mapred.JobClient:    Combine output records=484
```

With the preceding example run without the combiner as shown in Listing 5.17, these three counters were 0, 1955380, and 0, respectively. The reduce input records had been reduced from nearly 2M to 88 after the combiner was applied, which was what we expected from the combiner.

To demonstrate the pure effect out of the combiner, we copied the driver `SpendingPattern1f.java` to a new class of `SpendingPattern1g.java` as shown in Listing 5.20, removed the `StorePartitioner`, and ran the same example again. The output is presented in Listing 5.21. It is seen that the total execution time was 39 seconds, which was essentially the same as the preceding run with the Partitioner included (actually I was expecting less execution time, but it did not happen). Of course, after excluding the `StorePartitioner`, the McDonald and Six Flag transactions went to separate reducers.

This wraps up our discussion on Combiner and also this chapter on basic MapReduce programming. In the next chapter, we introduce some more advanced MapReduce programming features.

Listing 5.18 The Combiner example: the driver (#1)

```
import org.apache.hadoop.fs.Path;
import org.apache.hadoop.io.IntWritable;
import org.apache.hadoop.io.Text;
import org.apache.hadoop.io.BytesWritable;
import org.apache.hadoop.mapreduce.Job;
import org.apache.hadoop.mapreduce.lib.input.FileInputFormat;
import org.apache.hadoop.mapreduce.lib.input.KeyValueTextInputFormat;
import org.apache.hadoop.mapreduce.lib.output.FileOutputFormat;
import org.apache.hadoop.mapreduce.lib.output.TextOutputFormat;

import org.apache.hadoop.conf.Configured;
import org.apache.hadoop.util.Tool;
import org.apache.hadoop.util.ToolRunner;
import org.apache.hadoop.util.GenericOptionsParser;
import org.apache.hadoop.conf.*;

public class SpendingPattern1f extends Configured implements Tool {

    @Override
    public int run(String[] args) throws Exception {
        Configuration conf = new Configuration();
        String remainingArgs[] = new GenericOptionsParser(conf,
            args).getRemainingArgs();
        Job job = JobInit.init (this, getConf (), args);
        if (job == null) {
            return -1;
        }

        job.setJobName("Spending Pattern");
        job.setInputFormatClass(KeyValueTextInputFormat.class);
        job.setOutputFormatClass(TextOutputFormat.class);

        job.setMapperClass(SpendingPatternMapper1d.class);
        job.setCombinerClass(SpendingPatternReducer1d.class);
        job.setPartitionerClass(StorePartitioner.class);
```

```
        job.setReducerClass(SpendingPatternReducer1d.class);

        job.setOutputKeyClass(Text.class);
        job.setOutputValueClass(IntWritable.class);
        return job.waitForCompletion(true) ? 0 : 1;
    }

    public static void main(String[] args) throws Exception {
        int exitCode = ToolRunner.run(new SpendingPattern1f(), args);
        System.exit(exitCode);
    }
}
```

Listing 5.19 A test run with both custom StorePartitioner and Combiner applied.

```
henry@linux-1fsw:~/myapp/hadoop-1.0.3> hadoop jar spending-patterns.jar SpendingPattern1f
in0/credit_card_tx_0_out_kv.txt out1f
12/09/21 22:43:39 INFO input.FileInputFormat: Total input paths to process : 1
12/09/21 22:43:39 INFO util.NativeCodeLoader: Loaded the native-hadoop library
12/09/21 22:43:39 WARN snappy.LoadSnappy: Snappy native library not loaded
12/09/21 22:43:39 INFO mapred.JobClient: Running job: job_201209212204_0005
12/09/21 22:43:40 INFO mapred.JobClient:  map 0% reduce 0%
12/09/21 22:43:57 INFO mapred.JobClient:  map 45% reduce 0%
12/09/21 22:43:58 INFO mapred.JobClient:  map 95% reduce 0%
12/09/21 22:44:00 INFO mapred.JobClient:  map 100% reduce 0%
12/09/21 22:44:10 INFO mapred.JobClient:  map 100% reduce 50%
12/09/21 22:44:12 INFO mapred.JobClient:  map 100% reduce 100%
12/09/21 22:44:17 INFO mapred.JobClient: Job complete: job_201209212204_0005
12/09/21 22:44:17 INFO mapred.JobClient: Counters: 29
12/09/21 22:44:17 INFO mapred.JobClient:  Job Counters
12/09/21 22:44:17 INFO mapred.JobClient:    Launched reduce tasks=2
12/09/21 22:44:17 INFO mapred.JobClient:    SLOTS_MILLIS_MAPS=25661
12/09/21 22:44:17 INFO mapred.JobClient:    Launched map tasks=2
12/09/21 22:44:17 INFO mapred.JobClient:    Data-local map tasks=2
12/09/21 22:44:17 INFO mapred.JobClient:    SLOTS_MILLIS_REDUCES=20681
12/09/21 22:44:17 INFO mapred.JobClient:  File Output Format Counters
12/09/21 22:44:17 INFO mapred.JobClient:    Bytes Written=2094
12/09/21 22:44:17 INFO mapred.JobClient:  FileSystemCounters
12/09/21 22:44:17 INFO mapred.JobClient:    FILE_BYTES_READ=30534
12/09/21 22:44:17 INFO mapred.JobClient:    HDFS_BYTES_READ=93291334
12/09/21 22:44:17 INFO mapred.JobClient:    FILE_BYTES_WRITTEN=115220
12/09/21 22:44:17 INFO mapred.JobClient:    HDFS_BYTES_WRITTEN=2094
12/09/21 22:44:17 INFO mapred.JobClient:  File Input Format Counters
12/09/21 22:44:17 INFO mapred.JobClient:    Bytes Read=93291058
12/09/21 22:44:17 INFO mapred.JobClient:  Map-Reduce Framework
12/09/21 22:44:17 INFO mapred.JobClient:    Map output materialized bytes=4212
12/09/21 22:44:17 INFO mapred.JobClient:    Map input records=2000000
```

```
12/09/21 22:44:17 INFO mapred.JobClient:    Reduce shuffle bytes=4212
12/09/21 22:44:17 INFO mapred.JobClient:    Spilled Records=572
12/09/21 22:44:17 INFO mapred.JobClient:    Map output bytes=89147932
12/09/21 22:44:17 INFO mapred.JobClient:    CPU time spent (ms)=18690
12/09/21 22:44:17 INFO mapred.JobClient:    Total committed heap usage (bytes)=415436800
12/09/21 22:44:17 INFO mapred.JobClient:    Combine input records=1955776
12/09/21 22:44:17 INFO mapred.JobClient:    SPLIT_RAW_BYTES=276
12/09/21 22:44:17 INFO mapred.JobClient:    Reduce input records=88
12/09/21 22:44:17 INFO mapred.JobClient:    Reduce input groups=44
12/09/21 22:44:17 INFO mapred.JobClient:    Combine output records=484
12/09/21 22:44:17 INFO mapred.JobClient:    Physical memory (bytes) snapshot=493690880
12/09/21 22:44:17 INFO mapred.JobClient:    Reduce output records=44
12/09/21 22:44:17 INFO mapred.JobClient:    Virtual memory (bytes) snapshot=1439191040
12/09/21 22:44:17 INFO mapred.JobClient:    Map output records=1955380
henry@linux-1fsw:~/myapp/hadoop-1.0.3> hadoop fs -cat out1f/part-r-00000
76CR5754SUNNYVALE10080067 SUNNYVALE    CA    44637
......
MACY'S EAST #408    MOUNTAIN VIEW CA    44720
MCDONALD'S F20253    SUNNYVALE    CA  44382
MCDONALD'S F26393    SUNNYVALE    CA  44118
MCDONALD'S F33506    MOUNTAIN VIEW CA    44631
MCDONALD'S F5447    SUNNYVALE    CA  44508
MEMBERSHIP FEE AUG 12-JUL 13  44527
PETSMART INC 54    SUNNYVALE    CA 44522
PRETZEL TIME SUNRISE  CUPERTINO CA   44410
SAFEWAY STORE 00017947 SUNNYVALE    CA    44406
SAMSCLUB #6620    SUNNYVALE    CA44629
SIX FLAGS DISCOVERY KI 07076444000  CA    44492
SIX FLAGS DISCOVERY KI VALLEJO    CA  44638
SKECHERS-USA #119    SAN FRANCISCO  CA 44266
THAO FASHION MUSIC CTR SAN FRANCISCO   CA 44791
TOGOS BASKIN SUNNYVALE   SUNNYVALE    CA 44094
TRICKS GYMNASTICS DANC 916-3510024  CA 44284
henry@linux-1fsw:~/myapp/hadoop-1.0.3> hadoop fs -cat out1f/part-r-00001
76 10115095    SUNNYVALE    CA    44990
Chinese Gourmet Expres CUPERTINO CA   44577
......
WAL-MART #1760    SUNNYVALE    CA    44187
henry@linux-1fsw:~/myapp/hadoop-1.0.3>
```

Listing 5.20 The Combiner example: the driver (#2)

```java
import org.apache.hadoop.fs.Path;
import org.apache.hadoop.io.IntWritable;
import org.apache.hadoop.io.Text;
import org.apache.hadoop.io.BytesWritable;
import org.apache.hadoop.mapreduce.Job;
```

```java
import org.apache.hadoop.mapreduce.lib.input.FileInputFormat;
import org.apache.hadoop.mapreduce.lib.input.KeyValueTextInputFormat;
import org.apache.hadoop.mapreduce.lib.output.FileOutputFormat;
import org.apache.hadoop.mapreduce.lib.output.TextOutputFormat;

import org.apache.hadoop.conf.Configured;
import org.apache.hadoop.util.Tool;
import org.apache.hadoop.util.ToolRunner;
import org.apache.hadoop.util.GenericOptionsParser;
import org.apache.hadoop.conf.*;

public class SpendingPattern1g extends Configured implements Tool {

    @Override
    public int run(String[] args) throws Exception {
        Configuration conf = new Configuration();
        String remainingArgs[] = new GenericOptionsParser(conf, args).getRemainingArgs();
        Job job = JobInit.init (this, getConf (), args);
        if (job == null) {
            return -1;
        }

        job.setJobName("Spending Pattern");
        job.setInputFormatClass(KeyValueTextInputFormat.class);
        job.setOutputFormatClass(TextOutputFormat.class);

        job.setMapperClass(SpendingPatternMapper1d.class);
        job.setCombinerClass(SpendingPatternReducer1d.class);
        job.setReducerClass(SpendingPatternReducer1d.class);

        job.setOutputKeyClass(Text.class);
        job.setOutputValueClass(IntWritable.class);
        return job.waitForCompletion(true) ? 0 : 1;
    }

    public static void main(String[] args) throws Exception {
        int exitCode = ToolRunner.run(new SpendingPattern1g(), args);
        System.exit(exitCode);
    }
}
```

Listing 5.21 A test run with Combiner applied only.

```
henry@linux-1fsw:~/myapp/hadoop-1.0.3> hadoop jar spending-patterns.jar SpendingPattern1g
in0/credit_card_tx_0_out_kv.txt out1g
12/09/21 23:55:56 INFO input.FileInputFormat: Total input paths to process : 1
12/09/21 23:55:56 INFO util.NativeCodeLoader: Loaded the native-hadoop library
12/09/21 23:55:56 WARN snappy.LoadSnappy: Snappy native library not loaded
12/09/21 23:55:56 INFO mapred.JobClient: Running job: job_201209212204_0006
12/09/21 23:55:57 INFO mapred.JobClient:  map 0% reduce 0%
12/09/21 23:56:12 INFO mapred.JobClient:  map 50% reduce 0%
12/09/21 23:56:13 INFO mapred.JobClient:  map 87% reduce 0%
12/09/21 23:56:16 INFO mapred.JobClient:  map 99% reduce 0%
12/09/21 23:56:19 INFO mapred.JobClient:  map 100% reduce 0%
12/09/21 23:56:21 INFO mapred.JobClient:  map 100% reduce 8%
12/09/21 23:56:25 INFO mapred.JobClient:  map 100% reduce 58%
12/09/21 23:56:30 INFO mapred.JobClient:  map 100% reduce 100%
12/09/21 23:56:35 INFO mapred.JobClient: Job complete: job_201209212204_0006
12/09/21 23:56:35 INFO mapred.JobClient: Counters: 29
12/09/21 23:56:35 INFO mapred.JobClient:   Job Counters
12/09/21 23:56:35 INFO mapred.JobClient:     Launched reduce tasks=2
12/09/21 23:56:35 INFO mapred.JobClient:     SLOTS_MILLIS_MAPS=26161
12/09/21 23:56:35 INFO mapred.JobClient:     Launched map tasks=2
12/09/21 23:56:35 INFO mapred.JobClient:     Data-local map tasks=2
12/09/21 23:56:35 INFO mapred.JobClient:     SLOTS_MILLIS_REDUCES=27709
12/09/21 23:56:35 INFO mapred.JobClient:   File Output Format Counters
12/09/21 23:56:35 INFO mapred.JobClient:     Bytes Written=2094
12/09/21 23:56:35 INFO mapred.JobClient:   FileSystemCounters
12/09/21 23:56:35 INFO mapred.JobClient:     FILE_BYTES_READ=33855
12/09/21 23:56:35 INFO mapred.JobClient:     HDFS_BYTES_READ=93291334
12/09/21 23:56:35 INFO mapred.JobClient:     FILE_BYTES_WRITTEN=114848
12/09/21 23:56:35 INFO mapred.JobClient:     HDFS_BYTES_WRITTEN=2094
12/09/21 23:56:35 INFO mapred.JobClient:   File Input Format Counters
12/09/21 23:56:35 INFO mapred.JobClient:     Bytes Read=93291058
12/09/21 23:56:35 INFO mapred.JobClient:   Map-Reduce Framework
12/09/21 23:56:35 INFO mapred.JobClient:     Map output materialized bytes=4212
12/09/21 23:56:35 INFO mapred.JobClient:     Map input records=2000000
12/09/21 23:56:35 INFO mapred.JobClient:     Reduce shuffle bytes=3295
12/09/21 23:56:35 INFO mapred.JobClient:     Spilled Records=572
12/09/21 23:56:35 INFO mapred.JobClient:     Map output bytes=89147932
12/09/21 23:56:35 INFO mapred.JobClient:     CPU time spent (ms)=17500
12/09/21 23:56:35 INFO mapred.JobClient:     Total committed heap usage (bytes)=410980352
12/09/21 23:56:35 INFO mapred.JobClient:     Combine input records=1955776
12/09/21 23:56:35 INFO mapred.JobClient:     SPLIT_RAW_BYTES=276
12/09/21 23:56:35 INFO mapred.JobClient:     Reduce input records=88
12/09/21 23:56:35 INFO mapred.JobClient:     Reduce input groups=44
12/09/21 23:56:35 INFO mapred.JobClient:     Combine output records=484
12/09/21 23:56:35 INFO mapred.JobClient:     Physical memory (bytes) snapshot=481034240
12/09/21 23:56:35 INFO mapred.JobClient:     Reduce output records=44
12/09/21 23:56:35 INFO mapred.JobClient:     Virtual memory (bytes) snapshot=1436622848
12/09/21 23:56:35 INFO mapred.JobClient:     Map output records=1955380
```

```
henry@linux-1fsw:~/myapp/hadoop-1.0.3> hadoop fs -cat out1g/part-r-00000
76CR5754SUNNYVALE10080067 SUNNYVALE     CA  44637
BABIES R US #6447 QPS SUNNYVALE     CA  44272
......
LORI'S GIFTS STORE#233 SAN FRANCISCO  CA44249
MCDONALD'S F20253     SUNNYVALE     CA 44382
MCDONALD'S F33506     MOUNTAIN VIEW CA    44631
MCDONALD'S F5447      SUNNYVALE     CA  44508
PRETZEL TIME SUNRISE  CUPERTINO CA    44410
RUE21 # 384 SUNNYVALE     SUNNYVALE     CA   44319
SIX FLAGS DISCOVERY KI 07076444000  CA    44492
TARGET     00010983 SUNNYVALE     CA44805
WAL-MART #1760     SUNNYVALE     CA    44187
henry@linux-1fsw:~/myapp/hadoop-1.0.3> hadoop fs -cat out1g/part-r-00001
76 10115095          SUNNYVALE     CA    44990
.......
MARSHALLS # 821     SUNNYVALE     CA44491
MCDONALD'S F26393     SUNNYVALE     CA 44118
MEG*LEGOLANDCALIFORNIA 760-918-5346  CA    44445
......
SAVEMART 607 SUNNYVALE   SUNNYVALE     CA 44281
SIX FLAGS DISCOVERY KI VALLEJO     CA   44638
SKECHERS-USA #119     SAN FRANCISCO  CA 44266
......
henry@linux-1fsw:~/myapp/hadoop-1.0.3>
```

5.11 SUMMARY

In this chapter, we focused on the programming aspect of the Hadoop MapReduce framework. We started with reviewing Java data types and a few other relevant concepts such as generics, bounded types, wildcard arguments, and streams, which laid foundation for introducing Hadoop data types. We then introduced most of the classes that almost every MapReduce program needs, for example, InputFormat, OutputFormat, OutputCommitter, TaskAttemptContext, Mapper, Reducer, Partitioner, and Combiner. Whenever possible, we used concrete examples to demonstrate how to use some of these classes in developing MapReduce programs. This chapter is also helpful for understanding the subjects covered in all preceding chapters.

RECOMMENDED READING

Refer to the following link for the API hierarchy of the package *org.apache.hadoop.mapreduce*:

http://hadoop.apache.org/docs/r1.0.3/api/org/apache/hadoop/mapreduce/package-tree.html

EXERCISES

5.1 Explain why Hadoop needs its own data types.

5.2 Is an input split a logical or physical split? What's the difference conceptually between an input split and a block?

5.3 What's the major difference between the TextInputFormat class and the SequenceFileInputFormat class? Which one is more efficient?

5.4 Why does Hadoop need an OutputCommitter class?

5.5 What is a Hadoop task attempt? What is it based on?

5.6 What does a SecondarySort.Reducer do? Use an example to help explain how to implement it.

5.7 A MapReduce project: devise and implement a MapReduce program that uses a Mapper, a Reducer, a Partitioner and a Combiner.

6 Advanced MapReduce Programming

In this chapter, we continue covering Hadoop MapReduce programming with several more advanced subjects, such as:

- Chaining mappers with a reducer
- Compression
- MultipleInputs
- MultipleOutputs
- Counters
- Passing parameters/metadata to MapReduce programs

Let's start with chaining mappers with a reducer.

6.1 CHAINING MAPPERS WITH A REDUCER

The Hadoop MapReduce framework provides a mechanism for chaining multiple mappers with one reducer into one job. This mechanism can be expressed in the form of

[Map+ | Reduce | MAP*],

namely, one set of mappers can be invoked in sequence to preprocess the data, and after running the reduce task, another set of mappers can be invoked in sequence to post-process the data.

This chaining mechanism can potentially help avoid some intermediate disk I/O and network I/O operations, and thus improving the execution efficiency of MapReduce programs. In addition, all chained mappers and the associated reducer would be executed in one JVM, which would further help yield better performance than they were executed in separate JVMs of separate jobs.

Next, let's take a look at how mappers can be chained together with the ChainMapper API. We will not only introduce the ChainMapper API, but also provide a working example to demonstrate how multiple mappers can be chained together.

6.1.1 ChainMapper API

The ChainMapper class allows multiple Mapper classes to be chained into a single map task. Each Mapper class acts as an independent, reusable mapper. However, it is required to have the output of the nth Mapper used as the input of the $(n+1)^{th}$ Mapper. Since there is no internal conversion for the types of input/output keys and values among the mappers and the reducer, it is the programmer's responsibility to make sure the key and value types are valid between any two adjacent mappers, or between a mapper and the ensuing reducer and between the reducer and the ensuing mapper.

Contained in the package of `org.apache.hadoop.mapred.lib`, the `ChainMapper` class extends `Object` and `implements` the `Mapper` interface:

```
package org.apache.hadoop.mapred.lib;
...
public class ChainMapper extends Object implements Mapper {...}
```

It has a default constructor of

```
ChainMapper ()
```

It has four methods: `addMapper`, `configure`, `map`, and `close` as introduced next.

- **addMapper** (you might want to review the use of the Java wildcard argument <?> covered in §5.1.5):

  public static <K1,V1,K2,V2> void **addMapper**(JobConf **job**,
                       Class<? extends **Mapper**<K1,V1,K2,V2>> klass,
                       Class<? extends K1> **inputKeyClass**,
                       Class<? extends V1> **inputValueClass**,
                       Class<? extends K2> **outputKeyClass**,
                       Class<? extends V2> **outputValueClass**,
                       boolean **byValue**,
                       JobConf **mapperConf**)

  Parameters:
  `job` - A JobConf object for the job to add the Mapper class.
  `klass` - the Mapper class to add.
  `inputKeyClass` - mapper input key class.
  `inputValueClass` - mapper input value class.
  `outputKeyClass` - mapper output key class.
  `outputValueClass` - mapper output value class.
  `byValue` - indicates if key/values should be passed by value to the next Mapper in the chain, if any.
  `mapperConf` - a JobConf object for the Mapper class. It is recommended to use a JobConf object constrcuted with the constructor `JobConf(boolean loadDefaults)` with `loadDefaults` set to `false`.

This method adds a Mapper class to the chain defined within a `JobConf` object named `job`. There are a few things to note here:

1) Precedence: Since there are two JobConf objects (one for the job and one for the mapper), the mapper's configuration settings take higher precedence than the job's, or in other words, the mapper's configuration settings override the job's configuration settings.

2) By value or by reference: This parameter of byValue has something to do with whether the key-value pairs are allowed to be modified by its subsequent mapper. Setting byValue to true is safer and recommended in general. Setting byValue to false means that the subsequent mapper can reference the key-value pairs by reference or in memory in the same JVM, which may run faster but may result in undesirable effects.

■ **configure:**

```
public void configure (JobConf job)
Parameters:
job - the configuration
```

This method is used to configure the ChainMapper and all the Mappers in the chain.

■ **map:**

```
public void map(Object key,
                Object value,
                OutputCollector output,
                Reporter reporter) throws IOException
Parameters:
key - the input key.
value - the input value.
output - collects mapped keys and values.
reporter - reports progress.
```

This method performs the usual mapping task.

■ **close**:

```
public void close() throws IOException
```

This method closes the ChainMapper and all the Mappers in the chain.

Next, let us introduce the ChainReducer class.

6.1.2 ChainReducer API

The ChainReducer class allows multiple Mapper classes to be chained into a logically single Map task after the reducer. Each Mapper class acts as an independent, reusable mapper. However, similar to the chained mappers prior to the reducer, it is required to have the output of the nth Mapper used as the input of the $(n+1)^{th}$ Mapper. Since there is no internal conversion for the types of input/output keys and values among the mappers and the reducer, it is the programmer's responsibility to make sure the key and value types are valid between the reducer and the ensuing mapper, and between any two adjacent mappers after the reducer.

Contained in the package of org.apache.hadoop.mapred.lib, the ChainReducer class extends Object and implements the Reducer interface:

```
package org.apache.hadoop.mapred.lib;
```

```
...
public class ChainReducer extends Object implements Reducer {...}
```

It has a default constructor of

```
ChainReducer ()
```

It has five methods: setReducer, reduce, addMapper, configure, and close. They are introduced next.

- **setReducer**:

```
public static <k1, V1, K2, V2> void setReducer (JobConf job,
                Class<? extends Reducer<K1,V1,K2,V2>> klass,
                Class<? extends K1> inputKeyClass,
                Class<? extends V1> inputValueClass,
                Class<? extends K2> outputKeyClass,
                Class<? extends V2> outputValueClass,
                boolean byValue,
                JobConf reducerConf)
```

Parameters:

job - job's JobConf to add the Reducer class.

klass - the Reducer class to add.

inputKeyClass - reducer input key class.

inputValueClass - reducer input value class.

outputKeyClass - reducer output key class.

outputValueClass - reducer output value class.

byValue - indicates if key/values should be passed by value to the next Mapper in the chain, if any. In general, it should be set to true unless it is provable that setting it to false could result in significant performance gain.

reducerConf - a JobConf object for the Reducer class. It is recommended to set loadDefaults to false for the JobConf (boolean) constructor.

- **addMapper** (you might want to review the use of the Java wildcard argument <?> covered in Section 5.1.5):

```
public static <K1,V1,K2,V2> void addMapper(JobConf job,
                Class<? extends Mapper<K1,V1,K2,V2>> klass,
                Class<? extends K1> inputKeyClass,
                Class<? extends V1> inputValueClass,
                Class<? extends K2> outputKeyClass,
                Class<? extends V2> outputValueClass,
                boolean byValue,
                JobConf mapperConf)
```

Parameters:

    job - A JobConf object for the job to add the Mapper class.

klass - the Mapper class to add.
inputKeyClass - mapper input key class.
inputValueClass - mapper input value class.
outputKeyClass - mapper output key class.
outputValueClass - mapper output value class.
byValue - indicates if key/values should be passed by value to the next Mapper in the chain, if any.
mapperConf - a JobConf object for the Mapper class. It is recommended to use a JobConf object constrcuted with the constructor JobConf(boolean loadDefaults) with loadDefaults set to false.

This method adds a Mapper class after the Reducer to the chain. All previous discussions associated with the ChainMapper class apply here.

- **configure**:

    public void configure (JobConf job)

    Parameters:

        job - the configuration

This method is used to configure the ChainReducer and all the Mappers after the reducer in the chain.

- **reduce**:

    public void reduce   (Object key,
                           Iterator value,
                           OutputCollector output,
                           Reporter reporter) throws IOException

    Parameters:

                    key - the input key.
                    values - the input values from the prior mapper to reduce.
                    output - collects keys and reduced values.
                    reporter - reports progress.

This method chains the reduce (...) method of the Reducer with the map (...) methods of the Mappers in the chain.

- **close**:

    public void close() throws IOException {...}

This method closes the ChainReducer and all the Mappers in the chain.

Next, let us use an example to demonstrate how the ChainMapper class and the ChainReducer class work collaboratively to constitute a chained MapReduce program.

6.1.3 A Complete ChainMapper/ChainReducer Example

Let us re-use some of the Mapper and Reducer classes we presented previously to demonstrate how they can be chained together to form a chained MapReduce program. We are interested more in showing how to chain multiple mappers and the reducer together programmatically using the ChainMapper and ChainReducer APIs than in the details of the subject matter context, which is application dependent. In addition, we omit chaining mappers after the reducer, as the programmatic logic remains the same whether we chain mappers prior to or after the reducer.

Recall from our first MapReduce program presented in Chapter 1 that we once demonstrated how to construct a MapReduce program to find the maximum amount spent at each store with a large dataset of credit card transactions over a given period. The input data file is composed of credit card transactions with each transaction record formatted in the form of {*transaction date, description, amount*}. The *description* field contains the name and location of a store (physical or online). The Mapper (Listing 1.9) program transforms each record into a key-value pair with the description field mapped to the *key* parameter and the amount field mapped to the *value* parameter. The Reducer (Listing 1.10) takes the key-value pairs from the Mapper and reduces them to the max amount spent at a store for all stores.

Then in Chapter 5, we illustrated how a Mapper can take the key-value pairs from an input text file directly with a KeyValueTextInputFormat example (see Listing 5.5 for the Mapper program). In order to make this example work, we actually used a standalone program named MapIncrease2.java to make up a specified number of records that contain description/amount fields only to be mapped to key-value pairs. This seems to be a proper context for our chained MapReduce program, as we can first construct a mapper that maps a record with those three fields of {*transaction date, description, amount*} into a key-value pair of {*description-amount*}, which can then be used as the input for the second mapper that takes key-value pairs as input. The subsequent reducer would work exactly as it did with either of the previous two examples.

Now it's clear what we want the chained MapReduce program to do from the functional point of view. It appears that all we need to do is to make sure the output/input parameters match among the two mappers and the reducer. However, it looks like as of this writing, the ChainMapper and ChainReducer APIs have not been updated from 0.22 to 1.x, so we have to use Mappers and Reducers coded in 0.22 API. This can be verified with the required Mapper class in the addMapper method of both ChainMapper and ChainReducer that the Mapper must extend the MapReduceBase class and implement the Mapper interface, both of which are contained in the package of org.apache.hadoop.mapred, as is shown in Listing 6.1 (a). Otherwise, an error would occur during the compiling phase if the Mapper extends the Mapper class contained in the package of org.apache.hadoop.mapreduce.Mapper as we have done with all Mappers so far. Because of this incompatibility, we have to code the chained mappers, the reducer and the driver all in 0.22 APIs. Actually, according to Apache website http://hadoop.apache.org/releases.html, the feature of ChainMapper/ChainReducer was introduced in version 0.22.0, which was released on Dec. 10, 2011. It does not seem to have been updated to use the newer 1.x MapReduce API. In the future, I would definitely update the book to use newer ChainMapper and ChainReducer API, but for now, let's just take it as an opportunity to learn how 0.22 Mapper and Reducer API works, along with how to code the driver with the 0.22 API.

The two mappers to be chained are displayed in Listings 6.1 (a) and (b), named
`SpendingPatternMapper1b.java` and `SpendingPatternMapper1c.java`, respectively. Note
how the Mapper class is defined using the 0.22 API, for example, with the first Mapper as follows:

> public class SpendingPatternMapper1b **extends** MapReduceBase
> **implements** Mapper <...> {...}

If this Mapper were written in 1.x APIs, it would have been

> public class SpendingPatternMapper1b **extends** Mapper <...> {...}

This subtle difference applies to the reducer class shown in Listing 6.1 (c) and named
`SpendingPatternReducer1a.java` as well. In addition, the driver shown in Listing 6.1 (d) and
named `SpendingPattern1h.java` uses JobConf (0.22 API approach) rather than Job (1.x
approach) to configure the job. Listing 6.1 (e) shows the console output and final reduced data
from running this chained MapReduce program.

Let us examine these programs further to understand more about how they are coded. In addition
to how the Mapper and Reducer classes are defined, note the parameterized types of the two
mappers and the reducer as summarized in Table 6.1. The input key-value pair is <LongWritable,
Text> for Mapper0, whereas all the input/output key-value pairs afterwards are <Text,
FloatWritable>. This kind of type matching is required in order for a chained MapReduce program
to work.

Finally, let's take a look at how the `byValue` parameter was specified for the two mappers and the
reducer class. We once explained in the previous sections that this parameter determines whether
the intermediate key-value pairs are referenced in memory (yes if set to `false`). In non-chained
MapReduce programs, the equivalent setting of this parameter is *true*, because the intermediate
key-value pairs need to be serialized and written to disk. With chained mappers and the reducer,
those intermediate key-value pairs could be potentially referenced in memory without being
serialized and written to disk, thus saving some execution time and improving the overall
performance. In principle, this parameter can be set to false except in the first mapper and the
reducer. In other words, it can be set to *false* for all subsequent mappers of the chained mappers.
In order to prove this is true, we copied the driver program `SpendingPattern1h.java` to
`SpendingPattern1i.java` as shown in Listing 6.2 (a) with the `byValue` parameter set to false for
the second mapper. We then ran this modified job. The console output results are displayed in
Listing 6.2 (b). By comparing Listings 6.1 (e) and 6.2 (b), we see that the difference is between 29
seconds and 28 seconds for the two cases that only one second was saved, which is insignificant
for this example.

Table 6.2 following the end of Listing 6.2 (b) summarizes some of the differences between the old
0.22 and newer 1.x APIs associated with writing the Mapper, Reducer and MapReduce driver
classes for this example.

Listing 6.1(a) The ChainMapper example: Mapper0

```
import java.io.IOException;
import java.util.StringTokenizer;
```

```java
import org.apache.hadoop.io.FloatWritable;
import org.apache.hadoop.io.LongWritable;
import org.apache.hadoop.io.Text;

import org.apache.hadoop.mapred.Mapper;
import org.apache.hadoop.mapred.MapReduceBase;
import org.apache.hadoop.mapred.OutputCollector;
import org.apache.hadoop.mapred.Reporter;
public class SpendingPatternMapper1b extends MapReduceBase
 implements Mapper<LongWritable, Text, Text, FloatWritable> {

 @Override
 public void map(LongWritable key, Text value, OutputCollector <Text, FloatWritable>
output, Reporter reporter)
   throws IOException {

  String line = value.toString();
  if (!line.contains ("PAYMENT")) {
  StringTokenizer st = new StringTokenizer (line, "\t");
  String tranxDate = st.nextToken();
  String description = st.nextToken();
  float amount = Float.parseFloat(st.nextToken());
  output.collect(new Text(description), new FloatWritable(amount));
  }
 }
}
```

Listing 6.1 (b) The ChainMapper example: Mapper1

```java
import java.io.IOException;
import java.util.StringTokenizer;
import org.apache.hadoop.io.FloatWritable;
import org.apache.hadoop.io.LongWritable;
import org.apache.hadoop.io.Text;

import org.apache.hadoop.mapred.Mapper;
import org.apache.hadoop.mapred.MapReduceBase;
import org.apache.hadoop.mapred.OutputCollector;
import org.apache.hadoop.mapred.Reporter;

public class SpendingPatternMapper1c extends MapReduceBase implements Mapper<Text,
FloatWritable, Text, FloatWritable> {

 @Override
```

```
    public void map(Text key, FloatWritable value, OutputCollector <Text, FloatWritable>
output, Reporter reporter) throws IOException{

        if (!key.toString().contains("PAYMENT")) {
            float amount = Float.parseFloat(value.toString());
            output.collect (key, new FloatWritable(amount));
        }
    }
}
```

Listing 6.1 (c) The ChainMapper example: the Reducer

```
import java.io.IOException;
import java.util.Iterator;

import org.apache.hadoop.io.IntWritable;
import org.apache.hadoop.io.FloatWritable;
import org.apache.hadoop.io.Text;
import org.apache.hadoop.mapred.Reducer;
import org.apache.hadoop.mapred.MapReduceBase;
import org.apache.hadoop.mapred.OutputCollector;
import org.apache.hadoop.mapred.Reporter;

public class SpendingPatternReducer1a extends MapReduceBase implements
        Reducer<Text, FloatWritable, Text, FloatWritable> {

    @Override
    public void reduce(Text key, Iterator<FloatWritable> values,
            OutputCollector <Text, FloatWritable> output, Reporter reporter) throws
IOException {

        float maxValue = Float.MIN_VALUE;
        while (values.hasNext()) {
            maxValue = Math.max(maxValue, values.next().get());
        }
        output.collect(key, new FloatWritable(maxValue));
    }
}
```

Listing 6.1 (d) The ChainMapper example: the driver

```
import org.apache.hadoop.fs.Path;
import org.apache.hadoop.io.LongWritable;
import org.apache.hadoop.io.IntWritable;
```

```java
import org.apache.hadoop.io.FloatWritable;
import org.apache.hadoop.io.Text;
import org.apache.hadoop.io.BytesWritable;
import org.apache.hadoop.mapreduce.Job;
import org.apache.hadoop.mapred.FileInputFormat;
import org.apache.hadoop.mapred.FileOutputFormat;
import org.apache.hadoop.mapred.TextInputFormat;
import org.apache.hadoop.mapred.TextOutputFormat;

import org.apache.hadoop.mapred.JobConf;
import org.apache.hadoop.mapred.JobClient;
import org.apache.hadoop.mapred.lib.ChainMapper;
import org.apache.hadoop.mapred.lib.ChainReducer;

import org.apache.hadoop.conf.Configured;
import org.apache.hadoop.util.Tool;
import org.apache.hadoop.util.ToolRunner;
import org.apache.hadoop.util.GenericOptionsParser;
import org.apache.hadoop.conf.*;

public class SpendingPattern1h {

    public static void main (String[] args) throws Exception {
        Configuration conf = new Configuration();

        String remainingArgs[] = new GenericOptionsParser(conf,
            args).getRemainingArgs();
        if (args.length != 2) {
            System.exit (-1);
        }
        JobConf jobConf = new JobConf(conf);
        jobConf.setJarByClass(SpendingPattern1h.class);
        FileInputFormat.addInputPath(jobConf, new Path(args[0]));
        FileOutputFormat.setOutputPath(jobConf, new Path(args[1]));

        jobConf.setJobName("Spending Pattern ChainMapper");
        jobConf.setInputFormat(TextInputFormat.class);
        jobConf.setOutputFormat(TextOutputFormat.class);

        JobConf map0Conf = new JobConf (false);
        ChainMapper.addMapper(jobConf, SpendingPatternMapper1b.class,
                LongWritable.class, Text.class, Text.class,
                FloatWritable.class, true, map0Conf);
```

```
        JobConf map1Conf = new JobConf (false);
        ChainMapper.addMapper(jobConf, SpendingPatternMapper1c.class,
                Text.class, FloatWritable.class, Text.class,
                FloatWritable.class, true, map1Conf);
        JobConf reduceConf = new JobConf (false);
        ChainReducer.setReducer (jobConf, SpendingPatternReducer1a.class,
                Text.class, FloatWritable.class, Text.class,
                FloatWritable.class,true, reduceConf);
        JobClient.runJob (jobConf);
    }
}
```

Listing 6.1 (e) Console output of the chained MapReduce program

mc815ll:hadoop-1.0.3 henry$ bin/**hadoop jar spending-patterns.jar SpendingPattern1h
in0/credit_card_tx_0_out.txt out60**
12/09/24 23:42:22 WARN util.NativeCodeLoader: Unable to load native-hadoop library for your
platform... using builtin-java classes where applicable
12/09/24 23:42:22 WARN snappy.LoadSnappy: Snappy native library not loaded
12/09/24 23:42:22 INFO mapred.FileInputFormat: Total input paths to process : 1
12/09/24 23:42:23 INFO mapred.JobClient: Running job: job_local_0001
12/09/24 23:42:23 INFO mapred.Task: Using ResourceCalculatorPlugin : null
12/09/24 23:42:23 INFO mapred.MapTask: numReduceTasks: 1
12/09/24 23:42:23 INFO mapred.MapTask: io.sort.mb = 100
12/09/24 23:42:23 INFO mapred.MapTask: data buffer = 79691776/99614720
12/09/24 23:42:23 INFO mapred.MapTask: record buffer = 262144/327680
12/09/24 23:42:24 INFO mapred.JobClient: map 0% reduce 0%
12/09/24 23:42:26 INFO mapred.MapTask: Spilling map output: record full = true
12/09/24 23:42:27 INFO mapred.MapTask: Finished spill 0
12/09/24 23:42:28 INFO mapred.MapTask: Spilling map output: record full = true
12/09/24 23:42:29 INFO mapred.LocalJobRunner: file:/Users/henry/dev/hadoop-
1.0.3/in0/credit_card_tx_0_out.txt:0+33554432
12/09/24 23:42:29 INFO mapred.MapTask: Finished spill 1
12/09/24 23:42:29 INFO mapred.MapTask: Starting flush of map output
12/09/24 23:42:29 INFO mapred.MapTask: Finished spill 2
12/09/24 23:42:29 INFO mapred.Merger: Merging 3 sorted segments
12/09/24 23:42:29 INFO mapred.Merger: Down to the last merge-pass, with 3 segments left of total
size: 27085156 bytes
12/09/24 23:42:30 INFO mapred.JobClient: map 98% reduce 0%
12/09/24 23:42:30 INFO mapred.Task: Task:attempt_local_0001_m_000000_0 is done. And is in the
process of commiting
12/09/24 23:42:32 INFO mapred.LocalJobRunner: file:/Users/henry/dev/hadoop-
1.0.3/in0/credit_card_tx_0_out.txt:0+33554432
12/09/24 23:42:32 INFO mapred.LocalJobRunner: file:/Users/henry/dev/hadoop-
1.0.3/in0/credit_card_tx_0_out.txt:0+33554432
12/09/24 23:42:32 INFO mapred.Task: Task 'attempt_local_0001_m_000000_0' done.
12/09/24 23:42:32 INFO mapred.Task: Using ResourceCalculatorPlugin : null

12/09/24 23:42:32 INFO mapred.MapTask: numReduceTasks: 1
12/09/24 23:42:32 INFO mapred.MapTask: io.sort.mb = 100
12/09/24 23:42:32 INFO mapred.MapTask: data buffer = 79691776/99614720
12/09/24 23:42:32 INFO mapred.MapTask: record buffer = 262144/327680
12/09/24 23:42:33 INFO mapred.JobClient: map 100% reduce 0%
12/09/24 23:42:34 INFO mapred.MapTask: Spilling map output: record full = true
12/09/24 23:42:34 INFO mapred.MapTask: Finished spill 0
12/09/24 23:42:36 INFO mapred.MapTask: Spilling map output: record full = true
12/09/24 23:42:36 INFO mapred.MapTask: Starting flush of map output
12/09/24 23:42:36 INFO mapred.MapTask: Finished spill 1
12/09/24 23:42:36 INFO mapred.MapTask: Finished spill 2
12/09/24 23:42:36 INFO mapred.Merger: Merging 3 sorted segments
12/09/24 23:42:36 INFO mapred.Merger: Down to the last merge-pass, with 3 segments left of total size: 27083677 bytes
12/09/24 23:42:37 INFO mapred.Task: Task:attempt_local_0001_m_000001_0 is done. And is in the process of commiting
12/09/24 23:42:38 INFO mapred.LocalJobRunner: file:/Users/henry/dev/hadoop-1.0.3/in0/credit_card_tx_0_out.txt:33554432+33554432
12/09/24 23:42:38 INFO mapred.LocalJobRunner: file:/Users/henry/dev/hadoop-1.0.3/in0/credit_card_tx_0_out.txt:33554432+33554432
12/09/24 23:42:38 INFO mapred.Task: Task 'attempt_local_0001_m_000001_0' done.
12/09/24 23:42:38 INFO mapred.Task: Using ResourceCalculatorPlugin : null
12/09/24 23:42:38 INFO mapred.MapTask: numReduceTasks: 1
12/09/24 23:42:38 INFO mapred.MapTask: io.sort.mb = 100
12/09/24 23:42:38 INFO mapred.MapTask: data buffer = 79691776/99614720
12/09/24 23:42:38 INFO mapred.MapTask: record buffer = 262144/327680
12/09/24 23:42:40 INFO mapred.MapTask: Spilling map output: record full = true
12/09/24 23:42:40 INFO mapred.MapTask: Finished spill 0
12/09/24 23:42:42 INFO mapred.MapTask: Spilling map output: record full = true
12/09/24 23:42:42 INFO mapred.MapTask: Starting flush of map output
12/09/24 23:42:42 INFO mapred.MapTask: Finished spill 1
12/09/24 23:42:42 INFO mapred.MapTask: Finished spill 2
12/09/24 23:42:42 INFO mapred.Merger: Merging 3 sorted segments
12/09/24 23:42:43 INFO mapred.Merger: Down to the last merge-pass, with 3 segments left of total size: 27086619 bytes
12/09/24 23:42:43 INFO mapred.Task: Task:attempt_local_0001_m_000002_0 is done. And is in the process of commiting
12/09/24 23:42:44 INFO mapred.LocalJobRunner: file:/Users/henry/dev/hadoop-1.0.3/in0/credit_card_tx_0_out.txt:67108864+33554432
12/09/24 23:42:44 INFO mapred.LocalJobRunner: file:/Users/henry/dev/hadoop-1.0.3/in0/credit_card_tx_0_out.txt:67108864+33554432
12/09/24 23:42:44 INFO mapred.Task: Task 'attempt_local_0001_m_000002_0' done.
12/09/24 23:42:44 INFO mapred.Task: Using ResourceCalculatorPlugin : null
12/09/24 23:42:44 INFO mapred.MapTask: numReduceTasks: 1
12/09/24 23:42:44 INFO mapred.MapTask: io.sort.mb = 100
12/09/24 23:42:44 INFO mapred.MapTask: data buffer = 79691776/99614720
12/09/24 23:42:44 INFO mapred.MapTask: record buffer = 262144/327680
12/09/24 23:42:46 INFO mapred.MapTask: Starting flush of map output

12/09/24 23:42:46 INFO mapred.MapTask: Finished spill 0
12/09/24 23:42:46 INFO mapred.Task: Task:attempt_local_0001_m_000003_0 is done. And is in the process of commiting
12/09/24 23:42:47 INFO mapred.LocalJobRunner: file:/Users/henry/dev/hadoop-1.0.3/in0/credit_card_tx_0_out.txt:100663296+14624079
12/09/24 23:42:47 INFO mapred.Task: Task 'attempt_local_0001_m_000003_0' done.
12/09/24 23:42:47 INFO mapred.Task: Using ResourceCalculatorPlugin : null
12/09/24 23:42:47 INFO mapred.Merger: Merging 4 sorted segments
12/09/24 23:42:47 INFO mapred.Merger: Down to the last merge-pass, with 4 segments left of total size: 93059664 bytes
12/09/24 23:42:48 INFO mapred.Task: Task:attempt_local_0001_r_000000_0 is done. And is in the process of commiting
12/09/24 23:42:48 INFO mapred.Task: Task attempt_local_0001_r_000000_0 is allowed to commit now
12/09/24 23:42:48 INFO mapred.FileOutputCommitter: Saved output of task 'attempt_local_0001_r_000000_0' to file:/Users/henry/dev/hadoop-1.0.3/out60
12/09/24 23:42:50 INFO mapred.LocalJobRunner: reduce > reduce
12/09/24 23:42:50 INFO mapred.Task: Task 'attempt_local_0001_r_000000_0' done.
12/09/24 23:42:51 INFO mapred.JobClient: map 100% reduce 100%
12/09/24 23:42:51 INFO mapred.JobClient: Job complete: job_local_0001
12/09/24 23:42:51 INFO mapred.JobClient: Counters: 18
12/09/24 23:42:51 INFO mapred.JobClient: File Input Format Counters
12/09/24 23:42:51 INFO mapred.JobClient: Bytes Read=116233631
12/09/24 23:42:51 INFO mapred.JobClient: File Output Format Counters
12/09/24 23:42:51 INFO mapred.JobClient: Bytes Written=2122
12/09/24 23:42:51 INFO mapred.JobClient: FileSystemCounters
12/09/24 23:42:51 INFO mapred.JobClient: FILE_BYTES_READ=853726772
12/09/24 23:42:51 INFO mapred.JobClient: FILE_BYTES_WRITTEN=674035895
12/09/24 23:42:51 INFO mapred.JobClient: Map-Reduce Framework
12/09/24 23:42:51 INFO mapred.JobClient: Map output materialized bytes=93059680
12/09/24 23:42:51 INFO mapred.JobClient: Map input records=2000000
12/09/24 23:42:51 INFO mapred.JobClient: Reduce shuffle bytes=0
12/09/24 23:42:51 INFO mapred.JobClient: Spilled Records=5618663
12/09/24 23:42:51 INFO mapred.JobClient: Map output bytes=89148518
12/09/24 23:42:51 INFO mapred.JobClient: Total committed heap usage (bytes)=995926016
12/09/24 23:42:51 INFO mapred.JobClient: Map input bytes=115287375
12/09/24 23:42:51 INFO mapred.JobClient: SPLIT_RAW_BYTES=464
12/09/24 23:42:51 INFO mapred.JobClient: Combine input records=0
12/09/24 23:42:51 INFO mapred.JobClient: Reduce input records=1955569
12/09/24 23:42:51 INFO mapred.JobClient: Reduce input groups=44
12/09/24 23:42:51 INFO mapred.JobClient: Combine output records=0
12/09/24 23:42:51 INFO mapred.JobClient: Reduce output records=44
12/09/24 23:42:51 INFO mapred.JobClient: Map output records=1955569
mc815ll:hadoop-1.0.3 henry$ **cat out60/part-r-00000**
cat: out60/part-r-00000: No such file or directory
mc815ll:hadoop-1.0.3 henry$ ls out60
_SUCCESS part-00000
mc815ll:hadoop-1.0.3 henry$ cat out60/part-00000
76 10115095   SUNNYVALE   CA   99.99

```
76CR5754SUNNYVALE10080067 SUNNYVALE    CA   99.99
99 RANCH #1776     SAN FRANCISCO   CA    99.99
BABIES R US #6447  QPS SUNNYVALE      CA   99.99
......
TOYS R US #5808    QPS CUPERTINO CA     99.99
TRICKS GYMNASTICS DANC 916-3510024  CA 99.99
TRU HOLIDAY EXPRESSQPS SUNNYVALE     CA    99.99
WAL-MART #1760       SUNNYVALE    CA    99.99
mc815ll:hadoop-1.0.3 henry$
```

Table 6.1 Input/output key-value pairs of the two chained mappers and the reducer

class	Input {key, value} pair	Output {key, value} pair
Mapper0	LongWritable, Text	Text, FloatWritable
Mapper1	Text, FloatWritable	Text, FloatWritable
Reducer	Text, FloatWritable	Text, FloatWritable

Listing 6.2 (a) The ChainMapper byValue example: the driver

```
import org.apache.hadoop.fs.Path;
import org.apache.hadoop.io.LongWritable;
import org.apache.hadoop.io.IntWritable;
import org.apache.hadoop.io.FloatWritable;
import org.apache.hadoop.io.Text;
import org.apache.hadoop.io.BytesWritable;
import org.apache.hadoop.mapreduce.Job;
import org.apache.hadoop.mapred.FileInputFormat;
//import org.apache.hadoop.mapreduce.lib.input.FileInputFormat;
import org.apache.hadoop.mapreduce.lib.input.KeyValueTextInputFormat;
import org.apache.hadoop.mapred.FileOutputFormat;
import org.apache.hadoop.mapred.TextInputFormat;
import org.apache.hadoop.mapred.TextOutputFormat;

import org.apache.hadoop.mapred.JobConf;
import org.apache.hadoop.mapred.JobClient;
import org.apache.hadoop.mapred.lib.ChainMapper;
import org.apache.hadoop.mapred.lib.ChainReducer;

import org.apache.hadoop.conf.Configured;
import org.apache.hadoop.util.Tool;
import org.apache.hadoop.util.ToolRunner;
import org.apache.hadoop.util.GenericOptionsParser;
import org.apache.hadoop.conf.*;

public class SpendingPattern1i {
```

```
public static void main (String[] args) throws Exception {
    Configuration conf = new Configuration();

    String remainingArgs[] = new GenericOptionsParser(conf,
        args).getRemainingArgs();
  if (args.length != 2) {
    System.exit (-1);
  }
  JobConf jobConf = new JobConf(conf);
  jobConf.setJarByClass(SpendingPattern1h.class);
  FileInputFormat.addInputPath(jobConf, new Path(args[0]));
  FileOutputFormat.setOutputPath(jobConf, new Path(args[1]));

  jobConf.setJobName("Spending Pattern ChainMapper");
  jobConf.setInputFormat(TextInputFormat.class);
  jobConf.setOutputFormat(TextOutputFormat.class);

  JobConf map0Conf = new JobConf (false);
  ChainMapper.addMapper(jobConf, SpendingPatternMapper1b.class,
          LongWritable.class, Text.class, Text.class,
          FloatWritable.class, true, map0Conf);

  JobConf map1Conf = new JobConf (false);
  ChainMapper.addMapper(jobConf, SpendingPatternMapper1c.class,
          Text.class, FloatWritable.class, Text.class,
          FloatWritable.class, false, map1Conf);
  JobConf reduceConf = new JobConf (false);
  ChainReducer.setReducer (jobConf, SpendingPatternReducer1a.class,
          Text.class, FloatWritable.class, Text.class,
          FloatWritable.class,true, reduceConf);
   JobClient.runJob (jobConf);
 }
}
```

Listing 6.2 (b) Console output of the same job with the byValue parameter set to false for the second mapper

```
mc815ll:hadoop-1.0.3 henry$ bin/hadoop jar spending-patterns.jar SpendingPattern1i
in0/credit_card_tx_0_out.txt out61
12/09/25 12:30:09 WARN util.NativeCodeLoader: Unable to load native-hadoop library for your
platform... using builtin-java classes where applicable
12/09/25 12:30:09 WARN snappy.LoadSnappy: Snappy native library not loaded
12/09/25 12:30:09 INFO mapred.FileInputFormat: Total input paths to process : 1
```

```
12/09/25 12:30:09 INFO mapred.JobClient: Running job: job_local_0001
12/09/25 12:30:09 INFO mapred.Task: Using ResourceCalculatorPlugin : null
12/09/25 12:30:09 INFO mapred.MapTask: numReduceTasks: 1
12/09/25 12:30:10 INFO mapred.MapTask: io.sort.mb = 100
12/09/25 12:30:10 INFO mapred.MapTask: data buffer = 79691776/99614720
12/09/25 12:30:10 INFO mapred.MapTask: record buffer = 262144/327680
12/09/25 12:30:10 INFO mapred.JobClient:  map 0% reduce 0%
12/09/25 12:30:13 INFO mapred.MapTask: Spilling map output: record full = true
12/09/25 12:30:13 INFO mapred.MapTask: Finished spill 0
12/09/25 12:30:15 INFO mapred.MapTask: Spilling map output: record full = true
12/09/25 12:30:15 INFO mapred.MapTask: Starting flush of map output
12/09/25 12:30:15 INFO mapred.MapTask: Finished spill 1
12/09/25 12:30:15 INFO mapred.LocalJobRunner: file:/Users/henry/dev/hadoop-
1.0.3/in0/credit_card_tx_0_out.txt:0+33554432
12/09/25 12:30:16 INFO mapred.MapTask: Finished spill 2
12/09/25 12:30:16 INFO mapred.Merger: Merging 3 sorted segments
12/09/25 12:30:16 INFO mapred.Merger: Down to the last merge-pass, with 3 segments left of total
size: 27085156 bytes
12/09/25 12:30:16 INFO mapred.Task: Task:attempt_local_0001_m_000000_0 is done. And is in the
process of commiting
12/09/25 12:30:16 INFO mapred.JobClient:  map 100% reduce 0%
12/09/25 12:30:18 INFO mapred.LocalJobRunner: file:/Users/henry/dev/hadoop-
1.0.3/in0/credit_card_tx_0_out.txt:0+33554432
12/09/25 12:30:18 INFO mapred.LocalJobRunner: file:/Users/henry/dev/hadoop-
1.0.3/in0/credit_card_tx_0_out.txt:0+33554432
12/09/25 12:30:18 INFO mapred.Task: Task 'attempt_local_0001_m_000000_0' done.
12/09/25 12:30:18 INFO mapred.Task: Using ResourceCalculatorPlugin : null
12/09/25 12:30:18 INFO mapred.MapTask: numReduceTasks: 1
12/09/25 12:30:18 INFO mapred.MapTask: io.sort.mb = 100
12/09/25 12:30:19 INFO mapred.MapTask: data buffer = 79691776/99614720
12/09/25 12:30:19 INFO mapred.MapTask: record buffer = 262144/327680
12/09/25 12:30:21 INFO mapred.MapTask: Spilling map output: record full = true
12/09/25 12:30:21 INFO mapred.MapTask: Finished spill 0
12/09/25 12:30:23 INFO mapred.MapTask: Spilling map output: record full = true
12/09/25 12:30:23 INFO mapred.MapTask: Starting flush of map output
12/09/25 12:30:23 INFO mapred.MapTask: Finished spill 1
12/09/25 12:30:23 INFO mapred.MapTask: Finished spill 2
12/09/25 12:30:23 INFO mapred.Merger: Merging 3 sorted segments
12/09/25 12:30:23 INFO mapred.Merger: Down to the last merge-pass, with 3 segments left of total
size: 27083677 bytes
12/09/25 12:30:24 INFO mapred.Task: Task:attempt_local_0001_m_000001_0 is done. And is in the
process of commiting
12/09/25 12:30:24 INFO mapred.LocalJobRunner: file:/Users/henry/dev/hadoop-
1.0.3/in0/credit_card_tx_0_out.txt:33554432+33554432
12/09/25 12:30:24 INFO mapred.LocalJobRunner: file:/Users/henry/dev/hadoop-
1.0.3/in0/credit_card_tx_0_out.txt:33554432+33554432
12/09/25 12:30:25 INFO mapred.Task: Task 'attempt_local_0001_m_000001_0' done.
12/09/25 12:30:25 INFO mapred.Task: Using ResourceCalculatorPlugin : null
```

12/09/25 12:30:25 INFO mapred.MapTask: numReduceTasks: 1
12/09/25 12:30:25 INFO mapred.MapTask: io.sort.mb = 100
12/09/25 12:30:25 INFO mapred.MapTask: data buffer = 79691776/99614720
12/09/25 12:30:25 INFO mapred.MapTask: record buffer = 262144/327680
12/09/25 12:30:27 INFO mapred.MapTask: Spilling map output: record full = true
12/09/25 12:30:27 INFO mapred.MapTask: Finished spill 0
12/09/25 12:30:29 INFO mapred.MapTask: Spilling map output: record full = true
12/09/25 12:30:29 INFO mapred.MapTask: Starting flush of map output
12/09/25 12:30:29 INFO mapred.MapTask: Finished spill 1
12/09/25 12:30:29 INFO mapred.MapTask: Finished spill 2
12/09/25 12:30:29 INFO mapred.Merger: Merging 3 sorted segments
12/09/25 12:30:29 INFO mapred.Merger: Down to the last merge-pass, with 3 segments left of total
size: 27086619 bytes
12/09/25 12:30:30 INFO mapred.Task: Task:attempt_local_0001_m_000002_0 is done. And is in the
process of commiting
12/09/25 12:30:31 INFO mapred.LocalJobRunner: file:/Users/henry/dev/hadoop-
1.0.3/in0/credit_card_tx_0_out.txt:67108864+33554432
12/09/25 12:30:31 INFO mapred.LocalJobRunner: file:/Users/henry/dev/hadoop-
1.0.3/in0/credit_card_tx_0_out.txt:67108864+33554432
12/09/25 12:30:31 INFO mapred.Task: Task 'attempt_local_0001_m_000002_0' done.
12/09/25 12:30:31 INFO mapred.Task: Using ResourceCalculatorPlugin : null
12/09/25 12:30:31 INFO mapred.MapTask: numReduceTasks: 1
12/09/25 12:30:31 INFO mapred.MapTask: io.sort.mb = 100
12/09/25 12:30:31 INFO mapred.MapTask: data buffer = 79691776/99614720
12/09/25 12:30:31 INFO mapred.MapTask: record buffer = 262144/327680
12/09/25 12:30:33 INFO mapred.MapTask: Starting flush of map output
12/09/25 12:30:33 INFO mapred.MapTask: Finished spill 0
12/09/25 12:30:33 INFO mapred.Task: Task:attempt_local_0001_m_000003_0 is done. And is in the
process of commiting
12/09/25 12:30:34 INFO mapred.LocalJobRunner: file:/Users/henry/dev/hadoop-
1.0.3/in0/credit_card_tx_0_out.txt:100663296+14624079
12/09/25 12:30:34 INFO mapred.Task: Task 'attempt_local_0001_m_000003_0' done.
12/09/25 12:30:34 INFO mapred.Task: Using ResourceCalculatorPlugin : null
12/09/25 12:30:34 INFO mapred.LocalJobRunner:
12/09/25 12:30:34 INFO mapred.Merger: Merging 4 sorted segments
12/09/25 12:30:34 INFO mapred.Merger: Down to the last merge-pass, with 4 segments left of total
size: 93059664 bytes
12/09/25 12:30:34 INFO mapred.LocalJobRunner:
12/09/25 12:30:35 INFO mapred.Task: Task:attempt_local_0001_r_000000_0 is done. And is in the
process of commiting
12/09/25 12:30:35 INFO mapred.LocalJobRunner:
12/09/25 12:30:35 INFO mapred.Task: Task attempt_local_0001_r_000000_0 is allowed to commit
now
12/09/25 12:30:35 INFO mapred.FileOutputCommitter: Saved output of task
'attempt_local_0001_r_000000_0' to file:/Users/henry/dev/hadoop-1.0.3/out61
12/09/25 12:30:37 INFO mapred.LocalJobRunner: reduce > reduce
12/09/25 12:30:37 INFO mapred.Task: Task 'attempt_local_0001_r_000000_0' done.
12/09/25 12:30:37 INFO mapred.JobClient: map 100% reduce 100%
12/09/25 12:30:37 INFO mapred.JobClient: Job complete: job_local_0001

```
12/09/25 12:30:37 INFO mapred.JobClient: Counters: 18
12/09/25 12:30:37 INFO mapred.JobClient:   File Input Format Counters
12/09/25 12:30:37 INFO mapred.JobClient:     Bytes Read=116233631
12/09/25 12:30:37 INFO mapred.JobClient:   File Output Format Counters
12/09/25 12:30:37 INFO mapred.JobClient:     Bytes Written=2122
12/09/25 12:30:37 INFO mapred.JobClient:   FileSystemCounters
12/09/25 12:30:37 INFO mapred.JobClient:     FILE_BYTES_READ=853732987
12/09/25 12:30:37 INFO mapred.JobClient:     FILE_BYTES_WRITTEN=674042130
12/09/25 12:30:37 INFO mapred.JobClient:   Map-Reduce Framework
12/09/25 12:30:37 INFO mapred.JobClient:     Map output materialized bytes=93059680
12/09/25 12:30:37 INFO mapred.JobClient:     Map input records=2000000
12/09/25 12:30:37 INFO mapred.JobClient:     Reduce shuffle bytes=0
12/09/25 12:30:37 INFO mapred.JobClient:     Spilled Records=5618663
12/09/25 12:30:37 INFO mapred.JobClient:     Map output bytes=89148518
12/09/25 12:30:37 INFO mapred.JobClient:     Total committed heap usage (bytes)=999096320
12/09/25 12:30:37 INFO mapred.JobClient:     Map input bytes=115287375
12/09/25 12:30:37 INFO mapred.JobClient:     SPLIT_RAW_BYTES=464
12/09/25 12:30:37 INFO mapred.JobClient:     Combine input records=0
12/09/25 12:30:37 INFO mapred.JobClient:     Reduce input records=1955569
12/09/25 12:30:37 INFO mapred.JobClient:     Reduce input groups=44
12/09/25 12:30:37 INFO mapred.JobClient:     Combine output records=0
12/09/25 12:30:37 INFO mapred.JobClient:     Reduce output records=44
12/09/25 12:30:37 INFO mapred.JobClient:     Map output records=1955569
mc815ll:hadoop-1.0.3 henry$ cat out61/part-00000
76 10115095        SUNNYVALE    CA    99.99
76CR5754SUNNYVALE10080067 SUNNYVALE      CA   99.99
99 RANCH #1776      SAN FRANCISCO  CA    99.99
BABIES R US #6447  QPS SUNNYVALE      CA    99.99
......
TOYS R US #5808   QPS CUPERTINO CA    99.99
TRICKS GYMNASTICS DANC 916-3510024  CA 99.99
TRU HOLIDAY EXPRESSQPS SUNNYVALE     CA     99.99
WAL-MART #1760      SUNNYVALE    CA    99.99
```

Table 6.2 Some of the differences between 0.22 and 1.x Hadoop APIs

Difference in	0.22 API	1.x API
Mapper/Reducer package	org.apache.hadoop.**mapred** Mapper/Reducer	org.apache.hadoop. **mapreduce**
Mapper/Reducer Class Definition	*extends* MapReduceBase *implements* Mapper/Reducer	*extends* Mapper/Reducer
write method	output.collect (...)	context.write (...)
Job configuration	Configuration	Job
Job submission	JobClient	Job

Reduce output files	part-nnnnn	part-r-nnnnn
map/reduce methods throws	IOException	IOException, InterruptedException
reduce mthod passes values	java.lang.Iterator	java.lang.Iteraable

6.1.4 Apache Project Oozie

In the previous chapters, we have seen how Hadoop job orchestration and workflow APIs are used to wire various job and task flows so that a MapReduce program can be executed orderly. However, from the application point of view, this approach is too low-level. To make it more flexible, Apache provides a framework through one of its many projects named Ozzie for managing Hadoop job orchestration and workflows. With Oozie, Hadoop workflow jobs can be defined as directed acyclical graphs (DAG) of actions, while coordination jobs are defined as recurrent Oozie workflow jobs triggered by time (frequency) and data availability. A detailed coverage of Oozie is beyond the scope of this book, but that is where you should look if you want to pursue more advanced techniques in constructing more flexible job orchestration and workflow control for your applications.

6.2 COMPRESSION

Hadoop works on large datasets. Shuffling large volumes of data across nodes or networks is one of the major concerns for performance and scalability. There are several proven practices in helping speed up data movement, and compression is one of them as discussed next.

6.2.1 Why Compressing?

Compression is a general software performance optimization technique used to minimize storage space and speed up data I/O operations from and to disk or across network. This technique applies to Hadoop as well, since intermediate map output data needs to be stored to disk and shuffled across network to various data nodes. How much performance gain can be realized depends on many factors, such as the size of the dataset, compression format and associated compression/decompression algorithms, hardware raw capability, and available disk and network bandwidths, etc.

In this section, we are interested more in how to enable compression with a Hadoop MapReduce program, rather than in quantifying how much performance gain can be realized by tweaking various factors as mentioned above. Therefore, let's demonstrate first how to compress intermediate map output data with an example next.

6.2.2 Compressing Intermediate Map Output Data

To compress intermediate map output data, all we need to do is to specify whether to enable compression and what compression format or codec class to use. A codec is a representation of the compression format along with the implementation of its compression/decompression algorithm. For example, to enable compression with the DefaultCodec from a JDK, add the following statements in a driver program:

```
FileOutputFormat.setCompressOutput (job, true);
FileOutputFormat.setOutputCompressorClass (job, DefaultCodec.class);
SequenceFileAsBinaryOutputFormat.setOutputCompressionType (job,
    SequenceFile.CompressionType.BLOCK);
```

Listings 6.3 (a) – (d) show the drivers with no compression, the DefaultCodec, the GzipCodec, and the BZip2Codec, respectively. All these programs share the following common characteristics:

- The compression type is set to BLOCK, which means that blocks of records are compressed. The default compression type is set to RECORD, which would compress record by record.
- The output format is set to *SequenceFileAsBinaryOutputFormat*. This is an arbitrary, rather than a required, choice.
- The same mapper of SpendingPattern1 and the same reducer of SpendingPatternReducer1 are used. See Listing 5.4 and Listing 5.8 for the details of these two classes.

These MapReduce programs with different codecs were run with different size of dataset for the input data files. Table 6.3 summarizes the test results in terms of total elapsed time in seconds for each run. Figure 6.1 shows the same data in graphic form. It is interesting to see that with no compression, the throughput in terms of the input data size divided by the total job run time seems to be constant, while when compressions with various codec schemes were introduced, the throughput seems to decrease with the data size. For your project, you need to conduct similar tests to determine which scheme is the best.

Table 6.3 MapReduce job runs with different Codecs and different input file sizes

Data size (MB)	No compression	DefaultCodec	GzipCodec	BZip2Codec
93	52	55	48	47
466	93	107	88	93
933	174	170	170	173

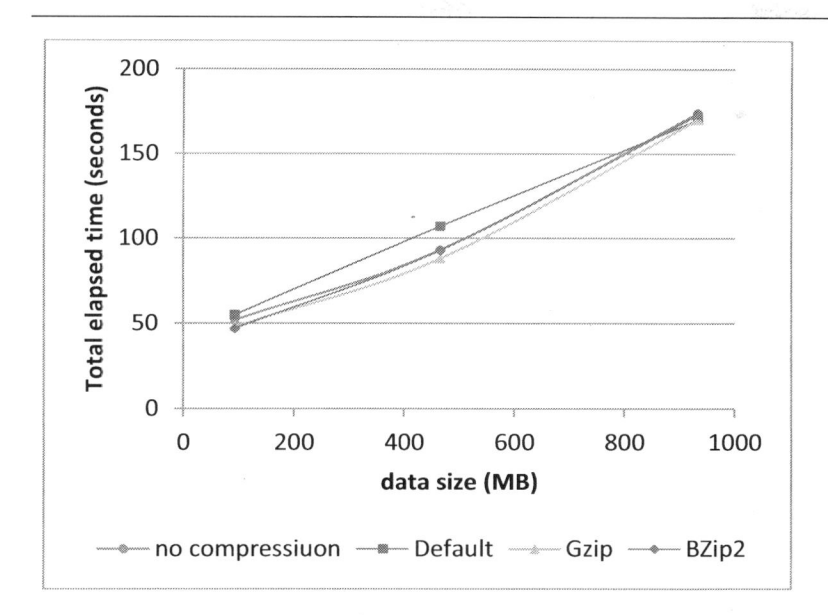

Figure 6.1 Total elapsed time in seconds versus input data size (MB) under different compression schemes

Listing 6.3 (e) shows the output of running *SpendingPattern1j3* with the BZip2 codec. The job was run on the four node Linux cluster as described in Chapter 2. An input file containing 20M credit card transactions was used. The associated file size was 933 MB or close to 1GB. Figure 6.2 shows the reduce output captured with the *cat* utility against the runs corresponding to GzipCodec (top), no compression (middle) and BZip2Codec (bottom), respectively. You can actually identify the Codec used from the header of a reduce output file (check out the GzipCodec and BZip2Codec shown in Figure 6.2).

This concludes our discussion on using compression with Hadoop MapReduce programs. Next, we discuss MultipleInputs.

Listing 6.3 (a) The Compression example: the driver with no compression

```
import org.apache.hadoop.fs.Path;
import org.apache.hadoop.io.FloatWritable;
import org.apache.hadoop.io.Text;
import org.apache.hadoop.io.BytesWritable;
import org.apache.hadoop.mapreduce.Job;
import org.apache.hadoop.mapreduce.lib.input.FileInputFormat;
import org.apache.hadoop.mapreduce.lib.input.KeyValueTextInputFormat;
import org.apache.hadoop.mapreduce.lib.output.FileOutputFormat;
import org.apache.hadoop.mapreduce.lib.output.SequenceFileAsBinaryOutputFormat;
import org.apache.hadoop.mapreduce.lib.output.SequenceFileOutputFormat;
```

```java
import org.apache.hadoop.io.compress.*;
import org.apache.hadoop.io.SequenceFile;
public class SpendingPattern1j0 {

  public static void main(String[] args) throws Exception {
   if (args.length != 2) {
    System.err.println("Usage: SpendingPattern <input path> <output path>");
    System.exit(-1);
   }

   Job job = new Job();
   job.setJarByClass(SpendingPattern1j0.class);
   job.setJobName("Spending Pattern");
   job.setInputFormatClass (KeyValueTextInputFormat.class);
   job.setOutputFormatClass (SequenceFileAsBinaryOutputFormat.class);

   FileInputFormat.addInputPath(job, new Path(args[0]));
   FileOutputFormat.setOutputPath(job, new Path(args[1]));

   job.setMapperClass(SpendingPatternMapper1.class);
   job.setReducerClass(SpendingPatternReducer1.class);

   job.setOutputKeyClass(Text.class);
   job.setOutputValueClass(FloatWritable.class);

   System.exit(job.waitForCompletion(true) ? 0 : 1);
  }
}
```

Listing 6.3 (b) The Compression example: the driver with the DefaultCodec

```java
import org.apache.hadoop.fs.Path;
import org.apache.hadoop.io.FloatWritable;
import org.apache.hadoop.io.Text;
import org.apache.hadoop.io.BytesWritable;
import org.apache.hadoop.mapreduce.Job;
import org.apache.hadoop.mapreduce.lib.input.FileInputFormat;
import org.apache.hadoop.mapreduce.lib.input.KeyValueTextInputFormat;
import org.apache.hadoop.mapreduce.lib.output.FileOutputFormat;
import org.apache.hadoop.mapreduce.lib.output.SequenceFileAsBinaryOutputFormat;
import org.apache.hadoop.mapreduce.lib.output.SequenceFileOutputFormat;
import org.apache.hadoop.io.compress.*;
import org.apache.hadoop.io.SequenceFile;
public class SpendingPattern1j1 {
```

```java
public static void main(String[] args) throws Exception {
 if (args.length != 2) {
  System.err.println("Usage: SpendingPattern <input path> <output path>");
  System.exit(-1);
 }

 Job job = new Job();
 job.setJarByClass(SpendingPattern1j1.class);
 job.setJobName("Spending Pattern");
 job.setInputFormatClass (KeyValueTextInputFormat.class);
 job.setOutputFormatClass (SequenceFileAsBinaryOutputFormat.class);

 FileInputFormat.addInputPath(job, new Path(args[0]));
 FileOutputFormat.setOutputPath(job, new Path(args[1]));
 FileOutputFormat.setCompressOutput (job, true);
 FileOutputFormat.setOutputCompressorClass (job, DefaultCodec.class);
 SequenceFileAsBinaryOutputFormat.setOutputCompressionType (job,
     SequenceFile.CompressionType.BLOCK);

 job.setMapperClass(SpendingPatternMapper1.class);
 job.setReducerClass(SpendingPatternReducer1.class);

 job.setOutputKeyClass(Text.class);
 job.setOutputValueClass(FloatWritable.class);

 System.exit(job.waitForCompletion(true) ? 0 : 1);
 }
}
```

Listing 6.3 (c) The Compression example: the driver with the GzipCodec

```java
import org.apache.hadoop.fs.Path;
import org.apache.hadoop.io.FloatWritable;
import org.apache.hadoop.io.Text;
import org.apache.hadoop.io.BytesWritable;
import org.apache.hadoop.mapreduce.Job;
import org.apache.hadoop.mapreduce.lib.input.FileInputFormat;
import org.apache.hadoop.mapreduce.lib.input.KeyValueTextInputFormat;
import org.apache.hadoop.mapreduce.lib.output.FileOutputFormat;
import org.apache.hadoop.mapreduce.lib.output.SequenceFileAsBinaryOutputFormat;
import org.apache.hadoop.mapreduce.lib.output.SequenceFileOutputFormat;
import org.apache.hadoop.io.compress.*;
import org.apache.hadoop.io.SequenceFile;
```

```java
public class SpendingPattern1j2 {

  public static void main(String[] args) throws Exception {
    if (args.length != 2) {
      System.err.println("Usage: SpendingPattern <input path> <output path>");
      System.exit(-1);
    }

    Job job = new Job();
    job.setJarByClass(SpendingPattern1j2.class);
    job.setJobName("Spending Pattern");
    job.setInputFormatClass (KeyValueTextInputFormat.class);
    job.setOutputFormatClass (SequenceFileAsBinaryOutputFormat.class);

    FileInputFormat.addInputPath(job, new Path(args[0]));
    FileOutputFormat.setOutputPath(job, new Path(args[1]));
    FileOutputFormat.setCompressOutput (job, true);
    FileOutputFormat.setOutputCompressorClass (job, GzipCodec.class);
    SequenceFileAsBinaryOutputFormat.setOutputCompressionType (job,
        SequenceFile.CompressionType.BLOCK);

    job.setMapperClass(SpendingPatternMapper1.class);
    job.setReducerClass(SpendingPatternReducer1.class);

    job.setOutputKeyClass(Text.class);
    job.setOutputValueClass(FloatWritable.class);

    System.exit(job.waitForCompletion(true) ? 0 : 1);
  }
}
```

Listing 6.3 (d) The Compression example: the driver with the BZip2Codec

```java
import org.apache.hadoop.fs.Path;
import org.apache.hadoop.io.FloatWritable;
import org.apache.hadoop.io.Text;
import org.apache.hadoop.io.BytesWritable;
import org.apache.hadoop.mapreduce.Job;
import org.apache.hadoop.mapreduce.lib.input.FileInputFormat;
import org.apache.hadoop.mapreduce.lib.input.KeyValueTextInputFormat;
import org.apache.hadoop.mapreduce.lib.output.FileOutputFormat;
import org.apache.hadoop.mapreduce.lib.output.SequenceFileAsBinaryOutputFormat;
import org.apache.hadoop.mapreduce.lib.output.SequenceFileOutputFormat;
import org.apache.hadoop.io.compress.*;
```

```
import org.apache.hadoop.io.SequenceFile;
public class SpendingPattern1j3 {

 public static void main(String[] args) throws Exception {
  if (args.length != 2) {
   System.err.println("Usage: SpendingPattern <input path> <output path>");
   System.exit(-1);
  }

  Job job = new Job();
  job.setJarByClass(SpendingPattern1j3.class);
  job.setJobName("Spending Pattern");
  job.setInputFormatClass (KeyValueTextInputFormat.class);
  job.setOutputFormatClass (SequenceFileAsBinaryOutputFormat.class);

  FileInputFormat.addInputPath(job, new Path(args[0]));
  FileOutputFormat.setOutputPath(job, new Path(args[1]));
  FileOutputFormat.setCompressOutput (job, true);
  FileOutputFormat.setOutputCompressorClass (job, BZip2Codec.class);
  SequenceFileAsBinaryOutputFormat.setOutputCompressionType (job,
     SequenceFile.CompressionType.BLOCK);

  job.setMapperClass(SpendingPatternMapper1.class);
  job.setReducerClass(SpendingPatternReducer1.class);

  job.setOutputKeyClass(Text.class);
  job.setOutputValueClass(FloatWritable.class);

  System.exit(job.waitForCompletion(true) ? 0 : 1);
 }
}
```

Listing 6.3 (e) Console output of the BZip2 codec example executed on the four node Linux cluster with an input file containing 20M credit card transactions

```
henry@linux-1fsw:~/myapp/hadoop-1.0.3> hadoop jar spending-patterns.jar SpendingPattern1j3
in0/credit_card_tx_2_out_kv.txt out4d
12/09/25 18:12:25 WARN mapred.JobClient: Use GenericOptionsParser for parsing the arguments.
Applications should implement Tool for the same.
12/09/25 18:12:25 INFO input.FileInputFormat: Total input paths to process : 1
12/09/25 18:12:25 INFO util.NativeCodeLoader: Loaded the native-hadoop library
12/09/25 18:12:25 WARN snappy.LoadSnappy: Snappy native library not loaded
12/09/25 18:12:25 INFO mapred.JobClient: Running job: job_201209212204_0020
12/09/25 18:12:26 INFO mapred.JobClient:  map 0% reduce 0%
12/09/25 18:12:44 INFO mapred.JobClient:  map 7% reduce 0%
```

```
12/09/25 18:12:47 INFO mapred.JobClient:  map 14% reduce 0%
12/09/25 18:12:50 INFO mapred.JobClient:  map 20% reduce 0%
12/09/25 18:12:53 INFO mapred.JobClient:  map 21% reduce 0%
12/09/25 18:12:56 INFO mapred.JobClient:  map 22% reduce 0%
12/09/25 18:12:59 INFO mapred.JobClient:  map 24% reduce 0%
12/09/25 18:13:02 INFO mapred.JobClient:  map 30% reduce 0%
12/09/25 18:13:05 INFO mapred.JobClient:  map 37% reduce 0%
12/09/25 18:13:08 INFO mapred.JobClient:  map 41% reduce 0%
12/09/25 18:13:11 INFO mapred.JobClient:  map 42% reduce 2%
12/09/25 18:13:17 INFO mapred.JobClient:  map 42% reduce 3%
12/09/25 18:13:20 INFO mapred.JobClient:  map 42% reduce 4%
12/09/25 18:13:23 INFO mapred.JobClient:  map 50% reduce 5%
12/09/25 18:13:26 INFO mapred.JobClient:  map 52% reduce 8%
12/09/25 18:13:29 INFO mapred.JobClient:  map 57% reduce 10%
12/09/25 18:13:32 INFO mapred.JobClient:  map 58% reduce 11%
12/09/25 18:13:35 INFO mapred.JobClient:  map 59% reduce 14%
12/09/25 18:13:38 INFO mapred.JobClient:  map 61% reduce 14%
12/09/25 18:13:41 INFO mapred.JobClient:  map 64% reduce 15%
12/09/25 18:13:44 INFO mapred.JobClient:  map 70% reduce 16%
12/09/25 18:13:47 INFO mapred.JobClient:  map 73% reduce 16%
12/09/25 18:13:48 INFO mapred.JobClient:  map 75% reduce 16%
12/09/25 18:13:50 INFO mapred.JobClient:  map 80% reduce 16%
12/09/25 18:13:51 INFO mapred.JobClient:  map 81% reduce 17%
12/09/25 18:13:54 INFO mapred.JobClient:  map 83% reduce 19%
12/09/25 18:13:57 INFO mapred.JobClient:  map 85% reduce 19%
12/09/25 18:14:02 INFO mapred.JobClient:  map 90% reduce 19%
12/09/25 18:14:05 INFO mapred.JobClient:  map 96% reduce 19%
12/09/25 18:14:06 INFO mapred.JobClient:  map 96% reduce 20%
12/09/25 18:14:08 INFO mapred.JobClient:  map 99% reduce 22%
12/09/25 18:14:11 INFO mapred.JobClient:  map 100% reduce 22%
12/09/25 18:14:12 INFO mapred.JobClient:  map 100% reduce 23%
12/09/25 18:14:14 INFO mapred.JobClient:  map 100% reduce 25%
12/09/25 18:14:20 INFO mapred.JobClient:  map 100% reduce 27%
12/09/25 18:14:24 INFO mapred.JobClient:  map 100% reduce 28%
12/09/25 18:14:26 INFO mapred.JobClient:  map 100% reduce 29%
12/09/25 18:14:27 INFO mapred.JobClient:  map 100% reduce 32%
12/09/25 18:14:29 INFO mapred.JobClient:  map 100% reduce 53%
12/09/25 18:14:32 INFO mapred.JobClient:  map 100% reduce 62%
12/09/25 18:14:34 INFO mapred.JobClient:  map 100% reduce 64%
12/09/25 18:14:38 INFO mapred.JobClient:  map 100% reduce 66%
12/09/25 18:14:46 INFO mapred.JobClient:  map 100% reduce 83%
12/09/25 18:14:49 INFO mapred.JobClient:  map 100% reduce 86%
12/09/25 18:14:52 INFO mapred.JobClient:  map 100% reduce 88%
12/09/25 18:14:55 INFO mapred.JobClient:  map 100% reduce 90%
12/09/25 18:14:58 INFO mapred.JobClient:  map 100% reduce 94%
12/09/25 18:15:04 INFO mapred.JobClient:  map 100% reduce 97%
12/09/25 18:15:13 INFO mapred.JobClient:  map 100% reduce 100%
12/09/25 18:15:18 INFO mapred.JobClient: Job complete: job_201209212204_0020
```

```
12/09/25 18:15:18 INFO mapred.JobClient: Counters: 29
12/09/25 18:15:18 INFO mapred.JobClient:   Job Counters
12/09/25 18:15:18 INFO mapred.JobClient:     Launched reduce tasks=3
12/09/25 18:15:18 INFO mapred.JobClient:     SLOTS_MILLIS_MAPS=382476
12/09/25 18:15:18 INFO mapred.JobClient:     Total time spent by all reduces waiting after reserving
slots (ms)=0
12/09/25 18:15:18 INFO mapred.JobClient:     Total time spent by all maps waiting after reserving slots
(ms)=0
12/09/25 18:15:18 INFO mapred.JobClient:     Launched map tasks=15
12/09/25 18:15:18 INFO mapred.JobClient:     Data-local map tasks=15
12/09/25 18:15:18 INFO mapred.JobClient:     SLOTS_MILLIS_REDUCES=247297
12/09/25 18:15:18 INFO mapred.JobClient:   File Output Format Counters
12/09/25 18:15:18 INFO mapred.JobClient:     Bytes Written=1500
12/09/25 18:15:18 INFO mapred.JobClient:   FileSystemCounters
12/09/25 18:15:18 INFO mapred.JobClient:     FILE_BYTES_READ=2012762589
12/09/25 18:15:18 INFO mapred.JobClient:     HDFS_BYTES_READ=933007035
12/09/25 18:15:18 INFO mapred.JobClient:     FILE_BYTES_WRITTEN=2943614146
12/09/25 18:15:18 INFO mapred.JobClient:     HDFS_BYTES_WRITTEN=1500
12/09/25 18:15:18 INFO mapred.JobClient:   File Input Format Counters
12/09/25 18:15:18 INFO mapred.JobClient:     Bytes Read=933005103
12/09/25 18:15:18 INFO mapred.JobClient:   Map-Reduce Framework
12/09/25 18:15:18 INFO mapred.JobClient:     Map output materialized bytes=930682012
12/09/25 18:15:18 INFO mapred.JobClient:     Map input records=20000000
12/09/25 18:15:18 INFO mapred.JobClient:     Reduce shuffle bytes=867433154
12/09/25 18:15:18 INFO mapred.JobClient:     Spilled Records=61862792
12/09/25 18:15:18 INFO mapred.JobClient:     Map output bytes=891570524
12/09/25 18:15:18 INFO mapred.JobClient:     CPU time spent (ms)=270180
12/09/25 18:15:18 INFO mapred.JobClient:     Total committed heap usage (bytes)=2485014528
12/09/25 18:15:18 INFO mapred.JobClient:     Combine input records=0
12/09/25 18:15:18 INFO mapred.JobClient:     SPLIT_RAW_BYTES=1932
12/09/25 18:15:18 INFO mapred.JobClient:     Reduce input records=19555660
12/09/25 18:15:18 INFO mapred.JobClient:     Reduce input groups=44
12/09/25 18:15:18 INFO mapred.JobClient:     Combine output records=0
12/09/25 18:15:18 INFO mapred.JobClient:     Physical memory (bytes) snapshot=2861121536
12/09/25 18:15:18 INFO mapred.JobClient:     Reduce output records=44
12/09/25 18:15:18 INFO mapred.JobClient:     Virtual memory (bytes) snapshot=5826785280
12/09/25 18:15:18 INFO mapred.JobClient:     Map output records=19555660
henry@linux-1fsw:~/myapp/hadoop-1.0.3>
```

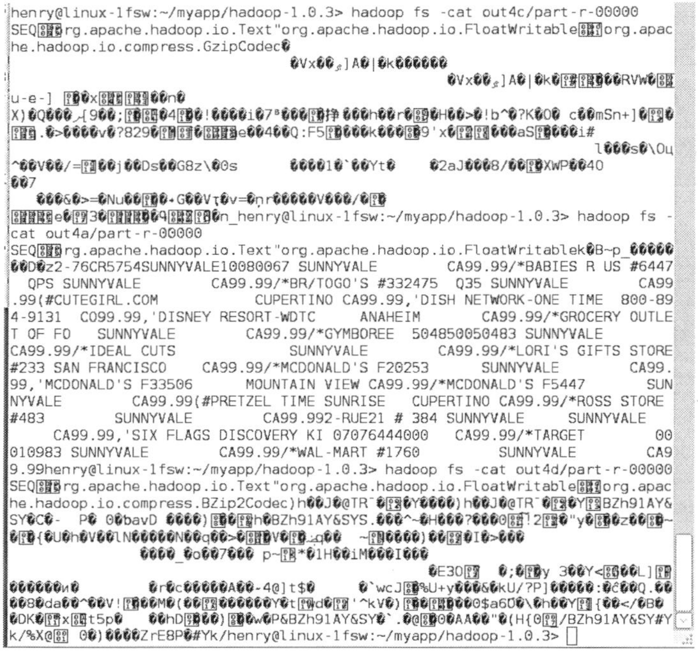

Figure 6.2 Reduce output from the runs with the GzipCodec (top), no compression (middle), and BZip2Codec (bottom)

6.3 MULTIPLEINPUTS

In Chapter 5, we discussed that a mapper can take multiple input files of the same format by using the `FileInputFormat.addPath` (...) method or `FileInputFormat.addPaths` (...) method. The multiple input files are stitched together internally and presented to the single mapper as one input. We also discussed earlier in this chapter that multiple mappers can be chained together with one input to the first mapper, and the output of the first mapper would become the input of the second mapper, and so forth. In this section, we discuss another Hadoop class named `MultipleInputs`, which can deal with the situation of multiple inputs with each input having its own mapper, forming multiple mapper branches to the same reducer or no reducer at all.

Next, let's see how the `MultipleInputs` class supports the above feature.

6.3.1 The MultipleInputs API

The `MultipleInputs` class is defined as follows:

```
package org.apache.hadoop.mapreduce.lib.input;
class MultipleInputs { ...}
```

It has only a default constructor of MultipleInputs () and the following two methods:

- **addInputPath**:

  public static void **addInputPath** (
            Job job,
            Path path,
            Class<? extends InputFormat> inputFormatClass)

This method adds a Path with a custom InputFormat to the list of inputs for the map-reduce job.

- **addInputPath**:

  public static void addInputPath(
            Job job,
            Path path,
            Class<? extends InputFormat> inputFormatClass,
            Class<? extends **Mapper**> mapperClass)

This method also adds a Path with a custom InputFormat to the list of inputs for the map-reduce job, but with a Mapper designating which mapper to add the path to.

The first addInputPath (...) assumes that there is only one mapper to add multiple inputs to, whereas the second addInputPath (...) method allows adding the input path to a designated mapper so that multiple, independent mappers can be placed prior to the reducer. Figure 6.3 shows this scenario of having multiple mappers with all their outputs fed to the same reducer.

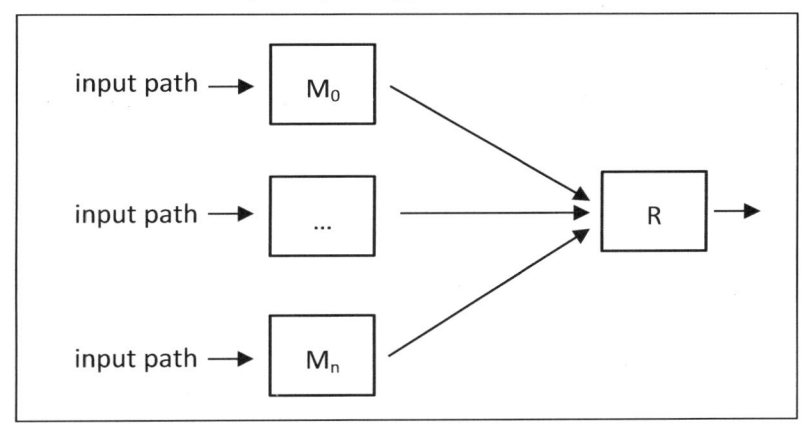

Figure 6.3 How MultipleInputs works

Next, let's use an example to demonstrate how to use the MultipleInputs API to form multiple mapping branches with multiple inputs.

6.3.2 A MultipleInputs Example

Recall that we presented two MapReduce program examples: one in Chapter 1 as our first MapReduce program and the other in Chapter 5 as a KeyValueTextInputFormat example. Those two programs share the same reducer that they both output the maximum amount spent at a store. The only difference is that they use input files with different number of fields for each record: one uses three fields of {*transaction date, description, amount*} for each record, while the other uses two fields of {*description, amount*} as key-value for each record. This appears to be a perfect situation for our MultipleInputs example that we can just re-use the same mappers and the reducer, and all we need to do is to write a new driver.

For convenience, the two mappers and the shared reducer are shown in Listings 6.4 (a), (b), and (c), respectively. You can take a quick look at the input/output key-value types to help refresh your memory on what they do. Our focus here is the driver, which is shown in Listing 6.4 (d). Note the following:

■ The driver has the following two statements to add multiple inputs to the two mappers (cross-check these two statements with the second addInputPath (...) method of the MultipleInputs class introduced in the previous section):

```
MultipleInputs.addInputPath (job, new Path(args[0]),
            TextInputFormat.class,
            SpendingPatternMapper.class);
MultipleInputs.addInputPath (job, new Path(args[1]),
            KeyValueTextInputFormat.class,
            SpendingPatternMapper1.class);
```

■ The example was run with the following command and the console output was collected and displayed in Listing 6.4 (e) (note the two input files specified):

```
$ hadoop jar spending-patterns.jar SpendingPattern1k0 in0/credit_card_tx_0_out.txt
in0/credit_card_tx_0_out_kv.txt out71
```

■ Check out the counters at the end of the console output and note the counter Reduce output records=44, which confirms that the job was completed successfully and correctly.

This example concludes our discussion on MultipleInputs. In the next section, we discuss MultipleOutputs, which is slightly more complicated than MultipleInputs.

Listing 6.4 (a) The MultipleInputs example: Mapper 0

```
import java.io.IOException;
import java.util.StringTokenizer;
import org.apache.hadoop.io.FloatWritable;
import org.apache.hadoop.io.LongWritable;
import org.apache.hadoop.io.Text;
import org.apache.hadoop.mapreduce.Mapper;


public class SpendingPatternMapper
```

```
extends Mapper<LongWritable, Text, Text, FloatWritable> {

    @Override
    public void map(LongWritable key, Text value, Context context)
        throws IOException, InterruptedException {

        String line = value.toString();
        if (!line.contains ("PAYMENT")) {
        StringTokenizer st = new StringTokenizer (line, "\t");
        String tranxDate = st.nextToken();
        String description = st.nextToken();
        float amount = Float.parseFloat(st.nextToken());
        context.write(new Text(description), new FloatWritable(amount));
        }
    }
}
```

Listing 6.4 (b) The MultipleInputs example: Mapper1

```
import java.io.IOException;
import java.util.StringTokenizer;
import org.apache.hadoop.io.FloatWritable;
import org.apache.hadoop.io.LongWritable;
import org.apache.hadoop.io.Text;
import org.apache.hadoop.mapreduce.Mapper;

public class SpendingPatternMapper1 extends
        Mapper<Text, Text, Text, FloatWritable> {

    @Override
    public void map(Text key, Text value, Context context) throws IOException,
            InterruptedException {
        if (!key.toString().contains("PAYMENT")) {
            float amount = Float.parseFloat(value.toString());
            context.write(key, new FloatWritable(amount));
        }
    }
}
```

Listing 6.4 (c) The MultipleInputs example: the Reducer

```
import java.io.IOException;

import org.apache.hadoop.io.IntWritable;
```

```java
import org.apache.hadoop.io.FloatWritable;
import org.apache.hadoop.io.BytesWritable;
import org.apache.hadoop.io.Text;
import org.apache.hadoop.mapreduce.Reducer;

public class SpendingPatternReducer extends
        Reducer<Text, FloatWritable, Text, FloatWritable> {

    @Override
    public void reduce(Text key, Iterable<FloatWritable> values,
            Context context) throws IOException, InterruptedException {

        float maxValue = Float.MIN_VALUE;
        for (FloatWritable value : values) {
            maxValue = Math.max(maxValue, value.get());
        }
        context.write(key, new FloatWritable(maxValue));
    }
}
```

Listing 6.4 (d) MultipleInputs example: the driver

```java
import org.apache.hadoop.fs.Path;
import org.apache.hadoop.io.FloatWritable;
import org.apache.hadoop.io.Text;

import org.apache.hadoop.mapreduce.lib.input.MultipleInputs;
import org.apache.hadoop.mapreduce.lib.input.KeyValueTextInputFormat;

import org.apache.hadoop.mapreduce.lib.input.FileInputFormat;
import org.apache.hadoop.mapreduce.lib.input.TextInputFormat;
import org.apache.hadoop.mapreduce.lib.output.FileOutputFormat;
import org.apache.hadoop.mapreduce.lib.output.TextOutputFormat;
import org.apache.hadoop.conf.*;
import org.apache.hadoop.mapreduce.Job;
import org.apache.hadoop.conf.Configured;
import org.apache.hadoop.util.Tool;
import org.apache.hadoop.util.ToolRunner;
import org.apache.hadoop.util.GenericOptionsParser;
import org.apache.hadoop.conf.*;

public class SpendingPattern1k0 extends Configured implements Tool {

    @Override
```

```java
public int run(String[] args) throws Exception {
    Configuration conf = new Configuration();
    String remainingArgs[] = new GenericOptionsParser
(conf, args).getRemainingArgs();

    Job job = new Job (conf);
    job.setJobName("Spending Pattern: Multiple Inputs");

    MultipleInputs.addInputPath (job, new Path(args[0]),
        TextInputFormat.class,
        SpendingPatternMapper.class);
    MultipleInputs.addInputPath (job, new Path(args[1]),
        KeyValueTextInputFormat.class,
        SpendingPatternMapper1.class);

    FileOutputFormat.setOutputPath(job, new Path(args[2]));
    job.setReducerClass(SpendingPatternReducer.class);
    job.setOutputKeyClass(Text.class);
    job.setOutputValueClass(FloatWritable.class);

    return job.waitForCompletion(true) ? 0 : 1;
}

public static void main(String[] args) throws Exception {
    int exitCode = ToolRunner.run(new SpendingPattern1k0(), args);
    System.exit(exitCode);
}
}
```

Listing 6.4 (e) Console output of the MultipleInputs example

```
$ hadoop jar spending-patterns.jar SpendingPattern1k0 in0/credit_card_tx_0_out.txt
in0/credit_card_tx_0_out_kv.txt out71
12/09/28 23:16:23 WARN util.NativeCodeLoader: Unable to load native-hadoop library for your
platform... using builtin-java classes where applicable
12/09/28 23:16:23 WARN mapred.JobClient: No job jar file set.  User classes may not be found. See
JobConf(Class) or JobConf#setJar(String).
12/09/28 23:16:23 INFO input.FileInputFormat: Total input paths to process : 1
12/09/28 23:16:23 WARN snappy.LoadSnappy: Snappy native library not loaded
12/09/28 23:16:23 INFO input.FileInputFormat: Total input paths to process : 1
12/09/28 23:16:23 INFO mapred.JobClient: Running job: job_local_0001
12/09/28 23:16:23 INFO mapred.Task:  Using ResourceCalculatorPlugin : null
12/09/28 23:16:23 INFO mapred.MapTask: io.sort.mb = 100
12/09/28 23:16:23 INFO mapred.MapTask: data buffer = 79691776/99614720
12/09/28 23:16:23 INFO mapred.MapTask: record buffer = 262144/327680
```

```
12/09/28 23:16:24 INFO mapred.JobClient:  map 0% reduce 0%
12/09/28 23:16:24 INFO mapred.MapTask: Spilling map output: record full = true
12/09/28 23:16:25 INFO mapred.MapTask: Finished spill 0
12/09/28 23:16:25 INFO mapred.MapTask: Spilling map output: record full = true
12/09/28 23:16:25 INFO mapred.MapTask: Starting flush of map output
12/09/28 23:16:25 INFO mapred.MapTask: Finished spill 1
12/09/28 23:16:26 INFO mapred.MapTask: Finished spill 2
12/09/28 23:16:26 INFO mapred.Merger: Merging 3 sorted segments
12/09/28 23:16:26 INFO mapred.Merger: Down to the last merge-pass, with 3 segments left of total
size: 27085156 bytes
12/09/28 23:16:26 INFO mapred.Task: Task:attempt_local_0001_m_000000_0 is done. And is in the
process of commiting
12/09/28 23:16:29 INFO mapred.LocalJobRunner:
12/09/28 23:16:29 INFO mapred.LocalJobRunner:
12/09/28 23:16:29 INFO mapred.Task: Task 'attempt_local_0001_m_000000_0' done.
12/09/28 23:16:29 INFO mapred.Task:  Using ResourceCalculatorPlugin : null
12/09/28 23:16:29 INFO mapred.MapTask: io.sort.mb = 100
12/09/28 23:16:29 INFO mapred.MapTask: data buffer = 79691776/99614720
12/09/28 23:16:29 INFO mapred.MapTask: record buffer = 262144/327680
12/09/28 23:16:29 INFO mapred.MapTask: Spilling map output: record full = true
12/09/28 23:16:30 INFO mapred.MapTask: Finished spill 0
12/09/28 23:16:30 INFO mapred.JobClient:  map 100% reduce 0%
12/09/28 23:16:30 INFO mapred.MapTask: Spilling map output: record full = true
12/09/28 23:16:30 INFO mapred.MapTask: Starting flush of map output
12/09/28 23:16:31 INFO mapred.MapTask: Finished spill 1
12/09/28 23:16:31 INFO mapred.MapTask: Finished spill 2
12/09/28 23:16:31 INFO mapred.Merger: Merging 3 sorted segments
12/09/28 23:16:31 INFO mapred.Merger: Down to the last merge-pass, with 3 segments left of total
size: 27083677 bytes
12/09/28 23:16:31 INFO mapred.Task: Task:attempt_local_0001_m_000001_0 is done. And is in the
process of commiting
12/09/28 23:16:32 INFO mapred.Task: Task 'attempt_local_0001_m_000001_0' done.
12/09/28 23:16:32 INFO mapred.Task:  Using ResourceCalculatorPlugin : null
12/09/28 23:16:32 INFO mapred.MapTask: io.sort.mb = 100
12/09/28 23:16:32 INFO mapred.MapTask: data buffer = 79691776/99614720
12/09/28 23:16:32 INFO mapred.MapTask: record buffer = 262144/327680
12/09/28 23:16:32 INFO mapred.MapTask: Spilling map output: record full = true
12/09/28 23:16:33 INFO mapred.MapTask: Finished spill 0
12/09/28 23:16:33 INFO mapred.MapTask: Spilling map output: record full = true
12/09/28 23:16:33 INFO mapred.MapTask: Starting flush of map output
12/09/28 23:16:34 INFO mapred.MapTask: Finished spill 1
12/09/28 23:16:34 INFO mapred.MapTask: Finished spill 2
12/09/28 23:16:34 INFO mapred.Merger: Merging 3 sorted segments
12/09/28 23:16:34 INFO mapred.Merger: Down to the last merge-pass, with 3 segments left of total
size: 27086619 bytes
12/09/28 23:16:34 INFO mapred.Task: Task:attempt_local_0001_m_000002_0 is done. And is in the
process of commiting
12/09/28 23:16:35 INFO mapred.Task: Task 'attempt_local_0001_m_000002_0' done.
```

12/09/28 23:16:35 INFO mapred.Task: Using ResourceCalculatorPlugin : null
12/09/28 23:16:35 INFO mapred.MapTask: io.sort.mb = 100
12/09/28 23:16:35 INFO mapred.MapTask: data buffer = 79691776/99614720
12/09/28 23:16:35 INFO mapred.MapTask: record buffer = 262144/327680
12/09/28 23:16:35 INFO mapred.MapTask: Spilling map output: record full = true
12/09/28 23:16:36 INFO mapred.MapTask: Finished spill 0
12/09/28 23:16:36 INFO mapred.MapTask: Spilling map output: record full = true
12/09/28 23:16:36 INFO mapred.MapTask: Finished spill 1
12/09/28 23:16:37 INFO mapred.MapTask: Starting flush of map output
12/09/28 23:16:37 INFO mapred.MapTask: Finished spill 2
12/09/28 23:16:37 INFO mapred.Merger: Merging 3 sorted segments
12/09/28 23:16:37 INFO mapred.Merger: Down to the last merge-pass, with 3 segments left of total
size: 33471433 bytes
12/09/28 23:16:38 INFO mapred.Task: Task:attempt_local_0001_m_000003_0 is done. And is in the
process of commiting
12/09/28 23:16:38 INFO mapred.Task: Task 'attempt_local_0001_m_000003_0' done.
12/09/28 23:16:38 INFO mapred.Task: Using ResourceCalculatorPlugin : null
12/09/28 23:16:38 INFO mapred.MapTask: io.sort.mb = 100
12/09/28 23:16:38 INFO mapred.MapTask: data buffer = 79691776/99614720
12/09/28 23:16:38 INFO mapred.MapTask: record buffer = 262144/327680
12/09/28 23:16:38 INFO mapred.MapTask: Spilling map output: record full = true
12/09/28 23:16:39 INFO mapred.MapTask: Finished spill 0
12/09/28 23:16:39 INFO mapred.MapTask: Spilling map output: record full = true
12/09/28 23:16:39 INFO mapred.MapTask: Finished spill 1
12/09/28 23:16:40 INFO mapred.MapTask: Starting flush of map output
12/09/28 23:16:40 INFO mapred.MapTask: Finished spill 2
12/09/28 23:16:40 INFO mapred.Merger: Merging 3 sorted segments
12/09/28 23:16:40 INFO mapred.Merger: Down to the last merge-pass, with 3 segments left of total
size: 33473173 bytes
12/09/28 23:16:41 INFO mapred.Task: Task:attempt_local_0001_m_000004_0 is done. And is in the
process of commiting
12/09/28 23:16:41 INFO mapred.Task: Task 'attempt_local_0001_m_000004_0' done.
12/09/28 23:16:41 INFO mapred.Task: Using ResourceCalculatorPlugin : null
12/09/28 23:16:41 INFO mapred.MapTask: io.sort.mb = 100
12/09/28 23:16:41 INFO mapred.MapTask: data buffer = 79691776/99614720
12/09/28 23:16:41 INFO mapred.MapTask: record buffer = 262144/327680
12/09/28 23:16:41 INFO mapred.MapTask: Spilling map output: record full = true
12/09/28 23:16:42 INFO mapred.MapTask: Finished spill 0
12/09/28 23:16:42 INFO mapred.MapTask: Spilling map output: record full = true
12/09/28 23:16:42 INFO mapred.MapTask: Starting flush of map output
12/09/28 23:16:42 INFO mapred.MapTask: Finished spill 1
12/09/28 23:16:42 INFO mapred.MapTask: Finished spill 2
12/09/28 23:16:42 INFO mapred.Merger: Merging 3 sorted segments
12/09/28 23:16:43 INFO mapred.Merger: Down to the last merge-pass, with 3 segments left of total
size: 26114104 bytes
12/09/28 23:16:43 INFO mapred.Task: Task:attempt_local_0001_m_000005_0 is done. And is in the
process of commiting
12/09/28 23:16:44 INFO mapred.Task: Task 'attempt_local_0001_m_000005_0' done.
12/09/28 23:16:44 INFO mapred.Task: Using ResourceCalculatorPlugin : null

```
12/09/28 23:16:44 INFO mapred.MapTask: io.sort.mb = 100
12/09/28 23:16:44 INFO mapred.MapTask: data buffer = 79691776/99614720
12/09/28 23:16:44 INFO mapred.MapTask: record buffer = 262144/327680
12/09/28 23:16:44 INFO mapred.MapTask: Starting flush of map output
12/09/28 23:16:45 INFO mapred.MapTask: Finished spill 0
12/09/28 23:16:45 INFO mapred.Task: Task:attempt_local_0001_m_000006_0 is done. And is in the
process of commiting
12/09/28 23:16:47 INFO mapred.Task: Task 'attempt_local_0001_m_000006_0' done.
12/09/28 23:16:47 INFO mapred.Task:  Using ResourceCalculatorPlugin : null
12/09/28 23:16:47 INFO mapred.Merger: Merging 7 sorted segments
12/09/28 23:16:47 INFO mapred.Merger: Down to the last merge-pass, with 7 segments left of total
size: 186118362 bytes
12/09/28 23:16:49 INFO mapred.Task: Task:attempt_local_0001_r_000000_0 is done. And is in the
process of commiting
12/09/28 23:16:49 INFO mapred.Task: Task attempt_local_0001_r_000000_0 is allowed to commit
now
12/09/28 23:16:49 INFO output.FileOutputCommitter: Saved output of task
'attempt_local_0001_r_000000_0' to out71
12/09/28 23:16:50 INFO mapred.LocalJobRunner: reduce > reduce
12/09/28 23:16:50 INFO mapred.Task: Task 'attempt_local_0001_r_000000_0' done.
12/09/28 23:16:51 INFO mapred.JobClient:  map 100% reduce 100%
12/09/28 23:16:51 INFO mapred.JobClient: Job complete: job_local_0001
12/09/28 23:16:51 INFO mapred.JobClient: Counters: 17
12/09/28 23:16:51 INFO mapred.JobClient:   File Output Format Counters
12/09/28 23:16:51 INFO mapred.JobClient:     Bytes Written=2122
12/09/28 23:16:51 INFO mapred.JobClient:   FileSystemCounters
12/09/28 23:16:51 INFO mapred.JobClient:     FILE_BYTES_READ=2258078677
12/09/28 23:16:51 INFO mapred.JobClient:     FILE_BYTES_WRITTEN=1920647122
12/09/28 23:16:51 INFO mapred.JobClient:   File Input Format Counters
12/09/28 23:16:51 INFO mapred.JobClient:     Bytes Read=0
12/09/28 23:16:51 INFO mapred.JobClient:   Map-Reduce Framework
12/09/28 23:16:51 INFO mapred.JobClient:     Map output materialized bytes=186118390
12/09/28 23:16:51 INFO mapred.JobClient:     Map input records=4000000
12/09/28 23:16:51 INFO mapred.JobClient:     Reduce shuffle bytes=0
12/09/28 23:16:51 INFO mapred.JobClient:     Spilled Records=11484803
12/09/28 23:16:51 INFO mapred.JobClient:     Map output bytes=178296450
12/09/28 23:16:51 INFO mapred.JobClient:     Total committed heap usage (bytes)=1598029824
12/09/28 23:16:51 INFO mapred.JobClient:     SPLIT_RAW_BYTES=1849
12/09/28 23:16:51 INFO mapred.JobClient:     Combine input records=0
12/09/28 23:16:51 INFO mapred.JobClient:     Reduce input records=3910949
12/09/28 23:16:51 INFO mapred.JobClient:     Reduce input groups=44
12/09/28 23:16:51 INFO mapred.JobClient:     Combine output records=0
12/09/28 23:16:51 INFO mapred.JobClient:     Reduce output records=44
12/09/28 23:16:51 INFO mapred.JobClient:     Map output records=3910949
mc815ll:hadoop-1.0.3 henry$ MultipleOutputs
```

6.4 MULTIPLEOUTPUTS

With all examples we have presented so far, there has always been a single job output by default. The `MultipleOutputs` class allows writing output data to multiple outputs. There are two scenarios associated with this feature:

- Writing output data to different directories designated by the user.
- Writing to user-defined outputs other than the job default output. Each user-defined output is called a *named output*, which can be configured with its own `OutputFormat`, and with its own key and value classes as well.

Next, let's take a look at the MultipleOutputs API and see how it supports the kind of outputs described above.

6.4.1 MultipleOutputs API

The `MutipleOutputs` class is defined as follows:

```
org.apache.hadoop.mapreduce.lib.out;
class MultipleOutputs <KEYOUT, VALUEOUT> {...}
```

It has a parameterized constructor as follows:

```
MultipleOutputs (TaskInputOutputContext <?, ? , KEYOUT, VALUEOUT> context)
```

This constructor creates and initializes multiple outputs support for a given task input/output context. It should be instantiated in the setup method of a mapper or reducer class.

The MultipleOutputs class has the following methods:

- **addNamedOutput**: This method adds a named output for the job with the parameters designated as follows:

```
public static void addNamedOutput (
                Job job,
                String namedOutput,
                Class<? extends OutputFormat> outputFormatClass,
                Class<?> keyClass,
                Class<?> valueClass)
```
Parameters:
```
                job - job to add the named output
                namedOutput - named output name, it has to be a word, letters and
                numbers only, and cannot be the word 'part' as that is reserved for the
                default output.
                outputFormatClass - OutputFormat class.
                keyClass - key class
                valueClass - value class
```

- **setCountersEnabled**: This method enables or disables counters for the named outputs. The counters group is the `MultipleOutputs` class name. The names of the counters are the same as the named outputs. These counters count the number of records written to each output name. By default these counters are disabled. Counters are discussed in the next section.

```
public static void setCountersEnabled (
                Job job,
                boolean enabled)
Parameters:
                job - job to enable
                enabled - indicates if the counters will be enabled or not.
```

- **getCountersEnabled**: Returns if the counters for the named outputs are enabled or not. By default these counters are disabled.

```
public static boolean getCountersEnabled (JobContext job)
Parameters: job - the job
```

- **write**: Writes keys and values to the namedOutput. Output path is a unique file generated for the namedOutput. For example, {namedOutput}-(m|r)-{part-number}

```
public <K,V> void write(
                String namedOutput,
                K key,
                V value) throws IOException, InterruptedException
Parameters:
                namedOutput - the named output name
                key - the key
                value - the value
```

- **write**: Writes keys and values to baseOutputPath using the namedOutput.

```
public <K,V> void write(
                String namedOutput,
                K key,
                V value,
                String baseOutputPath) throws IOException, InterruptedException
Parameters:
                namedOutput - the named output name
                key - the key
                value - the value
                baseOutputPath - base-output path to write the record to. The framework
                will generate unique filename for the baseOutputPath
```

- **write**: Writes keys and values to an output file name. Gets the record writer from job's output format. Job's output format should be a FileOutputFormat.

```
public void write(KEYOUT key,
                VALUEOUT value,
                String baseOutputPath)
```

> throws IOException, InterruptedException

Parameters:

> key - the key
> value - the value
> baseOutputPath - base-output path to write the record to. The framework will generate unique filename for the baseOutputPath

- **close**: Closes all opened outputs. This should be called from the `cleanup` method of a map/reduce task. If overridden, subclasses must invoke `super.close()` at the end of their close () call.

   public void close () throws IOException, InterruptedException

Next, we present two examples to illustrate how to generate multiple outputs with the `MultipleOutputs` API.

6.4.2 MultipleOutputs Example 1

Our first MultipleOutputs example has only one mapper without a reducer. The mapper class shown in Listing 6.5 (a) has an attribute typed `MultipleOutputs`. This attribute is initialized in the `setup` method with the job `context` object. Note the generics of `<NullWritable, Text>` tied to this class. The `NullWritable` class is a singleton writable with no data. The second parameter type `Text` specifies the data to write. The `close ()` method closes the `MultipleOutputs` instance. However, the most relevant part in terms of MultipleOutputs was contained in the `map` (...) method:

```
String fileName = generateFileNameForKeyValue (value);
multipleOutputs.write (NullWritable.get (), value, fileName);
```

The first statement retrieves a file name from the `generateFileNameForKeyValue` (...) method in the mapper class. This method generates a file name based on the transaction date of a transaction record in the format of mm/dd/yyyy, which was transformed with the "/" removed (otherwise, "dd" and "yyyy" would be interpreted as sub-directories). Therefore, we would expect all map intermediate outputs will be partitioned into many files according to the transaction date.

The driver shown in Listing 6.5 (b) has the following four statements relevant to MultipleOutputs:

```
job.setMapperClass(SpendingPatternMapper1f.class);
job.setOutputKeyClass(NullWritable.class);
job.setOutputValueClass(Text.class);
job.setNumReduceTasks (0);
```

The first statement sets the map class, which you have seen many times with the examples presented so far. The second statement specifies the output key class, which has to be `NullWritable.class`, as we are doing multiple outputs now. The fourth statements sets the number of reduce tasks to *zero*, as we want to see multiple outputs with the map intermediate outputs, which would have not persisted if a reducer were specified.

With both the mapper and driver in place, we are ready to run this example. Listing 6.5 (c) shows the console output when it was run in my environment with the following command:

$ hadoop jar spending-patterns.jar SpendingPattern1k1 in0/credit_card_tx_0_out.txt out73

Note that the output directory was *out73*. In order to see the contents of this directory, I issued a command of "*ls –l out73 | cat b*" at the command prompt, with the "*-b*" option for the *cat* command to place the line number at the beginning of each output line. This would allow us to know how many files had been generated. The output of this command is shown below, with many intermediate lines removed to save space:

```
mc815ll:hadoop-1.0.3 henry$ ls -l out73 | cat -b
   1   total 0
   2   drwxr-xr-x  10 henry  staff  340 Sep 26 14:08 01012008
   3   drwxr-xr-x  10 henry  staff  340 Sep 26 14:08 01012009
   4   drwxr-xr-x  10 henry  staff  340 Sep 26 14:08 01012010
   5   drwxr-xr-x  10 henry  staff  340 Sep 26 14:08 01012011
   6   drwxr-xr-x  10 henry  staff  340 Sep 26 14:08 01012012
   7   drwxr-xr-x  10 henry  staff  340 Sep 26 14:08 01022008
   8   drwxr-xr-x  10 henry  staff  340 Sep 26 14:08 01022009
   9   drwxr-xr-x  10 henry  staff  340 Sep 26 14:08 01022010
  10   drwxr-xr-x  10 henry  staff  340 Sep 26 14:08 01022011
  11   drwxr-xr-x  10 henry  staff  340 Sep 26 14:08 01022012
      ...... lines 12 – 1825 omitted to save space ....
1826 drwxr-xr-x  10 henry  staff  340 Sep 26 14:08 12312010
1827 drwxr-xr-x  10 henry  staff  340 Sep 26 14:08 12312011
1828 -rwxrwxrwx   1 henry  staff    0 Sep 26 14:08 _SUCCESS
1829 -rwxrwxrwx   1 henry  staff    0 Sep 26 14:06 part-m-00000
1830 -rwxrwxrwx   1 henry  staff    0 Sep 26 14:07 part-m-00001
1831 -rwxrwxrwx   1 henry  staff    0 Sep 26 14:07 part-m-00002
1832 -rwxrwxrwx   1 henry  staff    0 Sep 26 14:08 part-m-00003
mc815ll:hadoop-1.0.3 henry$
```

As you see, there had been 1825 output files generated from this multiple outputs example, corresponding to the transaction date range from Jan. 1, 2008 to Dec. 31, 2012 specific to that input file. This verified that the multiple outputs implementation worked.

However, those 1825 files were 1825 directories. To confirm this, I picked a specific item named "12312011" and issued the following command:

$ ls out73/12312011

which returned the contents of that directory as shown below. As is seen, it contained the four map output files from *part-m-00000* to *part-m-00003*, corresponding to each of the four mapping tasks.

```
mc815ll:hadoop-1.0.3 henry$ ls out73/12312011
part-m-00000
part-m-00001
part-m-00002
part-m-00003
```

To see exactly what those four files contained, I issued the following command to see just the beginning part of a file, which is shown as follows:

```
mc815ll:hadoop-1.0.3 henry$ head out73/12312011/part-m-00000
12/31/2011    MCDONALD'S F20253    SUNNYVALE    CA    51.91
12/31/2011    DISH NETWORK-ONE TIME  800-894-9131 CO 31.24
12/31/2011    WAL-MART #1760      SUNNYVALE    CA 96.13
12/31/2011    76CR5754SUNNYVALE10080067 SUNNYVALE    CA    2.51
12/31/2011    SAVEMART 607 SUNNYVALE  SUNNYVALE    CA 51.56
12/31/2011    IDEAL CUTS      SUNNYVALE    CA  36.61
12/31/2011    TRICKS GYMNASTICS DANC 916-3510024 CA  73.55
12/31/2011    IDEAL CUTS      SUNNYVALE    CA 27.47
12/31/2011    KP INTERNATIONAL MARKE MILPITAS CA    13.26
12/31/2011    DISNEY RESORT-WDTC    ANAHEIM    CA 50.89
mc815ll:hadoop-1.0.3 henry$
```

This output was determined by the `value` argument of the map method and it was indeed partitioned by transaction date.

This concludes our first `MultipleOutputs` example without a reducer. Our next example shows `MultipleOuts` with a reducer specified.

Listing 6.5 (a) MultipleOutputs example 1: the Mapper

```
import java.io.IOException;

import org.apache.hadoop.io.NullWritable;
import org.apache.hadoop.io.LongWritable;
import org.apache.hadoop.io.Text;
import org.apache.hadoop.mapreduce.Mapper;
import org.apache.hadoop.mapreduce.lib.output.MultipleOutputs;

public class SpendingPatternMapper1f
  extends Mapper<LongWritable, Text, NullWritable, Text> {
  private MultipleOutputs <NullWritable, Text> multipleOutputs;
  @Override
  protected void setup (Context context) throws IOException, InterruptedException {
     multipleOutputs = new MultipleOutputs <NullWritable, Text> (context);
  }
  @Override
  public void map(LongWritable key, Text value, Context context)
     throws IOException, InterruptedException {

  String line = value.toString();
  if (!line.contains ("PAYMENT")) {
   String fileName = generateFileNameForKeyValue (value);
   multipleOutputs.write (NullWritable.get (), value, fileName);
```

```
      }
    }
    @Override
     protected void cleanup (Context context) throws IOException,
      InterruptedException {
        multipleOutputs.close ();
    }
    protected String generateFileNameForKeyValue (Text value) {

        String line = value.toString();
        if (!line.contains ("PAYMENT")) {
         String[] arr = line.split("\t", 0);
         String txDate = arr [0].replaceAll ("/", "");
         return txDate +"/part";
        } else {
         return "payment/part";
        }
    }
  }
  }
```

Listing 6. 5 (b) MultipleOutputs example 1: the driver

```
import org.apache.hadoop.fs.Path;
import org.apache.hadoop.io.NullWritable;
import org.apache.hadoop.io.Text;
import org.apache.hadoop.mapreduce.Job;
import org.apache.hadoop.mapreduce.lib.input.FileInputFormat;
import org.apache.hadoop.mapreduce.lib.input.TextInputFormat;
import org.apache.hadoop.mapreduce.lib.output.FileOutputFormat;
import org.apache.hadoop.mapreduce.lib.output.TextOutputFormat;

import org.apache.hadoop.conf.Configured;
import org.apache.hadoop.util.Tool;
import org.apache.hadoop.util.ToolRunner;
import org.apache.hadoop.util.GenericOptionsParser;
import org.apache.hadoop.conf.*;

public class SpendingPattern1k1 extends Configured implements Tool {

   @Override
   public int run(String[] args) throws Exception {
      Configuration conf = new Configuration();
      String remainingArgs[] = new GenericOptionsParser(conf, args).getRemainingArgs();
      Job job = JobInit.init (this, getConf (), args);
```

```
        if (job == null) {
            return -1;
        }

        job.setJobName("Spending Pattern: Multiple Outputs 1");
        job.setInputFormatClass(TextInputFormat.class);
        job.setOutputFormatClass(TextOutputFormat.class);

        job.setMapperClass(SpendingPatternMapper1f.class);

        job.setOutputKeyClass(NullWritable.class);
        job.setOutputValueClass(Text.class);

        job.setNumReduceTasks (0);
        return job.waitForCompletion(true) ? 0 : 1;
    }

    public static void main(String[] args) throws Exception {
        int exitCode = ToolRunner.run(new SpendingPattern1k1(), args);
        System.exit(exitCode);
    }
}
```

Listing 6.5 (c) Console output from MultipleOutputs example 1

```
mc815ll:hadoop-1.0.3 henry$ hadoop jar spending-patterns.jar SpendingPattern1k1
in0/credit_card_tx_0_out.txt out73
12/09/26 14:06:56 WARN util.NativeCodeLoader: Unable to load native-hadoop library for your
platform... using builtin-java classes where applicable
12/09/26 14:06:56 INFO input.FileInputFormat: Total input paths to process : 1
12/09/26 14:06:56 WARN snappy.LoadSnappy: Snappy native library not loaded
12/09/26 14:06:56 INFO mapred.JobClient: Running job: job_local_0001
12/09/26 14:06:57 INFO mapred.Task:  Using ResourceCalculatorPlugin : null
12/09/26 14:06:57 INFO mapred.JobClient:  map 0% reduce 0%
12/09/26 14:07:03 INFO mapred.JobClient:  map 50% reduce 0%
12/09/26 14:07:06 INFO mapred.JobClient:  map 94% reduce 0%
12/09/26 14:07:09 INFO mapred.Task: Task:attempt_local_0001_m_000000_0 is done. And is in the
process of commiting
12/09/26 14:07:09 INFO mapred.Task: Task attempt_local_0001_m_000000_0 is allowed to commit
now
12/09/26 14:07:09 INFO mapred.JobClient:  map 100% reduce 0%
12/09/26 14:07:18 INFO output.FileOutputCommitter: Saved output of task
'attempt_local_0001_m_000000_0' to out73
12/09/26 14:07:21 INFO mapred.Task: Task 'attempt_local_0001_m_000000_0' done.
12/09/26 14:07:21 INFO mapred.Task:  Using ResourceCalculatorPlugin : null
12/09/26 14:07:28 INFO mapred.JobClient:  map 64% reduce 0%
```

```
12/09/26 14:07:31 INFO mapred.JobClient:  map 79% reduce 0%
12/09/26 14:07:34 INFO mapred.JobClient:  map 92% reduce 0%
12/09/26 14:07:37 INFO mapred.JobClient:  map 100% reduce 0%
12/09/26 14:07:39 INFO mapred.Task: Task:attempt_local_0001_m_000001_0 is done. And is in the
process of commiting
12/09/26 14:07:39 INFO mapred.Task: Task attempt_local_0001_m_000001_0 is allowed to commit
now
12/09/26 14:07:55 INFO output.FileOutputCommitter: Saved output of task
'attempt_local_0001_m_000001_0' to out73
12/09/26 14:07:57 INFO mapred.Task: Task 'attempt_local_0001_m_000001_0' done.
12/09/26 14:07:57 INFO mapred.Task:  Using ResourceCalculatorPlugin : null
12/09/26 14:08:04 INFO mapred.JobClient:  map 66% reduce 0%
12/09/26 14:08:07 INFO mapred.JobClient:  map 76% reduce 0%
12/09/26 14:08:10 INFO mapred.JobClient:  map 90% reduce 0%
12/09/26 14:08:13 INFO mapred.JobClient:  map 100% reduce 0%
12/09/26 14:08:14 INFO mapred.Task: Task:attempt_local_0001_m_000002_0 is done. And is in the
process of commiting
12/09/26 14:08:14 INFO mapred.Task: Task attempt_local_0001_m_000002_0 is allowed to commit
now
12/09/26 14:08:28 INFO output.FileOutputCommitter: Saved output of task
'attempt_local_0001_m_000002_0' to out73
12/09/26 14:08:30 INFO mapred.Task: Task 'attempt_local_0001_m_000002_0' done.
12/09/26 14:08:30 INFO mapred.Task:  Using ResourceCalculatorPlugin : null
12/09/26 14:08:36 INFO mapred.JobClient:  map 75% reduce 0%
12/09/26 14:08:39 INFO mapred.JobClient:  map 89% reduce 0%
12/09/26 14:08:42 INFO mapred.JobClient:  map 100% reduce 0%
12/09/26 14:08:42 INFO mapred.Task: Task:attempt_local_0001_m_000003_0 is done. And is in the
process of commiting
12/09/26 14:08:42 INFO mapred.Task: Task attempt_local_0001_m_000003_0 is allowed to commit
now
12/09/26 14:08:51 INFO output.FileOutputCommitter: Saved output of task
'attempt_local_0001_m_000003_0' to out73
12/09/26 14:08:54 INFO mapred.Task: Task 'attempt_local_0001_m_000003_0' done.
12/09/26 14:08:54 INFO mapred.JobClient: Job complete: job_local_0001
12/09/26 14:08:54 INFO mapred.JobClient: Counters: 9
12/09/26 14:08:54 INFO mapred.JobClient:  File Output Format Counters
12/09/26 14:08:54 INFO mapred.JobClient:   Bytes Written=32
12/09/26 14:08:54 INFO mapred.JobClient:  FileSystemCounters
12/09/26 14:08:54 INFO mapred.JobClient:   FILE_BYTES_READ=319418477
12/09/26 14:08:54 INFO mapred.JobClient:   FILE_BYTES_WRITTEN=316438829
12/09/26 14:08:54 INFO mapred.JobClient:  File Input Format Counters
12/09/26 14:08:54 INFO mapred.JobClient:   Bytes Read=116233631
12/09/26 14:08:54 INFO mapred.JobClient:  Map-Reduce Framework
12/09/26 14:08:54 INFO mapred.JobClient:   Map input records=2000000
12/09/26 14:08:54 INFO mapred.JobClient:   Spilled Records=0
12/09/26 14:08:54 INFO mapred.JobClient:   Total committed heap usage (bytes)=340000768
12/09/26 14:08:54 INFO mapred.JobClient:   Map output records=0
12/09/26 14:08:54 INFO mapred.JobClient:   SPLIT_RAW_BYTES=512
```

```
mc815ll:hadoop-1.0.3 henry$
```

6.4.3 MultipleOutputs Example 2

With this second `MultipleOutputs` example, the mapper as shown in Listing 6.6 (a) is a regular mapper that it takes an input file with the record format of {*transaction date, description, amount*} and outputs key-value pairs in the format of {*description, amount*}. In contrast with the preceding example, we have the `MultipleOutputs` attribute defined in the reducer class as shown in Listing 6.6 (b), as we'd like to show how to use `MultipleOutputs` with a reducer. It's not very different from our preceding MultipleOutputs example except that:

1) The file name is generated according to the name of the city where the store is located, rather than the transaction date as in the preceding example.
2) Since the types of the reduce output keys and values are defined as <*NullWritable, Text*>, we need to format the output values using the following statement so that both keys and values are output:

```
String outValue = key.toString () + "\t" + Float.toString (maxValue);
```

The driver for this example is shown in Listing 6.6 (c). It also is similar to the driver for the preceding example except that we now have to specify a reducer class. Similarly, this example was run with the following command:

```
$ hadoop jar spending-patterns.jar SpendingPattern1k2 in0/credit_card_tx_0_out.txt out85
```

The reduce output was directed to the directory named *out85*. The contents of this directory are shown below with the command *ls –l out85*:

```
mc815ll:hadoop-1.0.3 henry$ ls -l out85
total 72
-rwxrwxrwx  1 henry  staff    46 Sep 26 16:52 ANAHEIM_CA-r-00000
-rwxrwxrwx  1 henry  staff   168 Sep 26 16:52 CUPERTINO_CA-r-00000
-rwxrwxrwx  1 henry  staff    41 Sep 26 16:52 MILPITAS_CA-r-00000
-rwxrwxrwx  1 henry  staff    92 Sep 26 16:52 MOUNTAIN_VIEW_CA-r-00000
-rwxrwxrwx  1 henry  staff   245 Sep 26 16:52 SAN_FRANCISCO_CA-r-00000
-rwxrwxrwx  1 henry  staff  1029 Sep 26 16:52 SUNNYVALE_CA-r-00000
-rwxrwxrwx  1 henry  staff    35 Sep 26 16:52 UL_13-r-00000
-rwxrwxrwx  1 henry  staff    46 Sep 26 16:52 VALLEJO_CA-r-00000
-rwxrwxrwx  1 henry  staff     0 Sep 26 16:52 _SUCCESS
-rwxrwxrwx  1 henry  staff   392 Sep 26 16:52 other-r-00000
-rwxrwxrwx  1 henry  staff     0 Sep 26 16:52 part-r-00000
```

It is seen that the conventional reduce output file is empty and all outputs are partitioned according to the city name where the transaction occurred (note that the file names are in the format of <*cityname_state*>*-r-00000*). We have randomly picked three cities and checked their contents as shown below to confirm that the reduce outputs had indeed been partitioned according to the cities where they occurred. This wraps up our discussion on MultipleOutputs. In the next section, we discuss another advanced Hadoop feature: the Counters.

```
mc815ll:hadoop-1.0.3 henry$ cat out85/ANAHEIM_CA-r-00000
```

```
DISNEY RESORT-WDTC    ANAHEIM      CA 99.99
mc815ll:hadoop-1.0.3 henry$ cat out85/CUPERTINO_CA-r-00000
CUTEGIRL.COM        CUPERTINO CA  99.99
Chinese Gourmet Expres CUPERTINO CA   99.99
PRETZEL TIME SUNRISE  CUPERTINO CA   99.99
TOYS R US #5808    QPS CUPERTINO CA     99.99
mc815ll:hadoop-1.0.3 henry$ cat out85/SUNNYVALE_CA-r-00000
76 10115095        SUNNYVALE    CA    99.99
BABIES R US #6447  QPS SUNNYVALE     CA 99.99
BR/TOGO'S #332475  Q35 SUNNYVALE      CA 99.99
CENTURY THEATRES 41QPS SUNNYVALE       CA    99.99
CVS PHARMACY #9923    SUNNYVALE     CA 99.99
DOLRTREE 1228 00012286 SUNNYVALE     CA     99.99
GROCERY OUTLET OF FO   SUNNYVALE      CA 99.99
GYMBOREE  504850050483 SUNNYVALE      CA    99.99
IDEAL CUTS        SUNNYVALE      CA 99.99
KOHLS #0663        SUNNYVALE    CA   99.99
MARSHALLS # 821      SUNNYVALE      CA 99.99
MCDONALD'S F20253     SUNNYVALE     CA   99.99
MCDONALD'S F26393     SUNNYVALE     CA   99.99
MCDONALD'S F5447      SUNNYVALE     CA   99.99
PETSMART INC 54      SUNNYVALE    CA 99.98
ROSS STORE #483       SUNNYVALE    CA 99.98
SAFEWAY STORE 00017947 SUNNYVALE     CA     99.99
SAMSCLUB #6620       SUNNYVALE    CA99.99
TARGET      00010983 SUNNYVALE     CA99.99
TRU HOLIDAY EXPRESSQPS SUNNYVALE      CA     99.99
WAL-MART #1760        SUNNYVALE     CA    99.99
mc815ll:hadoop-1.0.3 henry$
```

Listing 6.6 (a) MultipleOutputs example 2: the Mapper

```java
import java.io.IOException;
import java.util.StringTokenizer;
import org.apache.hadoop.io.LongWritable;
import org.apache.hadoop.io.FloatWritable;
import org.apache.hadoop.io.Text;
import org.apache.hadoop.mapreduce.Mapper;

public class SpendingPatternMapper1g extends Mapper<LongWritable, Text,
Text, Text> {

@Override
public void map (LongWritable key, Text value, Context context)
   throws IOException, InterruptedException {
```

```
String line = value.toString();
if (!line.contains ("PAYMENT")) {
 StringTokenizer st = new StringTokenizer (line, "\t");
 String tranxDate = st.nextToken();
 String description = st.nextToken();
 String amount = st.nextToken ();
 context.write(new Text(description), new Text (amount));
 }
}
}
```

Listing 6.6 (b) MultipleOutputs example 2: the Reducer

```
import java.io.IOException;

import org.apache.hadoop.io.NullWritable;
import org.apache.hadoop.io.LongWritable;
import org.apache.hadoop.io.FloatWritable;
import org.apache.hadoop.io.Text;
import org.apache.hadoop.mapreduce.Reducer;
import org.apache.hadoop.mapreduce.lib.output.MultipleOutputs;

public class SpendingPatternReducer1e
 extends Reducer<Text, Text, NullWritable, Text> {
 private MultipleOutputs <NullWritable, Text> multipleOutputs;
 @Override
 protected void setup (Context context) throws IOException, InterruptedException {
    multipleOutputs = new MultipleOutputs <NullWritable, Text> (context);
 }
 @Override
 public void reduce(Text key, Iterable<Text> values, Context context)
   throws IOException, InterruptedException {

   String fileName = generateFileNameForKeyValue (key);
   System.out.println ("key=" + key + " fileName = " + fileName);

  float maxValue = Float.MIN_VALUE;
  for (Text value : values) {
  maxValue = Math.max(maxValue, Float.parseFloat (value.toString()));
  }
   String outValue = key.toString () + "\t" + Float.toString (maxValue);
   multipleOutputs.write (NullWritable.get (), new Text (outValue), fileName);
 }
 @Override
```

```java
    protected void cleanup (Context context) throws IOException, InterruptedException {
        multipleOutputs.close ();
    }
    protected String generateFileNameForKeyValue (Text key) {

        String city = key.toString().trim().substring(23);
        if (!city.contains ("PAYMENT")) {
          if (Character.isLetter(city.charAt (0))) {
              int index = city.lastIndexOf (" ");
              String state = city.substring(index + 1);
              city = city.substring(0, index).trim() + "_" + state;
              return city.replaceAll(" ", "_") + "";
          } else {
              return "other";
          }
        } else {
          return "payment";
        }
    }
}
}
```

Listing 6.6 (c) MultipleOutputs example 2: the driver

```java
    import org.apache.hadoop.fs.Path;
    import org.apache.hadoop.io.NullWritable;
    import org.apache.hadoop.io.Text;
    import org.apache.hadoop.mapreduce.Job;
    import org.apache.hadoop.mapreduce.lib.input.FileInputFormat;
    import org.apache.hadoop.mapreduce.lib.input.TextInputFormat;
    import org.apache.hadoop.mapreduce.lib.output.FileOutputFormat;
    import org.apache.hadoop.mapreduce.lib.output.TextOutputFormat;

    import org.apache.hadoop.conf.Configured;
    import org.apache.hadoop.util.Tool;
    import org.apache.hadoop.util.ToolRunner;
    import org.apache.hadoop.util.GenericOptionsParser;
    import org.apache.hadoop.conf.*;

    public class SpendingPattern1k2 extends Configured implements Tool {

      @Override
      public int run(String[] args) throws Exception {
          Configuration conf = new Configuration();
          String remainingArgs[] = new GenericOptionsParser (conf,
```

```
        args).getRemainingArgs();
    Job job = JobInit.init (this, getConf (), args);
    if (job == null) {
        return -1;
    }

    job.setJobName("Spending Pattern: Multiple Outputs 1");
    job.setInputFormatClass(TextInputFormat.class);
    job.setOutputFormatClass(TextOutputFormat.class);

    job.setMapperClass(SpendingPatternMapper1g.class);
    job.setReducerClass(SpendingPatternReducer1e.class);

    job.setMapOutputKeyClass(Text.class);
    job.setOutputKeyClass(NullWritable.class);
    job.setOutputValueClass(Text.class);

    return job.waitForCompletion(true) ? 0 : 1;
    }

    public static void main(String[] args) throws Exception {
        int exitCode = ToolRunner.run(new SpendingPattern1k2(), args);
        System.exit(exitCode);
    }
}
```

Listing 6.6 (d) Console output from the second MultipleOutputs example

```
mc815ll:hadoop-1.0.3 henry$ hadoop jar spending-patterns.jar SpendingPattern1k2
in0/credit_card_tx_0_out.txt out85
12/09/26 16:52:28 WARN util.NativeCodeLoader: Unable to load native-hadoop library for your
platform... using builtin-java classes where applicable
12/09/26 16:52:28 INFO input.FileInputFormat: Total input paths to process : 1
12/09/26 16:52:28 WARN snappy.LoadSnappy: Snappy native library not loaded
12/09/26 16:52:28 INFO mapred.JobClient: Running job: job_local_0001
12/09/26 16:52:29 INFO mapred.Task:  Using ResourceCalculatorPlugin : null
12/09/26 16:52:29 INFO mapred.MapTask: io.sort.mb = 100
12/09/26 16:52:29 INFO mapred.MapTask: data buffer = 79691776/99614720
12/09/26 16:52:29 INFO mapred.MapTask: record buffer = 262144/327680
12/09/26 16:52:29 INFO mapred.JobClient:  map 0% reduce 0%
12/09/26 16:52:30 INFO mapred.MapTask: Spilling map output: record full = true
12/09/26 16:52:30 INFO mapred.MapTask: Finished spill 0
12/09/26 16:52:31 INFO mapred.MapTask: Spilling map output: record full = true
12/09/26 16:52:31 INFO mapred.MapTask: Starting flush of map output
12/09/26 16:52:31 INFO mapred.MapTask: Finished spill 1
12/09/26 16:52:31 INFO mapred.MapTask: Finished spill 2
```

12/09/26 16:52:31 INFO mapred.Merger: Merging 3 sorted segments
12/09/26 16:52:31 INFO mapred.Merger: Down to the last merge-pass, with 3 segments left of total size: 28098975 bytes
12/09/26 16:52:32 INFO mapred.Task: Task:attempt_local_0001_m_000000_0 is done. And is in the process of commiting
12/09/26 16:52:35 INFO mapred.Task: Task 'attempt_local_0001_m_000000_0' done.
12/09/26 16:52:35 INFO mapred.Task: Using ResourceCalculatorPlugin : null
12/09/26 16:52:35 INFO mapred.MapTask: io.sort.mb = 100
12/09/26 16:52:35 INFO mapred.MapTask: data buffer = 79691776/99614720
12/09/26 16:52:35 INFO mapred.MapTask: record buffer = 262144/327680
12/09/26 16:52:35 INFO mapred.MapTask: Finished spill 0
12/09/26 16:52:35 INFO mapred.JobClient: map 100% reduce 0%
12/09/26 16:52:36 INFO mapred.MapTask: Spilling map output: record full = true
12/09/26 16:52:36 INFO mapred.MapTask: Starting flush of map output
12/09/26 16:52:36 INFO mapred.MapTask: Finished spill 1
12/09/26 16:52:36 INFO mapred.MapTask: Finished spill 2
12/09/26 16:52:36 INFO mapred.Merger: Merging 3 sorted segments
12/09/26 16:52:36 INFO mapred.Merger: Down to the last merge-pass, with 3 segments left of total size: 28097151 bytes
12/09/26 16:52:37 INFO mapred.Task: Task:attempt_local_0001_m_000001_0 is done. And is in the process of commiting
12/09/26 16:52:38 INFO mapred.Task: Task 'attempt_local_0001_m_000001_0' done.
12/09/26 16:52:38 INFO mapred.Task: Using ResourceCalculatorPlugin : null
12/09/26 16:52:38 INFO mapred.MapTask: io.sort.mb = 100
12/09/26 16:52:38 INFO mapred.MapTask: data buffer = 79691776/99614720
12/09/26 16:52:38 INFO mapred.MapTask: record buffer = 262144/327680
12/09/26 16:52:38 INFO mapred.MapTask: Spilling map output: record full = true
12/09/26 16:52:38 INFO mapred.MapTask: Finished spill 0
12/09/26 16:52:39 INFO mapred.MapTask: Spilling map output: record full = true
12/09/26 16:52:39 INFO mapred.MapTask: Starting flush of map output
12/09/26 16:52:39 INFO mapred.MapTask: Finished spill 1
12/09/26 16:52:39 INFO mapred.MapTask: Finished spill 2
12/09/26 16:52:39 INFO mapred.Merger: Merging 3 sorted segments
12/09/26 16:52:39 INFO mapred.Merger: Down to the last merge-pass, with 3 segments left of total size: 28099975 bytes
12/09/26 16:52:40 INFO mapred.Task: Task:attempt_local_0001_m_000002_0 is done. And is in the process of commiting
12/09/26 16:52:41 INFO mapred.Task: Task 'attempt_local_0001_m_000002_0' done.
12/09/26 16:52:41 INFO mapred.Task: Using ResourceCalculatorPlugin : null
12/09/26 16:52:41 INFO mapred.MapTask: io.sort.mb = 100
12/09/26 16:52:41 INFO mapred.MapTask: data buffer = 79691776/99614720
12/09/26 16:52:41 INFO mapred.MapTask: record buffer = 262144/327680
12/09/26 16:52:41 INFO mapred.MapTask: Starting flush of map output
12/09/26 16:52:41 INFO mapred.MapTask: Finished spill 0
12/09/26 16:52:41 INFO mapred.Task: Task:attempt_local_0001_m_000003_0 is done. And is in the process of commiting
12/09/26 16:52:44 INFO mapred.Task: Task 'attempt_local_0001_m_000003_0' done.
12/09/26 16:52:44 INFO mapred.Task: Using ResourceCalculatorPlugin : null

```
12/09/26 16:52:44 INFO mapred.Merger: Merging 4 sorted segments
12/09/26 16:52:44 INFO mapred.Merger: Down to the last merge-pass, with 4 segments left of total
size: 96541860 bytes
12/09/26 16:52:44 INFO mapred.LocalJobRunner:
key=76 10115095        SUNNYVALE       CA fileName = SUNNYVALE_CA
key=76CR5754SUNNYVALE10080067 SUNNYVALE       CA fileName = other
......
key=WAL-MART #1760       SUNNYVALE      CA fileName = SUNNYVALE_CA
12/09/26 16:52:45 INFO mapred.Task: Task:attempt_local_0001_r_000000_0 is done. And is in the
process of commiting
12/09/26 16:52:45 INFO mapred.Task: Task attempt_local_0001_r_000000_0 is allowed to commit
now
12/09/26 16:52:45 INFO output.FileOutputCommitter: Saved output of task
'attempt_local_0001_r_000000_0' to out85
12/09/26 16:52:47 INFO mapred.LocalJobRunner: reduce > reduce
12/09/26 16:52:47 INFO mapred.Task: Task 'attempt_local_0001_r_000000_0' done.
12/09/26 16:52:48 INFO mapred.JobClient:  map 100% reduce 100%
12/09/26 16:52:48 INFO mapred.JobClient: Job complete: job_local_0001
12/09/26 16:52:48 INFO mapred.JobClient: Counters: 17
12/09/26 16:52:48 INFO mapred.JobClient:   File Output Format Counters
12/09/26 16:52:48 INFO mapred.JobClient:     Bytes Written=8
12/09/26 16:52:48 INFO mapred.JobClient:   FileSystemCounters
12/09/26 16:52:48 INFO mapred.JobClient:     FILE_BYTES_READ=869452550
12/09/26 16:52:48 INFO mapred.JobClient:     FILE_BYTES_WRITTEN=699308868
12/09/26 16:52:48 INFO mapred.JobClient:   File Input Format Counters
12/09/26 16:52:48 INFO mapred.JobClient:     Bytes Read=116233631
12/09/26 16:52:48 INFO mapred.JobClient:   Map-Reduce Framework
12/09/26 16:52:48 INFO mapred.JobClient:     Map output materialized bytes=96541876
12/09/26 16:52:48 INFO mapred.JobClient:     Map input records=2000000
12/09/26 16:52:48 INFO mapred.JobClient:     Reduce shuffle bytes=0
12/09/26 16:52:48 INFO mapred.JobClient:     Spilled Records=5618663
12/09/26 16:52:48 INFO mapred.JobClient:     Map output bytes=92630714
12/09/26 16:52:48 INFO mapred.JobClient:     Total committed heap usage (bytes)=995069952
12/09/26 16:52:48 INFO mapred.JobClient:     SPLIT_RAW_BYTES=512
12/09/26 16:52:48 INFO mapred.JobClient:     Combine input records=0
12/09/26 16:52:48 INFO mapred.JobClient:     Reduce input records=1955569
12/09/26 16:52:48 INFO mapred.JobClient:     Reduce input groups=44
12/09/26 16:52:48 INFO mapred.JobClient:     Combine output records=0
12/09/26 16:52:48 INFO mapred.JobClient:     Reduce output records=0
12/09/26 16:52:48 INFO mapred.JobClient:     Map output records=1955569
mc815ll:hadoop-1.0.3 henry$
```

6.5 COUNTERS

Throughout this text, you have seen that there is always a section at the end of the console output of a MapReduce program run, which summarizes various counters. For example, the following part was copied to here from the console output of the last example showing nine counters. Following each counter group, which was underlined for convenience, pairs of counter-values are listed. These are standard built-in Hadoop system counters that apply to every MapReduce job. To some extent, these counters constitute a profile about how the job was executed *quantitatively*.

```
12/09/26 14:08:54 INFO mapred.JobClient: Job complete: job_local_0001
12/09/26 14:08:54 INFO mapred.JobClient: Counters: 9
12/09/26 14:08:54 INFO mapred.JobClient:   File Output Format Counters
12/09/26 14:08:54 INFO mapred.JobClient:     Bytes Written=32
12/09/26 14:08:54 INFO mapred.JobClient:   FileSystemCounters
12/09/26 14:08:54 INFO mapred.JobClient:     FILE_BYTES_READ=319418477
12/09/26 14:08:54 INFO mapred.JobClient:     FILE_BYTES_WRITTEN=316438829
12/09/26 14:08:54 INFO mapred.JobClient:   File Input Format Counters
12/09/26 14:08:54 INFO mapred.JobClient:     Bytes Read=116233631
12/09/26 14:08:54 INFO mapred.JobClient:   Map-Reduce Framework
12/09/26 14:08:54 INFO mapred.JobClient:     Map input records=2000000
12/09/26 14:08:54 INFO mapred.JobClient:     Spilled Records=0
12/09/26 14:08:54 INFO mapred.JobClient:     Total committed heap usage (bytes)=340000768
12/09/26 14:08:54 INFO mapred.JobClient:     Map output records=0
12/09/26 14:08:54 INFO mapred.JobClient:     SPLIT_RAW_BYTES=512
```

Can we create our own counters and how do we do that if possible? For example, we might want to know with our spending pattern sample that out of all records processed, how many of them were PAYMENT records. This is made possible with Hadoop's Counter class and Context class, as is explained next.

6.5.1 Static Custom Counters

To implement static custom counters, follow the below steps:

- Creating a Java enum type such as the following:

```
enum TxType {
   PAYMENT
}
```

- In the map (...) method or reduce (...) method, using the increment (int) method of the Counter class via the getCounter (String counterName) of the context object to increment the value of the counter. For example, the following is what we would do for the PAYMENT record:

```
context.getCounter (TxType.PAYMENT).increment(1);
```

- Creating an external properties file to define the counter group and a more readable name for the counter. For example, we can put the following two lines in a file named *SpendingPatternMapper1h_TxType.properties*, which is named in the format of <MapperClassName>_<enumTypeName>.properties (note that this properties file should be placed in the same directory as the top level class containing the enum type):

```
SpendingPatternMapper1h_TxType.properties
CounterGroupName=Special Transaction Types
```

```
PAYMENT.name=Payment
```

That's all we need to do to implement a static custom counter. Next, let's see how to create a non-enum dependent custom dynamic counter.

6.5.2 Dynamic Custom Counters

It's simpler to create a custom dynamic counter than to create a custom static counter, as there is no need to have an enum type and a properties file to go with the enum type. One can simply add one statement in the map (...) method of the mapper class or the reduce (...) method of the reducer class as follows:

```
context.getCounter (counterGroupName, counter).increment (1);
```

where counterGroupName can be hard-coded in the program, and counter is created dynamically during program execution. Together with the custom static counter, we use an example to demonstrate how to create a custom dynamic counter next.

6.5.3 A Counter Example

With this example, we would like to achieve two objectives:

1) Creating a static counter to counter the number of PAYMENT records encountered in the mapper class.
2) Creating a dynamic counter group that contains all records from which the city name could not be parsed properly. The city name is determined dynamically during program execution, so this is a good case to help demonstrate how to create dynamic counters. This exercise would be done with the reducer class, as we would like to partition transactions by city (note that the name of the city is extracted from the description field of the input file).

Given the objectives stated above, we have modified the previous MapReduce example to accommodate both the static and dynamic custom counters. The static customer counter has been implemented in the mapper class shown in Listing 6.7 (a), whereas the dynamic counter has been implemented in the reducer class shown in Listing 6.7 (b). The static counter implementation is self-explanatory, while the dynamic counter implementation calls for a little bit more explanation.

The key to the dynamic counter implementation is to determine the counter with a given counter group. For our example, each transaction record is like the following:

```
MCDONALD'S F5447    SUNNYVALE    CA 99.99
MEG*LEGOLANDCALIFORNIA 760-918-5346 CA   99.99
MEMBERSHIP FEE AUG 12-JUL 13 99.99
PETSMART INC 54    SUNNYVALE    CA 99.99
PRETZEL TIME SUNRISE  CUPERTINO CA   99.99
......
```

The first part is the description field that contains the city name of the store, whereas the last numeric part represents the maximum amount spent at the store. The generateFileNameForKeyValue (...) method of the reducer class returns the file name named with the city name, which is used for the filepath argument (the last one) for the multipleOutputs.write (...) method as shown below:

multipleOutputs.write (NullWritable.get (), new Text (outValue), **fileName**);

This way, the reducer outputs will be partitioned by the city name. However, not all records can be properly parsed with a proper city name. Such records are classified into a file named '*other*', which is the dynamic counter we are trying to implement here. This is done with the following statement in the reducer class:

```
if (fileName.contains("other")) {
  context.getCounter ("City names not parsed properly ",
  key.toString()).increment (1);
    }
```

As is seen, the counter group is named "City names not parsed properly", and the corresponding counter is the key of the record or the description field of the record.

In order to run this example, we have to modify the driver as well for proper mapper and reducer classes, and the modified driver is shown in Listing 6.7 (c). The properties file required for the static counter is shown in Listing 6.7 (d). After running this example, the console output was collected and shown in Listing 6.7 (e). You can identify the dynamic counters and static counters under their respective counter groups as stated above.

This concludes our discussion on creating custom counters. In the next section, we discuss the subject of passing parameters and metadata to MapReduce programs.

Listing 6.7 (a) The Counter example: the Mapper

```java
import java.io.IOException;
import java.util.StringTokenizer;
import org.apache.hadoop.io.LongWritable;
import org.apache.hadoop.io.FloatWritable;
import org.apache.hadoop.io.Text;
import org.apache.hadoop.mapreduce.Mapper;

enum TxType {
  PAYMENT
}
public class SpendingPatternMapper1h extends Mapper<LongWritable, Text, Text, Text> {

@Override
public void map(LongWritable key, Text value, Context context)
  throws IOException, InterruptedException {

String line = value.toString();
```

```
  if (!line.contains ("PAYMENT")) {
    StringTokenizer st = new StringTokenizer (line, "\t");
    String tranxDate = st.nextToken();
    String description = st.nextToken();
    String amount = st.nextToken ();
    context.write(new Text(description), new Text (amount));
  } else {
      context.getCounter (TxType.PAYMENT).increment(1);
  }
 }
 }
```

Listing 6.7 (b) The Counter example: the Reducer

```
import java.io.IOException;

import org.apache.hadoop.io.NullWritable;
import org.apache.hadoop.io.LongWritable;
import org.apache.hadoop.io.FloatWritable;
import org.apache.hadoop.io.Text;
import org.apache.hadoop.mapreduce.Reducer;
import org.apache.hadoop.mapreduce.lib.output.MultipleOutputs;

public class SpendingPatternReducer1f
  extends Reducer<Text, Text, NullWritable, Text> {
  private MultipleOutputs <NullWritable, Text> multipleOutputs;
  @Override
  protected void setup (Context context) throws IOException, InterruptedException {
      multipleOutputs = new MultipleOutputs <NullWritable, Text> (context);
  }
  @Override
  public void reduce(Text key, Iterable<Text> values, Context context)
    throws IOException, InterruptedException {

    String fileName = generateFileNameForKeyValue (key);
    System.out.println ("key=" + key + " fileName = " + fileName);
    if (fileName.contains("other")) {
context.getCounter ("City names not parsed properly ", key.toString()).increment (1);
    }
  float maxValue = Float.MIN_VALUE;
  for (Text value : values) {
  maxValue = Math.max(maxValue, Float.parseFloat (value.toString()));
  }
  String outValue = key.toString () + "\t" + Float.toString (maxValue);
```

```
        multipleOutputs.write (NullWritable.get (), new Text (outValue), fileName);
    }
    @Override
    protected void cleanup (Context context) throws IOException, InterruptedException {
        multipleOutputs.close ();
    }
    protected String generateFileNameForKeyValue (Text key) {

        String city = key.toString().trim().substring(23);
        if (!city.contains ("PAYMENT")) {
          if (Character.isLetter(city.charAt (0))) {
            int index = city.lastIndexOf (" ");
            String state = city.substring(index + 1);
            city = city.substring(0, index).trim() + "_" + state;
            return city.replaceAll(" ", "_") + "";
          } else {
            return "other";
          }
        } else {
          return "payment";
        }
    }
}
}
```

Listing 6.7 (c) The Counter example: the driver

```
import org.apache.hadoop.fs.Path;
import org.apache.hadoop.io.NullWritable;
import org.apache.hadoop.io.Text;
import org.apache.hadoop.mapreduce.Job;
import org.apache.hadoop.mapreduce.lib.input.FileInputFormat;
import org.apache.hadoop.mapreduce.lib.input.TextInputFormat;
import org.apache.hadoop.mapreduce.lib.output.FileOutputFormat;
import org.apache.hadoop.mapreduce.lib.output.TextOutputFormat;

import org.apache.hadoop.conf.Configured;
import org.apache.hadoop.util.Tool;
import org.apache.hadoop.util.ToolRunner;
import org.apache.hadoop.util.GenericOptionsParser;
import org.apache.hadoop.conf.*;

public class SpendingPattern1l extends Configured implements Tool {

    @Override
```

```
public int run(String[] args) throws Exception {
    Configuration conf = new Configuration();
    String remainingArgs[] = new GenericOptionsParser(conf, args).getRemainingArgs();
    Job job = JobInit.init (this, getConf (), args);
    if (job == null) {
        return -1;
    }

    job.setJobName("Spending Pattern: Counter example");
    job.setInputFormatClass(TextInputFormat.class);
    job.setOutputFormatClass(TextOutputFormat.class);

    job.setMapperClass(SpendingPatternMapper1h.class);
    job.setReducerClass(SpendingPatternReducer1f.class);

    job.setMapOutputKeyClass(Text.class);
    job.setOutputKeyClass(NullWritable.class);
    job.setOutputValueClass(Text.class);

    return job.waitForCompletion(true) ? 0 : 1;
}

public static void main(String[] args) throws Exception {
    int exitCode = ToolRunner.run(new SpendingPattern1l(), args);
    System.exit(exitCode);
}
}
```

Listing 6.7 (d) The Counter example property file: SpendingPatternMapper1h_TxType.properties

```
CounterGroupName=Special Transaction Types
PAYMENT.name=Payment
```

Listing 6.7 (e) The Counter example run: console output

```
mc815ll:hadoop-1.0.3 henry$ hadoop jar spending-patterns.jar SpendingPattern1l
in0/credit_card_tx_0_out.txt out86
12/09/27 11:47:36 WARN util.NativeCodeLoader: Unable to load native-hadoop library for your
platform... using builtin-java classes where applicable
12/09/27 11:47:36 INFO input.FileInputFormat: Total input paths to process : 1
12/09/27 11:47:36 WARN snappy.LoadSnappy: Snappy native library not loaded
12/09/27 11:47:36 INFO mapred.JobClient: Running job: job_local_0001
12/09/27 11:47:36 INFO mapred.Task:  Using ResourceCalculatorPlugin : null
12/09/27 11:47:36 INFO mapred.MapTask: io.sort.mb = 100
```

```
12/09/27 11:47:36 INFO mapred.MapTask: data buffer = 79691776/99614720
12/09/27 11:47:36 INFO mapred.MapTask: record buffer = 262144/327680
12/09/27 11:47:37 INFO mapred.JobClient:  map 0% reduce 0%
12/09/27 11:47:37 INFO mapred.MapTask: Spilling map output: record full = true
12/09/27 11:47:38 INFO mapred.MapTask: Finished spill 0
12/09/27 11:47:38 INFO mapred.MapTask: Spilling map output: record full = true
12/09/27 11:47:38 INFO mapred.MapTask: Starting flush of map output
12/09/27 11:47:39 INFO mapred.MapTask: Finished spill 1
12/09/27 11:47:39 INFO mapred.MapTask: Finished spill 2
12/09/27 11:47:39 INFO mapred.Merger: Merging 3 sorted segments
12/09/27 11:47:39 INFO mapred.Merger: Down to the last merge-pass, with 3 segments left of total
size: 28098975 bytes
12/09/27 11:47:40 INFO mapred.Task: Task:attempt_local_0001_m_000000_0 is done. And is in the
process of commiting
12/09/27 11:47:42 INFO mapred.Task: Task 'attempt_local_0001_m_000000_0' done.
12/09/27 11:47:42 INFO mapred.Task:  Using ResourceCalculatorPlugin : null
12/09/27 11:47:42 INFO mapred.MapTask: io.sort.mb = 100
12/09/27 11:47:42 INFO mapred.MapTask: data buffer = 79691776/99614720
12/09/27 11:47:42 INFO mapred.MapTask: record buffer = 262144/327680
12/09/27 11:47:43 INFO mapred.MapTask: Spilling map output: record full = true
12/09/27 11:47:43 INFO mapred.MapTask: Finished spill 0
12/09/27 11:47:43 INFO mapred.JobClient:  map 100% reduce 0%
12/09/27 11:47:44 INFO mapred.MapTask: Spilling map output: record full = true
12/09/27 11:47:44 INFO mapred.MapTask: Starting flush of map output
12/09/27 11:47:44 INFO mapred.MapTask: Finished spill 1
12/09/27 11:47:44 INFO mapred.MapTask: Finished spill 2
12/09/27 11:47:44 INFO mapred.Merger: Merging 3 sorted segments
12/09/27 11:47:44 INFO mapred.Merger: Down to the last merge-pass, with 3 segments left of total
size: 28097151 bytes
12/09/27 11:47:45 INFO mapred.Task: Task:attempt_local_0001_m_000001_0 is done. And is in the
process of commiting
12/09/27 11:47:45 INFO mapred.Task: Task 'attempt_local_0001_m_000001_0' done.
12/09/27 11:47:45 INFO mapred.Task:  Using ResourceCalculatorPlugin : null
12/09/27 11:47:45 INFO mapred.MapTask: io.sort.mb = 100
12/09/27 11:47:45 INFO mapred.MapTask: data buffer = 79691776/99614720
12/09/27 11:47:45 INFO mapred.MapTask: record buffer = 262144/327680
12/09/27 11:47:46 INFO mapred.MapTask: Spilling map output: record full = true
12/09/27 11:47:46 INFO mapred.MapTask: Finished spill 0
12/09/27 11:47:47 INFO mapred.MapTask: Spilling map output: record full = true
12/09/27 11:47:47 INFO mapred.MapTask: Starting flush of map output
12/09/27 11:47:47 INFO mapred.MapTask: Finished spill 1
12/09/27 11:47:47 INFO mapred.MapTask: Finished spill 2
12/09/27 11:47:47 INFO mapred.Merger: Merging 3 sorted segments
12/09/27 11:47:47 INFO mapred.Merger: Down to the last merge-pass, with 3 segments left of total
size: 28099975 bytes
12/09/27 11:47:48 INFO mapred.Task: Task:attempt_local_0001_m_000002_0 is done. And is in the
process of commiting
12/09/27 11:47:48 INFO mapred.Task: Task 'attempt_local_0001_m_000002_0' done.
```

```
12/09/27 11:47:48 INFO mapred.Task:  Using ResourceCalculatorPlugin : null
12/09/27 11:47:48 INFO mapred.MapTask: io.sort.mb = 100
12/09/27 11:47:48 INFO mapred.MapTask: data buffer = 79691776/99614720
12/09/27 11:47:48 INFO mapred.MapTask: record buffer = 262144/327680
12/09/27 11:47:49 INFO mapred.MapTask: Starting flush of map output
12/09/27 11:47:49 INFO mapred.MapTask: Finished spill 0
12/09/27 11:47:49 INFO mapred.Task: Task:attempt_local_0001_m_000003_0 is done. And is in the
process of commiting
12/09/27 11:47:51 INFO mapred.Task: Task 'attempt_local_0001_m_000003_0' done.
12/09/27 11:47:51 INFO mapred.Task:  Using ResourceCalculatorPlugin : null
12/09/27 11:47:51 INFO mapred.Merger: Merging 4 sorted segments
12/09/27 11:47:51 INFO mapred.Merger: Down to the last merge-pass, with 4 segments left of total
size: 96541860 bytes
key=76 10115095        SUNNYVALE      CA fileName = SUNNYVALE_CA
key=76CR5754SUNNYVALE10080067 SUNNYVALE      CA fileName = other
key=99 RANCH #1776      SAN FRANCISCO   CA fileName = SAN_FRANCISCO_CA
key=BABIES R US #6447  QPS SUNNYVALE      CA fileName = SUNNYVALE_CA
......
key=WAL-MART #1760       SUNNYVALE      CA fileName = SUNNYVALE_CA
12/09/27 11:47:53 INFO mapred.Task: Task:attempt_local_0001_r_000000_0 is done. And is in the
process of commiting
12/09/27 11:47:53 INFO mapred.LocalJobRunner:
12/09/27 11:47:53 INFO mapred.Task: Task attempt_local_0001_r_000000_0 is allowed to commit
now
12/09/27 11:47:53 INFO output.FileOutputCommitter: Saved output of task
'attempt_local_0001_r_000000_0' to out86
12/09/27 11:47:54 INFO mapred.LocalJobRunner: reduce > reduce
12/09/27 11:47:54 INFO mapred.Task: Task 'attempt_local_0001_r_000000_0' done.
12/09/27 11:47:55 INFO mapred.JobClient:  map 100% reduce 100%
12/09/27 11:47:55 INFO mapred.JobClient: Job complete: job_local_0001
12/09/27 11:47:55 INFO mapred.JobClient: Counters: 26
12/09/27 11:47:55 INFO mapred.JobClient: City names not parsed properly
12/09/27 11:47:55 INFO mapred.JobClient: DISH NETWORK-ONE TIME  800-894-9131  CO=1
12/09/27 11:47:55 INFO mapred.JobClient: SAVEMART 607 SUNNYVALE    SUNNYVALE CA=1
12/09/27 11:47:55 INFO mapred.JobClient: MEG*LEGOLANDCALIFORNIA 760-918-5346 CA=1
12/09/27 11:47:55 INFO mapred.JobClient: TRICKS GYMNASTICS DANC 916-3510024 CA=1
12/09/27 11:47:55 INFO mapred.JobClient: RUE21 # 384 SUNNYVALE    SUNNYVALE CA=1
12/09/27 11:47:55 INFO mapred.JobClient: SIX FLAGS DISCOVERY KI 07076444000  CA=1
12/09/27 11:47:55 INFO mapred.JobClient: 76CR5754SUNNYVALE10080067 SUNNYVALE CA=1
12/09/27 11:47:55 INFO mapred.JobClient: TOGOS BASKIN SUNNYVALE    SUNNYVALE CA=1
12/09/27 11:47:55 INFO mapred.JobClient:  File Output Format Counters
12/09/27 11:47:55 INFO mapred.JobClient:   Bytes Written=8
12/09/27 11:47:55 INFO mapred.JobClient:  FileSystemCounters
12/09/27 11:47:55 INFO mapred.JobClient:   FILE_BYTES_READ=869479000
12/09/27 11:47:55 INFO mapred.JobClient:   FILE_BYTES_WRITTEN=699335508
12/09/27 11:47:55 INFO mapred.JobClient:  TxType
12/09/27 11:47:55 INFO mapred.JobClient:    PAYMENT=44431
12/09/27 11:47:55 INFO mapred.JobClient:  File Input Format Counters
12/09/27 11:47:55 INFO mapred.JobClient:   Bytes Read=116233631
```

```
12/09/27 11:47:55 INFO mapred.JobClient:   Map-Reduce Framework
12/09/27 11:47:55 INFO mapred.JobClient:   Map output materialized bytes=96541876
12/09/27 11:47:55 INFO mapred.JobClient:   Map input records=2000000
12/09/27 11:47:55 INFO mapred.JobClient:   Reduce shuffle bytes=0
12/09/27 11:47:55 INFO mapred.JobClient:   Spilled Records=5618663
12/09/27 11:47:55 INFO mapred.JobClient:   Map output bytes=92630714
12/09/27 11:47:55 INFO mapred.JobClient:   Total committed heap usage (bytes)=995565568
12/09/27 11:47:55 INFO mapred.JobClient:   SPLIT_RAW_BYTES=512
12/09/27 11:47:55 INFO mapred.JobClient:   Combine input records=0
12/09/27 11:47:55 INFO mapred.JobClient:   Reduce input records=1955569
12/09/27 11:47:55 INFO mapred.JobClient:   Reduce input groups=44
12/09/27 11:47:55 INFO mapred.JobClient:   Combine output records=0
12/09/27 11:47:55 INFO mapred.JobClient:   Reduce output records=0
12/09/27 11:47:55 INFO mapred.JobClient:   Map output records=1955569
mc815ll:hadoop-1.0.3 henry$
```

6.6   PASSING PARAMETERS/METADATA TO MAPREDUCE PROGRAMS

Like any other programs written in Java or any other languages, Hadoop MapReduce programs may require some parameters externalized so that one does not have to recompile and deploy every time when a parameter needs to be set to a different value. Besides, during startup, MapReduce programs might need to read and cache some static metadata in order to function properly. For example, with our SpendingPattern MapReduce program, we might want to pass some filters into the Mapper or Reducer program to filter certain types of credit card transactions that are not shopping related such as payments and membership fees, etc.

In this section, we demonstrate how to pass parameters and metadata to MapReduce programs as you would with any other programs you are familiar with. There are two approaches to dealing with these requirements: using the Hadoop job *Configuration* object and using the Hadoop *Distributed Cache* mechanism. Next, we describe each of these two methods, followed with a working sample to illustrate exactly how to make them work. The subject matter contexts may not be exactly what you are looking for, but the programming bits would be similar no matter what parameters or metadata you want to pass into your MapReduce programs.

6.6.1 Using the Job Configuration

Recall that in §5.7.1 we introduced a few Hadoop classes such as the *Configuration, JobConf, Job* and *JobContext* classes that are used to facilitate configuring and executing mapping and reducing tasks. Recall also that in that same section we once introduced Hadoop generic options feature that allows both built-in and user-defined parameters to be passed in and then retrieved internally in a map or reduce program. This feature and those classes make it possible to specify a parameter at the command line and retrieve it internally at the proper place. Next, let's use an example to illustrate how this works.

Suppose we want to pass a parameter named `record.ignore.type` to instruct the mapper or reducer program to ignore certain types of transactions such as *payment* (note that it makes no sense to find the maximum amount paid by a credit card holder. Those records are there simply because they are part of a credit card account monthly statement, so we want to filter them out from being included in the reduce output). This can be done as follows:

1) Add the Hadoop generic option "`-D record.ignore.type=PAYMENT`" following the main class specified in your Hadoop job launching command of "`hadoop jar <your jar file> <your main class> <your generic option> <your command option>`".

2) Inside your mapper or reducer class, declare a variable for holding this parameter. For this example, let's say we declare it as `String recordToIgnore`.

3) Use the `context` object in you `map` or `reduce` method to retrieve this parameter into the variable declared in your mapper or reducer class. With our example in question, it can be done as follows (note that the second parameter is the default value):

```
recordToIgnore = (context.getConfiguration()).get
➥("record.ignore.type", "PAYMENT");
```

So far, we have hard-coded this parameter into the Mapper classes we have presented, but that's exactly how we would parameterize in the example we present after we discuss how to pass metadata into a mapper or reducer program using the Distributed Cache mechanism next.

6.6.2 Using the Distributed Cache

The previous approach to passing parameters into a MapReduce program works well when we do not have many parameters to pass in. However, it would become clumsy quickly when we have too many parameters to pass in. For example, we may also want to ignore the membership fee transactions, because they are not related to shopping. In this case, if we continue to use the Hadoop generic options feature, we would need to add another option like "`-D record.ignore.type=MEMBERSHIP`". What if we have additional transaction types to ignore? A better approach is putting all ignorable transaction types into a file and specify a "`-files <filename>`" generic option to pass them in, where <filename> represents the name of the file that contains all ignorable transaction types. This is the approach to using the Distributed Cache as is discussed next.

The "`- files`" option takes a comma-separated list of files to be distributed to all nodes of a Hadoop cluster (note the plural form and the singular form would not work even if you have only one file to distribute). The files specified would be copied to the HDFS first. Then before a task on a node needs them, the files would be copied from the HDFS to the local filesystem of the node. From this point on, when the program starts to execute, these files would be read into the memory as if they were regular files on the local filesystem. Note that in this context, the term *distributed cache* means that files are *localized* onto the local filesystem of each node in the cluster.

For our example in question, we would put the PAYMENT and MEMBERSHIP transaction types into a text file named *tx-type-filter.txt* as two separate lines. Then, the file can be passed in with the option of "- *files tx-type-filter.txt*", similar to the "–D" option we discussed in the preceding section except that we are passing in a metadata file instead of a parameter. Then the metadata would be cached internally in a mapper or reducer program. The example to be presented next shows how it is done exactly.

Before moving to the next section, let me mention that there are two other options similar to the "-files ..." option: the "- `libjars`" option and the "- `archives`" option, which can be used to add the jar files and archives to the distributed cache. The difference between the two options is that jar files are not un-archived while the archive files are un-archived. The jar files would be added to the *classpath* of the mapper and reducer programs if they were not included in the jar file following the Hadoop jar command.

Next, let's use a single example to demonstrate how the above two approaches work to help pass parameters and metadata into mapper and reducer programs.

6.6.3 Parameter/Metadata Passing Example

Before presenting the example, let me state what we want to accomplish. We would like to accomplish two things:

1) We would like to pass the "-D `record.ignore.type=PAYMENT`" parameter into the mapper class so that we do not have to hard-code a specific type of transactions to ignore. We would specify "PAYMENT" but it could be any other types as we see fit. We would use the Configuration and Context classes to accomplish this in the mapper class.

2) To demonstrate the approach to using the distributed cache mechanism to pass in metadata to a mapper or a reducer program, we put the PAYMENT and MEMBERSHIP transaction types into a text file and pass them in. This seems to be partially redundant with the preceding approach, but our purpose here is to show the *method* rather than what makes sense and what doesn't from the application's point of view. What metadata we are passing in is less a concern for the moment.

Similar to all MapReduce examples we have presented so far, we would need a mapper, a reducer and a driver. Let's start with the mapper class first.

The mapper class is shown in listing 6.8 (a). Note that we have a `String recordToIgnore` variable defined. The configuration object is obtained with the `context.getConfiguration ()` method. Refer to §5.7.1 and you would find that the `Configuration` class has a method `get (String, String)`, which can be used to retrieve a property with the name of the property specified in the first argument and the default value specified in the second argument. The retrieved value is assigned to the variable defined as an attribute of the class. Next, the application logic uses this attribute to determine whether the current record should be discarded. If it should be, then the corresponding counter is incremented.

This mapper class demonstrates how to pass a parameter to a mapper program. The reducer class shown in Listing 6.8 (b) demonstrates how to pass metadata into a reducer program via Hadoop Distributed Cache mechanism. This reducer class has an `ArrayList` data structure to hold the metadata to be passed in. It has a `setup (...)` method for reading the metadata from the specified file "*tx-type-filter.txt*", which will be specified as a Hadoop generic option in the format of "– *files* <*files*>" as we discussed earlier. How the metadata information is read is purely Java, which is easy to follow. There is another method named txTypeIsValid (...) that compares each filter item with the key of the current transaction to determine if the current transaction record is valid or should be filtered. This method is used in the reduce (...) method to switch the logic based on the boolean value returned from the txTypeIsValid (...) method. The bulk of the application logic is executed only if the transaction record being processed is valid. The programming itself is Java and easy to understand. The importance is to understand how everything works in Hadoop's context.

The driver is shown in Listing 6.8 (c). There is nothing special in terms of parameter and metadata passing except that it needs to extend Configured class and implement Tool interface to enable Hadoop generic options feature. Of course, it needs to specify the proper mapper and reducer classes. Besides, this example was adapted based on the MultipleOutputs example presented in the previous section, so you need to refer back to that example for any MultipleOutputs related statements.

Before running the example, make sure the file *tx-type-filter.txt* specified in the reducer class is placed in the Hadoop installation directory. As is shown in Listing 6.8 (d) and discussed previously, the metadata file *tx-type-filter.txt* contains only two lines: PAYMENT and MEMBERSHIP. It doesn't seem to be a lot, but suffices for illustrating how to use Hadoop distributed cache feature to pass metadata into a mapper or reducer class.

Listing 6.8 (e) shows the console output of running this example. Once again, you need to copy the packaged *spending-patterns.jar* file to Hadoop's installation directory and execute the following command as can be found from the beginning of Listing 6.8 (e) (note that no space should be placed following the dash sign in both "-D" and "-files"):

```
$ hadoop jar spending-patterns.jar SpendingPattern1m
 ↪-D record.ignore.type=PAYMENT -files tx-type-filter.txt in0/credit_card_tx_0_out.txt out91
```

The console output was directed to the directory named *out91*. To verify the effect of applying the transaction type filter passed in as metadata as shown in Listing 6.8 (d), the reduce output from the previous example, which did not have this filter applied, was appended to the end of Listing 6.8 (e). You can see that the MEMBERSHIP record that appeared in the output of the previous example did not show up in the reduce output of this example. This concludes our coverage of passing parameters and metadata to MapReduce programs.

Listing 6.8 (a) The parameter/metadata passing example: the Mapper

```
import java.io.IOException;
import java.util.StringTokenizer;
import org.apache.hadoop.io.LongWritable;
import org.apache.hadoop.io.FloatWritable;
import org.apache.hadoop.io.Text;
import org.apache.hadoop.mapreduce.Mapper;
public class SpendingPatternMapper1i extends
```

```
Mapper<LongWritable, Text, Text, Text> {
    String recordToIgnore;
@Override
public void map (LongWritable key, Text value, Context context)
    throws IOException, InterruptedException {
    recordToIgnore = (context.getConfiguration()).get
("record.ignore.type", "PAYMENT");
 String line = value.toString();
 if (!line.contains (recordToIgnore)) {
    StringTokenizer st = new StringTokenizer (line, "\t");
    String tranxDate = st.nextToken();
    String description = st.nextToken();
    String amount = st.nextToken ();
    context.write(new Text(description), new Text (amount));
 } else {
    context.getCounter (recordToIgnore).increment(1);
 }
}
}
```

Listing 6.8 (b) The parameter/metadata passing example: the Reducer

```
import java.io.*;
import java.util.*;
import org.apache.hadoop.io.NullWritable;
import org.apache.hadoop.io.LongWritable;
import org.apache.hadoop.io.FloatWritable;
import org.apache.hadoop.io.Text;
import org.apache.hadoop.mapreduce.Reducer;
import org.apache.hadoop.mapreduce.lib.output.MultipleOutputs;

public class SpendingPatternReducer1g extends
        Reducer<Text, Text, NullWritable, Text> {
    private ArrayList <String> txFilter;
    private MultipleOutputs<NullWritable, Text> multipleOutputs;

    @Override
    protected void setup(Context context) throws IOException,
            InterruptedException {
        multipleOutputs = new MultipleOutputs<NullWritable, Text>(context);
        // populate the txFilter ArrayList
        txFilter = new ArrayList<String>();
        BufferedReader reader = null;
        try {
```

```java
        reader = new BufferedReader(new InputStreamReader(
                new FileInputStream("tx-type-filter.txt")));
        String line;
        while ((line = reader.readLine()) != null) {
            txFilter.add(line.trim());
        }
    } finally {
        if (reader!= null) reader.close();
    }
}

@Override
public void reduce (Text key, Iterable<Text> values,
        Context context) throws IOException, InterruptedException {
    if (txTypeIsValid(key.toString())) {
        String fileName = generateFileNameForKeyValue(key);
        System.out.println(key + " fileName = " + fileName);
        if (fileName.contains("other")) {
            context.getCounter("City names not parsed properly ",
                    key.toString()).increment(1);
        }
        float maxValue = Float.MIN_VALUE;
        for (Text value : values) {
            maxValue = Math.max(maxValue,
                    Float.parseFloat(value.toString()));
        }
        String outValue = key.toString() + "\t" + Float.toString(maxValue);
        multipleOutputs.write(NullWritable.get(), new Text(outValue),
                fileName);
    }
}

@Override
protected void cleanup(Context context) throws IOException,
        InterruptedException {
    multipleOutputs.close();
}

protected String generateFileNameForKeyValue(Text key) {

    String city = key.toString().trim().substring(23);
    if (!city.contains ("PAYMENT")) {
        if (Character.isLetter(city.charAt(0))) {
            int index = city.lastIndexOf(" ");
```

```
                String state = city.substring(index + 1);
                city = city.substring(0, index).trim() + "_" + state;
                return city.replaceAll(" ", "_") + "";
            } else {
                return "other";
            }
        } else {
            return "payment";
        }
    }


    protected boolean txTypeIsValid(String key) {
        boolean valid = true;
        for (int i = 0; i < txFilter.size(); i++) {
            if (key.startsWith(txFilter.get(i))) {
                valid = false;
                break;
            }
        }
        return valid;
    }
}
```

Listing 6.8 (c) The parameter/metadata passing example: the driver

```
import org.apache.hadoop.fs.Path;
import org.apache.hadoop.io.NullWritable;
import org.apache.hadoop.io.Text;
import org.apache.hadoop.mapreduce.Job;
import org.apache.hadoop.mapreduce.lib.input.FileInputFormat;
import org.apache.hadoop.mapreduce.lib.input.TextInputFormat;
import org.apache.hadoop.mapreduce.lib.output.FileOutputFormat;
import org.apache.hadoop.mapreduce.lib.output.TextOutputFormat;

import org.apache.hadoop.conf.Configured;
import org.apache.hadoop.util.Tool;
import org.apache.hadoop.util.ToolRunner;
import org.apache.hadoop.util.GenericOptionsParser;
import org.apache.hadoop.conf.*;

public class SpendingPattern1m extends Configured implements Tool {

    @Override
    public int run(String[] args) throws Exception {
```

```
        Configuration conf = new Configuration();
        String remainingArgs[] = new GenericOptionsParser
(conf, args).getRemainingArgs();
        Job job = JobInit.init (this, getConf (), args);
        if (job == null) {
            return -1;
        }

        job.setJobName("Spending Pattern: param and metadata passing  example");
        job.setInputFormatClass(TextInputFormat.class);
        job.setOutputFormatClass(TextOutputFormat.class);

        job.setMapperClass(SpendingPatternMapper1i.class);
        job.setReducerClass(SpendingPatternReducer1g.class);

        job.setMapOutputKeyClass(Text.class);
        job.setOutputKeyClass(NullWritable.class);
        job.setOutputValueClass(Text.class);

        return job.waitForCompletion(true) ? 0 : 1;
    }

    public static void main(String[] args) throws Exception {
        int exitCode = ToolRunner.run(new SpendingPattern1m(), args);
        System.exit(exitCode);
    }
}
```

Listing 6.8 (d) The parameter/metadata passing example: tx-type-filter.txt

```
MEMBERSHIP
PAYMENT
```

Listing 6.8 (e) The parameter/metadata passing example: console output

```
mc815ll:hadoop-1.0.3 henry$ hadoop jar spending-patterns.jar SpendingPattern1m -D
record.ignore.type=PAYMENT -files tx-type-filter.txt in0/credit_card_tx_0_out.txt out91
12/09/27 22:21:31 WARN util.NativeCodeLoader: Unable to load native-hadoop library for your
platform... using builtin-java classes where applicable
12/09/27 22:21:31 INFO input.FileInputFormat: Total input paths to process : 1
12/09/27 22:21:31 WARN snappy.LoadSnappy: Snappy native library not loaded
12/09/27 22:21:32 INFO filecache.TrackerDistributedCacheManager: Creating tx-type-filter.txt in
/tmp/hadoop-henry/mapred/local/archive/3952051824995222739_-
78324236_188808684/file/Users/henry/dev/hadoop-1.0.3-work--649232234911577571 with rwxr-xr-x
```

12/09/27 22:21:32 INFO filecache.TrackerDistributedCacheManager: Cached
file:/Users/henry/dev/hadoop-1.0.3/tx-type-filter.txt#tx-type-filter.txt as /tmp/hadoop-
henry/mapred/local/archive/3952051824995222739_-
78324236_188808684/file/Users/henry/dev/hadoop-1.0.3/tx-type-filter.txt
12/09/27 22:21:32 INFO filecache.TrackerDistributedCacheManager: Cached
file:/Users/henry/dev/hadoop-1.0.3/tx-type-filter.txt#tx-type-filter.txt as /tmp/hadoop-
henry/mapred/local/archive/3952051824995222739_-
78324236_188808684/file/Users/henry/dev/hadoop-1.0.3/tx-type-filter.txt
12/09/27 22:21:32 WARN mapred.LocalJobRunner: LocalJobRunner does not support symlinking into
current working dir.
12/09/27 22:21:32 INFO mapred.TaskRunner: **Creating symlink**: /tmp/hadoop-
henry/mapred/local/archive/3952051824995222739_-
78324236_188808684/file/Users/henry/dev/hadoop-1.0.3/tx-type-filter.txt <- /tmp/hadoop-
henry/mapred/local/localRunner/tx-type-filter.txt
12/09/27 22:21:32 INFO mapred.JobClient: Running job: job_local_0001
12/09/27 22:21:32 INFO mapred.Task: Using ResourceCalculatorPlugin : null
12/09/27 22:21:32 INFO mapred.MapTask: io.sort.mb = 100
12/09/27 22:21:32 INFO mapred.MapTask: data buffer = 79691776/99614720
12/09/27 22:21:32 INFO mapred.MapTask: record buffer = 262144/327680
12/09/27 22:21:33 INFO mapred.JobClient: map 0% reduce 0%
12/09/27 22:21:33 INFO mapred.MapTask: Spilling map output: record full = true
12/09/27 22:21:33 INFO mapred.MapTask: Finished spill 0
12/09/27 22:21:34 INFO mapred.MapTask: Spilling map output: record full = true
12/09/27 22:21:34 INFO mapred.MapTask: Starting flush of map output
12/09/27 22:21:34 INFO mapred.MapTask: Finished spill 1
12/09/27 22:21:34 INFO mapred.MapTask: Finished spill 2
12/09/27 22:21:34 INFO mapred.Merger: Merging 3 sorted segments
12/09/27 22:21:34 INFO mapred.Merger: Down to the last merge-pass, with 3 segments left of total
size: 28098975 bytes
12/09/27 22:21:35 INFO mapred.Task: Task:attempt_local_0001_m_000000_0 is done. And is in the
process of commiting
12/09/27 22:21:38 INFO mapred.Task: Task 'attempt_local_0001_m_000000_0' done.
12/09/27 22:21:38 INFO mapred.Task: Using ResourceCalculatorPlugin : null
12/09/27 22:21:38 INFO mapred.MapTask: io.sort.mb = 100
12/09/27 22:21:38 INFO mapred.MapTask: data buffer = 79691776/99614720
12/09/27 22:21:38 INFO mapred.MapTask: record buffer = 262144/327680
12/09/27 22:21:38 INFO mapred.MapTask: Spilling map output: record full = true
12/09/27 22:21:39 INFO mapred.JobClient: map 100% reduce 0%
12/09/27 22:21:39 INFO mapred.MapTask: Finished spill 0
12/09/27 22:21:39 INFO mapred.MapTask: Spilling map output: record full = true
12/09/27 22:21:39 INFO mapred.MapTask: Starting flush of map output
12/09/27 22:21:39 INFO mapred.MapTask: Finished spill 1
12/09/27 22:21:39 INFO mapred.MapTask: Finished spill 2
12/09/27 22:21:39 INFO mapred.Merger: Merging 3 sorted segments
12/09/27 22:21:40 INFO mapred.Merger: Down to the last merge-pass, with 3 segments left of total
size: 28097151 bytes
12/09/27 22:21:40 INFO mapred.Task: Task:attempt_local_0001_m_000001_0 is done. And is in the
process of commiting

12/09/27 22:21:41 INFO mapred.Task: Task 'attempt_local_0001_m_000001_0' done.
12/09/27 22:21:41 INFO mapred.Task: Using ResourceCalculatorPlugin : null
12/09/27 22:21:41 INFO mapred.MapTask: io.sort.mb = 100
12/09/27 22:21:41 INFO mapred.MapTask: data buffer = 79691776/99614720
12/09/27 22:21:41 INFO mapred.MapTask: record buffer = 262144/327680
12/09/27 22:21:41 INFO mapred.MapTask: Spilling map output: record full = true
12/09/27 22:21:42 INFO mapred.MapTask: Finished spill 0
12/09/27 22:21:42 INFO mapred.MapTask: Spilling map output: record full = true
12/09/27 22:21:42 INFO mapred.MapTask: Starting flush of map output
12/09/27 22:21:42 INFO mapred.MapTask: Finished spill 1
12/09/27 22:21:43 INFO mapred.MapTask: Finished spill 2
12/09/27 22:21:43 INFO mapred.Merger: Merging 3 sorted segments
12/09/27 22:21:43 INFO mapred.Merger: Down to the last merge-pass, with 3 segments left of total size: 28099975 bytes
12/09/27 22:21:43 INFO mapred.Task: Task:attempt_local_0001_m_000002_0 is done. And is in the process of commiting
12/09/27 22:21:44 INFO mapred.Task: Task 'attempt_local_0001_m_000002_0' done.
12/09/27 22:21:44 INFO mapred.Task: Using ResourceCalculatorPlugin : null
12/09/27 22:21:44 INFO mapred.MapTask: io.sort.mb = 100
12/09/27 22:21:44 INFO mapred.MapTask: data buffer = 79691776/99614720
12/09/27 22:21:44 INFO mapred.MapTask: record buffer = 262144/327680
12/09/27 22:21:44 INFO mapred.MapTask: Starting flush of map output
12/09/27 22:21:45 INFO mapred.MapTask: Finished spill 0
12/09/27 22:21:45 INFO mapred.Task: Task:attempt_local_0001_m_000003_0 is done. And is in the process of commiting
12/09/27 22:21:47 INFO mapred.Task: Task 'attempt_local_0001_m_000003_0' done.
12/09/27 22:21:47 INFO mapred.Task: Using ResourceCalculatorPlugin : null
12/09/27 22:21:47 INFO mapred.Merger: Merging 4 sorted segments
12/09/27 22:21:47 INFO mapred.Merger: Down to the last merge-pass, with 4 segments left of total size: 96541860 bytes
76 10115095   SUNNYVALE   CA fileName = SUNNYVALE_CA
76CR5754SUNNYVALE10080067 SUNNYVALE   CA fileName = other
99 RANCH #1776   SAN FRANCISCO   CA fileName = SAN_FRANCISCO_CA
BABIES R US #6447 QPS SUNNYVALE   CA fileName = SUNNYVALE_CA
……
WAL-MART #1760   SUNNYVALE   CA fileName = SUNNYVALE_CA
12/09/27 22:21:48 INFO mapred.Task: Task:attempt_local_0001_r_000000_0 is done. And is in the process of commiting
12/09/27 22:21:48 INFO mapred.Task: Task attempt_local_0001_r_000000_0 is allowed to commit now
12/09/27 22:21:48 INFO output.FileOutputCommitter: Saved output of task 'attempt_local_0001_r_000000_0' to out91
12/09/27 22:21:50 INFO mapred.LocalJobRunner: reduce > reduce
12/09/27 22:21:50 INFO mapred.Task: Task 'attempt_local_0001_r_000000_0' done.
12/09/27 22:21:51 INFO mapred.JobClient: map 100% reduce 100%
12/09/27 22:21:51 INFO mapred.JobClient: Job complete: job_local_0001
12/09/27 22:21:51 INFO mapred.JobClient: Counters: 26
12/09/27 22:21:51 INFO mapred.JobClient: City names not parsed properly
12/09/27 22:21:51 INFO mapred.JobClient: DISH NETWORK-ONE TIME 800-894-9131CO=1

```
12/09/27 22:21:51 INFO mapred.JobClient: SAVEMART 607 SUNNYVALE    SUNNYVALE CA=1
12/09/27 22:21:51 INFO mapred.JobClient: MEG*LEGOLANDCALIFORNIA 760-918-5346 CA=1
12/09/27 22:21:51 INFO mapred.JobClient: TRICKS GYMNASTICS DANC 916-3510024   CA=1
12/09/27 22:21:51 INFO mapred.JobClient: RUE21 # 384 SUNNYVALE     SUNNYVALE CA=1
12/09/27 22:21:51 INFO mapred.JobClient: SIX FLAGS DISCOVERY KI 07076444000   CA=1
12/09/27 22:21:51 INFO mapred.JobClient: 76CR5754SUNNYVALE10080067 SUNNYVALE CA=1
12/09/27 22:21:51 INFO mapred.JobClient: TOGOS BASKIN SUNNYVALE    SUNNYVALE CA=1
12/09/27 22:21:51 INFO mapred.JobClient:  File Output Format Counters
12/09/27 22:21:51 INFO mapred.JobClient:   Bytes Written=8
12/09/27 22:21:51 INFO mapred.JobClient:  FileSystemCounters
12/09/27 22:21:51 INFO mapred.JobClient:   FILE_BYTES_READ=869504600
12/09/27 22:21:51 INFO mapred.JobClient:   FILE_BYTES_WRITTEN=699369061
12/09/27 22:21:51 INFO mapred.JobClient:  TxType
12/09/27 22:21:51 INFO mapred.JobClient:   PAYMENT=44431
12/09/27 22:21:51 INFO mapred.JobClient:  File Input Format Counters
12/09/27 22:21:51 INFO mapred.JobClient:   Bytes Read=116233631
12/09/27 22:21:51 INFO mapred.JobClient:  Map-Reduce Framework
12/09/27 22:21:51 INFO mapred.JobClient:   Map output materialized bytes=96541876
12/09/27 22:21:51 INFO mapred.JobClient:   Map input records=2000000
12/09/27 22:21:51 INFO mapred.JobClient:   Reduce shuffle bytes=0
12/09/27 22:21:51 INFO mapred.JobClient:   Spilled Records=5618663
12/09/27 22:21:51 INFO mapred.JobClient:   Map output bytes=92630714
12/09/27 22:21:51 INFO mapred.JobClient:   Total committed heap usage (bytes)=999362560
12/09/27 22:21:51 INFO mapred.JobClient:   SPLIT_RAW_BYTES=512
12/09/27 22:21:51 INFO mapred.JobClient:   Combine input records=0
12/09/27 22:21:51 INFO mapred.JobClient:   Reduce input records=1955569
12/09/27 22:21:51 INFO mapred.JobClient:   Reduce input groups=44
12/09/27 22:21:51 INFO mapred.JobClient:   Combine output records=0
12/09/27 22:21:51 INFO mapred.JobClient:   Reduce output records=0
12/09/27 22:21:51 INFO mapred.JobClient:   Map output records=1955569
mc815ll:hadoop-1.0.3 henry$ ls out91
ANAHEIM_CA-r-00000       MILPITAS_CA-r-00000
SAN_FRANCISCO_CA-r-00000 VALLEJO_CA-r-00000       other-r-00000
CUPERTINO_CA-r-00000        MOUNTAIN_VIEW_CA-r-00000 SUNNYVALE_CA-r-00000
  _SUCCESS           part-r-00000
mc815ll:hadoop-1.0.3 henry$ cat out91/other-r-00000
76CR5754SUNNYVALE10080067 SUNNYVALE    CA 99.99
DISH NETWORK-ONE TIME 800-894-9131 CO 99.99
MEG*LEGOLANDCALIFORNIA 760-918-5346 CA   99.99
RUE21 # 384 SUNNYVALE    SUNNYVALE    CA   99.99
SAVEMART 607 SUNNYVALE   SUNNYVALE    CA 99.99
SIX FLAGS DISCOVERY KI 07076444000   CA   99.99
TOGOS BASKIN SUNNYVALE   SUNNYVALE    CA 99.99
TRICKS GYMNASTICS DANC 916-3510024   CA 99.99
mc815ll:hadoop-1.0.3 henry$ ls out86
ANAHEIM_CA-r-00000       MOUNTAIN_VIEW_CA-r-00000 UL_13-r-00000        other-r-00000
CUPERTINO_CA-r-00000        SAN_FRANCISCO_CA-r-00000  VALLEJO_CA-r-00000       part-r-00000
MILPITAS_CA-r-00000      SUNNYVALE_CA-r-00000        _SUCCESS
```

```
mc815ll:hadoop-1.0.3 henry$ cat out86/UL_13-r-00000
MEMBERSHIP FEE AUG 12-JUL 13  99.99
mc815ll:hadoop-1.0.3 henry$
```

6.7 SUMMARY

In this chapter, we focused on the subject of advanced MapReduce programming beyond writing basic MapReduce programs. We covered chaining mappers with a reducer, compressing map intermediate output data, using MultipleInputs and MultipleOutputs for more complicated input and output situations, adding custom counters, and passing parameters and metadata into map and reduce programs. However, when application logic gets more complicated, it's not always a good choice to write everything using the Hadoop MapReduce API exclusively. You might want to refer back to Table 1.1 for more information on what other Apache projects to look for to meet your more sophisticated needs, such as more complicated sorting, data joining, more flexible job orchestration and workflow composition, etc. These more advanced topics are beyond the scope of this text for the moment.

However, there is one more interesting subject that I'd like to introduce in the next chapter: Hadoop Streaming. As you will see, the Hadoop Streaming feature provides an alternative to writing MapReduce programs in Java, namely, you can use any other language of your choice to compose your map and reduce tasks. However, keep in mind that when you move away from writing Mappers and Reducers using the Hadoop MapReduce Java API, you gain more flexibility but at the cost of less control over what you can do. Besides, you might compromise the performance and scalability that you could have achieved with the MapReduce programs written with the Hadoop MapReduce Java API. These concerns need to be gauged carefully when you make your own decisions.

RECOMMENDED READING

The following link describes Hadoop ChainMapper class:

http://hadoop.apache.org/docs/r1.0.3/api/org/apache/hadoop/mapred/lib/ChainMapper.html .

EXERCISES

6.1 Explain the concept of Hadoop chaining mappers. What's the general form for describing this concept? What's the purpose of having chained mappers after the reducer?

6.2 Is it possible to chain multiple reducers in a chained MapReduce program?

6.3 Explain the implications of setting the `byValue` parameter in the `addMapper` method of the `ChainMapper` class.

6.4 What are the pros and cons of each of the three compression schemes of `DefaultCodec`, `GzipCodec`, and `BZip2Codec`?

6.5 Explain why there is a need for `MultipleInputs` given the possibility that one can chain mappers with the `ChainMapper` and `ChainReducer` classes.

6.6 Devise a use case for static and dynamic counters and then implement it.

6.7 How do you decide whether you would use the job configuration or distributed cache to pass data into your MapReduce program?

7 Hadoop Streaming

So far, all Hadoop MapReduce programs presented in the previous chapters have been written in Java. However, the Hadoop MapReduce framework provides a mechanism for using any executable scripts and/or programs as mappers and/or reducers through its *streaming* feature. The term *streaming* essentially means the *stdin* input stream and *stdout* output stream as we have learnt in Chapter 5. This is an interesting feature, as it makes it possible to reuse existing scripts or programs or even well-known Unix utilities as mappers and reducers. Of course, the Hadoop streaming feature does not exclude using Hadoop's own built-in mappers and reducers in streaming in a similar way to using scripts/programs written in other languages.

In this chapter, we focus on presenting the Hadoop streaming feature. Given what you have learnt from the previous chapters, it is actually quite easy to comprehend how Hadoop streaming works, as the underlying mechanism and concepts are still the same. Some other books spread presenting the Hadoop streaming feature across many separate chapters with one piece here and one piece there, but it might be more effective, more efficient, and more consistent if we get through with it in one standalone chapter as we are doing here. This would also give those who do not plan to use this feature a chance to skip it once without being interrupted throughout many chapters.

Let's start with a Hadoop streaming example next.

7.1 A HADOOP STREAMING EXAMPLE

Similar to the all-coded-in-Java MapReduce examples we presented in the previous chapters, Hadoop streaming requires specifying the input path, output path, mapper, and optionally reducer as well. However, these entries are specified at the command line rather than in the driver as we have seen before. For example, let's say we would like to count the number of lines contained in one of the input files we used before. This can be done easily with the Unix word counting command "*wc –l*", where the option "*-l*" instructs the utility to output the number of lines of the file operated on. Let's pick the *credit_card_tx_0_out.txt* file in the *in0* directory that we have used many times in the previous chapters. Here are the command and the output of this command:

```
$ wc –l in0/credit_card_tx_0_out.txt
2000000
$ in0/credit_card_tx_0_out.txt
```

It reports that this file contains 2M lines. In fact, this input file contains 2M credit card transactions and that command just confirms that.

Now, as an example of how one can run UNIX utility programs with Hadoop, let's demonstrate how we can turn it into a Hadoop MapReduce job. We can run it in one of the two ways as follows:

- No reducer:

```
$ hadoop jar contrib/streaming/hadoop-streaming-1.0.3.jar \
  -input in0/credit_card_tx_0_out.txt \
  -output sout1 \
  -mapper 'wc -l' \
  -numReduceTasks 0
```

- With a reducer:

```
$ hadoop jar contrib/streaming/hadoop-streaming-1.0.3.jar \
  -input in0/credit_card_tx_0_out.txt \
  -output sout2 \
  -mapper 'cat' \
  -reducer 'wc -l'
```

After the job was completed without a reducer, the output directory *sout1* contains the following four files prefixed with '*part*' as is shown with the "*ls sout1*" command:

```
mc815ll:hadoop-1.0.3 henry$ ls sout1
_SUCCESS part-00000 part-00001 part-00002 part-00003
mc815ll:hadoop-1.0.3 henry$ cat sout1/part-00000
582098
mc815ll:hadoop-1.0.3 henry$ cat sout1/part-00001
582136
mc815ll:hadoop-1.0.3 henry$ cat sout1/part-00002
582060
mc815ll:hadoop-1.0.3 henry$ cat sout1/part-00003
253706
mc815ll:hadoop-1.0.3 henry$
```

Following the above command, the contents of the first file were queried with the *cat* command. If we add the number of lines in all those four files, that's 2M, which agrees with the fact that the input file contains 2M credit card transaction records.

Listing 7.1 shows the console output of the job with a reducer. After the job was completed, the output directory *sout2* contains one file prefixed with '*part*' as is shown with the "*ls –l sout2*" command (following this command, the contents of the file were queried with the *cat* command, which shows the number of 2M credit card transaction records contained in the input file):

```
$ mc815ll:hadoop-1.0.3 henry$ ls -l sout2
total 8
-rwxrwxrwx  1 henry  staff   0 Oct  1 11:28 _SUCCESS
-rwxrwxrwx  1 henry  staff  10 Oct  1 11:27 part-00000
mc815ll:hadoop-1.0.3 henry$ cat sout2/part-00000
```

2000000
mc815ll:hadoop-1.0.3 henry$

We leave analyzing the above console output to the next section.

You might wonder if we could do it with a UNIX utility, why we would need to run it with Hadoop streaming. Yes – with this example, we are like *"shooting a fly with a cannon."* However, what if the dataset we need to process is orders of magnitude larger? What if we need to break a similar job down to multiple parallel tasks so that it could complete much faster? And what if we do not want to worry about potential failures mid-way ourselves? All these *"what-if's"* have been handled by Hadoop streaming so that we could be worry-free. That's the power of Hadoop streaming that UNIX utilities do not possess.

In the next section, we use this example to explore how Hadoop streaming works.

Listing 7.1 Console out of the Hadoop streaming word counting example

```
mc815ll:hadoop-1.0.3 henry$ hadoop jar contrib/streaming/hadoop-streaming-1.0.3.jar -input
in0/credit_card_tx_0_out.txt -output sout2 -mapper 'cat' -reducer 'wc -l'
12/10/01 11:27:42 WARN util.NativeCodeLoader: Unable to load native-hadoop library for your
platform... using builtin-java classes where applicable
12/10/01 11:27:42 WARN mapred.JobClient: No job jar file set.  User classes may not be found. See
JobConf(Class) or JobConf#setJar(String).
12/10/01 11:27:42 WARN snappy.LoadSnappy: Snappy native library not loaded
12/10/01 11:27:42 INFO mapred.FileInputFormat: Total input paths to process : 1
12/10/01 11:27:43 WARN mapred.LocalJobRunner: LocalJobRunner does not support symlinking into
current working dir.
12/10/01 11:27:43 INFO streaming.StreamJob: getLocalDirs(): [/tmp/hadoop-henry/mapred/local]
12/10/01 11:27:43 INFO streaming.StreamJob: Running job: job_local_0001
12/10/01 11:27:43 INFO streaming.StreamJob: Job running in-process (local Hadoop)
12/10/01 11:27:43 INFO mapred.Task:  Using ResourceCalculatorPlugin : null
12/10/01 11:27:43 INFO mapred.MapTask: numReduceTasks: 1
12/10/01 11:27:43 INFO mapred.MapTask: io.sort.mb = 100
12/10/01 11:27:43 INFO mapred.MapTask: data buffer = 79691776/99614720
12/10/01 11:27:43 INFO mapred.MapTask: record buffer = 262144/327680
12/10/01 11:27:43 INFO streaming.PipeMapRed: PipeMapRed exec [/bin/cat]
12/10/01 11:27:43 INFO streaming.PipeMapRed: R/W/S=1/0/0 in:NA [rec/s] out:NA [rec/s]
12/10/01 11:27:43 INFO streaming.PipeMapRed: R/W/S=10/0/0 in:NA [rec/s] out:NA [rec/s]
12/10/01 11:27:43 INFO streaming.PipeMapRed: R/W/S=100/0/0 in:NA [rec/s] out:NA [rec/s]
12/10/01 11:27:43 INFO streaming.PipeMapRed: R/W/S=1000/0/0 in:NA [rec/s] out:NA [rec/s]
12/10/01 11:27:43 INFO streaming.PipeMapRed: Records R/W=2499/1
12/10/01 11:27:43 INFO streaming.PipeMapRed: R/W/S=10000/7585/0 in:NA [rec/s] out:NA [rec/s]
12/10/01 11:27:43 INFO streaming.PipeMapRed: R/W/S=100000/97759/0 in:NA [rec/s] out:NA [rec/s]
12/10/01 11:27:43 INFO streaming.PipeMapRed: R/W/S=200000/197754/0 in:NA [rec/s] out:NA [rec/s]
12/10/01 11:27:44 INFO mapred.MapTask: Spilling map output: record full = true
12/10/01 11:27:44 INFO mapred.MapTask: bufstart = 0; bufend = 15110352; bufvoid = 99614720
12/10/01 11:27:44 INFO mapred.MapTask: kvstart = 0; kvend = 262144; length = 327680
12/10/01 11:27:44 INFO streaming.PipeMapRed: R/W/S=300000/297827/0 in:NA [rec/s] out:NA [rec/s]
12/10/01 11:27:44 INFO streaming.StreamJob:  map 0%  reduce 0%
```

12/10/01 11:27:44 INFO mapred.MapTask: **Finished spill 0**
12/10/01 11:27:44 INFO streaming.PipeMapRed: R/W/S=400000/397617/0 in:400000=400000/1 [rec/s] out:397630=397630/1 [rec/s]
12/10/01 11:27:44 INFO streaming.PipeMapRed: R/W/S=500000/497008/0 in:500000=500000/1 [rec/s] out:497008=497008/1 [rec/s]
12/10/01 11:27:45 INFO mapred.MapTask: Spilling map output: record full = true
12/10/01 11:27:45 INFO streaming.PipeMapRed: MRErrorThread done
12/10/01 11:27:45 INFO streaming.PipeMapRed: mapRedFinished
12/10/01 11:27:45 INFO mapred.MapTask: **Starting flush of map output**
12/10/01 11:27:45 INFO mapred.MapTask: **Finished spill 1**
12/10/01 11:27:45 INFO mapred.MapTask: **Finished spill 2**
12/10/01 11:27:45 INFO mapred.Merger: **Merging 3 sorted segments**
12/10/01 11:27:45 INFO mapred.Merger: **Down to the last merge-pass**, with 3 segments left of total size: 34718674 bytes
12/10/01 11:27:46 INFO mapred.Task: Task:**attempt_local_0001_m_000000_0 is done. And is in the process of commiting**
12/10/01 11:27:49 INFO mapred.LocalJobRunner: Records R/W=2499/1
12/10/01 11:27:49 INFO mapred.LocalJobRunner: Records R/W=2499/1
12/10/01 11:27:49 INFO mapred.Task: **Task 'attempt_local_0001_m_000000_0' done**.
12/10/01 11:27:49 INFO mapred.Task: Using ResourceCalculatorPlugin : null
12/10/01 11:27:49 INFO mapred.MapTask: numReduceTasks: 1
12/10/01 11:27:49 INFO mapred.MapTask: io.sort.mb = 100
12/10/01 11:27:49 INFO mapred.MapTask: data buffer = 79691776/99614720
12/10/01 11:27:49 INFO mapred.MapTask: record buffer = 262144/327680
12/10/01 11:27:49 INFO streaming.PipeMapRed: PipeMapRed exec [/bin/cat]
12/10/01 11:27:49 INFO streaming.PipeMapRed: R/W/S=1/0/0 in:NA [rec/s] out:NA [rec/s]
12/10/01 11:27:49 INFO streaming.PipeMapRed: R/W/S=10/0/0 in:NA [rec/s] out:NA [rec/s]
12/10/01 11:27:49 INFO streaming.PipeMapRed: R/W/S=100/0/0 in:NA [rec/s] out:NA [rec/s]
12/10/01 11:27:49 INFO streaming.PipeMapRed: R/W/S=1000/0/0 in:NA [rec/s] out:NA [rec/s]
12/10/01 11:27:49 INFO streaming.PipeMapRed: Records R/W=2342/1
12/10/01 11:27:49 INFO streaming.PipeMapRed: R/W/S=10000/7755/0 in:NA [rec/s] out:NA [rec/s]
12/10/01 11:27:49 INFO streaming.PipeMapRed: R/W/S=100000/97336/0 in:NA [rec/s] out:NA [rec/s]
12/10/01 11:27:49 INFO streaming.PipeMapRed: R/W/S=200000/197388/0 in:NA [rec/s] out:NA [rec/s]
12/10/01 11:27:49 INFO mapred.MapTask: Spilling map output: record full = true
12/10/01 11:27:49 INFO streaming.PipeMapRed: R/W/S=300000/296776/0 in:NA [rec/s] out:NA [rec/s]
12/10/01 11:27:50 INFO streaming.StreamJob: map 100% reduce 0%
12/10/01 11:27:50 INFO mapred.MapTask: Finished spill 0
12/10/01 11:27:50 INFO streaming.PipeMapRed: R/W/S=400000/397584/0 in:NA [rec/s] out:NA [rec/s]
12/10/01 11:27:50 INFO streaming.PipeMapRed: R/W/S=500000/497423/0 in:NA [rec/s] out:NA [rec/s]
12/10/01 11:27:50 INFO mapred.MapTask: Spilling map output: record full = true
12/10/01 11:27:50 INFO streaming.PipeMapRed: MRErrorThread done
12/10/01 11:27:50 INFO streaming.PipeMapRed: mapRedFinished
12/10/01 11:27:50 INFO mapred.MapTask: Starting flush of map output
12/10/01 11:27:50 INFO mapred.MapTask: Finished spill 1
12/10/01 11:27:51 INFO mapred.MapTask: Finished spill 2
12/10/01 11:27:51 INFO mapred.Merger: Merging 3 sorted segments
12/10/01 11:27:51 INFO mapred.Merger: Down to the last merge-pass, with 3 segments left of total size: 34718679 bytes

```
12/10/01 11:27:51 INFO mapred.Task: Task:attempt_local_0001_m_000001_0 is done. And is in the
process of commiting
12/10/01 11:27:52 INFO mapred.LocalJobRunner: Records R/W=2342/1
12/10/01 11:27:52 INFO mapred.Task: Task 'attempt_local_0001_m_000001_0' done.
12/10/01 11:27:52 INFO mapred.Task:  Using ResourceCalculatorPlugin : null
12/10/01 11:27:52 INFO mapred.MapTask: numReduceTasks: 1
12/10/01 11:27:52 INFO mapred.MapTask: io.sort.mb = 100
12/10/01 11:27:52 INFO mapred.MapTask: data buffer = 79691776/99614720
12/10/01 11:27:52 INFO mapred.MapTask: record buffer = 262144/327680
12/10/01 11:27:52 INFO streaming.PipeMapRed: PipeMapRed exec [/bin/cat]
12/10/01 11:27:52 INFO streaming.PipeMapRed: R/W/S=1/0/0 in:NA [rec/s] out:NA [rec/s]
12/10/01 11:27:52 INFO streaming.PipeMapRed: R/W/S=10/0/0 in:NA [rec/s] out:NA [rec/s]
12/10/01 11:27:52 INFO streaming.PipeMapRed: R/W/S=100/0/0 in:NA [rec/s] out:NA [rec/s]
12/10/01 11:27:52 INFO streaming.PipeMapRed: R/W/S=1000/0/0 in:NA [rec/s] out:NA [rec/s]
12/10/01 11:27:52 INFO streaming.PipeMapRed: Records R/W=2279/1
12/10/01 11:27:52 INFO streaming.PipeMapRed: R/W/S=10000/7805/0 in:NA [rec/s] out:NA [rec/s]
12/10/01 11:27:52 INFO streaming.PipeMapRed: R/W/S=100000/97307/0 in:NA [rec/s] out:NA [rec/s]
12/10/01 11:27:52 INFO streaming.PipeMapRed: R/W/S=200000/197511/0 in:NA [rec/s] out:NA [rec/s]
12/10/01 11:27:52 INFO mapred.MapTask: Spilling map output: record full = true
12/10/01 11:27:52 INFO mapred.MapTask: bufstart = 0; bufend = 15113185; bufvoid = 99614720
12/10/01 11:27:52 INFO mapred.MapTask: kvstart = 0; kvend = 262144; length = 327680
12/10/01 11:27:52 INFO streaming.PipeMapRed: R/W/S=300000/297800/0 in:NA [rec/s] out:NA [rec/s]
12/10/01 11:27:53 INFO mapred.MapTask: Finished spill 0
12/10/01 11:27:53 INFO streaming.PipeMapRed: R/W/S=400000/397412/0 in:NA [rec/s] out:NA [rec/s]
12/10/01 11:27:53 INFO streaming.PipeMapRed: R/W/S=500000/497388/0 in:NA [rec/s] out:NA [rec/s]
12/10/01 11:27:53 INFO mapred.MapTask: Spilling map output: record full = true
12/10/01 11:27:53 INFO streaming.PipeMapRed: MRErrorThread done
12/10/01 11:27:53 INFO streaming.PipeMapRed: mapRedFinished
12/10/01 11:27:53 INFO mapred.MapTask: Starting flush of map output
12/10/01 11:27:53 INFO mapred.MapTask: Finished spill 1
12/10/01 11:27:54 INFO mapred.MapTask: Finished spill 2
12/10/01 11:27:54 INFO mapred.Merger: Merging 3 sorted segments
12/10/01 11:27:54 INFO mapred.Merger: Down to the last merge-pass, with 3 segments left of total
size: 34718606 bytes
12/10/01 11:27:54 INFO mapred.Task: Task:attempt_local_0001_m_000002_0 is done. And is in the
process of commiting
12/10/01 11:27:55 INFO mapred.LocalJobRunner: Records R/W=2279/1
12/10/01 11:27:55 INFO mapred.Task: Task 'attempt_local_0001_m_000002_0' done.
12/10/01 11:27:55 INFO mapred.Task:  Using ResourceCalculatorPlugin : null
12/10/01 11:27:55 INFO mapred.MapTask: numReduceTasks: 1
12/10/01 11:27:55 INFO mapred.MapTask: io.sort.mb = 100
12/10/01 11:27:55 INFO mapred.MapTask: data buffer = 79691776/99614720
12/10/01 11:27:55 INFO mapred.MapTask: record buffer = 262144/327680
12/10/01 11:27:55 INFO streaming.PipeMapRed: PipeMapRed exec [/bin/cat]
12/10/01 11:27:55 INFO streaming.PipeMapRed: R/W/S=1/0/0 in:NA [rec/s] out:NA [rec/s]
12/10/01 11:27:55 INFO streaming.PipeMapRed: R/W/S=10/0/0 in:NA [rec/s] out:NA [rec/s]
12/10/01 11:27:55 INFO streaming.PipeMapRed: R/W/S=100/0/0 in:NA [rec/s] out:NA [rec/s]
12/10/01 11:27:55 INFO streaming.PipeMapRed: R/W/S=1000/0/0 in:NA [rec/s] out:NA [rec/s]
12/10/01 11:27:55 INFO streaming.PipeMapRed: Records R/W=2465/1
```

```
12/10/01 11:27:55 INFO streaming.PipeMapRed: R/W/S=10000/7671/0 in:NA [rec/s] out:NA [rec/s]
12/10/01 11:27:55 INFO streaming.PipeMapRed: R/W/S=100000/97347/0 in:NA [rec/s] out:NA [rec/s]
12/10/01 11:27:55 INFO streaming.PipeMapRed: R/W/S=200000/197423/0 in:NA [rec/s] out:NA [rec/s]
12/10/01 11:27:55 INFO streaming.PipeMapRed: MRErrorThread done
12/10/01 11:27:55 INFO streaming.PipeMapRed: mapRedFinished
12/10/01 11:27:55 INFO mapred.MapTask: Starting flush of map output
12/10/01 11:27:56 INFO mapred.MapTask: Finished spill 0
12/10/01 11:27:56 INFO mapred.Task: Task:attempt_local_0001_m_000003_0 is done. And is in the
process of commiting
12/10/01 11:27:58 INFO mapred.LocalJobRunner: Records R/W=2465/1
12/10/01 11:27:58 INFO mapred.Task: Task 'attempt_local_0001_m_000003_0' done.
12/10/01 11:27:58 INFO mapred.Task:  Using ResourceCalculatorPlugin : null
12/10/01 11:27:58 INFO mapred.Merger: Merging 4 sorted segments
12/10/01 11:27:58 INFO mapred.Merger: Down to the last merge-pass, with 4 segments left of total
size: 119287383 bytes
12/10/01 11:27:58 INFO streaming.PipeMapRed: PipeMapRed exec [/usr/bin/wc, -l]
12/10/01 11:27:58 INFO streaming.PipeMapRed: R/W/S=1/0/0 in:NA [rec/s] out:NA [rec/s]
12/10/01 11:27:58 INFO streaming.PipeMapRed: R/W/S=10/0/0 in:NA [rec/s] out:NA [rec/s]
12/10/01 11:27:58 INFO streaming.PipeMapRed: R/W/S=100/0/0 in:NA [rec/s] out:NA [rec/s]
12/10/01 11:27:58 INFO streaming.PipeMapRed: R/W/S=1000/0/0 in:NA [rec/s] out:NA [rec/s]
12/10/01 11:27:58 INFO streaming.PipeMapRed: R/W/S=10000/0/0 in:NA [rec/s] out:NA [rec/s]
12/10/01 11:27:58 INFO streaming.PipeMapRed: R/W/S=100000/0/0 in:NA [rec/s] out:NA [rec/s]
......
12/10/01 11:27:59 INFO streaming.PipeMapRed: R/W/S=2000000/0/0 in:2000000=2000000/1 [rec/s]
out:0=0/1 [rec/s]
12/10/01 11:27:59 INFO streaming.PipeMapRed: MRErrorThread done
12/10/01 11:27:59 INFO streaming.PipeMapRed: Records R/W=2000000/1
12/10/01 11:27:59 INFO streaming.PipeMapRed: mapRedFinished
12/10/01 11:27:59 INFO mapred.Task: Task:attempt_local_0001_r_000000_0 is done. And is in the
process of commiting
12/10/01 11:27:59 INFO mapred.Task: Task attempt_local_0001_r_000000_0 is allowed to commit
now
12/10/01 11:27:59 INFO mapred.FileOutputCommitter: Saved output of task
'attempt_local_0001_r_000000_0' to file:/Users/henry/dev/hadoop-1.0.3/sout2
12/10/01 11:28:01 INFO mapred.LocalJobRunner: Records R/W=2000000/1 > reduce
12/10/01 11:28:01 INFO mapred.Task: Task 'attempt_local_0001_r_000000_0' done.
12/10/01 11:28:02 INFO streaming.StreamJob:  map 100%  reduce 100%
12/10/01 11:28:02 INFO streaming.StreamJob: Job complete: job_local_0001
12/10/01 11:28:02 INFO streaming.StreamJob: Output: sout2
mc815ll:hadoop-1.0.3 henry$
```

7.2 HOW HADOOP STREAMING WORKS

By looking at the console output of the previous streaming example shown in Listing 7.1, it is obvious that the map tasks and reduce task executed are similar to those experienced in our first MapReduce example shown in Listing 1.14. By examining the timestamps, we see that the four map tasks and one reduce task were executed in the following sequence:

1) 11:27:43 – 11:27:49: the first map task
2) 11:27:49 – 11:27.52: the second map task
3) 11:27:52 – 11:27:55 the third map task
4) 11:27:55 – 11:27:58: the fourth map task
5) 11:27:58 – 11:28:02: the reduce task

We could easily identify at what points the mapper and reducer processes were spawned as separate processes and the subsequent steps of splitting, spilling, merging, output committing, etc., except that there were extra reports from the `streaming.PipeMapRed` API. Besides, there is an important convention about the input/output key-values pairs as follows:

- By default, the prefix of a line up to the first tab separator is considered the *key*, and the rest of the line is considered the *value*.
- If there is no tab separator in the line, then the entire line is considered the *key* and the *value* is *null*. This kind of behavior can be customized, though, as we will see later.

Next, let's take a look at streaming command options.

7.3   STREAMING COMMAND OPTIONS

Through the previous streaming example, we have seen several streaming command options such as *–input, -output, -mapper,* and *–reducer*. These are required streaming command options. Similar to the general Hadoop command syntax we introduced in Chapter 6, a Hadoop streaming command follows the below command syntax:

$ bin/hadoop command [genericOptions] [streamingOptions]

Table 7.1 lists all Hadoop streaming options including those four *required* options we have demonstrated. The following additional options should look familiar to you since they have been covered in the previous chapters:

- –file <filename>
- –inputformat <JavaClassName>
- –outputformat <JavaClassName>
- –partitioner <JavaClassName>
- –combiner <streamingCommand> or <JavaClassName>
- –numReduceTasks <n> (note that if you set n to zero, no reducer needs to be specified)

The following remaining options are unique to streaming and you can use them if you need to:

- –cmdenv <name=value>
- –inputreader
- –verbose
- –mapdebug
- -reducedebug

For example, when the "-verbose" option was appended to the following command as shown below, the standard console output was preceded with the job configuration information as shown in Listing 7.2 following Table 7.1:

```
$ hadoop jar contrib/streaming/hadoop-streaming-1.0.3.jar \
  -input in0/credit_card_tx_0_out.txt \
  -output sout2 \
  -mapper 'cat' \
  -reducer 'wc –l'
  -verbose
```

You can take a quick look at this output, and most of it should look familiar to you given what we have covered in the previous chapters.

In addition to streaming command options, you can also use the generic options as we described in the previous chapter. You can refer to the resources given at the end of this chapter for more information and examples about how to use those generic options.

Table 7.1 Hadoop streaming command options

option	Required?	Description
-input directoryname or filename	Required	Input path for mapper
-output directoryname	Required	Output path for reducer
-mapper executable or JavaClassName	Required	Mapper executable
-reducer executable or JavaClassName	Required	Reducer executable
-file <file>	Optional	The equivalent distributed cache mechanism for shipping the specified file/dir in the Job jar file to the compute nodes
-inputformat JavaClassName	Optional	If not specified, TextInputFormat is used as the default. The class you supply should return key/value pairs of Text class.
-outputformat JavaClassName	Optional	If not specified, TextOutputformat is used as the default. The class you supply should take key/value pairs of Text class.
-partitioner JavaClassName	Optional	The class that determines which reduce task a key should be sent to
-combiner streamingCommand or	Optional	Combiner executable for map output
-cmdenv name=value	Optional	Passes environment variable to streaming commands

-inputreader	Optional	Specifies a record reader class (instead of an input format class) for backwards-
-verbose	Optional	Verbose output
-numReduceTasks	Optional	Specifies the number of reducers
-mapdebug <path>	Optional	Script to call when map task fails
-reducedebug <path>	Optional	Script to call when reduce task fails

Listing 7.2 A typical console output from the "-verbose" streaming command option

```
mc815ll:hadoop-1.0.3 henry$ hadoop jar contrib/streaming/hadoop-streaming-1.0.3.jar -input
in0/credit_card_tx_0_out.txt -output sout7 -mapper 'cat' -reducer 'wc -l' -verbose
STREAM: addTaskEnvironment=
STREAM: shippedCanonFiles_=[]
STREAM: shipped: false /Users/henry/dev/hadoop-1.0.3/cat
STREAM: cmd=cat
STREAM: cmd=null
STREAM: shipped: false /Users/henry/dev/hadoop-1.0.3/wc
STREAM: cmd=wc -l
STREAM: Found runtime classes in: /tmp/hadoop-henry/hadoop-unjar3715429478604475468/
STREAM: ==== JobConf properties:
STREAM: fs.checkpoint.dir=${hadoop.tmp.dir}/dfs/namesecondary
STREAM: fs.checkpoint.edits.dir=${fs.checkpoint.dir}
STREAM: fs.checkpoint.period=3600
STREAM: fs.checkpoint.size=67108864
STREAM: fs.default.name=file:///
STREAM: fs.file.impl=org.apache.hadoop.fs.LocalFileSystem
STREAM: fs.ftp.impl=org.apache.hadoop.fs.ftp.FTPFileSystem
STREAM: fs.har.impl=org.apache.hadoop.fs.HarFileSystem
STREAM: fs.har.impl.disable.cache=true
STREAM: fs.hdfs.impl=org.apache.hadoop.hdfs.DistributedFileSystem
STREAM: fs.hftp.impl=org.apache.hadoop.hdfs.HftpFileSystem
STREAM: fs.hsftp.impl=org.apache.hadoop.hdfs.HsftpFileSystem
STREAM: fs.kfs.impl=org.apache.hadoop.fs.kfs.KosmosFileSystem
STREAM: fs.ramfs.impl=org.apache.hadoop.fs.InMemoryFileSystem
STREAM: fs.s3.block.size=67108864
STREAM: fs.s3.buffer.dir=${hadoop.tmp.dir}/s3
STREAM: fs.s3.impl=org.apache.hadoop.fs.s3.S3FileSystem
STREAM: fs.s3.maxRetries=4
STREAM: fs.s3.sleepTimeSeconds=10
STREAM: fs.s3n.impl=org.apache.hadoop.fs.s3native.NativeS3FileSystem
STREAM: fs.trash.interval=0
STREAM: fs.webhdfs.impl=org.apache.hadoop.hdfs.web.WebHdfsFileSystem
STREAM: hadoop.logfile.count=10
STREAM: hadoop.logfile.size=10000000
STREAM: hadoop.native.lib=true
```

```
STREAM: hadoop.rpc.socket.factory.class.default=org.apache.hadoop.net.StandardSocketFactory
STREAM: hadoop.security.authentication=simple
STREAM: hadoop.security.authorization=false
STREAM: hadoop.security.group.mapping=org.apache.hadoop.security.ShellBasedUnixGroupsMapping
STREAM: hadoop.security.token.service.use_ip=true
STREAM: hadoop.security.uid.cache.secs=14400
STREAM: hadoop.tmp.dir=/tmp/hadoop-${user.name}
STREAM: hadoop.util.hash.type=murmur
STREAM: io.bytes.per.checksum=512
STREAM:
io.compression.codecs=org.apache.hadoop.io.compress.DefaultCodec,org.apache.hadoop.io.compress
.GzipCodec,org.apache.hadoop.io.compress.BZip2Codec,org.apache.hadoop.io.compress.SnappyCodec
STREAM: io.file.buffer.size=4096
STREAM: io.map.index.skip=0
STREAM: io.mapfile.bloom.error.rate=0.005
STREAM: io.mapfile.bloom.size=1048576
STREAM: io.seqfile.compress.blocksize=1000000
STREAM: io.seqfile.lazydecompress=true
STREAM: io.seqfile.sorter.recordlimit=1000000
STREAM: io.serializations=org.apache.hadoop.io.serializer.WritableSerialization
STREAM: io.skip.checksum.errors=false
STREAM: io.sort.factor=10
STREAM: io.sort.mb=100
STREAM: io.sort.record.percent=0.05
STREAM: io.sort.spill.percent=0.80
STREAM: ipc.client.connect.max.retries=10
STREAM: ipc.client.connection.maxidletime=10000
STREAM: ipc.client.idlethreshold=4000
STREAM: ipc.client.kill.max=10
STREAM: ipc.client.tcpnodelay=false
STREAM: ipc.server.listen.queue.size=128
STREAM: ipc.server.tcpnodelay=false
STREAM: job.end.retry.attempts=0
STREAM: job.end.retry.interval=30000
STREAM: jobclient.output.filter=FAILED
STREAM: keep.failed.task.files=false
STREAM: local.cache.size=10737418240
STREAM: map.sort.class=org.apache.hadoop.util.QuickSort
STREAM: mapred.acls.enabled=false
STREAM: mapred.child.java.opts=-Xmx200m
STREAM: mapred.child.tmp=./tmp
STREAM: mapred.cluster.map.memory.mb=-1
STREAM: mapred.cluster.max.map.memory.mb=-1
STREAM: mapred.cluster.max.reduce.memory.mb=-1
STREAM: mapred.cluster.reduce.memory.mb=-1
STREAM: mapred.combine.recordsBeforeProgress=10000
STREAM: mapred.compress.map.output=false
STREAM: mapred.create.symlink=yes
```

```
STREAM: mapred.healthChecker.interval=60000
STREAM: mapred.healthChecker.script.timeout=600000
STREAM: mapred.heartbeats.in.second=100
STREAM: mapred.inmem.merge.threshold=1000
STREAM: mapred.input.dir=file:/Users/henry/dev/hadoop-1.0.3/in0/credit_card_tx_0_out.txt
STREAM: mapred.input.format.class=org.apache.hadoop.mapred.TextInputFormat
STREAM: mapred.job.map.memory.mb=-1
STREAM: mapred.job.queue.name=default
STREAM: mapred.job.reduce.input.buffer.percent=0.0
STREAM: mapred.job.reduce.memory.mb=-1
STREAM: mapred.job.reuse.jvm.num.tasks=1
STREAM: mapred.job.shuffle.input.buffer.percent=0.70
STREAM: mapred.job.shuffle.merge.percent=0.66
STREAM: mapred.job.tracker=local
STREAM: mapred.job.tracker.handler.count=10
STREAM: mapred.job.tracker.http.address=0.0.0.0:50030
STREAM: mapred.job.tracker.jobhistory.lru.cache.size=5
STREAM: mapred.job.tracker.persist.jobstatus.active=false
STREAM: mapred.job.tracker.persist.jobstatus.dir=/jobtracker/jobsInfo
STREAM: mapred.job.tracker.persist.jobstatus.hours=0
STREAM: mapred.job.tracker.retiredjobs.cache.size=1000
STREAM: mapred.jobtracker.blacklist.fault-bucket-width=15
STREAM: mapred.jobtracker.blacklist.fault-timeout-window=180
STREAM: mapred.jobtracker.completeuserjobs.maximum=100
STREAM: mapred.jobtracker.job.history.block.size=3145728
STREAM: mapred.jobtracker.maxtasks.per.job=-1
STREAM: mapred.jobtracker.restart.recover=false
STREAM: mapred.jobtracker.taskScheduler=org.apache.hadoop.mapred.JobQueueTaskScheduler
STREAM: mapred.line.input.format.linespermap=1
STREAM: mapred.local.dir=${hadoop.tmp.dir}/mapred/local
STREAM: mapred.local.dir.minspacekill=0
STREAM: mapred.local.dir.minspacestart=0
STREAM: mapred.map.max.attempts=4
STREAM: mapred.map.output.compression.codec=org.apache.hadoop.io.compress.DefaultCodec
STREAM: mapred.map.runner.class=org.apache.hadoop.streaming.PipeMapRunner
STREAM: mapred.map.tasks=2
STREAM: mapred.map.tasks.speculative.execution=true
STREAM: mapred.mapoutput.key.class=org.apache.hadoop.io.Text
STREAM: mapred.mapoutput.value.class=org.apache.hadoop.io.Text
STREAM: mapred.mapper.class=org.apache.hadoop.streaming.PipeMapper
STREAM: mapred.max.tracker.blacklists=4
STREAM: mapred.max.tracker.failures=4
STREAM: mapred.merge.recordsBeforeProgress=10000
STREAM: mapred.min.split.size=0
STREAM: mapred.output.compress=false
STREAM: mapred.output.compression.codec=org.apache.hadoop.io.compress.DefaultCodec
STREAM: mapred.output.compression.type=RECORD
STREAM: mapred.output.dir=file:/Users/henry/dev/hadoop-1.0.3/sout7
STREAM: mapred.output.format.class=org.apache.hadoop.mapred.TextOutputFormat
```

```
STREAM: mapred.output.key.class=org.apache.hadoop.io.Text
STREAM: mapred.output.value.class=org.apache.hadoop.io.Text
STREAM: mapred.queue.default.state=RUNNING
STREAM: mapred.queue.names=default
STREAM: mapred.reduce.max.attempts=4
STREAM: mapred.reduce.parallel.copies=5
STREAM: mapred.reduce.slowstart.completed.maps=0.05
STREAM: mapred.reduce.tasks=1
STREAM: mapred.reduce.tasks.speculative.execution=true
STREAM: mapred.reducer.class=org.apache.hadoop.streaming.PipeReducer
STREAM: mapred.skip.attempts.to.start.skipping=2
STREAM: mapred.skip.map.auto.incr.proc.count=true
STREAM: mapred.skip.map.max.skip.records=0
STREAM: mapred.skip.reduce.auto.incr.proc.count=true
STREAM: mapred.skip.reduce.max.skip.groups=0
STREAM: mapred.submit.replication=10
STREAM: mapred.system.dir=${hadoop.tmp.dir}/mapred/system
STREAM: mapred.task.cache.levels=2
STREAM: mapred.task.profile=false
STREAM: mapred.task.profile.maps=0-2
STREAM: mapred.task.profile.reduces=0-2
STREAM: mapred.task.timeout=600000
STREAM: mapred.task.tracker.http.address=0.0.0.0:50060
STREAM: mapred.task.tracker.report.address=127.0.0.1:0
STREAM: mapred.task.tracker.task-controller=org.apache.hadoop.mapred.DefaultTaskController
STREAM: mapred.tasktracker.dns.interface=default
STREAM: mapred.tasktracker.dns.nameserver=default
STREAM: mapred.tasktracker.expiry.interval=600000
STREAM: mapred.tasktracker.indexcache.mb=10
STREAM: mapred.tasktracker.map.tasks.maximum=2
STREAM: mapred.tasktracker.reduce.tasks.maximum=2
STREAM: mapred.tasktracker.taskmemorymanager.monitoring-interval=5000
STREAM: mapred.tasktracker.tasks.sleeptime-before-sigkill=5000
STREAM: mapred.temp.dir=${hadoop.tmp.dir}/mapred/temp
STREAM: mapred.used.genericoptionsparser=true
STREAM: mapred.user.jobconf.limit=5242880
STREAM: mapred.userlog.limit.kb=0
STREAM: mapred.userlog.retain.hours=24
STREAM: mapred.working.dir=file:/Users/henry/dev/hadoop-1.0.3
STREAM: mapreduce.job.acl-modify-job=
STREAM: mapreduce.job.acl-view-job=
STREAM: mapreduce.job.complete.cancel.delegation.tokens=true
STREAM: mapreduce.job.counters.limit=120
STREAM: mapreduce.job.split.metainfo.maxsize=10000000
STREAM: mapreduce.jobtracker.staging.root.dir=${hadoop.tmp.dir}/mapred/staging
STREAM: mapreduce.reduce.input.limit=-1
STREAM: mapreduce.reduce.shuffle.connect.timeout=180000
STREAM: mapreduce.reduce.shuffle.maxfetchfailures=10
```

```
STREAM: mapreduce.reduce.shuffle.read.timeout=180000
STREAM: mapreduce.tasktracker.outofband.heartbeat=false
STREAM: mapreduce.tasktracker.outofband.heartbeat.damper=1000000
STREAM: stream.addenvironment=
STREAM: stream.map.input.writer.class=org.apache.hadoop.streaming.io.TextInputWriter
STREAM: stream.map.output.reader.class=org.apache.hadoop.streaming.io.TextOutputReader
STREAM: stream.map.streamprocessor=cat
STREAM: stream.numinputspecs=1
STREAM: stream.reduce.input.writer.class=org.apache.hadoop.streaming.io.TextInputWriter
STREAM: stream.reduce.output.reader.class=org.apache.hadoop.streaming.io.TextOutputReader
STREAM: stream.reduce.streamprocessor=wc+-l
STREAM: tasktracker.http.threads=40
STREAM: topology.node.switch.mapping.impl=org.apache.hadoop.net.ScriptBasedMapping
STREAM: topology.script.number.args=100
STREAM: webinterface.private.actions=false
STREAM: ====
```

7.4   A STREAMING EXAMPLE USING A PYTHON SCRIPT

In this section, we present a streaming example using a Python script. You might wonder why we chose Python instead of some other similar scripting languages like Ruby. I actually pondered on whether to use Python or Ruby. I finally decided to use Python rather than Ruby based on the following factors:

- I tried to upgrade both Python and Ruby on my Mac OS X machine on which most of the examples illustrated in this book were developed and tested in local mode. The Python upgrade succeeded while Ruby upgrade failed.
- On the OpenSuse 12.1 Linux machines that formed a Linux cluster for running Hadoop in fully distributed mode, Python was bundled out of the box, whereas Ruby was not.

In fact, it doesn't matter whether we chose Python or Ruby here. They should be equally applicable as long as you find one or the other readily available or you are willing to spend time to make it work if it doesn't.

With this example, we would like to mirror the KeyValueTextInputFormat example we presented in §5.3.3. We will use the file *credit_card_tx_0_out_kv.txt* file located in the *in0* directory to run the example. This input file contains key-value records with the key and value separated by a tab delimiter. This is a better fit as Hadoop streaming assumes that the input stream consists of key-value lines with the key and value separated by a tab delimiter. We can continue to use the UNIX *'cat'* utility as the mapper as we demonstrated in the previous example. All we need to do is to write a reducer in Python, which would find and output the maximum amount customers spent at each store. This is a simple script and is shown in Listing 7.3.

Since the input lines to the reducer are key-value pairs separated with a tab delimiter, the key and value are separated and assigned with the following statement for each input line:

```
(key, amount) = line.split("\t")
```

Then if a new key is found, the previous key and the max amount are output with the `maxAmount` variable reset. Otherwise, the max amount comparison is performed, followed with proper assignment when applicable. Eventually, the max amount is output for transactions that occurred at each store except the PAYMENT transaction type.

Listing 7.3 A Python script named FindMaxAmount.py to be used as a reducer for a streaming example.

```
#!/usr/bin/env python

import sys

(prev_key, maxAmount) = ("", -0.001)

for line in sys.stdin:
    (key, amount) = line.split("\t")

    if prev_key and prev_key != key:
        print prev_key + "\t" + str(maxAmount)
        maxAmount = -0.001

    prev_key = key
    if maxAmount < float(amount):
        maxAmount = float (amount)

if (not prev_key.find("PAYMENT")):
    print prev_key + "\t" + str(maxAmount)
```

This example was run with the following command:

```
$ hadoop jar contrib/streaming/hadoop-streaming-1.0.3.jar \
    -input in0/credit_card_tx_0_out_kv.txt \
    -output sout9 \
    -mapper 'cat' \
    -reducer '/usr/bin/python FindMaxAmount.py'
```

The console output is shown in Listing 7.4. Since the map task output part is redundant with the preceding example, it has been removed from Listing 7.4. The correctness of the Python script *FinaMaxAmount.py* is verifiable by querying the output of the reduce task as shown below:

```
mc815ll:hadoop-1.0.3 henry$ cat sout9/part-00000
76 10115095        SUNNYVALE     CA    99.98
......
TOYS R US #5808    QPS CUPERTINO CA    99.98
TRICKS GYMNASTICS DANC 916-3510024  CA 99.99
TRU HOLIDAY EXPRESSQPS SUNNYVALE     CA     99.99
mc815ll:hadoop-1.0.3 henry$
```

This concludes our discussion on Hadoop streaming. In the next chapter, we cover Hadoop administration and performance tuning.

Listing 7.4 Console output of the streaming example using a python script as the reducer

mc815ll:hadoop-1.0.3 henry$ **hadoop jar contrib/streaming/hadoop-streaming-1.0.3.jar -input in0/credit_card_tx_0_out_kv.txt -output sout9 -mapper 'cat' -reducer '/usr/bin/python FindMaxAmount.py'**
12/10/01 15:03:04 WARN util.NativeCodeLoader: Unable to load native-hadoop library for your platform... using builtin-java classes where applicable
12/10/01 15:03:04 WARN mapred.JobClient: No job jar file set. User classes may not be found. See JobConf(Class) or JobConf#setJar(String).
12/10/01 15:03:04 WARN snappy.LoadSnappy: Snappy native library not loaded
12/10/01 15:03:04 INFO mapred.FileInputFormat: Total input paths to process : 1
......
12/10/01 15:03:16 INFO mapred.Task: Task 'attempt_local_0001_m_000002_0' done.
12/10/01 15:03:16 INFO mapred.Task: Using ResourceCalculatorPlugin : null
12/10/01 15:03:16 INFO mapred.Merger: Merging 3 sorted segments
12/10/01 15:03:16 INFO mapred.Merger: Down to the last merge-pass, with 3 segments left of total size: 97286967 bytes
12/10/01 15:03:16 INFO streaming.PipeMapRed: PipeMapRed exec [/usr/bin/python, FindMaxAmount.py]
12/10/01 15:03:16 INFO streaming.PipeMapRed: R/W/S=1/0/0 in:NA [rec/s] out:NA [rec/s]
12/10/01 15:03:16 INFO streaming.PipeMapRed: R/W/S=10/0/0 in:NA [rec/s] out:NA [rec/s]
12/10/01 15:03:16 INFO streaming.PipeMapRed: R/W/S=100/0/0 in:NA [rec/s] out:NA [rec/s]
12/10/01 15:03:16 INFO streaming.PipeMapRed: R/W/S=1000/0/0 in:NA [rec/s] out:NA [rec/s]
12/10/01 15:03:16 INFO streaming.PipeMapRed: R/W/S=10000/0/0 in:NA [rec/s] out:NA [rec/s]
12/10/01 15:03:16 INFO streaming.PipeMapRed: R/W/S=**100000**/0/0 in:NA [rec/s] out:NA [rec/s]
12/10/01 15:03:17 INFO streaming.PipeMapRed: R/W/S=**200000**/0/0 in:NA [rec/s] out:NA [rec/s]
......
12/10/01 15:03:18 INFO streaming.PipeMapRed: R/W/S=**900000**/0/0 in:900000=900000/1 [rec/s] out:0=0/1 [rec/s]
......
12/10/01 15:03:20 INFO streaming.PipeMapRed: R/W/S=2000000/0/0 in:666666=2000000/3 [rec/s] out:0=0/3 [rec/s]
12/10/01 15:03:20 INFO streaming.PipeMapRed: MRErrorThread done
12/10/01 15:03:20 INFO streaming.PipeMapRed: Records R/W=2000000/1
12/10/01 15:03:20 INFO streaming.PipeMapRed: mapRedFinished
12/10/01 15:03:20 INFO mapred.Task: Task:attempt_local_0001_r_000000_0 is done. And is in the process of commiting
12/10/01 15:03:20 INFO mapred.Task: Task attempt_local_0001_r_000000_0 is allowed to commit now
12/10/01 15:03:20 INFO mapred.FileOutputCommitter: Saved output of task 'attempt_local_0001_r_000000_0' to file:/Users/henry/dev/hadoop-1.0.3/sout9
12/10/01 15:03:22 INFO mapred.LocalJobRunner: Records R/W=2000000/1 > reduce
12/10/01 15:03:22 INFO mapred.LocalJobRunner: Records R/W=2000000/1 > reduce
12/10/01 15:03:22 INFO mapred.Task: Task 'attempt_local_0001_r_000000_0' done.
12/10/01 15:03:23 INFO streaming.StreamJob: map 100% reduce 100%

```
12/10/01 15:03:23 INFO streaming.StreamJob: Job complete: job_local_0001
12/10/01 15:03:23 INFO streaming.StreamJob: Output: sout9
mc815ll:hadoop-1.0.3 henry$
```

7.5 SUMMARY

In this chapter, we focused on understanding how Hadoop streaming works, facilitated with a few representative examples. One example used UNIX utilities as mappers and reducer, whereas the other used a Python script as the reducer. The key to understanding Hadoop streaming is to know how to use various streaming command options and how to process input/output key-value pairs for a seamless connection between the mapper and the reducer.

This chapter wraps up our coverage on Hadoop MapReduce programming – both basic and advanced. The next chapter covers Hadoop administration from a developer's perspective so that one would know how to trouble shoot various issues encountered while developing Hadoop MapReduce programs.

RECOMMENDED READING

For a summary of the Hadoop Streaming API, refer to the following URL:

http://hadoop.apache.org/docs/r1.0.3/api/org/apache/hadoop/streaming/package-summary.html

To learn more about Hadoop streaming, check out the following URL:

http://hadoop.apache.org/docs/r1.0.3/streaming.html

EXERCISES

7.1 What are the pros and cons with Hadoop streaming versus the purely Java-based, mapper-reducer-driver approach as introduced in the previous chapters?

7.2 Does Hadoop distributed cache feature apply to Hadoop streaming? How would you use it?

7.3 Is it possible to implement advanced features such as ChainMapper/ChainReducer, compression, counters, MultipleInputs and MultipleOutputs with Hadoop streaming?

8 Hadoop Administration

Administering a production cluster is a demanding job. It is impractical to cover all aspects in this regard in this chapter. Our objective for this chapter would be to help a developer understand some basic concepts and simple procedures in order to be able to trouble shoot a Hadoop environment when something goes awry during developing and testing MapReduce programs. This kind of knowledge is also indispensable when developers work with professional Hadoop administrators to resolve issues encountered after their MapReduce programs have been deployed in production.

We first explore Hadoop storage settings. This is an important aspect in managing and maintaining a Hadoop environment, as Hadoop is file-centric and the HDFS plays a fundamental role in this regard.

8.1 HADOOP STORAGE SETTINGS

Even though you are not a full-time Hadoop administrator, it's beneficial to know all major Hadoop environment parameters. The first category of such parameters is with the HDFS, which provides all file related services. Let's take a look at some of those parameters. Since the HDFS consists of three components of the namenode, the secondary namenode, and the datanodes, we divide them into three sub-categories. We start with the namenode next.

8.1.1 The NameNode Storage

If you look up Table A.1, which lists all configuration parameters generated from a Hadoop MapReduce job that processed 2M credit card transactions on a four-node Linux cluster, you would find a parameter named ${hadoop.tmp.dir}. This parameter defines the top directory for storing all Hadoop related activities for each component as mentioned above. It is set to /tmp/hadoop-${user.name} by default, which would be /tmp/hadoop-henry in my case, as I used my name as the Hadoop user name on each node of the Linux cluster.

To find out what sub-directories and files are contained underneath the top directory defined by the parameter ${hadoop.tmp.dir}, I executed the following two commands on my namenode:

```
henry@linux-1fsw:~/myapp/hadoop-1.0.3> $JAVA_HOME/bin/jps
28380 NameNode
28573 JobTracker
26108 Jps
henry@linux-1fsw:~/myapp/hadoop-1.0.3>
```

```
henry@linux-1fsw:~/myapp/hadoop-1.0.3> ls  -R /tmp/hadoop-henry
/tmp/hadoop-henry:
dfs  mapred

/tmp/hadoop-henry/dfs:
name

/tmp/hadoop-henry/dfs/name:
current  image  in_use.lock  previous.checkpoint

/tmp/hadoop-henry/dfs/name/current:
edits  edits.new  fsimage  fstime  VERSION

/tmp/hadoop-henry/dfs/name/image:
fsimage

/tmp/hadoop-henry/dfs/name/previous.checkpoint:
edits  fsimage  fstime  VERSION

/tmp/hadoop-henry/mapred:
local

/tmp/hadoop-henry/mapred/local:
jobTracker

/tmp/hadoop-henry/mapred/local/jobTracker:
```

With above two commands, the first command of "$JAVA_HOME/bin/jps" shows that the *NameNode* and *JobTracker* daemons were running, which confirmed that this was indeed the namenode, while the second command "*ls –R /tmp/hadoop-henry*" displayed all sub-directories and files under the top directory of *tmp/hadoop-henry* recursively. It's actually easier to look at the entire directory structure under the top directory as shown in Figure 8.1.

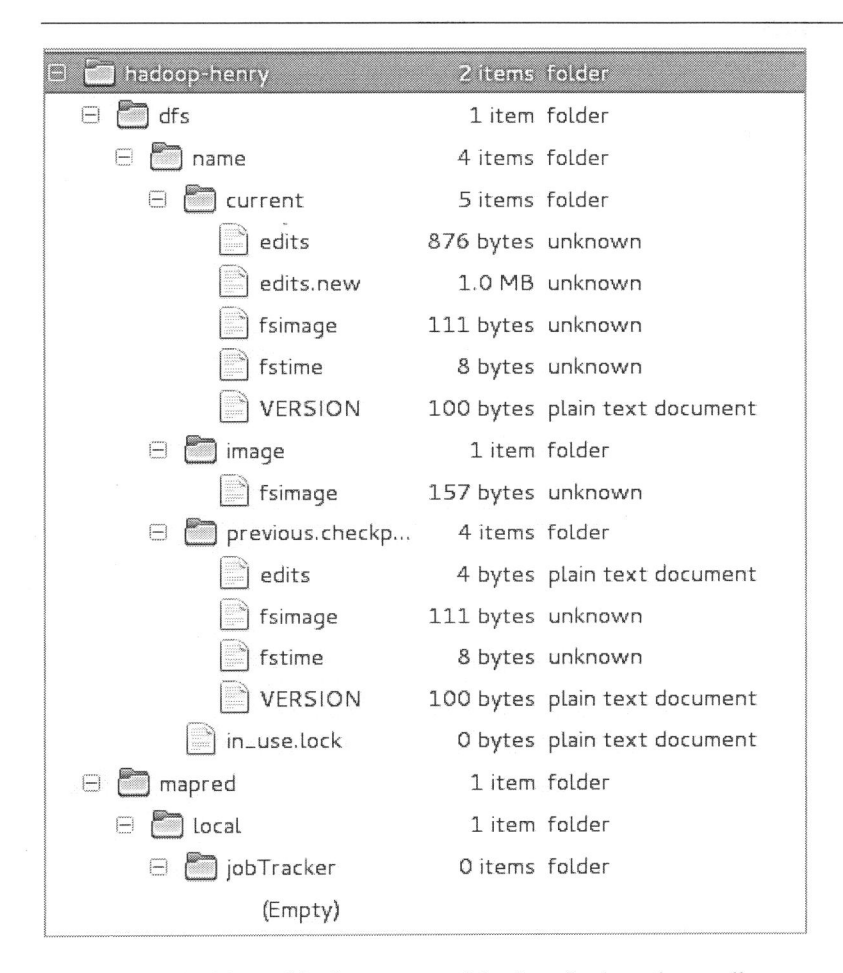

⊟ 🗀 hadoop-henry	2 items	folder
⊟ 🗀 dfs	1 item	folder
⊟ 🗀 name	4 items	folder
⊟ 🗀 current	5 items	folder
📄 edits	876 bytes	unknown
📄 edits.new	1.0 MB	unknown
📄 fsimage	111 bytes	unknown
📄 fstime	8 bytes	unknown
📄 VERSION	100 bytes	plain text document
⊟ 🗀 image	1 item	folder
📄 fsimage	157 bytes	unknown
⊟ 🗀 previous.checkp...	4 items	folder
📄 edits	4 bytes	plain text document
📄 fsimage	111 bytes	unknown
📄 fstime	8 bytes	unknown
📄 VERSION	100 bytes	plain text document
📄 in_use.lock	0 bytes	plain text document
⊟ 🗀 mapred	1 item	folder
⊟ 🗀 local	1 item	folder
⊟ 🗀 jobTracker	0 items	folder
(Empty)		

Figure 8.1 The hierarchical structure of the /tmp/hadoop-henry directory on the namenode of the four-node Linux cluster

On the namenode, there are two directories: one is *dfs/name* for the HDFS and the other is *mapred/local* for the JobTracker, which are defined by the variables

${dfs.name.dir}=${hadoop.tmp.dir}/dfs/name
${mapred.local.dir}=${hadoop.tmp.dir}/local/dir,

respectively. These sub directories and files therein are generated and maintained by the Hadoop system. In general, you should not try to modify them yourself. Especially, the *current* sub-directory under *dfs/name* contains the current version of the HDFS in use together with a history of *edits* and *fsimage* (filesystem image) to keep Hadoop running. For whatever reason if the namenode is corrupt, you might need to re-create them by using the command "*hadoop –format namenode*" (note: this is not recommended in a production environment and it will essentially erase your data in the HDFS).

8.1.2 The Secondary NameNode Storage

Similarly, the secondary namenode was verified with the following command:

```
$JAVA_HOME/bin/jps
31150 SecondaryNameNode
1890 Jps
```

See Figure 8.2 for the Hadoop storage structure on the secondary namenode.

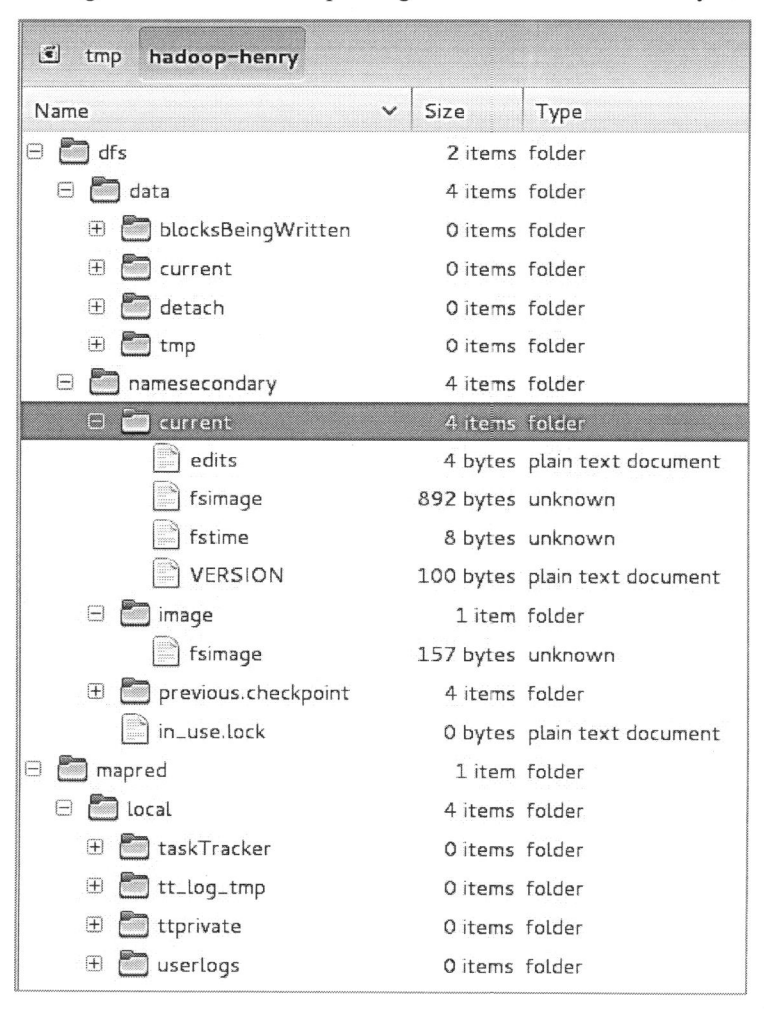

Figure 8.2 The hierarchical structure of the /tmp/hadoop-henry directory on the secondary namenode of the four-node Linux cluster

It is seen that the secondary namenode has a *dfs/namesecondary* directory, which is a backup of the *dfs/name* directory on the namenode. Because of the checkpointing process, both the namenode and the secondary namenode maintain a copy of the *previous.checkpoint* directory for recovery purposes.

8.1.3 The DataNode Storage

Similarly, one of the datanodes was verified with the following command:

```
$JAVA_HOME/bin/jps
2718 DataNode
11802 Jps
2851 TaskTracker
```

See Figure 8.3 for the Hadoop storage structure on this datanode.

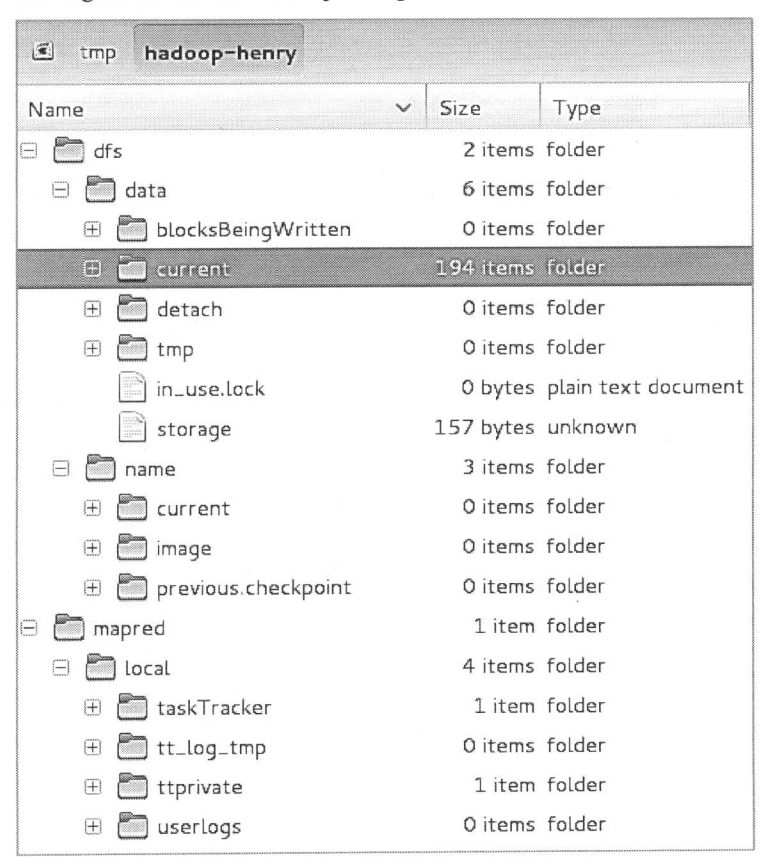

Figure 8.3 The hierarchical structure of the /tmp/hadoop-henry directory on one of the datanodes of the four-node Linux cluster

As you see, the *current* directory on this *datanode* contains 194 items. Those items are partially block files that contain raw bytes, partially block metadata and partially subdirectories as shown below:

```
/tmp/hadoop-henry/dfs/data/current:
blk_1057974575516506032
blk_1057974575516506032_1054.meta
blk_-1101235861842575430
blk_-1101235861842575430_1068.meta
blk_1360426629255365812
blk_1360426629255365812_1057.meta
blk_-1580417785072859522
blk_-1580417785072859522_1057.meta
......
dncp_block_verification.log.curr
subdir0
subdir1
subdir10
subdir11
subdir12
```

It is interesting to note that out of those 194 items in the *current* directory, there are 64 subdirectories, 64 block files, 64 metadata files, plus two additional files of *VERSION* and *dncp_block_verification.log.curr*. The number "64" is determined by a configuration parameter named *dfs.datanode.numblocks*, which is set to 64 by default. The purpose for this setting is to have a tree with a reasonable fan-out structure so that it would not end up with too many files in a single directory. Having an unlimited number of files in a directory is detrimental to the performance of a filesystem.

As we know, Hadoop operates on large datasets, which are divided into *blocks*. Those data blocks are not replicated locally. Instead, they are replicated across the nodes in a cluster. To help improve I/O throughput, it's helpful to configure the ${*dfs.data.dir*} parameter with a list of individual drives on each datanode so that I/O operations would be spread out among multiple drives as evenly as possible. This is not a concern in a development environment, but would be crucial in performance testing and production environments. Hadoop provides a convenient approach to configuring multiple drives for the directory specified by the parameter *dfs.data.dir*, which is as simple as just specifying a list of comma-separated paths for the *dfs.data.dir* parameter. An even easier approach would be to override the default parameter ${*hadoop.tmp.dir*} with a list of comma-separated paths, as all other directory related parameters derive their settings from this parameter.

8.1.4 The Concept of Safe Mode

Although in a development environment, we do not manipulate the mode in which Hadoop runs specifically, it's important to understand the concept of *safe mode*, because this may affect what you can do and what you can't do depending on whether safe mode in on or off.

The concept of safe mode comes from the requirement that Hadoop must provide a mechanism for preventing data from being corrupted in a cluster. When a namenode starts up, it reconstructs a new *fsimage* by loading the stored *fsimage* and applying edits from the *edits* log file. It also needs to construct a map of block locations from the datanodes. Hadoop would be in safe mode until these operations have successfully completed. In other words, when Hadoop is in safe mode, it is shielded from accepting write operations from user MapReduce programs. In a bare-minimum development environment, this typically is not an issue, but it may cause trouble sometimes.

Figure 8.4 shows how to manage safe mode using *dfsadmin* commands. The first *get* command from the upper window shows that safe mode is OFF, which means that Hadoop is ready for use. The second *wait* command immediately returned as the safe mode was off. Then the *enter/leave/enter* commands toggled the safe mode to on/off/on sequentially. At that point, a *wait* command put Hadoop in safe mode ON state and it stayed there. In order to get it back to *off* state, I had to open up another shell prompt and enter a *leave* command, which ended the *wait* state of the safe mode and got it back to *off* state. These commands are handy when you need to trouble shoot safe mode related issues.

```
                   henry@linux-1fsw:...myapp/hadoop-1.0.3

 File  Edit  View  Search  Terminal  Help
henry@linux-1fsw:~/myapp/hadoop-1.0.3> bin/hadoop dfsadmin -safemode get
Safe mode is OFF
henry@linux-1fsw:~/myapp/hadoop-1.0.3> bin/hadoop dfsadmin -safemode wait
Safe mode is OFF
henry@linux-1fsw:~/myapp/hadoop-1.0.3> bin/hadoop dfsadmin -safemode enter
Safe mode is ON
henry@linux-1fsw:~/myapp/hadoop-1.0.3> bin/hadoop dfsadmin -safemode leave
Safe mode is OFF
henry@linux-1fsw:~/myapp/hadoop-1.0.3> bin/hadoop dfsadmin -safemode enter
Safe mode is ON
henry@linux-1fsw:~/myapp/hadoop-1.0.3> bin/hadoop dfsadmin -safemode wait
Safe mode is OFF
henry@linux-1fsw:~/myapp/hadoop-1.0.3> █


 File  Edit  View  Search  Terminal  Help
henry@linux-1fsw:~> pwd
/home/henry
henry@linux-1fsw:~> cd myapp
henry@linux-1fsw:~/myapp> cd hadoop-1.0.3/
henry@linux-1fsw:~/myapp/hadoop-1.0.3> bin/hadoop dfsadmin -safemode leave
Safe mode is OFF
henry@linux-1fsw:~/myapp/hadoop-1.0.3> □
```

Figure 8.4 dfsadmin commands for managing safe mode

8.1.5 Filesystem Health Check

Whenever you suspect whether your filesystem is healthy, run the following command against a path:

```
$ hadoop fsck <path>
```

On my namenode, the above command produced the following output against the root directory "/":

```
FSCK started by henry from /192.168.1.102 for path / at Tue Oct 02 09:45:14 PDT 2012

.
/tmp/hadoop-henry/mapred/staging/henry/.staging/job_201209212204_0007/job.jar: Under
replicated blk_-993370391260890914_1059. Target Replicas is 10 but found 2 replica(s).
.
......

.
/user/henry/out4e/part-r-00001:  Under replicated blk_3979692530517378686_1204. Target Replicas
is 3 but found 2 replica(s).
Status: HEALTHY
 Total size: 1493697065 B
 Total dirs: 64
 Total files:    90
 Total blocks (validated):    93 (avg. block size 16061258 B)
 Minimally replicated blocks:  93 (100.0 %)
 Over-replicated blocks:    0 (0.0 %)
 Under-replicated blocks:  93 (100.0 %)
 Mis-replicated blocks:        0 (0.0 %)
 Default replication factor: 3
 Average block replication: 2.0
 Corrupt blocks:        0
 Missing replicas:      100 (53.76344 %)
 Number of data-nodes:      2
 Number of racks:      1
FSCK ended at Tue Oct 02 09:45:14 PDT 2012 in 23 milliseconds


The filesystem under path '/' is HEALTHY
```

You would see many lines reported on each file checked. At the end of the report, it would give a status of *HEALTHY* most of the time. In general, you can ignore over-/under-/mis-replicated blocks, because these issues would be taken care of by Hadoop itself. However, you might need to use the "*-move*" option to move corrupt blocks to the */lost+found* directory if any so that Hadoop could repair those blocks by replicating them again.

You can add more options to the *fsck* command for other information in addition to the default report as shown above. For example, you can issue the following command to query about the location related information for a given path:

```
$hadoop fsck <path> –files –blocks –locations –racks
```

This commanded generated the following output against my */tmp/hadoop-henry* directory on my namenode:

```
FSCK started by henry from /192.168.1.102 for path /tmp/hadoop-henry at Tue Oct 02 09:48:26 PDT
2012
```

```
/tmp/hadoop-henry <dir>
/tmp/hadoop-henry/mapred <dir>
/tmp/hadoop-henry/mapred/staging <dir>
/tmp/hadoop-henry/mapred/staging/henry <dir>
/tmp/hadoop-henry/mapred/staging/henry/.staging <dir>
/tmp/hadoop-henry/mapred/staging/henry/.staging/job_201209212204_0007 <dir>
/tmp/hadoop-henry/mapred/staging/henry/.staging/job_201209212204_0007/job.jar 43568 bytes, 1
block(s):  Under replicated blk_-993370391260890914_1059. Target Replicas is 10 but found 2
replica(s).
0. blk_-993370391260890914_1059 len=43568 repl=2 [/default-rack/192.168.1.108:50010, /default-
rack/192.168.1.101:50010]
```

```
/tmp/hadoop-henry/mapred/system <dir>
/tmp/hadoop-henry/mapred/system/jobtracker.info 4 bytes, 1 block(s):  Under replicated blk_-
8794234436348050293_1001. Target Replicas is 3 but found 2 replica(s).
0. blk_-8794234436348050293_1001 len=4 repl=2 [/default-rack/192.168.1.108:50010, /default-
rack/192.168.1.101:50010]
```

```
Status: HEALTHY
 Total size: 43572 B
 Total dirs: 7
 Total files:     2
 Total blocks (validated):   2 (avg. block size 21786 B)
 Minimally replicated blocks:   2 (100.0 %)
 Over-replicated blocks:    0 (0.0 %)
 Under-replicated blocks:  2 (100.0 %)
 Mis-replicated blocks:      0 (0.0 %)
 Default replication factor: 3
 Average block replication: 2.0
 Corrupt blocks:       0
 Missing replicas:      9 (225.0 %)
 Number of data-nodes:      2
 Number of racks:      1
 FSCK ended at Tue Oct 02 09:48:26 PDT 2012 in 2 milliseconds
```

```
    The filesystem under path '/tmp/hadoop-henry' is HEALTHY
```

As you see, the above command tells where the replicated blocks are located. In this case, they were on the two datanodes identified by their respective IP addresses of 192.168.1.108 (linux-w9ms) and 192.168.1.101 (linux-sgpx).

To check the disk usage on the datanodes, use the following command:

```
$hadoop dfsadmin -report
```

This command generated the following output on my namenode:

```
Configured Capacity: 42274381824 (39.37 GB)
Present Capacity: 32881545216 (30.62 GB)
DFS Remaining: 29869010944 (27.82 GB)
```

```
DFS Used: 3012534272 (2.81 GB)
DFS Used%: 9.16%
Under replicated blocks: 93
Blocks with corrupt replicas: 0
Missing blocks: 0


-------------------------------------------------

Datanodes available: 2 (2 total, 0 dead)

Name: 192.168.1.108:50010
Decommission Status : Normal
Configured Capacity: 21137190912 (19.69 GB)
DFS Used: 1506267136 (1.4 GB)
Non DFS Used: 4725813248 (4.4 GB)
DFS Remaining: 14905110528(13.88 GB)
DFS Used%: 7.13%
DFS Remaining%: 70.52%
Last contact: Tue Oct 02 09:46:26 PDT 2012

Name: 192.168.1.101:50010
Decommission Status : Normal
Configured Capacity: 21137190912 (19.69 GB)
DFS Used: 1506267136 (1.4 GB)
Non DFS Used: 4667023360 (4.35 GB)
DFS Remaining: 14963900416(13.94 GB)
DFS Used%: 7.13%
DFS Remaining%: 70.79%
Last contact: Tue Oct 02 09:46:25 PDT 2012
```

As you see, it reported the storage usage on each of the two datanodes.

If you are curious and want to know the current activities on the namenode, execute the following command:

```
$hadoop dfsadmin –metasave <filename>
```

which would save all meta data into the file specified (this file can be found in the *logs* directory of your Hadoop installation). To find more usages of the *dfsadmin* utility, refer to the link given at the end of this chapter.

8.1.6 Balancer

In the preceding section, the *dfsadmin* utility reported the DFS usage on each datanode with the – *report* option. It turned out that the two datanodes were well-balanced with a 7.13% usage on each node. However, it's very possible that block distributions may become skewed among the datanodes available over time. Hadoop provides a balancer utility that can be used to cure this issue easily. The balancer can be launched with the following command by running the *start-balancer.sh* script in Hadoop's *bin* directory:

```
$bin/start-balancer.sh
```

The above command generated the following output on my namenode:

```
henry@linux-1fsw:~/myapp/hadoop-1.0.3> bin/start-balancer.sh
starting balancer, logging to /home/henry/myapp/hadoop-1.0.3/libexec/../logs/hadoop-henry-
balancer-linux-1fsw.out
Time Stamp         Iteration# Bytes Already Moved  Bytes Left To Move  Bytes Being Moved
The cluster is balanced. Exiting...
Balancing took 448.0 milliseconds
henry@linux-1fsw:~/myapp/hadoop-1.0.3>
```

Since this cluster was already balanced, there were no output under the title starting with *Time Stamp*. Also, it took 448 ms only for the same reason. In a production environment, it might take much longer. In addition, in order to minimize the impact of a running balancer job, you can limit the I/O bandwidth for the balancer by overwriting the configuration parameter *dfs.balance.bandwidthPerSec* in the *hdfs-site.xml* file with a setting specified in *bytes*.

8.2 PERFORMANCE TUNING

Hadoop performance tuning can be divided into two parts:

1) Writing efficient MapReduce programs that use least amount of system resources while getting the job done.
2) Optimally configuring system parameters to condition an environment in which efficient MapReduce programs can reach their potentials in both performance and scalability.

In order to be able to write efficient MapReduce programs and optimally configuring Hadoop system parameters for maximum performance and scalability, a developer needs to understand how a Hadoop environment is configured, as is discussed next.

8.2.1 Default Configuration

As we have introduced in the previous chapters, Hadoop configuration is divided into two parts: environment settings and site-specific settings. Environment settings are set in the *conf/hadoop-env.sh* file, whereas the site-specific settings set site-specific parameters. Hadoop has many configuration parameters set as the default configuration settings out of the box. The default settings are contained in the *core-default.xml*, *hdfs-default.xml* and *mapred-default.xml* files bundled in the *hadoop*.jar* file as shown in Figure 8.5, whereas the site-specific configuration files are located in the *conf* directory and named *core-site.xml*, *hdfs-site.xml* and *mapred-site.xml*, respectively. You can refer to Table A.1 for all default settings obtained in a job control configuration file from running a 2M credit card transaction MapReduce job.In general, we do not edit the default settings directly in their respective XML files. Instead, we overwrite the default settings to customize a site in the site-specific XML files.

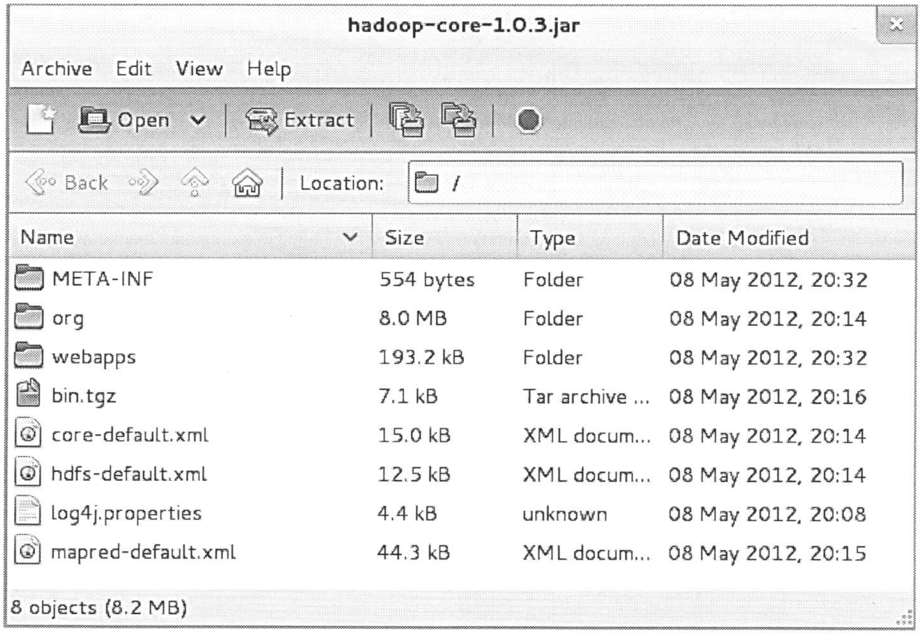

Figure 8.5 Hadoop default configuration files

Next, we introduce some of the performance sensitive parameters that can be set in the hadoop-env.sh script file and site-specific configuration files.

8.2.2 Configuring the Environment of the Hadoop Daemons

Listing 8.1 displays the *hadoop-env.sh* file I used on my Mac OS X. As it is noted, only the *JAVA_HOME* variable is mandatory; all others are optional. If performance is important, you should use newer JDKs, as I have benchmarked and documented in my other book *Java Performance and Scalability* (available on Amazon) with real products that newer JDKs may perform significantly better than older JDKs. The book also contains many JVM garbage collection tuning practices that are applicable to tuning Hadoop MapReduce programs, as all MapReduce programs are Java programs. It's worthwhile to check it out if you are interested in knowing more about Java performance and scalability.

Listing 8.1 The hadoop-env.sh file

```
# Set Hadoop-specific environment variables here.

# The only required environment variable is JAVA_HOME.  All others are
# optional.  When running a distributed configuration it is best to
# set JAVA_HOME in this file, so that it is correctly defined on
```

```
# remote nodes.

# The java implementation to use.  Required.

export JAVA_HOME=/Library/Java/Home
export HADOOP_OPTS="-Djava.security.krb5.realm=OX.AC.UK -
Djava.security.krb5.kdc=kdc0.ox.ac.uk:kdc1.ox.ac.uk"
# Extra Java CLASSPATH elements.  Optional.
# export HADOOP_CLASSPATH=

# The maximum amount of heap to use, in MB. Default is 1000.
export HADOOP_HEAPSIZE=2000

# Extra Java runtime options.  Empty by default.
# export HADOOP_OPTS=-server

# Command specific options appended to HADOOP_OPTS when specified
export HADOOP_NAMENODE_OPTS="-Dcom.sun.management.jmxremote
↪$HADOOP_NAMENODE_OPTS"
export HADOOP_SECONDARYNAMENODE_OPTS="-↪Dcom.sun.management.jmxremote
$HADOOP_SECONDARYNAMENODE_OPTS"
export HADOOP_DATANODE_OPTS="-Dcom.sun.management.jmxremote
↪$HADOOP_DATANODE_OPTS"
export HADOOP_BALANCER_OPTS="-Dcom.sun.management.jmxremote
↪$HADOOP_BALANCER_OPTS"
export HADOOP_JOBTRACKER_OPTS="-Dcom.sun.management.jmxremote
↪$HADOOP_JOBTRACKER_OPTS"
# export HADOOP_TASKTRACKER_OPTS=
# The following applies to multiple commands (fs, dfs, fsck, distcp etc)
# export HADOOP_CLIENT_OPTS

# Extra ssh options.  Empty by default.
# export HADOOP_SSH_OPTS="-o ConnectTimeout=1 -o ↪SendEnv=HADOOP_CONF_DIR"

# Where log files are stored.  $HADOOP_HOME/logs by default.
# export HADOOP_LOG_DIR=${HADOOP_HOME}/logs

# File naming remote slave hosts.  $HADOOP_HOME/conf/slaves by default.
# export HADOOP_SLAVES=${HADOOP_HOME}/conf/slaves

# host:path where hadoop code should be rsync'd from.  Unset by default.
# export HADOOP_MASTER=master:/home/$USER/src/hadoop

# Seconds to sleep between slave commands.  Unset by default.  This
# can be useful in large clusters, where, e.g., slave rsyncs can
# otherwise arrive faster than the master can service them.
# export HADOOP_SLAVE_SLEEP=0.1

# The directory where pid files are stored. /tmp by default.
```

```
# export HADOOP_PID_DIR=/var/hadoop/pids

# A string representing this instance of hadoop. $USER by default.
# export HADOOP_IDENT_STRING=$USER

# The scheduling priority for daemon processes.  See 'man nice'.
# export HADOOP_NICENESS=10
```

In the above file, the JVM heap size was set to 2 GB uniformly. You can configure individual daemons as shown in Table 8.1 using the configuration options *HADOOP_*_OPTS*. For example, to configure the NameNode to use the parallelGC garbage collection algorithm, add the following statement in your hadoop-env.sh:

    export HADOOP_NAMENODE_OPTS="-XX:+UseParallelGC ↪${HADOOP_NAMENODE_OPTS}"

You can add other JVM tuning options to any daemons you deem as helpful similarly.

Table 8.1 Hadoop daemon JVM option variables

Daemon	Configure Options
NameNode	HADOOP_NAMENODE_OPTS
DataNode	HADOOP_DATANODE_OPTS
SecondaryNamenode	HADOOP_SECONDARYNAMENODE_OPTS
JobTracker	HADOOP_JOBTRACKER_OPTS
TaskTracker	HADOOP_TASKTRACKER_OPTS

8.2.3 Configuring the Hadoop Daemons

This section lists performance sensitive parameters that can be overwritten in each site-specific XML configuration file (see Tables 8.2 – 8.4). How much performance gain you can actually get by adjusting a parameter depends on your application, environment and workload intensity. You would need to conduct rigorous performance and scalability tests to determine most applicable and accurate sizing guidelines for your application. You may want to refer to those proven procedures derived using real products and presented in my other book *Java Performance and Scalability*.

Table 8.2 Performance sensitive parameters to be overwritten in core-site.xml

Parameter	Value	description
io.sort.factor	100	More streams merged at once while sorting files.
io.sort.mb	200	Higher memory-limit while sorting data.
io.file.buffer.size	131072	Size of read/write buffer used in SequenceFiles.

Table 8.3 Performance sensitive parameters to be overwritten in hdfs-site.xml

Parameter	Value	Description
dfs.name.dir	Path on the local filesystem where the NameNode stores the namespace and transactions logs persistently.	If this is a comma-delimited list of directories then the name table is replicated in all of the directories, for redundancy.
dfs.data.dir	Comma separated list of paths on the local filesystem of a DataNode where it should store its blocks.	If this is a comma-delimited list of directories, then data will be stored in all named directories, typically on different devices.
dfs.block.size	134217728	HDFS blocksize of 128MB for large file-systems.
dfs.namenode.handler.count	40	More NameNode server threads to handle RPCs from large number of DataNodes.

Table 8.4 Performance sensitive parameters to be overwritten in mapred-site.xml

Parameter	Value	Description
mapred.system.dir	Path on the HDFS where the MapReduce framework stores system files	This is in the default filesystem (HDFS) and must be accessible from both the server and client machines.
mapred.local.dir	Comma-separated list of paths on the local filesystem where temporary MapReduce	Multiple paths help spread disk i/o.
tasktracker.http.threads	50	More worker threads for the TaskTracker's http server. The http server is used by reduces to fetch intermediate map-outputs.
mapred.tasktracker .{map|reduce}.tasks. maximum	The maximum number of MapReduce tasks to run simultaneously in each TaskTracker daemon.	Defaults to 2 (2 maps and 2 reduces), but eventually determined by Hadoop.

mapred.acls.enabled	Boolean, specifying whether checks for queue ACLs and job ACLs are to be done for authorizing users for doing queue operations and job operations.	If *true*, queue ACLs are checked while submitting and administering jobs and job ACLs are checked for authorizing view and modification of jobs.
mapred.reduce.parallel.copies	20	Higher number of parallel copies run by reduces to fetch outputs from very large number of maps.
mapred.map.child.java.opts	-Xmx512M	Larger heap-size for child jvms of maps.
mapred.reduce.child.java.opts	-Xmx512M	Larger heap-size for child jvms of reduces.
fs.inmemory.size.mb	200	Larger amount of memory allocated for the in-memory file-system used to merge map-outputs at the reduces.

8.3 SUMMARY

In this chapter, we introduced Hadoop administration from a developer's perspective so that developers can trouble shoot issues in their development environment without recourse to professional administrators. This kind of knowledge is also desirable for developers to be able to communicate with full time Hadoop administrators in solving performance and scalability issues in production effectively and efficiently. We summarized some of the most performance sensitive parameters that would help developers determine what parameters to tune in pre-production environment before having their MapReduce programs deployed in production.

This wraps up our introduction to Hadoop essentials. If you are interested in learning some Hadoop components such as Pig, Hive, etc., you should refer to those dedicated texts readily available elsewhere.

RECOMMENDED READING

For Hadoop administration commands, refer to the URL below:

http://hadoop.apache.org/docs/r1.0.3/commands_manual.html

For Hadoop HDFS management, refer to the URL below:

http://hadoop.apache.org/docs/r1.0.3/hdfs_user_guide.html

For more information on Hadoop cluster configuration parameters, refer to the URL below:

http://hadoop.apache.org/docs/r1.0.3/cluster_setup.html

EXERCISES

8.1 Hadoop storage uses the *tmp* directory by default. How would you change it to a non-temporary directory?

8.2 The RAID technology is used in general with conventional relational database systems. Is it also preferable for Hadoop storage?

8.3 How would you determine what configuration parameters might affect Hadoop performance and scalability significantly?

Appendix A Developing Hadoop on Linux (Ubuntu 12.10)

This appendix describes how to set up a Hadoop dev environment on Linux as an alternative to Mac OS X. This task should be performed first before creating the MyHadoop-1.0.3 project as described in Section 1.2.2. Note that we use Ubuntu 12.10, but the procedure should apply to other Linux variants as well.

A.1 INSTALLING JDK AND MAVEN ON YOUR UBUNTU MACHINE

Perform the following tasks:

1) Install a latest JDK 1.6.0 release

2) Run "*sudo apt-get install maven*"

3) Download and install Hadoop 1.0.3

4) Add the lines similar to the following in your *.bashrc* file based on where you installed the JDK and Hadoop on your machine (note that you need to replace myapp if you use a different path):

```
export JAVA_HOME=$HOME/myapp/jdk1.6.0_35
export PATH="$JAVA_HOME/bin:$PATH"

export HADOOP_INSTALL=$HOME/myapp/hadoop-1.0.3
export PATH="$HADOOP_INSTALL/bin:$HADOOP_INSTALL/sbin:$PATH"
```

5) Run "mvn --version" to verify your Maven has been installed properly

6) Add a line similar to the following in your $HADOOP_INSTALL/conf/hadoop-env.sh file:

```
export JAVA_HOME=$HOME/myapp/jdk1.6.0_35
```

7) Run "hadoop version" to verify that Hadoop has been installed properly on your machine

The next step is to enable Maven on Eclipse, as is discussed next.

A.2 ENABLING MAVEN ON ECLIPSE

The Maven plug-in for Eclipse is named *m2eclipse or m2e*. It is now bundled with the latest (Indigo or Juno) version of Eclipse Java EE IDE for Web Developers. Next, I assume that you already installed Indigo or Juno on your Linux machine, or download and install it if not.

To enable Maven plug-in on your Eclipse IDE, start up your Eclipse IDE. Click *Help -> Install New Software...* In the dialog box of *Available Software*, enter http://download.eclipse.org/releases/juno and click *Add*, as shown in Figure A.1. Under the *Collaboration* category, make sure you select the two m2e entries. Click *Next* and finish the install. You are ready to use Maven 3 with Eclipse to create a Hadoop project. Refer to Section 1.2.2 for specific instructions.

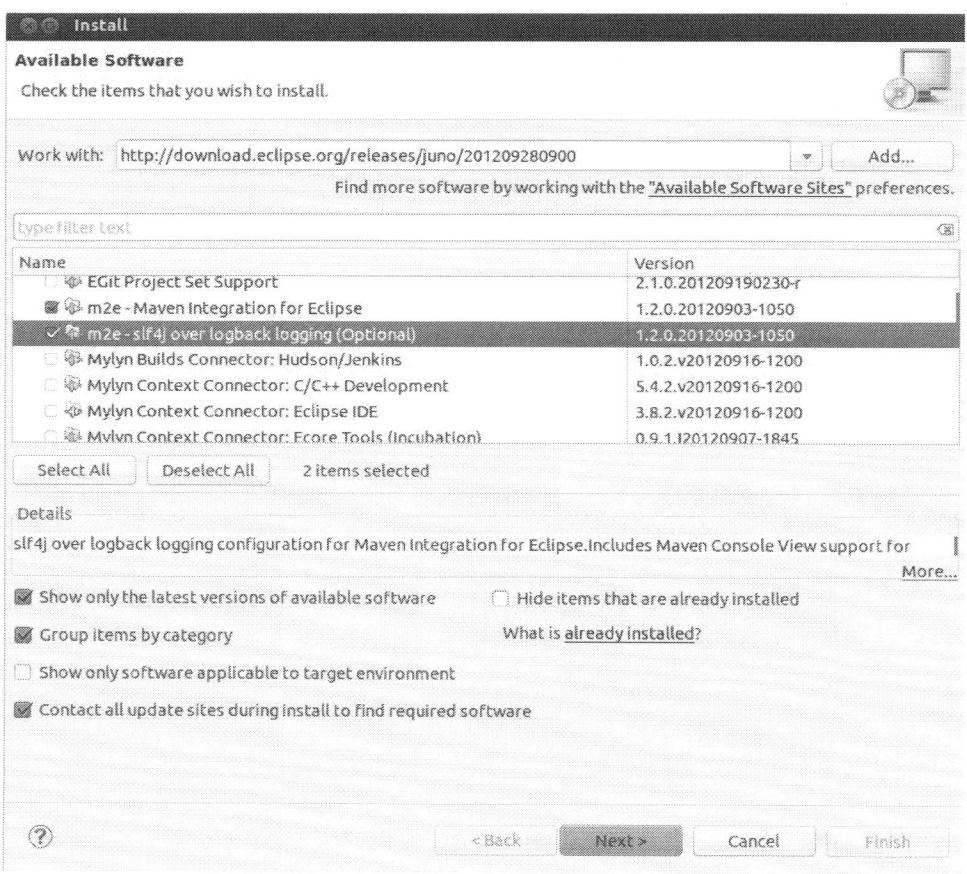

Figure A.1 Maven plug-in m2e bundled with Eclipse Juno

Appendix B Hadoop Default Job Configurations

This appendix presents all default Hadoop job configuration parameters, obtained from a 2M credit card transaction MapReduce program run on a four-node Linux cluster (the original file name was *job_201209021930_0001_conf.xml*). This is a convenient place to check whenever we need to look up a Hadoop configuration parameter.

Table B.1 Hadoop default job configuration parameters from a test run described in detail in §4.2.2

Name	Value
fs.s3n.impl	org.apache.hadoop.fs.s3native. NativeS3FileSystem
mapred.task.cache.levels	2
hadoop.tmp.dir	/tmp/hadoop-${user.name}
hadoop.native.lib	true
map.sort.class	org.apache.hadoop.util.QuickSort
dfs.namenode.decommission.nodes.per. interval	5
dfs.https.need.client.auth	false
ipc.client.idlethreshold	4000
dfs.datanode.data.dir.perm	755
mapred.system.dir	${hadoop.tmp.dir}/mapred/system
mapred.job.tracker.persist.jobstatus. hours	0

dfs.datanode.address	0.0.0.0:50010
dfs.namenode.logging.level	info
dfs.block.access.token.enable	false
io.skip.checksum.errors	false
fs.default.name	hdfs://linux-1fsw.perfmath.com
mapred.cluster.reduce.memory.mb	-1
mapred.reducer.new-api	true
mapred.child.tmp	./tmp
fs.har.impl.disable.cache	true
dfs.safemode.threshold.pct	0.999f
mapred.skip.reduce.max.skip.groups	0
dfs.namenode.handler.count	10
dfs.blockreport.initialDelay	0
mapred.heartbeats.in.second	100
mapred.tasktracker.dns.nameserver	default
io.sort.factor	10
mapred.task.timeout	600000
mapred.max.tracker.failures	4
hadoop.rpc.socket.factory.class. default	org.apache.hadoop.net. StandardSocketFactory
mapred.job.tracker.jobhistory.lru. cache.size	5
fs.hdfs.impl	org.apache.hadoop.hdfs. DistributedFileSystem
mapred.queue.default.acl-administer-jobs	*
mapred.output.key.class	org.apache.hadoop.io.Text
dfs.block.access.key.update.interval	600
mapred.skip.map.auto.incr.proc. count	true
mapreduce.job.complete.cancel. delegation.tokens	true

io.mapfile.bloom.size	1048576
mapreduce.reduce.shuffle.connect.timeout	180000
dfs.safemode.extension	30000
mapred.jobtracker.blacklist.fault-timeout-window	180
tasktracker.http.threads	40
mapred.job.shuffle.merge.percent	0.66
fs.ftp.impl	org.apache.hadoop.fs.ftp.FTPFileSystem
user.name	henry
mapred.output.compress	false
io.bytes.per.checksum	512
mapred.combine.recordsBeforeProgress	10000
mapred.healthChecker.script.timeout	60000
topology.node.switch.mapping.impl	org.apache.hadoop.net.ScriptBasedMapping
dfs.https.server.keystore.resource	ssl-server.xml
mapred.reduce.slowstart.completed.maps	0.05
mapred.reduce.max.attempts	4
mapred.reduce.max.attempts	org.apache.hadoop.fs.InMemoryFileSystem
dfs.block.access.token.lifetime	600
dfs.name.edits.dir	${dfs.name.dir}
mapred.skip.map.max.skip.records	0
mapred.cluster.map.memory.mb	true
hadoop.security.group.mapping	org.apache.hadoop.security.ShellBasedUnixGroupsMapping
mapred.job.tracker.persist.jobstatus.dir	/jobtracker/jobsInfo
mapred.jar	hdfs://linux-1fsw.perfmath.com/tmp/hadoop-henry/mapred/staging/henry/.staging/job_201209021930_0001/job.jar

dfs.block.size	67108864
fs.s3.buffer.dir	${hadoop.tmp.dir}/s3
job.end.retry.attempts	0
fs.file.impl	org.apache.hadoop.fs. LocalFileSystem
mapred.local.dir.minspacestart	0
mapred.output.compression.type	RECORD
dfs.datanode.ipc.address	0.0.0.0:50020
dfs.permissions	true
topology.script.number.args	100
io.mapfile.bloom.error.rate	0.005
mapred.cluster.max.reduce.memory.mb	-1
mapred.max.tracker.blacklists	4
mapred.task.profile.maps	0-2
dfs.datanode.https.address	0.0.0.0:50475
mapred.userlog.retain.hours	24
dfs.secondary.http.address	0.0.0.0:50090
dfs.replication.max	512
mapred.job.tracker.persist.jobstatus. active	false
hadoop.security.authorization	false
local.cache.size	10737418240
dfs.namenode.delegation.token. renew-interval	86400000
mapred.min.split.size	0
mapred.map.tasks	2
mapred.child.java.opts	-Xmx200m
mapreduce.job.counters.limit	120
mapred.output.value.class	org.apache.hadoop.io. FloatWritable
dfs.https.client.keystore.resource	ssl-client.xml

mapred.job.queue.name	default
dfs.https.address	0.0.0.0:50470
mapred.job.tracker.retiredjobs.cache.size	1000
dfs.balance.bandwidthPerSec	1048576
ipc.server.listen.queue.size	128
job.end.retry.interval	30000
mapred.inmem.merge.threshold	1000
mapred.skip.attempts.to.start.skipping	2
mapreduce.tasktracker.outofband.heartbeat.damper	1000000
fs.checkpoint.dir	${hadoop.tmp.dir}/dfs/namesecondary
mapred.reduce.tasks	1
mapred.merge.recordsBeforeProgress	10000
mapred.userlog.limit.kb	0
mapred.job.reduce.memory.mb	-1
dfs.max.objects	0
webinterface.private.actions	false
hadoop.security.token.service.use_ip	true
io.sort.spill.percent	0.80
mapred.job.shuffle.input.buffer.percent	0.70
mapred.job.name	Spending Pattern
dfs.datanode.dns.nameserver	default
mapred.map.tasks.speculative.execution	true
hadoop.util.hash.type	murmur
dfs.blockreport.intervalMsec	3600000
mapred.map.max.attempts	4
mapreduce.job.acl-view-job	

dfs.client.block.write.retries	3
mapred.job.tracker.handler.count	10
mapreduce.reduce.shuffle.read. timeout	180000
mapred.tasktracker.expiry.interval	600000
dfs.https.enable	false
mapred.jobtracker.maxtasks.per.job	1
mapred.jobtracker.job.history.block.size	3145728
keep.failed.task.files	false
dfs.datanode.failed.volumes. tolerated	0
ipc.client.tcpnodelay	false
mapred.task.profile.reduces	0-2
mapred.output.compression.codec	org.apache.hadoop.io.compress. DefaultCodec
io.map.index.skip	0
mapred.working.dir	hdfs://linux-1fsw.perfmath.com/user/henry
ipc.server.tcpnodelay	false
mapred.jobtracker.blacklist. fault-bucket-width	15
dfs.namenode.delegation.key. update-interval	86400000
mapred.mapper.new-api	true
mapred.job.map.memory.mb	-1
dfs.default.chunk.view.size	32768
hadoop.logfile.size	10000000
mapred.reduce.tasks.speculative. execution	true
mapreduce.job.dir	hdfs://linux-1fsw.perfmath.com/tmp/hadoop-henry/mapred/staging/henry/ .staging/job_201209021930_0001
mapreduce.tasktracker.outofband. heartbeat	false

mapreduce.reduce.input.limit	-1
dfs.datanode.du.reserved	0
hadoop.security.authentication	simple
fs.checkpoint.period	3600
dfs.web.ugi	webuser,webgroup
mapred.job.reuse.jvm.num.tasks	1
mapred.jobtracker.completeuserjobs.maximum	100
dfs.df.interval	60000
dfs.data.dir	${hadoop.tmp.dir}/dfs/data
mapred.task.tracker.task-controller	org.apache.hadoop.mapred.DefaultTaskController
fs.s3.maxRetries	4
dfs.datanode.dns.interface	default
mapred.cluster.max.map.memory.mb	-1
dfs.support.append	false
mapreduce.reduce.shuffle.maxfetchfailures	10
mapreduce.job.acl-modify-job	
dfs.permissions.supergroup	supergroup
mapred.local.dir	${hadoop.tmp.dir}/mapred/local
fs.hftp.impl	org.apache.hadoop.hdfs.HftpFileSystem
fs.trash.interval	0
fs.s3.sleepTimeSeconds	10
dfs.replication.min	1
mapred.submit.replication	10
fs.har.impl	org.apache.hadoop.fs.HarFileSystem
mapred.map.output.compression.codec	org.apache.hadoop.io.compress.DefaultCodec
mapred.tasktracker.dns.interface	default

dfs.namenode.decommission.interval	30
dfs.http.address	linux-1fsw.perfmath.com:50070
dfs.heartbeat.interval	3
mapred.job.tracker	linux-1fsw.perfmath.com:8021
mapreduce.job.submithost	linux-1fsw
io.seqfile.sorter.recordlimit	1000000
dfs.name.dir	${hadoop.tmp.dir}/dfs/name
mapred.line.input.format. linespermap	1
mapred.jobtracker.taskScheduler	org.apache.hadoop.mapred. JobQueueTaskScheduler
dfs.datanode.http.address	0.0.0.0:50075
fs.webhdfs.impl	org.apache.hadoop.hdfs.web. WebHdfsFileSystem
mapred.local.dir.minspacekill	0
dfs.replication.interval	3
io.sort.record.percent	0.05
mapreduce.reduce.class	SpendingPatternReducer
fs.kfs.impl	org.apache.hadoop.fs.kfs. KosmosFileSystem
mapred.temp.dir	${hadoop.tmp.dir}/mapred/temp
mapred.tasktracker.reduce.tasks. maximum	2
dfs.replication	3
fs.checkpoint.edits.dir	${fs.checkpoint.dir}
mapred.tasktracker.tasks. sleeptime-before-sigkill	5000
mapred.job.reduce.input.buffer. percent	0.0
mapred.tasktracker.indexcache.mb	10
mapreduce.job.split.metainfo. maxsize	10000000
hadoop.logfile.count	10

mapred.skip.reduce.auto.incr.proc. count	true
mapreduce.job.submithostaddress	192.168.1.103
io.seqfile.compress.blocksize	1000000
fs.s3.block	67108864
mapred.tasktracker.taskmemory manager.monitoring-interval	5000
mapred.queue.default.state	RUNNING
mapred.acls.enabled	false
mapreduce.jobtracker.staging.root. dir	${hadoop.tmp.dir}/mapred/staging
mapred.queue.names	default
dfs.access.time.precision	3600000
fs.hsftp.impl	org.apache.hadoop.hdfs. HsftpFileSystem
mapred.task.tracker.http.address	0.0.0.0:50060
mapred.reduce.parallel.copies	5
io.seqfile.lazydecompress	true
mapred.output.dir	out30
io.sort.mb	100
ipc.client.connection.maxidletime	10000
mapred.compress.map.output	false
hadoop.security.uid.cache.secs	14400
mapred.task.tracker.report.address	127.0.0.1:0
mapred.healthChecker.interval	60000
ipc.client.kill.max	10
ipc.client.connect.max.retries	10
mapreduce.map.class	SpendingPatternMapper
fs.s3.impl	org.apache.hadoop.fs.s3. S3FileSystem
mapred.user.jobconf.limit	5242880

mapred.input.dir	hdfs://linux-1fsw.perfmath.com/user/henry/input/credit_card_tx_1_out.txt
mapred.job.tracker.http.address	0.0.0.0:50030
io.file.buffer.size	4096
mapred.jobtracker.restart.recover	false
io.serializations	org.apache.hadoop.io.serializer.WritableSerialization
dfs.datanode.handler.count	3
mapred.task.profile	false
mapreduce.input.num.files	1
dfs.replication.considerLoad	true
jobclient.output.filter	FAILED
dfs.namenode.delegation.token.max-lifetime	604800000
mapred.tasktracker.map.tasks.maximum	2
io.compression.codecs	org.apache.hadoop.io.compress.DefaultCodec,org.apache.hadoop.io.compress.GzipCodec,org.apache.hadoop.io.compress.BZip2Codec, org.apache.hadoop.io.compress.SnappyCodec
fs.checkpoint.size	67108864

Index

Other texts by the same author:

- A quantitative text on *Java Performance and Scalability*
- Developing Enterprise Applications with Spring: An End-to-End Approach

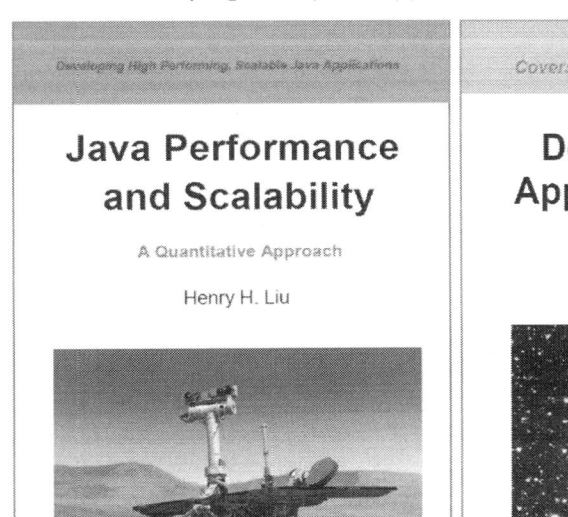

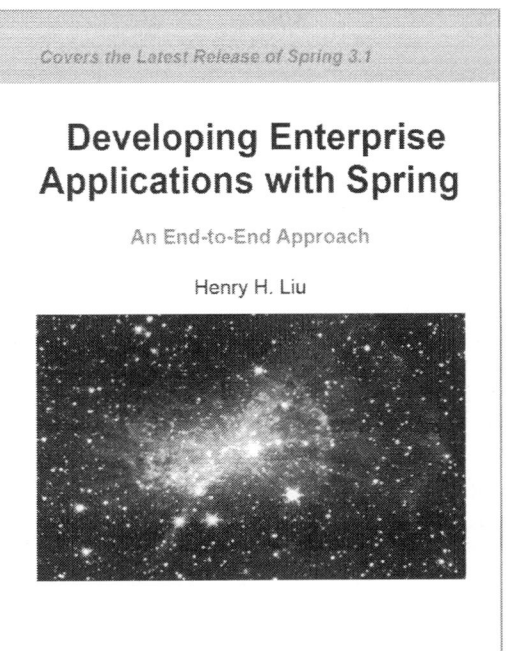

21814983R00190

Made in the USA
Lexington, KY
30 March 2013